MW00639635

Dear Grandpa~

Happy Father's Day!

I love you.

♡,

Alexandra

2218

THE PENINSULA CAMPAIGN &
THE NECESSITY OF EMANCIPATION

To
Wade Curry,
a fellow history
And battlefield
lover,
Best wishes,
Glen R. Brn
5/2/2018

CIVIL WAR AMERICA

Gary W. Gallagher, Peter S. Carmichael,
Caroline E. Janney, and Aaron Sheehan-Dean,
editors

The Peninsula Campaign & the Necessity of Emancipation

AFRICAN AMERICANS &

THE FIGHT FOR FREEDOM

GLENN DAVID BRASHER

THE UNIVERSITY OF NORTH

CAROLINA PRESS

Chapel Hill

This book was published with the assistance of the Fred W. Morrison Fund for Southern Studies of the University of North Carolina Press.

© 2012 The University of North Carolina Press
All rights reserved
Manufactured in the United States of America

Set in Arnhem and The Serif types
by Rebecca Evans

The paper in this book meets the guidelines for permanence
and durability of the Committee on Production Guidelines for
Book Longevity of the Council on Library Resources.

The University of North Carolina Press has been a member of
the Green Press Initiative since 2003.

Library of Congress Cataloging-in-Publication Data to come
Brasher, Glenn David.
The Peninsula Campaign and the necessity of emancipation: African
Americans and the fight for freedom / Glenn David Brasher.—1st ed.
p. cm.—(Civil War America)
Includes bibliographical references and index.
ISBN 978-0-8078-3544-9 (cloth : alk. paper)
1. Peninsular Campaign, 1862. 2. United States—History—Civil War,
1861–1865—Participation, African American. 3. Slaves—Emancipation—
United States. I. Title.
E473.6.B73 2012   973.7'415—dc23   2011036321

16 15 14 13 12   5 4 3 2 1

For them . . .

CONTENTS

ILLUSTRATIONS AND MAPS

Illustrations

Maps

INTRODUCTION AN EVENING ON MALVERN HILL

On July 1, 2001, 139 years after the Battle of Malvern Hill, I stood before a small crowd that had gathered to tour the site. It was my seventh year as a seasonal park ranger for the Richmond National Battlefield Park, and I had spent untold hours walking the ground and researching the fighting. I was capable of providing the visitors with what most came for: descriptions of troop movements, anecdotal stories of bravery, and heartrending tales of sacrifice. However, I planned to offer more than the standard battlefield tour.

Weeks earlier, the park's supervisory ranger, Michael J. Andrus, had asked me to lead the anniversary tour. He had suggested that I discuss the battle as more than just the climactic engagement of the 1862 Peninsula Campaign. He knew that I had researched the connections between Virginia slavery and the Richmond battles, and he wanted the tour to include more content than just "guns and glory." Andrus hoped visitors would leave with a better understanding of why Northerners and Southerners slaughtered each other on that field in such horrific numbers and how the battles around Richmond had affected the institution of slavery.

I knew what Andrus was looking for, and why. In the early 1990s, the National Park Service had received much criticism for doing little more at its battlefields than explaining who shot whom and where. Understanding that many adult Americans receive much of their continuing education at the national parks, a 1998 meeting of park superintendents resolved to expand historic interpretation at Civil War battlefield sites. The agency also asked teams of professional historians to evaluate these sites and make recommendations. Richmond National Battlefield Park was one of many locations the scholars criticized for having embarrassingly outdated exhibits that failed to offer visitors a broader understanding of the Civil War. The Park Service accepted these assessments, and soon many battlefield sites began the process of overhauling their interpretations.[1] Richmond National Battlefield Park eventually opened a state-of-the-art visitors' center at the site of the historic Tredegar Iron Works, and it impressively adhered to the Park Service's new goals.

Nevertheless, for many observers the changes were not occurring rapidly enough, and they correctly pointed out that the Park Service's battlefield interpretations still did not reflect the centrality of slavery to the

American Civil War. An African American congressman who had visited many battlefield parks, for example, was distressed to find that most did not "address the interests of *all* the American people." In reaction, in 1999 the House approved an amendment to an appropriations bill that required all federally funded battlefield sites to educate its visitors about slavery's role in causing the Civil War and its impact "if any, at the individual battle sites."[2]

This directive created considerable controversy, but even as a white Alabamian I could appreciate Congress's action. I always found it disturbing that although the Civil War was a crucial event in African American history, very few blacks ever visited the battlefields. When encountering the infrequent black visitor, I often asked about this apparent indifference to Civil War history among the African American community. The answer was usually the same—despite movies such as *Glory*, much of Civil War popular culture tended to glorify the Confederacy and largely ignored any African American role in the war.[3] Sadly, this trend has continued even into the era of our first black president. In early 2010, the governor of Virginia proclaimed a revival of the state's "Confederate History Month" and in doing so failed to acknowledge the South's fight to preserve slavery. Responding to widespread criticism for the omission, the governor stated that his proclamation had only mentioned those issues that were "most significant for Virginians."[4]

Thus, the National Park Service has hardly been alone in lagging behind in its interpretations of the Civil War, and the Peninsula Campaign in particular has suffered from relative neglect. Although hundreds of works have been written about the Battle of Gettysburg, the events from April to July 1862 have received far less attention. For years, four books dominated the subject, only two of which took the Peninsula Campaign as the central topic. Furthermore, three of the books presented the event only from the Confederate perspective. Not until 1992, with the publication of Stephen Sears's *To the Gates of Richmond*, was there a truly comprehensive study of the campaign.[5] Since then, several fine studies have appeared, including collections of essays by both Gary W. Gallagher and William J. Miller, a campaign study by Kevin Dougherty and J. Michael Moore, and a detailed examination of the Seven Days Battles by Brian K. Burton. Nevertheless, with the exception of several excellent essays in Gallagher's book (most notably by James Marten and William A. Blair), these works focused almost exclusively on military aspects of the campaign.[6]

Drawing on knowledge gleaned from such sources, however, I was able to craft a tour that met my supervisor's expectations. After greeting the visitors, I explained that in the spring of 1862 the Army of the Potomac, under the command of General George B. McClellan, had slowly advanced up the Virginia Peninsula toward Richmond. Arriving just outside the city, it outnumbered the southern army defending the Confederate capital. Yet during a week of almost continuous fighting initiated by General Robert E. Lee, the Confederates used bold and aggressive attacks to drive the northern army away from the city and south toward the James River. Before it could reach the safety of Union gunboats, however, the Army of the Potomac had to fend off one last Rebel attack. Pointing to the high ground on Malvern Hill, I explained to my audience how it provided the Federals with an exceptionally strong defensive position.

Having described the military situation that existed on July 1, 1862, I expanded the focus of the tour by explaining the political context. As the Peninsula Campaign was reaching its climax, Northerners were sharply divided over the issue of emancipation, and General McClellan insisted that the war could be won without resorting to such a radical measure. With his army just outside of the capital of the Confederacy, it appeared that he might be correct. Therefore, I informed the group, the outcome of the Seven Days Battles would likely determine the fate of the institution of slavery. As I ventured into this discussion, I noticed some members of my audience becoming visibly disturbed. Not surprisingly, I saw no black faces in the crowd.

As we set off down the trail, the group was no doubt relieved to discover that I was adept at describing the fighting. I explained the confused orders, the failure of Confederate artillery, and the role of the terrain. As we followed in the footsteps of southern soldiers, I used their words to convey the hell of charging into Union artillery and the futility of the assault. Upon reaching the Union side of the field, I put a human face on the staggering casualty rates and explained why, despite its victory, the Union army continued its retreat to a new base on the James River. The Federals would not be as close to the southern capital again until 1864.

My audience seemed riveted, but as the sun began to set, shadows crept over the battlefield, becoming my cue to conclude the presentation. Had McClellan captured the Confederate capital in the summer of 1862, I told my audience, this might have shortened the war and saved thousands of lives. Returning to the slavery issue, I maintained that an end to the war at that time would likely have left the institution largely intact. I explained that because McClellan's failure to capture Richmond exasperated Northerners, many began to see the necessity for radical measures. Just weeks after the battle, Lincoln presented the first draft of the Emancipation

Proclamation to his cabinet. Therefore, I concluded, the Peninsula Campaign that culminated at Malvern Hill had played a pivotal role in ending slavery. This analysis was a standard interpretation; historians have long recognized that the Peninsula Campaign's results influenced Lincoln's decision to issue the Emancipation Proclamation.[7]

The audience members applauded my efforts, although I suspected their accolades were mostly in appreciation of the details I had supplied about the fighting. As most headed for their cars, the usual number of visitors asked more questions and engaged in conversation. I received no questions or comments about the slavery element of my tour. Nevertheless, Andrus praised me for effectively incorporating slavery into the presentation. The Richmond National Battlefield Park's superintendent had also attended, and she too was pleased. The tour had gone well.

I was not satisfied, however. True, I had brought slavery into the discussion of the battlefield, but not the slaves themselves. I knew that African Americans had helped the Union army locate the best roads to the James River, and yet when discussing the logistics of the battle, I had failed to mention this fact. To some degree, the two armies were on Malvern Hill because of information supplied by slaves. Certainly, this made them important actors in the story, not just passive individuals who stood to benefit the most from the campaign.

I came to see that the problem with my tour and the military studies on which it was based was that they left the role of Virginia slaves and free blacks in the Peninsula Campaign largely unexplored. This book attempts to fill that void, uncovering the ways in which Virginia blacks were involved in one of the largest campaigns of the American Civil War. In doing so, the work blends military, social, and political history.[8]

Examining the efforts of African Americans in the Civil War has a long history in its own right. In the years following the war, writers such as William Wells Brown, George Washington Williams, and Joseph T. Wilson chronicled black participation in the conflict. They passionately argued that members of their race did not simply have freedom handed to them but that they were instrumental in winning it for themselves.[9] Professional historians such as Herbert Aptheker, Bell Irvin Wiley, Benjamin Quarles, Ervin Jordan, and James McPherson have added detail and nuance to that central argument. In addition, Dudley Taylor Cornish, Joseph T. Glatthaar, and Noah Trudeau have produced excellent works that detail the Union decision to organize black troops, the relationships between black soldiers and their white officers, and the combat experiences of black regiments. Perhaps most notably, Ira Berlin and the editors of the Freedmen and

Southern Society project have effectively demonstrated how the actions of Africans Americans influenced changes in Union war policy and significantly affected the purposes and outcomes of the war.[10]

What scholars have not done is examine the ways in which the activities of African Americans shaped the course of particular campaigns. Because the Peninsula Campaign played a crucial role in bringing about emancipation, it is important to uncover the degree to which blacks were a part of the campaign's history. In this study, I argue that African Americans influenced the strategy and tactics of both the Union and Confederate armies before and during the campaign and helped shape its results. More important, I maintain that the ways in which African Americans participated in the campaign helped prepare Northerners to accept emancipation as a military necessity.

As any good battlefield tour guide knows, the words of the participants themselves make for a more compelling story. I have constructed a narrative based on military records and correspondence, soldier and civilian diaries, letters, and memoirs, political speeches, the WPA (Works Progress Administration) slave interviews, material from Lincoln's cabinet members, abolitionist publications, and various other barometers of northern public opinion. This work quotes heavily from Civil War era newspapers. These sources frequently provided inaccurate information about events, but they are enormously important for telling us what people at the time believed was happening and their immediate reactions to news from the front.

A note of caution. This study quotes from primary sources in which people claim to have witnessed or heard rumors of African Americans fighting in Confederate armies. Such evidence can easily be misread, especially because some writers have used it to argue that many blacks voluntarily supported the Confederacy, and thus the South did not fight to defend the institution of slavery.[11] One historian has fittingly labeled this misguided thesis the "black confederate legend." However, because such modern-day "Lost Cause" arguments are flawed and based on questionable logic and because the evidence is usually anecdotal and hearsay in nature, many professional historians have too quickly dismissed any claims that blacks fought with the Confederates. As a result, we often do not quite know what to make of such testimonials.[12]

The accounts presented here are varied; they come from newspaper correspondents, interviews with slaves conducted by northern intelligence officers, Union soldier diaries and letters, and, to a much smaller degree, Confederate recollections (some recorded just days after the events). Taken individually, one could question the reliability of each source. Collectively, however, the sheer number tells us that in fact, to at least some small degree, this was happening early in the war. When contemporaries maintained that Southerners were using blacks in combat roles, they were not manufacturing it out of the whole cloth.

However, this work emphatically rejects claims of widespread slave support for the Confederacy. Instead, I maintain that the few slaves who may have fought alongside their masters did so because their owners had cajoled or forced them, impressed their labor, hinted at possible rewards, and deceived them about the intentions of Union troops. In order to understand the choices made by African Americans at the start of the Civil War, a brief overview of the historic relationship between war and slavery is necessary. The first chapter demonstrates that it should not be surprising to find slaves willingly or unwillingly fighting alongside those who held them in bondage. In fact, this was common throughout the history of the world in various times and locales, including previous wars fought on the Virginia Peninsula.

More important, one primary goal of this work is to demonstrate how in pushing for emancipation, some abolitionists and radical Republicans widely publicized these stories of blacks fighting alongside their masters. In propaganda-like fashion they greatly exaggerated these incidents to further their agenda, and thus they were the first to give these reports more credence and attention than they may have deserved. It is profoundly ironic that modern Confederate apologists now use these emancipationist exaggerations to support their own interpretations of southern motives.

Instead of ignoring or explaining away these accounts, this book takes them out of the hands of those who attempt to use them to glorify the Confederacy, puts them back into the context of the emancipation debate in which they first appeared, and in doing so reveals their true importance. While these sources do not prove black support for the South, they do illuminate one large reason why Northerners came to embrace emancipation as a war aim.

As much as possible, I have attempted to highlight the activities of African Americans. The actions and choices of slaves and free blacks are the backbone of the work, demonstrating that their involvement in the campaign mattered a great deal. One of the problems with a "bottom-up" approach, however, is that historians often overemphasize the importance of their subjects and devalue the influence of political and military leaders who wielded significant power. In an attempt to challenge traditional interpretations and methods, some historians portray such leaders and other elites as merely carried along by social and cultural forces put in motion through the "agency" of the lower ranks of society. Historians such as Vincent Harding and Barbara J. Fields have advanced the thesis that by fleeing to Union lines, slaves forced emancipation upon Union officers, Congress, and ultimately the president. In short, this "self-emancipation thesis" argues that the slaves freed themselves.[13]

Although this work emphasizes the role of African Americans, I do not attempt to argue that the activities of slaves and free blacks were the primary force that determined the outcome of the Peninsula Campaign and brought about the liberation of slaves. As this study reveals, generals and other officers made strategic and tactical decisions that helped shape the military course of the war; and the Union army, abolitionists, politicians, and other leaders were crucial to emancipation. Had the Union army uniformly turned away runaway slaves at the start of the conflict, had McClellan captured Richmond in 1862, had abolitionists and radicals not passionately and convincingly argued that it was a military necessity to free the slaves, and had Lincoln not come to agree, the course of both the war and emancipation would have been quite different. Nevertheless, I maintain that the actions of slaves made the military necessity argument more persuasive. This work demonstrates that no one individual, group, or historical force freed the slaves and reveals that a convergence of many factors, contingencies, and individual efforts produced emancipation.

This work concludes that the issue of slaves fleeing to Union lines was less important in the debate over emancipation than was the military contribution of African Americans to both the North and the South. This argument adds another dimension to our understanding of the Peninsula Campaign and its role in bringing freedom to slaves, concluding that the event was more important for bringing about emancipation than was the Battle of Antietam. By demonstrating the ways that blacks affected the outcome of the campaign and how Union leaders used those activities to push for the military necessity of emancipation, I hope to provide a more comprehensive understanding of the role that blacks played in winning their freedom. In short, the story that follows is the one I wish I had been better prepared to tell that evening on Malvern Hill.

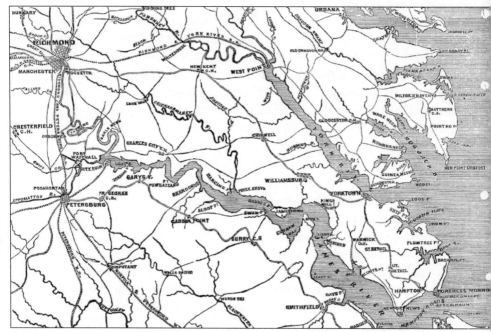

"The Seat of War in Southeastern Virginia." On April 9, 1862, the Philadelphia Enquirer *provided its readers with this map of the Virginia Peninsula and Richmond and surrounding areas.*

1

PRELUDES WAR, SLAVERY, AND THE VIRGINIA PENINSULA

In May 1862, a debate raged in the U.S. Congress as the Army of the Potomac prepared to attack the capital of the Confederacy. For months, radical Republicans had insisted that because slaves were a Confederate asset it was a "military necessity" to liberate them. Slaves labored for the southern army, and several congressmen also claimed that Rebel troops were using some blacks in combat. Ohio's abolitionist senator Benjamin Wade, for example, was outraged to "see black regiments put forward to shoot down my sons who are in the war . . . [and to] see these black chattels thrust forth in front of their 'chivalrous' owners to shoot down, murder, and destroy our men." Such allegations were not new—many Northerners had widely published and discussed these controversial and provocative claims since the early days of the war. At the same time, however, several congressmen pointed out that slaves on the Virginia Peninsula were demonstrating their desire to aid the Union army by providing military intelligence and labor. Referring to the American Revolution to illustrate his point, New York representative Charles B. Sedgwick summarized the military rationale for emancipation by maintaining that when fighting an enemy that possessed slaves, "no civilized nation ever failed" to weaken its opponent and strengthen itself by "proclaim[ing] the freedom of the slaves."[1]

As Sedgewick pointed out, the Peninsula Campaign is only one example of the connection between war and slavery. During the Civil War, Northerners were shocked to hear reports of slaves fighting alongside their masters. They should not have been surprised to find slaves laboring and fighting on both sides of the conflict, however. Throughout history, warfare has frequently served as a means of emancipation, and although most often slaves have gained freedom by aiding their masters' enemies, they frequently have done so by demonstrating "loyalty" to their owners.

"We had used them to good advantage"

For as long as slavery has existed, warfare has been one of the primary liberators of slaves. For example, during the Persian and Peloponnesian wars of the ancient world, slaves gained their freedom either by fighting for their masters or by joining the invaders. During the Punic Wars, even the Romans offered freedom to their slaves if they would fight for the Republic. In the fifteenth century, the Portuguese began the transatlantic African slave trade, and they ironically led the way in offering freedom to their African slaves as a reward for military service. During the seventeenth century, slaves won their freedom fighting for both sides as the Dutch and the Portuguese sought control over Brazil. In the Caribbean, all the European powers offered freedom to slaves who would fight. In the eighteenth and early nineteenth centuries, for example, the British army recruited and employed large numbers of blacks in the region. As a result, thousands received their freedom by fighting for the side that had previously held them in bondage.[2]

In contrast, slaves in the pre-Revolutionary North American colonies seldom served in the military. In 1619, a Dutch ship brought the first Africans known to have arrived in the British North American colonies to the Virginia Peninsula. Planters there attempted to solve the young colony's labor shortage by importing both slaves and indentured servants. By the end of the seventeenth century, however, the supply of indentured servants dramatically declined and death rates stabilized, making slaves a better investment than servants. As the number of slaves rapidly expanded, Virginia and the other southern colonies increasingly enacted laws that placed restrictions on the black population and drew significant color lines between the races. Because of economic self-interest, sensitivity to property rights, and the obvious fear of arming slaves, most colonial legislatures forbade the regular military enlistment of Africans.[3]

Wartime necessity, however, led to occasional black enlistments. For example, during the War of Spanish Succession (Queen Anne's War), with the South Carolina frontier threatened by isolated Indian raids, the colonial legislature authorized "stout negro men to be enlisted" in the militia. As an incentive, lawmakers decreed that any slave who killed or captured a member of the enemy's forces or was wounded while fighting for the colony would be freed. South Carolina repeated this offer a few times over the next few decades during times of military crisis, freeing those few slaves who fought alongside their masters. However, the Stono Rebellion in 1739 put an abrupt end to the idea of arming slaves. For the next two decades, few colonies allowed blacks to serve in the militia.[4]

Nevertheless, at the outbreak of the Seven Years War, white colonists called upon blacks yet again. For the most part, this service was limited to the northern colonies, but there were instances in which southern militia units also resorted to the practice of using blacks. In addition, British general Edward Braddock carried slaves from the Virginia Peninsula with him during his campaign into Pennsylvania. The black men fought side by side with the white soldiers and suffered casualties. Later in the war, George Washington used black laborers to construct defenses on the Virginia frontier.[5]

At the start of the American Revolution, a small group of slaves from the Virginia Peninsula appeared at the governor's house in Williamsburg and offered to help suppress the impending rebellion of their masters. Lord Dunmore sent them away, but the slaves had confirmed his belief that if a rebellion occurred he could count "all slaves on the side of the Government." The royal governor later declared "all indented servants, Negroes, or others, free, that are able and willing to bear arms."[6]

As a result, some blacks made their way down the Peninsula to the sheltering arms of Dunmore's forces. Talk of a Negro "stampede" led to increased patrols and other measures to prevent a mass exodus of slaves. Masters told their slaves that the British were no friends of the black man and would only sell them to the West Indies, where they would endure much harsher conditions. Nevertheless, despite the increased vigilance of whites, within a week of the proclamation approximately 300 blacks had evaded the patrols and made it behind British lines. Dunmore quickly put them to work in small-scale raiding, and they saw action at the Battle of Great Bridge, where they performed admirably. In time, the regiment grew to perhaps as many as 800 black soldiers. Aside from their limited role in combat, Dunmore's Ethiopian Regiment engaged in foraging for supplies badly needed by the troops stationed on ships in Chesapeake Bay.[7]

Dunmore's military use of slaves infuriated white Americans, but as in other wars, the colonists eventually proved willing to raise black troops themselves. Many colonial legislatures initially opposed the use of slaves, but once the crisis worsened, and especially after the British offered freedom to slaves who would join them, the northern colonies began to see the value in enlisting both free blacks and slaves in their militia units. The southern colonies, however, rarely allowed blacks to serve in the militia. Nevertheless, as early as December 1775, manpower shortages led Washington to accept the enlistment of black troops into the Continental army, especially because he feared that if African Americans were not allowed to serve, "they [might] Seek employ in the [British] Army." At any given time during the war, between 6 and 12 percent of Washington's forces were black. Many of these were slaves who eventually earned their freedom by serving with Patriot troops.[8]

Even Virginia found uses for blacks in the war against the British. Like most of the southern states, Virginia opposed using slaves in their militia units but did allow the enlistment of free blacks. Many of them enlisted as substitutes for whites who chose to buy their way out of military service. In addition, white owners often passed their slaves off as free men, placed them on the militia rolls as their substitutes, and thus avoided the draft. Other slaves ran away from their owners and pretended to be free men in order to enlist. African Americans served in the various Virginia units of the Continental army, fighting side by side with white soldiers in each of Washington's major engagements. Black men also acted as spies, gathering intelligence behind British lines by posing as runaways. In addition, Virginia authorized the military to purchase and hire slaves to help construct forts and other defenses.[9]

Nevertheless, the British were far more successful at exploiting Virginia's black labor. Lord Dunmore's promise of freedom eventually became official British policy, and thus when Lord Cornwallis arrived on the Virginia Peninsula in 1781, his troops brought hundreds of blacks they had gathered in the southern states. So many runaways accompanied Cornwallis that one Hessian officer recalled, perhaps with some exaggeration, that "every soldier had his Negro who carried his provisions and bundles." On his march up from North Carolina, Cornwallis had used African Americans to forage, and now he put these black laborers to work on the fortification of the lower Peninsula around Portsmouth, Gloucester, and Yorktown.[10]

Eventually, the Patriots hemmed Cornwallis into his lines around Yorktown, and the fateful siege by American forces began. Inside the British lines were 4,000 to 5,000 blacks who had taken refuge with the redcoats and constructed the fortifications standing between them and their former masters. Meanwhile, the Continental army and navy also benefited from the services of hundreds of blacks. No less than white Americans, blacks who fought in the American Revolution were committed to bettering their condition. For some, that meant casting their lot with the side that had openly offered freedom—the British—while others sided with those who had enslaved them—the Patriots. Whichever side gave them the best hope of obtaining the "inalienable rights" that Jefferson spoke of was likely to find a willing recruit.[11]

As conditions inside besieged Yorktown grew bleaker and provisions scarcer, Cornwallis decided that he could no longer keep the blacks within his lines. Sadly, the men and women who had rushed to his banner, who had foraged for him, acted as servants for his troops, and helped construct the lines that protected him, were now forced out and back into the hands of their former masters. One Hessian officer watched in shame and later recalled how "we had used them to good advantage and set them free, and now, with fear and trembling, they had to face the reward of their cruel masters."[12]

Washington ordered the slaves returned to their owners and opened up the lines so that masters could reclaim their property. He also decreed that any unclaimed blacks should be put to work immediately and that advertisements be placed to help locate their owners. After Cornwallis's surrender and the evacuation of British troops from Yorktown, Americans discovered the ravages that smallpox had inflicted upon many of the blacks who had been with the redcoats. The town and its surroundings contained the bodies of the barely living and the dead.[13]

During the American Revolution, African Americans had willingly gambled by using the war to gain their freedom. Aside from the slaves that were with Cornwallis, the British carried most of these runaways to freedom when they withdrew, but the sight of slaves being returned to the mercy of their vindictive owners at Yorktown, as well as the hundreds of smallpox-ridden bodies stacked for burial, graphically demonstrates that the gamble had not paid off for many of the slaves who had sided with their masters' enemy.

Ironically, however, the American victory resulted in a dramatic increase in the number of free blacks in Virginia. Many of the thousands of slaves who had escaped during the war managed to avoid recapture and now passed themselves off as free men. Other slaves were given their freedom as a reward for supporting the Patriot cause. The Virginia legislature, disturbed by reports that owners who had used their slaves during the war as conscript substitutes were now re-enslaving them, declared that such acts were "contrary to the principles of justice" and passed legislation that freed all such men. In addition, for those masters who were troubled by the philosophical incompatibility of fighting for freedom while denying it to others, many southern states made it easier for them to free their slaves. Repealing a fifty-nine-year-old law, Virginia made it possible for owners to liberate their slaves by will or deed. Most slaves who were freed had demonstrated loyalty to their masters during the Revolutionary War.[14]

The Peninsula's slaves were able to again use war as a means of liberation during the War of 1812. For a second time, the area became the target of British raiding parties designed to stir up the slave population. The memory of the redcoats acting as liberators during the Revolution perhaps lingered in the slave community, and the British again extended the offer of freedom to anyone who would rally to their flag.[15]

In the spring of 1813, British forces began a series of hit-and-run raids along the Virginia coastline designed to damage the American economy and cause general chaos that would disrupt the collaboration of state militia units with the American army. The British offered runaways the chance to enlist in a special regiment or be transported to British possessions in the West Indies. From the beginning, the redcoats underestimated how many blacks would accept such an offer. Throughout the summer of 1813, escapees crowded the decks of British ships. Transports carried most of these slaves to the West Indies, but many demonstrated a desire to fight. One British captain claimed that some slaves came aboard declaring, "Me free man, me go cut massa's throat, give me a musket."[16]

In the spring and summer of 1814, the British presence in the region suddenly increased, and a new commander, Sir Alexander Cochrane, took charge of blockading the coast. The commander established a camp on Tangier Island in the Chesapeake to receive runaway slaves. With black labor used to fortify the position with entrenchments, the camp became a base of operations for the British. Cochrane trained and equipped a number of these blacks as soldiers, and runaway slaves fought in every significant engagement in the Chesapeake region until the end of the war. In August, these former slaves served in the advance unit that routed the Americans at Bladensburg and went on to sack and burn Washington.[17]

As in the Revolution, Americans also benefited from black laborers during the war. When Cochrane's forces moved on Washington and Baltimore, they contended with fortifications constructed and defended with the aid of both slaves and free blacks. Of course the most famous African Americans serving with U.S. forces during the war were in Louisiana. Despite criticism, General Andrew Jackson gladly welcomed a few hundred free blacks and slaves into his army, and they played a prominent role in his successful defense of New Orleans. Thus, African Americans served on both sides in the War of 1812, and by the end of the conflict, between 3,000 and 5,000 Chesapeake slaves had seized the opportunity to liberate themselves.[18]

Whenever armies and navies had come to the Virginia Peninsula, thousands of slaves had used the moment to obtain freedom, if only temporarily. In 1861, forty-six years after the flow of slaves to the British stopped, armies would again arrive on the Peninsula and in numbers unheard of in 1776 or 1812. As could have been predicted by anyone familiar with the historical relationship between slavery and warfare, slaves would be active on both sides of the struggle. Whether a few chose to fight for their enslavers in the hope that their owners would reward their loyalty, or others sought freedom by helping their masters' enemies, Peninsula slaves would seize any advantages they might secure from the tumult and bloodshed of war.

Antebellum life on the Virginia Peninsula and in Richmond prepared the region's African Americans to become valuable assets to both the Confederate and Union armies during the Civil War. The area's relatively diversified economy made blacks skilled in the types of labor needed to support a military campaign, and both sides would come to greatly depend on their physical exertions. Moreover, although the Peninsula's small farms usually did not require slaves to work quite as hard as those in the lower South or in other parts of the state, Peninsula slaves felt all the injustices of slavery and were more than ready to exploit any wartime opportunities to lighten or even escape their burdens. To resist complete domination by their owners, slaves had developed unique skills and talents. Fooling their masters, slipping off the plantation at night, and evading patrols were forms of daily resistance practiced by the slaves, and these experiences gave them expertise and knowledge that would make them valuable assets to the Union army as more than just laborers.

"No one could desire to live in a more favorable place"
In the years after the War of 1812, two centuries of irresponsible land use had made the Tidewater soil incapable of sustaining a successful tobacco crop any longer, and thus the center of tobacco farming shifted to Virginia's central and western regions. In those areas, tobacco continued to thrive, causing a boom in processing and warehousing in Richmond. Water-powered tobacco factories and grain mills flourished due to the city's location on the James River, where the water accelerated at a fall line as it flowed from the Piedmont to the Tidewater. By 1860, Richmond was the nation's leading tobacco processor and the hub for a rail network that crisscrossed the state, tying central Virginia to raw materials, larger markets, and the Shenandoah Valley's blast furnaces. The city developed a highly profitable iron industry, and increasingly Virginians bought a variety of goods and finished iron products from Richmond's merchants

rather than from northern suppliers. Industrial expansion drew more people to the city, and multiplying numbers of shops, taverns, hotels, and other service industries grew up along the busy streets.[19]

In turn, Richmond's urban development helped rescue the Peninsula from economic stagnation. Before the Civil War, Virginia's Peninsula region was made up of the counties of Charles City, Elizabeth City, James City, New Kent, York, and Warwick and bordered (but did not include) the environs of Richmond on its western side and the Chesapeake Bay on its eastern side. In this area, agriculture shifted away from tobacco to food, which farmers sold to Richmond's expanding population or sent through Hampton to northern markets. Corn, peas, oats, potatoes, cabbages, tomatoes, melons, pears, peaches, apples, cherries, and even grapes began to spring from the Peninsula soil in abundance, with wheat the closest thing to a staple crop. Because the roads on the Peninsula were notoriously poor, both the York River, which formed the area's northern border, and the James River, which formed the southern border, carried much of the shipping. Jobs were readily available in loading and unloading cargo, navigating the river, and manning the vessels. In addition, on the lower Peninsula many people earned a good living by fishing and harvesting oysters.[20]

The Peninsula's shift to grains and truck farming reduced labor demand, leaving many of the area's slaveholders with surplus slaves. Owners solved this problem by selling slaves to tobacco planters in the Piedmont region of the state and to the ever-expanding cotton frontier of the Deep South, where slave prices were rising. Nevertheless, African Americans remained the majority of the Peninsula's population: approximately 14,000 slaves and 3,000 free blacks lived and toiled among 12,000 whites. Blacks outnumbered whites in every Peninsula county but one, despite the large number of slaves sold to the Piedmont and the Deep South.[21]

Large planters also sold or hired out many of their surplus slaves to the Peninsula's smaller farmers or to factory and mill owners in Richmond, where these bondsmen became an essential source of labor. By 1860, slaves represented approximately 48 percent of all adult male workers in Richmond. Slaves worked in tobacco warehouses, flourmills, sawmills, and stores. They also labored as stevedores on river docks or unloaded and loaded freight at railroad depots. Many worked in iron foundries, including the famous Tredegar Iron Works, whose owner, Joseph R. Anderson, did not hesitate to use slaves in jobs that required sound judgment and finely honed skills. By 1848, he had placed slaves in most of the skilled positions at his iron works.[22]

The large group of free blacks in Richmond and on the Peninsula also worked at many of these jobs. There were only 58,000 free blacks in the state of Virginia, but they were concentrated in the Tidewater region and were close to 11 percent of the population on the Peninsula in 1860.[23] Most toiled in the fields, but substantial numbers of free blacks worked in skilled crafts or as factory hands or on the York and James Rivers as pilots, fishermen, and oystermen. Slave owners also paid free blacks for work they considered too dangerous or harmful for their slaves, such as well digging or landscaping. As a result, many free blacks specialized in ditching and terracing, work that whites came to view as degrading and unfit for anyone other than blacks. (As we will see, this fact later created considerable difficulty for Confederate leaders).[24]

As the number of African Americans increased in Richmond and decreased on the Peninsula, the size of Peninsula farms shrank. In addition to selling and hiring out their slaves, many Peninsula planters made money by selling off land or leasing it to tenant farmers. As a result, farms were more numerous but considerably smaller than during the colonial era, when the region boasted some of the grandest plantations in North America. Although farmers still reaped modest profits from wheat and vegetable farming as well as from hiring out and selling slaves, the value of Peninsula land fell to about six dollars an acre. Land in other parts of the state was worth two to three times as much. Most Peninsula planters seeking to substantially increase their wealth moved to the more fertile tobacco lands in the Piedmont region or to the cotton frontier of the Deep South.[25]

Those who remained were content to live off inherited wealth from the great tobacco profits of the past, modest profits from wheat and vegetable farming, proceeds of land sales, returns from tenant farms, and income from hiring out and selling surplus slaves. George Benjamin West, who was twenty-two when the Civil War began, later romanticized his family's home near Hampton: "No one could desire to live in a more favorable place," he maintained. As for his neighbors, "None of them were rich, but all were well-to-do, owned their farms, and had sufficient slaves for household and farm work." His life on the Peninsula, surrounded by slowly declining homes and small farms, had been "free from care." Williamsburg's Charles S. Jones agreed: "Most of our people were educated and refined" and "having a sufficiency of the world's goods, were happy and content."[26]

"Twas slavery no matter whar you war"

Archie Booker, a slave from Charles City County, recalled that his owner, Gus Crenshaw, "owned jes an average plantashun" and claimed he had never seen his master whip a slave. Booker remembered Mrs. Crenshaw as well: "Marstuh's wife ol mistess wuz ve'y nice." Another Peninsula slave, Robert Ellett, had similar praise: "My mistess was a nice woman," he reflected. "In fact, she was an angel." Such positive assessments of the personal qualities of owners were common among the slaves on the Virginia Peninsula. The small size of Peninsula farms allowed for close relationships between owners and slaves and helped to foster this apparently benign temperament among some of the region's slaveholders. In addition, wheat and truck farming required relatively less work than tobacco or cotton planting. As Hampton slave Matilda Carter maintained, "All de slaves in dis section was treat ve'y nice."[27]

Nevertheless, slaves easily separated feelings of affection for masters who treated them comparatively well from their general hatred of slavery. "Kind treatment is a good thing," a black Richmonder who had purchased his own freedom maintained during an interview in the 1850s, "but it isn't liberty." Although some Peninsula slaves regarded their masters as kind, this did not diminish their desire for freedom. In fact, it may have heightened it. "Beat and cuff your slave, keep him hungry and spiritless, and he will follow the chain of his master like a dog," claimed Frederick Douglass. "But feed and clothe him well, work him moderately, surround him with physical comfort, and dreams of freedom intrude. Give him a bad master, and he aspires to a good master; give him a good master, and he wishes to become his own master."[28]

However much Peninsula slaveholders may have been "good masters," their slaves experienced most of the cruelties of the peculiar institution. "We wuked for ole Marsa Woods in Virginia jes' as hawd as we wuked down Mississippi," recalled Charles Grandy, who had toiled in the Deep South before being brought to the village of Hampton on the tip of the Peninsula. "Yes, got beatin's too. 'Twas slavery no matter whar you war."[29]

Although the workload for Peninsula slaves was relatively lighter than in other parts of the South, there were still times when Tidewater masters worked their slaves beyond endurance. "As slaves, the Negroes did some real work," declared Virginia Hayes Shepherd from nearby Portsmouth, "but even the Negro had his limit." She remembered a time when her mother "had worked and worked and worked until she just couldn't go any faster." The plantation's overseer noticed that she was slowing down, so he threatened her with a beating if she did not speed up. "She simply stopped and told them 'Go a-head, kill me if you want. I'm working as fast as I can and I just can't do more.' They saw she was at the place where she didn't care whether she died or not; so they left her alone."[30]

Others were not so fortunate. As in other parts of the South, whipping remained a common form of punishment on the Peninsula. "Whip em? Yes . . . I done seen 'em whipped," recalled Samuel Walter Chilton of Richmond. "Dey take yo' shirt off an' beat you bare back." Charles Grandy of Hampton explained that his master laid his slaves face down and tied their hands and feet to stakes. "Den dey whup you 'till de blood come." The owner used a bullwhip on his slaves, and Grandy had been its victim several times before he decided to resist. "I got tired him whuppin' me. You know, an' I stole de ole whup. He left it hangin' on de post. I took it an' hid it in de woods." Richard Eppes, who owned several large plantations in the region, including one on the Peninsula, claimed that he found whipping to be "the worst feature" of slavery and that it gave him "a distaste for the whole institution." However, "Let it once be known on the plantation that master will not whip," he insisted, and it would lead to "an end to all management" of the slaves. In typical paternalistic fashion, he compared the whipping of slaves to a father's punishment of his children. "Spare the rod you spoil the child," he maintained.[31]

Eliza Baker, a former slave, vividly recalled the location of a whipping post in a ravine at the corner of Francis and South England Streets in Williamsburg, as well as a cage in which those being whipped were held. "After they had whipped you," she remembered, "you had to pay a dollar to get out of the cage." Owners usually paid this fee for their slaves, but free blacks were also punished at the whipping post and were forced to pay a dollar to free themselves. "If you was caught out after nine o'clock," Baker maintained, "you would be whipped—given nine and thirty [lashes]."[32]

Whippings, however, did not arouse nearly as much fear as being sold. Selling slaves was so extensive that several historians have asserted that Virginians may have been in the business of slave breeding for the direct purpose of selling to the Deep South.[33] While traveling through the Virginia Tidewater during the 1850s, Frederick Law Olmsted observed "labourers . . . being constantly sent away. I have not been on or seen a railroad train, departing southward, that did not convey a considerable number of the best class of negro labourers, in the charge of a trader who was intending to sell them to cotton planters." He further claimed that "the slaves [are] drawn off almost as fast as they grow up." Thomas R. Dew, president of the College of William and Mary in Williamsburg, remarked in 1832 that Virginia had become "a Negro raising State for the other States." Peninsula slaves lived with the constant threat of being "sold south," where slavery was rumored to be harsher and the masters crueler. "If you didn't do what they wanted you to," Williamsburg's Eliza

Baker bitterly recalled, "they put you in their pocket. That means the nig-ger trader would get you."[34]

On the auction block, slaves had their muscles and teeth examined as if they were livestock, and their backs were examined for whipping scars. Slave women underwent an even more degrading examination. William I. Johnson, a hired slave living in Richmond before the war, explained that "when they put the women up on the auction block bidders would come up and feel the women's legs—lift up her [g]arments and examine their hips, feel their breast, and examine them to see if they could bear chil-dren." The degradation of slave women by white male owners all too often went beyond these auction block examinations. "In those days," declared Robert Ellet, a slave from West Point, "if you was a slave and had a good looking daughter, she was taken from you. . . . The young masters could have the run of her."[35]

Selling slaves meant separating families. "White folks in my part of the country didn't think anything of breaking up a family and selling the chil-dren in one section of the south and the parents in some other section," claimed William I. Johnson. "If they got short of cash and wanted four or five hundred dollars—they would say, 'John, Mary, James, I want you to get ready and go to the courthouse with me this morning.' They would take you on down there and that's the last we'd see of them." One histo-rian has argued that slaveholders in the upper South were far from "reluc-tant sellers," even when selling meant the breakup of families. He con-cludes that masters dissolved as many as one-third of all marriages in the upper South by either interregional or local slave trading and separated one out of every two slave children from their parents. Slaveholders de-luded themselves in such a way that they could regularly separate families and yet still consider themselves paternalists. "It is a truly painful thing to sell a really troublesome negro," Peninsula planter Richard Eppes admit-ted, "but it must be done for the good of the others."[36]

Matilda Carter of Hampton, who had declared that "all de slaves in dis section was treated ve'y nice," nevertheless recalled that the most unjust thing she ever endured was the selling of her "po' lil sis down South." She remembered that her "mother never did git over dis ack of sellin' her baby to dem slave drivers down New Orleans." Eliza Baker vividly described the slave auction block that stood on the Courthouse Green in Williamsburg and the separation of families that took place there. "I have heard many a crying out on the block," she recalled. In a particularly pointed remark while discussing the history of the city, Baker bitterly noted that there were numerous belles on the Peninsula before the Civil War. "They were good looking. They should have been, for their families were selling us to make pocket change to send them to the Springs every summer and to school in the fall."[37]

"In some instances they are very unfaithful"

For Peninsula and Richmond slaves longing to flee from the humiliations and abuses of slavery, the York and James Rivers beckoned. Throughout the 1850s, Virginia authorities discovered that increased shipping traffic on the rivers created opportunities for slaves to make their escape by hiding on steamers and other boats. Richard Slaughter, a former slave who grew up on the James River, recalled that "in those days a good captain would hide a slave way up in the top sail and carry him out of Virginia to New York and Boston." It is unlikely that many slaves successfully escaped in this manner, but there were clearly enough waterborne fugitives to compel the state to take action. In 1855, the legislature considered a bill to station an armed ship at the mouth of the James, the sole purpose of which would be to catch fugitive slaves. In 1856, Virginia passed a law that required a search for runaways on all out-of-state vessels before they left the commonwealth and mandated a $500 fine for all vessels that left without the inspection. The law resulted in several highly publicized captures and the imprisonment of ship's captains who knowingly or unknowingly had fugitives aboard their vessels.[38]

The many hired-out slaves on the Peninsula and particularly in Richmond were typically the most discontented and independent minded of all slaves, and thus they were likely candidates to run away. Slaves who were hired out in towns and cities had more mobility than those on the plantation, better access to information, and often some choice in their placement. Because owners earned larger profits by hiring out their most skilled people, hired slaves generally possessed a greater degree of self-confidence and individuality. They knew the worth of their labor, had more access to information from the outside world, and had a small taste of what freedom felt like. Such slaves often took advantage of their quasi-independence to pass themselves off as freemen, and their work in close proximity to Richmond's docks gave them access to outgoing ships.[39]

Hired slaves may have also been at the center of an organization that was helping other slaves escape from Tidewater Virginia. In 1858, officials in Norfolk discovered the existence of a group known as the Norfolk Nine, which was assisting runaways. The arrests and subsequent investigation exposed the existence of a network that allegedly stretched from Norfolk up the Peninsula to Richmond. Apparently, hired-out slaves partially funded the organization's efforts to help runaways obtain disguises, guides, and transportation. Several white ship captains helped hide runaways in the false bottoms of their boats.[40]

Although northern captains with abolitionist leanings sometimes assisted Peninsula runaways, the slaves more often received aid from the numerous free blacks working along the York and James Rivers. A free black steward named Meekins, for example, was known among the slave community for helping to stow runaways. Another free black named Lott Mundy, a cook on the schooner *Danville*, apparently hid runaways in the boat and charged ten dollars for his services. Officials eventually discovered Mundy's activities and sentenced him to ten years in prison. In the mid-1850s, the state legislature increased the punishments for free blacks who helped runaways, mandating longer jail sentences and public whippings.[41] The large concentration of free blacks in Richmond and on the Peninsula, coupled with the large number of hired-out slaves, helps account for the apparent frequency of runaways in the region.

Most slaves, of course, were not willing to risk running away or participating in a revolt. Gabriel's Rebellion in 1800 and especially Nat Turner's in 1831 had shown them that such violent resistance was rarely successful and was crushed mercilessly and only led to a further tightening of restrictions. Consequently, the slaves learned that the best way to resist complete degradation was to do so in small ways, on a day-to-day basis, and to reach down within themselves to create a social life and culture that was separate from the white world.[42]

Individual acts of resistance could take the form of slowing down on the job, damaging farm instruments, committing crimes, setting fire to outbuildings, playing simple tricks, or performing tasks inadequately. "They very frequently cannot be made to do their master's will," Frederick Law Olmsted observed after traveling through the Virginia Tidewater. "Not that they often directly refuse to obey an order, but when they are directed to do anything for which they have a disinclination, they undertake it in such a way that the desired result is sure not to be accomplished." In a prewar description of his home, William S. Forrest, a white resident near the lower Peninsula, predictably maintained that slaves in the area were loyal and content but added, "It must be admitted, that in some instances they are very unfaithful, and sometimes shamefully betray the confidence of their owners."[43]

Striving to create their own social order, slaves routinely left their quarters at night without permission. Illegally traveling away from their masters' jurisdiction allowed slaves to create an alternate realm in which they

Slaves at Foller's House, Cumberland Landing, Virginia. This famous 1862 photograph is of slaves in New Kent County on the Virginia Peninsula. (Library of Congress)

retained a degree of control of their lives. They often slipped away to find food, spent time with spouses and children who lived on other plantations, found amusements and rest, or temporarily absented themselves in individual acts of defiance against their masters for cruel treatment. For example, Cornelia Carney of Williamsburg claimed that her father ran away to the woods after a particularly harsh beating and came back only on Saturday nights and Sunday mornings when his owners had gone to church. He was not alone. "Father wasn't de onlies one hidin' in de woods. Der was his cousin, Gabriel, dat was hidin' an' a man name Charlie."[44]

While "laying out" in this fashion, some slaves were in effect negotiating with their masters. George Benjamin West remembered that one of his family's slaves ran away to the woods "and sent father word he wished to be sold and would never be any account to him unless he was sold." West's father refused to sell, but true to his word, the slave gave the owner nothing but trouble. Finally, "Father exchanged him for a man . . . and we never heard of him again."[45]

Slaves also frequently drifted off their plantations at night to meet deep in the woods. These social gatherings helped slaves to release pent-up emotions and rejuvenate the spirit and were often of a religious nature. Some slave owners, especially those of a paternalistic bent, were concerned with the spiritual lives of their slaves and took measures to instruct them in the basics of Christianity. However, as Charles City County's Sister Robinson explained, the doctrine that slaves heard most often was "be nice to massa an' missus, . . . be obedient, . . . an' wuk hard." But when slaves gathered away from white control, they worshipped a God who promised relief from the oppressions of the world. The dominant theme at these emotional meetings was freedom and hope, and it manifested itself in the prayers and songs of the slaves.[46]

Drawn to these spiritual meetings as a place of release, even slaves with no underlying inclination to escape risked punishment by stealing away from their cabins. Charles Grandy recalled how slaves on his plantation who wanted to "talk wid Jesus" would "go 'cross de fields nights to a old tobacco barn on de side of a hill." Peter Randolph, a slave in nearby Prince George County, explained how they arranged these meetings. The slaves, he wrote in 1855, "have an understanding among themselves as to the time and place of getting together. This is often done by the first one arriving breaking boughs from the trees, and bending them in the direction of the selected spot."[47]

As a precaution during these gatherings, the attendees kept someone on the lookout for slave patrols. Commonly referred to as "paddyrollers" by the slaves, these locally organized groups were infamous for their harsh punishments. However, slaves who had to contend with these units were adept at avoidance and trickery, and "baiting" patrols away from slave gatherings was a common practice. Beverly Jones, a slave from nearby Gloucester, recalled the tactic: "[We] used to station niggers in relays from the trail to the meetin' place an' when the patterollers would show up, [the slave] who was always the one farthest out, would whistle like a bobcat to warn the others." This would end the meeting and send the slaves scurrying for home. To buy time, the "bait" slave would flee before the patrols in the opposite direction and slip away into the darkness.[48]

In addition to attending parties and religious meetings, slaves left the plantations to gather news. Cornelius Garner explained that "evenings after we finished wuk we'd walk up to de store . . . and listen to de ole white folks talk." There they heard their masters discussing secession and the possibility of war. Domestic slaves heard the news by listening carefully around the master's home. When slaves could not gather news themselves, it traveled to them along the famous slave "grapevine." Slaves gathered information in a variety of ways and adeptly and secretly passed it along. Horace Muse, a slave near the Peninsula in King George County, remembered, "When de war came, de news spread like whirlwin! We heard it whispered 'roun' dat a war come to set de niggers free."[49]

"Some negroes have had their hopes unduly excited"
After the election of Abraham Lincoln in the fall of 1860, the number one topic on the grapevine was the possibility of war, causing many slaves to rejoice. "Ev'ybody was happy when de war came," Hampton's Charles Grandy later claimed.[50] The subsequent actions of many slaves before, during, and after the Peninsula Campaign lend credence to this recollection. In a culture that relied heavily on oral tradition, slaves handed down such lore from generation to generation, so Peninsula slaves were possibly aware of the opportunities that the Revolution and the War of 1812 had brought to their ancestors. More important, from listening to the conversations of their masters, slaves understood that their owners believed that Lincoln and northern society threatened the institution of slavery. The arrival of Union soldiers might well mean freedom.

Richard Eppes realized that some of his bondsmen interpreted white concerns over the election of Lincoln as good news. In response, he hired out a slave named Sandy, who was apparently exerting "a bad influence on my other negroes especially at this time." Eppes also instructed the overseer on his Peninsula plantation to "not allow meetings among negroes for the present & never at night." Shortly after the election, one of Williamsburg's largest slaveholders, Robert Page Waller, reported that the captain of the local militia company called a meeting "to form a guard for the town for the night. This was caused by an anonymous letter . . . dropped at Capt Henley's door, warning them of an insurrection to kill & destroy & burn the town." The threat never materialized, but Williamsburg's militia company spent a sleepless night on alert.[51]

Richmond slaves took advantage of their ready access to information and spread word to the enslaved community outside the city. With several Deep South states already out of the Union and others debating the question in January 1861, slaves in Richmond eavesdropped on whites gathered around telegraph offices waiting for news and discussing events. In one instance, blacks relayed their impressions of these conversations to other slaves across the river in Manchester. The news was then discussed at a gathering in the home of a local free black family. Some of the slaves present maintained that the coming of war meant that freedom was as little as two months away. Apparently, some of those in the group discussed the idea of burning one of the bridges leading out of the city so that blacks in Richmond could kill their trapped masters. Sensing the day of deliverance, one slave reportedly declared that "God had ordained it to be so," and another wished for a crowbar so that he could pluck out the eyes of his owner.[52]

Someone present at the gathering betrayed these would-be plotters and informed their owner. Local authorities arrested approximately fifteen slaves and free blacks. They all denied having taken part in this discussion, but each received as many as thirty-nine lashes. Although much of the fear of slave insurrection in the wake of Lincoln's election was the product of white paranoia, slaves could not help but sense the concerns of their masters and realize that war and perhaps freedom were coming. Whether this clandestine meeting represented the planning stage of an actual slave insurrection or was nothing more than slaves engaged in wishful thinking and boastful talk, it does demonstrate that some blacks were spreading the belief that the North was committed to ending slavery and were thus optimistic about the coming of the war. Many in the slave community recognized the possibilities that lay ahead. The *Richmond Daily Dispatch* discounted the Manchester gathering as nothing more than rumor and talk but admitted that "some negroes have had their hopes unduly excited, we have no doubt."[53]

The lives of African Americans had prepared them to take advantage of much of what was to come. The decline of staple crop agriculture on the Virginia Peninsula and the widespread system of hiring out had diversified their labor, which made the slaves and free blacks in the region a great source of skilled and unskilled labor for the two armies about to confront one another. Although slaves on the Virginia Peninsula enjoyed relatively better conditions than those in the Deep South, their desire for freedom remained strong. They had seen and suffered the familiar cruelties of slavery, and many of their families had been broken apart by sale. Hired-out slaves tended to be the most discontented of all, and there was a high concentration of them in the region. Years of daily resistance to slavery, as well as a degree of mobility and knowledge of the land, had taught the slaves how to fool their masters so they could flee into the woods and avoid recapture. They had learned how to sneak away for secret gatherings, and they knew all the places in the region where a slave could hide and later slip away to, unseen in the darkness. Perhaps no one understood the Peninsula's geography, road conditions, and hidden trails better than did the slaves, and this would soon make them invaluable to Union armies. When war came once again to the Virginia Peninsula in 1861, the enslaved community was prepared and more than willing to use it as a means of liberation.

2

CONTRABAND OF WAR
APRIL–JULY 1861

On April 23, 1861, eleven days after the firing on Fort Sumter and six days after the Virginia legislature approved an ordinance of secession, the steamship *Logan* left the city of Baltimore bound for Fredericksburg, Virginia. William Ringgold, a free black working as a steward, was aboard the vessel as it ventured south. When the ship landed, Confederates impressed it and the crew, sending both to the York River to transport workers and troops from West Point to Yorktown and Gloucester Point. For the next eight months, Ringgold helped deliver thousands of black workers to construct vital fortifications on the lower Peninsula.[1] The Confederacy's basic defensive strategy soon became dependent on their labor.

From the start of the war, some members of the Virginia Peninsula's enslaved community viewed the conflict as a potential path to liberation. Because many people in the North were not yet ready to support emancipation, however, it was unclear whether the Federals offered blacks the best opportunity for improving their lives, especially since masters went to great effort to deceive their slaves concerning Yankee intentions. Nevertheless, many slaves on the lower Peninsula quickly made contact with Federal troops, setting in motion a process that resulted in the Lincoln administration's policy of protecting runaways who had been forced to labor for the Confederacy. When Union troops first arrived in the area, white Virginians fled the lower Peninsula and left hundreds of their slaves behind, creating a situation that helped to cause one of the first land battles of the Civil War. As in previous wars, African Americans labored and may have even fought for both armies as they slowly gathered in the region. Just weeks after the war began, Northerners were already paying close attention to the activities of African Americans on the Virginia Peninsula.

"Matters pertaining to insurrection"

Once Virginia seceded, the defense of its borders became an immediate Confederate priority. In the state's eastern section, there were hundreds of miles of navigable water, and on the tip of the Virginia Peninsula sat Fort Monroe, the largest coastal fort in the United States. The federal government resupplied Monroe after the fall of Fort Sumter, and with its masonry walls and massive guns it was too formidable for the few Virginia troops on the Peninsula to attack. Confederate leaders quickly realized that this strong Federal presence hindered their control of the Chesapeake Bay and the rivers that led from it into the heart of the state.

On the same day that William Ringgold left Baltimore, Virginia placed Robert E. Lee in command of its military forces. The state had previously seized the arsenal at Harpers Ferry and the navy yard at Norfolk, and in response, President Lincoln gave the South until May 5 to cease such acts of rebellion. This gave Lee just twelve days to prepare Virginia for possible invasion. On April 26, he ordered the state's engineer, Colonel Andrew Talcott, to prepare batteries and fortifications along the seacoast and on the Peninsula. Confessing "ignorance of the James river," Lee left the placement of the works to Talcott's own judgment. The assignment was urgent because Federal gunboats could use the rivers to come within effective range of Richmond.[2]

Under Talcott's direction, engineers set stakes for the defensive works and the state's navy stood ready to mount the heavy artillery pieces. The colonel's biggest challenge was to find sufficient labor for the digging and construction. New recruits arriving from various parts of the Confederacy would have to spend their time drilling and organizing. Just as vexing, many whites deemed extensive digging as work fit only for blacks. "It appears that where negro slavery has long existed," Frederick Law Olmsted explained, "certain occupations are, by custom, assigned to the slaves, and a white man is not only reluctant to engage in those occupations, but is greatly disinclined to employ other whites in them." Such sentiments quickly created enormous difficulties for Confederate commanders. Talcott decided to mobilize the state's free blacks and slaves, many of whom specialized in ditching and terracing. It was not difficult to find African American turfers, carpenters, bricklayers, sawyers, wagon drivers, and ditchers on the Peninsula. Many slave owners quickly volunteered their slaves' services and were paid fifty cents per day for unskilled workers and a dollar a day for carpenters and bricklayers.[3]

Many free blacks also signed up for these wages. In Petersburg, for example, a gathering of about 300 free blacks listened as the mayor encouraged them to help defend the state. They left for the lower Peninsula and labored for the Confederacy. In Richmond, the *Dispatch* reported that free blacks laboring on the city's defenses "march in every evening with drums beating and colors flying," which the editors took as an indication that the black Virginians were not "displeased at having to contribute towards defending their native place from a foreign invader."[4] Community spirit and the festive air may indeed have motivated these laborers, but a more compelling factor was the income which was so difficult for free blacks to obtain.

Slaves also marched off to the lower Peninsula carrying picks and shovels, singing songs, and deceptively demonstrating "loyalty" to their masters. Although the prospect of freedom clearly excited many African Americans, they could not be certain that their owners would lose the war. The vast number of Rebel soldiers arriving in the capital city was intimidating. "Thousands of Troops were Sent to Richmond from all parts of the South," hired slave John Washington recalled. "So many troops of all discription was landed there that it appeared to be an impossiability, to us, Colored people that they could ever be conquord."[5] In the face of such overwhelming force, most slaves initially did little to either support or hinder the Confederacy. As in other wars throughout history, however, some slaves may have offered their services in the hope that their loyalty would earn short-term rewards or perhaps even freedom.

Always looking for revenue, Peninsula planter Richard Eppes recruited among his slaves and local free blacks to work on the fortifications. He told them that "labor was wanted and promised to give them meat and meal . . . for a week if they would go." They seemed less than enthused by the offer. "[I] don't know how many, if any, will go," the planter confessed.[6]

But Eppes had even bigger problems. On May 8, the overseer on his Peninsula plantation reported that a slave named William had "disappeared." Eppes seemed unconcerned, instructing the overseer to just "let him go," attributing the flight to the slave's "timidity" at working on the fortifications. Eppes worried, however, that William's "example will cause several of the others to disappear before morning."[7] His fears were justified; less than a month after the firing on Fort Sumter, Eppes's Peninsula plantation became a breeding ground for plans to flee to the Union army.

On May 24, the day after Virginians voted to ratify the state's secession ordinance, officials brought two of Richard Eppes's slaves, a female named Amy and a young teenage boy, before William Eppes, the magistrate of Prince George County. The woman "said on oath that she heard one of [Richard] Eppes' men, now ran away, declare that he would run off rather than go down the river to work on the batteries being there erected, and that he intended to remain in the woods until the arrival of the Northern army and join them." Perhaps this man was Richard Eppes's missing slave William. He was not alone. Amy explained that for the last six months, slaves on both sides of the James River, and especially in Charles City County on the Peninsula, had discussed how the Yankees would help them "get their freedom." The teenage boy was more specific, testifying that "since the election of Lincoln these negroes had been holding . . . meetings on the different farms in the neighborhood, ostensibly for the purpose of singing and praying, but at which the men would collect together and talk about matters pertaining to insurrection." Explaining all this to Hill Carter of Shirley Plantation, the magistrate warned that slaves at Shirley were also "in favor of the insurrection under favorable conditions."[8]

Troubled by the situation, fellow planter Edmund Ruffin speculated about why the slaves might believe Union soldiers would help them. "There have been the most ample facilities," he wrote, "for indoctrinating and deluding slaves with free intercourse with Northern sailors, and . . . with free negroes forming crews of vessels from the North." Besides this, "The negroes have received very general . . . impressions that the Northerners were operating for Negro emancipation, or as friends, real or pretended, to the slaves."[9]

These "impressions" did not come from the U.S. government. Although President Lincoln detested slavery and fervently hoped it would eventually end, his inaugural address sought to calm the upper South and the Border States by repeating his assurances not to "interfere with the institution of slavery where it exists." These promises were consistent with his belief that the Constitution protected southern slavery and that the government could only prevent its expansion. Lincoln hoped that restrictions on slavery's growth would put the institution on the path to ultimate extinction. The war was necessary only to prevent the South from breaking up the Union, because letting the South peacefully separate from the United States would essentially legitimize secession as a viable recourse for the minority. If that occurred, representative democracy could not work. Because he believed secession was unconstitutional, Lincoln saw himself as the chief executive for the entire nation and thus bound to protect the constitutional rights of southern slaveholders. He repeated these assurances in his April 15 call for 75,000 troops to end the rebellion.[10]

With the significant exception of abolitionists and radicals within the Republican Party, the president's sentiments mirrored those of most

Northerners. "The war is not an anti-slavery crusade of the North against the South," the *National Anti-Slavery Standard* grudgingly admitted. "Had this so much as been hinted at in the President's Proclamation, not a regiment would have volunteered." Democratic and Republican congressmen, newspaper editorialists, and military recruiting agents assured the nation that the purpose of the war was not to bring about the liberation of southern slaves. From the start, military commanders showed little sympathy for African Americans. General Benjamin Butler of Massachusetts, for example, offered the services of his soldiers to Maryland for the suppression of any possible slave insurrections as his troops made their way to Washington.[11]

Even antislavery editors and politicians seemed timid on the issue at the start of the war. Although they immediately hoped that the conflict would result in freedom for the slaves, they feared that criticizing the government by promoting emancipation during the surge of patriotic fervor after Fort Sumter would only further alienate them from the northern population. Radical Republicans made few public statements pushing emancipation as a war aim, and abolitionists brooded and debated among themselves about whether to even support the war. The *National Anti-Slavery Standard* encouraged its readers to suspend their criticism of the government and "watch the sequence of events." This momentary compromise of principle troubled many abolitionists, but they hoped that slaves would grasp the potential for freedom the war offered. "I will tell you what I once heard a negro say," Boston attorney George Smalley counseled famed abolitionist Wendell Philips. "When my massa and somebody else quarrel, I'm on the somebody else's side."[12]

Emancipationists would have been encouraged had they heard Amy's testimony before the Prince George County magistrate. Ironically, southern whites were the reason some slaves already believed the war would lead to emancipation. In an effort to ensure that their slaves would not assist Federal troops, masters had been telling horror stories about Northerners. They spoke of Yankees who bored holes in black skin, cut off limbs, harnessed slaves like horses, and drove them under the lash of the cruelest masters in the world. The big story was that money-hungry Yankees would sell slaves to work in the jungles of Cuba to pay for the war. Many slaves may have been deceived, but others realized that if slave owners concocted such tales about Northerners, the Yankees must be a threat to their masters and thus a friend to the slaves.[13]

Other evidence confirmed these slave suspicions. The election of 1860 and its aftermath featured an outpouring of southern rhetoric claiming that Lincoln was an abolitionist and that he and the Republicans would destroy slavery. Typical was the Southerner who denounced Lincoln as "an illiterate partisan . . . possessed only of his inveterate hatred of slavery and his openly avowed predilections of negro equality." (Such racially charged invectives frequently came from northern Democrats as well). The magistrate of Prince William County, William Eppes, discovered the connection between slave hopes and anti-Lincoln rhetoric after questioning Amy and the young slave boy. "As the Negroes have heard much through newspapers," he explained, "which some of them read, as also from the political] stump and in the family circles of their owners about the objects of the 'black Republican Party' it is very natural that some of it should be repeated in the quarters and among themselves."[14] Future runaways would soon confirm the accuracy of Eppes's assessment.

The testimony of Amy and the young boy convinced Edmund Ruffin that the danger was real. The evidence was "very full and confirming," and there was "no doubt of the guilt." Nevertheless, William Eppes decided that it would be "imprudent . . . to give publicity to the idea of such a thing as an insurrection among the slaves." Because he feared that a more severe punishment would arouse the attention of the public, he ordered thirty lashes for most of the guilty and thirty-nine for "the chief instigator and the leader in their 'prayer-meetings.'" Nevertheless, he told Hill Carter, "You and your citizens . . . [should] take such action or use such vigilance as your discretion will suggest." Ruffin also downplayed the event but believed it demonstrated that whites "ought to be always vigilant, and be ready to meet attacks, whether from Northern invaders or negro insurgents." He decided "to use means for defense which I never did before, in keeping loaded guns by my bedside."[15] The war was only a few weeks old, Lincoln and the northern public were disavowing emancipation as a war aim, and Union troops had not set foot on the Virginia Peninsula, but many Peninsula slaves were already prepared to use the conflict as a means of liberation.

"The readiness of slaves to flee . . . I did not expect"

Despite these alarming events, or perhaps because of them, the work on the lower Peninsula continued at a feverish pace. Black laborers and white soldiers rode the York River railroad from Richmond to West Point and then boarded steamers for the trip down the river. William Ringgold and the crew of the *Logan* plied the river daily delivering workers to the lower Peninsula. Thanks to the supply of black laborers, the building of defensive works progressed smoothly and required little of General Lee's attention. Virginia's enslaved community was proving to be an invaluable asset. "Our late Southern brethren are . . . teaching us that the negro has a part to play in the war," the *National Anti-Slavery Standard* sarcastically pointed out on May 18. "Desire as we may to rule him out, the slaveocrats of Virginia . . . will not allow it. . . . They place him in the ranks with the First Families of Virginia."[16]

During his time on the York River, William Ringgold witnessed fellow blacks engaged in exceptionally arduous labor. Civil War–era field fortifications required extensive and skilled labor to excavate the earth, create the parapet and glacis embankments, provide for drainage, and construct the platforms, slopes, and powder magazines.[17] Directed by the state's engineers, several hundred slaves and free blacks were laboring on the works on the lower Peninsula and around Norfolk. Besides skill, the work required stamina and strength. In stifling humidity, the men were constantly digging, cutting, clearing, and lifting logs and stones into place. Often they were required to work in water and mud up to their waists. Rations were inadequate, consisting of rice in the morning and little more than a pint of meal at night. The ten-hour workdays and poor diet took their toll, but the Confederates compelled the slaves to keep working. By the end of Lincoln's twelve-day grace period, the Confederates were developing a line of formidable entrenchments with felled trees and cleared fields in front and with the rivers well protected by batteries.[18] Ringgold took mental note of it all.

With the Federals nearby at Fort Monroe, many of the black laborers increasingly thought of freedom, especially since they were working harder than they had for their Peninsula masters. On May 22, Major General Benjamin Butler took command of Union forces at the fort. The next day, Virginia voters ratified the state's ordinance of secession, and Butler ordered a reconnoitering expedition under the command of Colonel John W. Phelps of the 1st Vermont. The soldiers crossed a bridge to the mainland and into the city of Hampton. They discovered that most of the white inhabitants had evacuated the town, leaving behind a few men to watch over the slaves.[19]

Private Edward Pierce recalled that the slaves greeted the Union soldiers warmly that day with "glad to see you, Massa." The bluecoats happily returned the sentiment. These New Englanders were the right people, in the right place, at the right time to encourage human freedom. From the colonel down to the privates, they held strong antislavery sentiments.[20] Because owners had filled their slaves' minds with all kinds of stories about the evil intentions of Yankees, if the first contact that Hampton slaves made with Federal troops had been with men who were unsympathetic or hostile, the relationship of trust between Peninsula slaves and the Yankees would have developed much more slowly.

Frank Baker, James Townsend, and Sheppard Mallory, three slaves who had worked on the Confederate fortifications, noticed how friendly the Vermonters had been to the blacks and decided that the Union army was too close not to make a run for it. During the day, they slipped into the woods and used their "laying out" skills to wait until the cover of darkness. As night fell, they set out on the bay in a small skiff and paddled as quietly as possible. They had no way of knowing for sure how they would be received, but they boldly presented themselves to the Federal picket guards and no doubt prayed their gamble would pay off. The soldiers offered shelter for the night but explained that in the morning they would have to present the runaways to General Butler.[21]

On the same day that Amy and the teenage boy were testifying in Prince George County, Butler separately interviewed Baker, Townsend, and Mallory about the work they had been doing for the Confederacy. Anxious to help in any way they could and begging the general not to return them to their masters, the three slaves pleaded their case. Realizing that their labor only benefited the Union's enemies, Butler decided to protect the men and put them to work on a new bakery near the fort. The runaways were no doubt relieved that the work did not require them to be harnessed or shipped to Cuba.[22]

The next day, Major John B. Cary of the Confederate army came to see Butler and demanded the return of the slaves. Butler had been one of the most successful criminal trial lawyers in the state of Massachusetts, and he put his courtroom skills to good use. He informed Cary that he intended to "retain" the slaves. "Do you mean then," Cary asked, "to set aside your constitutional obligations [to return fugitive slaves]?"

"I mean to abide by the decision of Virginia as expressed in her ordinance of secession," Butler coolly replied. "I am under no Constitutional obligations to a foreign country, which Virginia now claims to be."

Cary reminded Butler that Lincoln maintained that the southern states could not secede and were still a part of the nation. To be consistent with that reasoning, he declared, "you cannot . . . detain the Negroes."

Challenged by the logic, Butler shot back, "But you say that you have seceded, and [thus] you cannot consistently claim them." Then Butler went for the kill by declaring that if the owner wished to come into the fort "and take the oath of allegiance to the United States," he could have the men back.[23]

That ended the matter. In his official report, Butler defended his action by calling the three slaves "contraband of war." Since Southerners held slaves as a form of property and were using that property to build their fortifications, Butler concluded that slaves were subject to confiscation under rules of war that allowed the seizure of property that aided an enemy's war efforts. Butler was no abolitionist; he was not freeing these slaves, only confiscating their labor. Nevertheless, he set a precedent of refusing to return fugitive slaves. In forwarding the report to the War Department, Lieutenant General Winfield Scott, general in chief of the army, added his approval. "There is much to praise in this report and little to condemn."[24]

Baker, Townsend, and Mallory explained to Union soldiers that other slaves would soon know that Northerners had sheltered them and that as a result more would come. They were correct. Two days after Cary's visit, eight more slaves showed up at Fort Monroe. "Will you send us back?" they asked the Federals. "We want to know because if you don't, our friends will follow. They wait to learn how we are treated" by Union soldiers. The next day, fifty-nine slaves came to the gates of what they were now calling "Fort Freedom." Three days later, Butler estimated that $60,000 worth of slaves was now inside the fort. "We had heard it since last fall," explained one runaway, "that if Lincoln was elected, you would come down and set us free." As William Eppes learned after his questioning of Amy and the teenage slave in Prince George County, their masters had been the source of this information. "But they don't talk so now. The colored people have talked it all over; we heard that if we could get in here we should be free, or at any rate, we should be among friends." Arriving from all over the Virginia Peninsula—in canoes, on homemade rafts, and in hollowed-out logs—the escapees floated down streams into either the York River or the James River and then on to the fort. Those on foot made their way through familiar woods and secret trails. "They continued to come in [groups of] twenties, thirties and forties," Private Edward Pierce recalled.[25]

Butler was soon overwhelmed with entire families of runaways. On May 27, he wrote General Scott that he was "in the utmost doubt" about what to do with the women and children. He could justify taking slaves who were working on the fortifications because, he asserted, "without them, the [Confederate] batteries could not have been erected at least for many weeks. As a military question it would seem a necessity to deprive their masters of their services." But, he added, "as a political question and a question of humanity, can I receive the services of the father and mother and not take the children? Of the humanitarian aspect, I have no doubt.

Bridge and main entrance to Fort Monroe. Taken during the war, the photograph contains a blurred image of what appears to be African Americans congregating at the fort's entrance. (Library of Congress)

Of the political one, I have no right to judge." Until he received a response, Butler kept the men at work and issued rations. Because he was uncertain about what the Lincoln administration would do, he ordered that the slaves' "names, descriptions, and the names of their owners will . . . be correctly kept for future use."[26]

Before the president's cabinet met to discuss the issue, Postmaster General Montgomery Blair, who was from the border slave state of Maryland and had grown up in Kentucky, assured Butler in writing that he had made a wise choice in accepting the able-bodied men. However, he advised letting "the rest go, so as not to be required to feed unproductive laborers, or indeed any that you do not require or cannot conveniently manage." Nevertheless, he was familiar with the particular skills of slaves and suggested a use for them other than as laborers. "I have no doubt," he astutely asserted, "that you can get your best spies from among them, because they are accustomed to travel in the night time, and can go where no one, not accustomed to the sly tricks they practice from infancy to old age, could penetrate."[27] This was valuable advice, and Butler soon took it.

The cabinet met on May 30 to consider "Butler's fugitive slave law," as Lincoln jokingly styled it. The decision, as reported by Secretary Simon Cameron, was that Butler's actions "in respect to the negroes who came within your lines from the service of the rebels is approved." As for the families of the men, Lincoln said that "the government neither should, nor would send back into bondage such as came to our armies." Butler was instructed not to encourage runaways to come but to "refrain from surrendering to alleged masters any persons who may come within your lines." With these directives, the administration created its first unofficial policy on runaway slaves: commanders were not obligated to return them to their masters. Other Peninsula slaves were closely monitoring the situation, and had Lincoln instructed Butler to send the fugitives back it would have discouraged future runaways from coming to Union lines. The new policy was only a temporary solution, however. Their "final disposition" was to be determined later. The War Department told Butler to keep a list of the names of the slaves and their owners. Lincoln expressed concern that slaves in camp would become a nuisance and pondered the idea of colonizing them outside the country.[28] Nevertheless, a policy was established, the direct result of events put in motion by three Peninsula slaves who had decided to take a gamble.

Peninsula slave owners were shocked when their slaves ran away. Many of their bondsmen had pretended to be content, as a means of ensuring lax discipline from masters who saw themselves as paternalists. Now owners were learning the truth, leading Ruffin to admit, "The readiness of slaves to flee to the enemy . . . I did not expect." One Hampton slave owner was so troubled that he came to see Butler. "I have always treated my Negroes kindly," he informed the Union general, "[and] I supposed they loved me." However, he came home from church one Sunday to find that "there was no one in the kitchen. I went into the garden. There was no one in the garden. I went to the Negro quarters. There was no one in the Negro quarters. All my Negroes had departed, sir, while I was at the house of God." Eventually he found one slave at home, a man named James. The master ordered the servant to hitch a cart and drive him to the home of a relative. "The next morning," he continued, "James was gone! Then I

THE (FORT) **MONROE DOCTRINE**.

"The (Fort) Monroe Doctrine." This 1861 cartoon both satirizes and celebrates the Union contraband policy. A slave master stands at right brandishing a whip and demands, "Come back you black rascal." The slave answers, "Can't come back nohow massa. Dis chile's contraban." Meanwhile, other slaves flee to the fort. (Library of Congress)

came here," he told Butler, "and the first thing I saw . . . was James peddling cabbages to your men out of that very cart." All he wanted, the erstwhile slaveholder begged, was for "just one" of his slaves back.[29]

The several hundred slaves coming to Fort Monroe excited abolitionists and radical Republicans. Butler sent his communications with the Lincoln administration to various northern newspapers, and they quickly latched on to the term "contraband" to describe fugitive slaves seeking shelter with Federal troops.[30] "Butler is right," the *Chicago Tribune* proclaimed. "Let him treat every slave belonging to a rebel as contraband, and confiscate him as he would a musket or a cannon, and if he can't give them freedom, he can give them employment." The *Philadelphia Inquirer* agreed but was quick to point out that taking in the slaves was not abolitionism. "The approval is based upon the superior obligations of the Government to suppress rebellion," they argued. The military could not save the Union by "returning to their traitor masters the slaves who are notoriously employed as mere animals of labor . . . in the work of constructing fortifications to be used in the war levied by the rebels against the government."[31]

The dilemma of how to deal with runaways such as those at Fort Monroe forced many Northerners to consider questions they preferred to avoid. "It is quite apparent," the *Boston Herald* predicted, "that when our forces shall have advanced farther into the slaveholding country, and large crowds of slaves of all ages and sexes shall fly to our forces for protection, the question will then assume much larger proportions." The *New York Times*, which was in many ways the best barometer for moderate Republican sentiment, called Butler's contraband policy "a happy fancy" that settled the problem of the first few slaves who came into Fort Monroe. "But when the number swells as it is likely to do, to 10,000, 20,000, or 50,000," the government would have to devise a more permanent solution. "It is now certain," added the *Boston Herald*, "that the escape of slaves and their claims to the protection of [Fort Monroe], is going to be one of the most marked features of the war."[32]

"Dey . . . run like the old boy was after 'em"

Even as Peninsula slaves continued to run away, the work on the Confederate defenses proceeded. On the same day that the slave woman Amy testified in Prince George County and Butler first interviewed the three runaways, William Ringgold and the steamship *Logan* carried Confederate general John Bankhead Magruder down the York River. Known as "Prince John" because of his affinity for finery and showmanship, he had been sent by General Lee to take over the defense of the lower Peninsula.[33]

During the last week of May, Butler received reinforcements and pushed inland from Fort Monroe to Newport News. Lee feared that the Federals intended to seize the works at Yorktown, opening the York River as a line of advance. In response, he shuffled as many troops as possible to Magruder, but there were not nearly enough. Soldiers were arriving in Richmond, but Virginia faced invasion from at least three other routes. Exacerbating the problem was the fact that early in the war Virginia militia units were often reluctant to serve outside of their local areas. After arriving on the lower Peninsula, Magruder kept asking for more troops. Few were available, and he would need to strengthen the Peninsula's entrenchments. Lee instructed Prince John to push the work forward with great urgency.[34]

A former engineer in the U.S. army, Lee was earning a reputation as the "king of spades" because he believed in digging in for the defense. Given the few soldiers available to Magruder, Lee's basic strategy for defending his state from invasion on the Peninsula depended heavily on how many African Americans the Confederates could mobilize.[35] Peninsula slave owners soon became as irritated by Magruder's request for more slaves as Richmond was by his call for more troops.

As Butler's forces pushed inland into Hampton and Newport News, white Virginians hastily fled to Confederate lines. "The women and children have been passing here all day from Hampton," Magruder wrote on May 27. On that day, the 5th New York Zouaves, outfitted in their distinctive gaudy red pantaloons, moved into Hampton. The white citizens "didn't care for dem oder sojers," a slave told Private Thomas Southwick, "but when dey seen you red-legged debbils comin' right past, dey grab up eberything dey kin and run like the old boy was after 'em."[36] In most cases, these white refugees brought their house servants and left behind their field hands, increasing the number of slaves seeking shelter with Butler.

George Benjamin West and his family were among the white refugees of the lower Peninsula. Once the Federals arrived, his family's slaves stopped working and stayed in their quarters, leaving all the animals in the field. Roaming his neighborhood, West found that slaves were "loafing" and were "in a state of great excitement and jollification." They also "took possession of what was left by their owners." West encountered a white elderly couple who refused to leave their home and were frantically trying to protect their property. They had no living children but "kept two or three negro children about the house and petted them like they were their own, though they were not treated as equals." The couple was "particularly fond" of a sixteen- or seventeen-year-old mulatto boy whom they were raising "almost like a son." After the arrival of Federal troops, the boy showed no loyalty to them, broke into the house, and stole all their money. "The young rascal," West recalled, "went off, and neither I nor anyone about here ever knew what became of him."[37]

When West returned to his family, they decided to leave and sent him to obtain permission from the Federals. The young man took the opportunity to complain about the looting and the fact the Yankees were not returning runaway slaves. Soldiers harassed and teased him as he made his way through the camp of the 1st Vermont. When he finally reached Colonel John W. Phelps, West was feeling "very mad and indignant."[38]

Phelps was a West Point graduate and a leader in the abolitionist movement. He saw the war as "a great struggle for one of the highest of all objects, human rights." A London *Times* reporter who met Phelps on the Peninsula described him as a man "who places John Brown on a level with the great martyrs of the Christian world." The officer asserted, "Southern slaveholders are a false, licentious, godless people." Those who knew him commented on his zeal and his eyes that were so fiery with passion that he looked insane. Now he stood face-to-face with the very thing he hated most, a slaveholder, who was asking for help and complaining about his loss of slaves.[39]

Phelps quickly approved George Benjamin West's request to leave. However, because none of the slaves still with the West family had been working on Confederate fortifications, the colonel could not hold them as contraband and had no choice but to let West take any of his slaves who would willingly go. West claimed that Phelps also offered to let him take even the slaves who did not want to go, saying, "When you get your family in the Confederate lines, you can come back and I will send all your negroes with you."[40] Given his strong abolitionist sentiments, he was likely teasing and having as much fun with West as had the other Vermont soldiers.

West then confronted Phelps about "several Negroes . . . lounging about the tents." The abolitionist was not about to turn any slaves over to West: "He denied that any of ours, or anyone else's, slaves were in his camp." West argued that he had seen runaways as he had come into camp that very day. Phelps "then insisted that I go through the camp . . . and report all I found. I was very unwilling to do so, but he overruled all my excuses." Suddenly, all but one of the slaves vanished. Because these slaves had not been laboring for the Confederacy (and thus were technically not contraband), the only way for the abolitionist soldiers in the 1st Vermont to protect the runaways was to hide them. An irritated West returned to Phelps and "reported that I had seen but one negro, but I still believed that there were others." He did find his brother's buggy parked in front of the tent of a Massachusetts colonel. Phelps ordered it returned and promised to protect his other property but told West that "he thought it best that we leave."[41]

West returned to find his family packing up their belongings. He talked to his slave cook, Aunt Lucy, and her daughters and asked if they wanted to come along. Lucy had been with the family since 1842. She had two sons who had already gone to the Federals and a husband on another plantation who had apparently done the same. Nevertheless, she decided to take her chances with the West family and insisted on bringing her husband's clothing. "She was persuaded in her mind that he would follow her and she could not bear the thought of telling him she had left his clothes behind." Perhaps Lucy doubted that her husband had made the right choice in trusting the Northerners. If his gamble in going to Union lines did not pay off, she was not going to let him be stuck without clothing.[42]

With the wagon packed, the West family, along with Lucy and her two daughters and two granddaughters, left behind the rest of their slaves and property and joined their neighbors journeying to Richmond. When West and other lower Peninsula slaveholders fled, hundreds of abandoned slaves became available to work for both armies. This circumstance helped precipitate one of the Civil War's first battles.

"He fit in dat battle at Big Bethel"

Magruder watched the long line of refugees file through his camp, and he grew curious about Butler's activities. He ordered his cavalry forward to probe the Federal picket lines. During these excursions, Confederates eagerly grabbed up slaves whose masters had absconded, adding them to the labor gangs working on the defenses. Inching ever closer to the Federal lines, Daniel Harvey Hill posted his 1st North Carolina at a crossroads church known as Big Bethel. The position had little strategic value. "It looked as if Magruder was only sending us down . . . as a dare to General Butler," one of Hill's staff officers recalled.[43]

The Big Bethel site had been part of Lord Cornwallis's lines during the American Revolution, and the Confederates went to work restructuring the old earthen fortifications to suit their needs. "We do all of this work ourselves," one soldier remarked. This seemed a great novelty for white men: "[We] have no negroes to help us. . . . It goes right tough with some, who have never been used to any thing of the kind before."[44]

A runaway slave named George Scott covertly watched as Hill's men entrenched. He had escaped his owner two years earlier and was living in the woods around Hampton. As it routinely did with other slaves who were "laying out," the African American community kept Scott fed and informed about attempts to capture him. Whites were aware that he was out there, but his reputation as a fierce and powerful man made even bounty hunters reluctant to bring him in. He was agile and swift and evaded all slave patrols that sought to capture him. His owner had once managed to corner the fugitive, but Scott outfought him, took away his pistol and bowie knife, and darted off into the woods. This tough and resourceful African American would soon help spark one of the first land battles of the war.[45]

Taking note of Hill's forward position at Big Bethel, Scott made his way to Federal lines and eventually fell in with the 8th Massachusetts. Brought before Major Theodore Winthrop, he reported on the work he had seen the North Carolinians performing and led the officer back for a closer look. Accustomed to evading slave patrols, he stealthily dodged Confederate cavalry and took Winthrop right to the Confederate lines. The major discovered that the runaway's report was accurate. Magruder's "dare" was about to be accepted.[46]

To obtain better knowledge of Hill's lines and Magruder's intentions, Butler had Winthrop and Scott return several times to the Confederate works. Once Scott advanced so close to the North Carolinians that he had to lie flat for twenty-four hours before getting a chance to return. As he emerged from the bushes, a Confederate picket fired at his fleeing shadow. A bullet ripped Scott's sleeve, but he escaped otherwise unscathed.[47]

Winthrop was convinced that the Tar Heels were about to attack the Federals on the lower Peninsula. Meeting with General Butler, he suggested striking first. The general concurred, especially because he feared that Magruder was attempting to move forward to obtain more of the abandoned slaves to work on his lines at Yorktown. Using the information gleaned with the help of Scott, Butler and Winthrop devised a plan of attack. Winthrop insisted that "George Scott . . . have a shooting iron," thus making the runaway slave likely the first black man to carry a weapon for the Union cause on a Civil War battlefield. On the march out to Bethel, Federal soldiers recalled passing runaway slaves looking for "the freedom fort" and the Yankees were happy to point the way. In the minor engagement that followed, both sides fought like bumbling neophytes, but inexperience favored the defenders. The North Carolinians easily repulsed the attack and killed Major Winthrop at the head of his regiment.[48]

It is possible that during the skirmish a few blacks were carrying weapons for the Confederacy. As in other southern regiments, some of the North Carolinians had brought their body servants with them to war. Masters sometimes allowed these men to carry firearms, and as we will see in several later incidents, they may have cajoled some of their servants into doing their share in repulsing the Federal attack. Sadly, a bullet fired by a body servant may have been the one that killed Major Winthrop. After the war, a Confederate captain claimed that although there were many men firing at Winthrop as he gallantly led his men toward the Confederate position, his own body servant fired the fatal shot. Members of the Wythe Rifles of Hampton also maintained that one of their body servants had delivered the deadly round. The unit's captain had allegedly coaxed the slave into fighting by convincing him that if the Yankees won they would take the body servant's entire family to Cuba. Ex-slave Moble Hopson later recalled a slave named Shep Brown who "long 'fore de Yankees came . . . jined up wid de 'fedeartes. He fit in dat battle at Big Bethel but he ain't get uh scratch." Hopson's memory is certainly suspect, as Brown was most likely in the Rebel army as a body servant. However, it is not difficult to believe that he and perhaps a few of the other slaves were deceived by their masters' lies about evil Yankees coming to capture them. Such an erroneous belief provided an understandable motive to fight alongside their owners in the battle.[49]

Butler later sent condolences to Major Winthrop's family. In return, Mrs. Butler received a letter of thanks from the officer's sister expressing "great satisfaction to . . . know from Theodore's letters that some of the last acts of his life were kindnesses to an oppressed race." The day after the battle, Butler found George Scott "mourning bitterly" over the loss of his new friend. The runaway slave had been in the thick of the fight, and Butler asked if he was afraid to go back to the field, look for wounded, and find out if the North Carolinians intended to exploit their success. Although deeply saddened by the loss of his friend, Scott "started with alacrity," Butler remembered. Scott found that the Confederates had removed their casualties, so he crawled up to the Confederate works. Hearing nothing, he climbed into the lines and "found not a soul there." The Rebels had abandoned the position.[50]

The small fight revealed to both armies that the lower Peninsula was becoming dangerous. General Lee shifted additional troops to Magruder and suggested improvements in the defensive works. Despite the number of blacks toiling for the Confederacy, the army called on white soldiers to do much of the labor. An Alabama colonel was not alone when he protested against the "diversion from the legitimate duties of a Volunteer soldier . . . [while] there are Negroes & hirelings enough to do the menial labor of unloading transports." To limit these complaints and get the work done, Magruder increased the number of scouting parties sent out to round up slaves abandoned by fleeing whites and asked the citizens of the Peninsula to loan his army half of their male slaves. The scouting parties were largely unsuccessful at bringing in slaves who knew how to avoid slave patrols and who were increasingly seeking shelter within Federal lines.[51]

"This was what they had been praying for"

At Fort Monroe, the Union army used black laborers on its entrenchments as well. On July 8, Butler assigned Private Edward Pierce, a staunch abolitionist, to organize the contrabands into a labor force. His comrades laughed at the sight of the abolitionist "converted into a Virginia slavemaster." Nevertheless, Pierce took the work seriously. "To me it seemed rather an opportunity to lead them from the house of bondage never to return."[52]

The slaves were required to work for the Federals as hard as or harder than they had for their masters, but they did so more willingly. Pierce explained to the contrabands that the Confederates had been digging faster and creating better works due to their slave labor and that now the Federals needed black labor in order to keep up. "I told them . . . that they would be required to do only such labor as we ourselves had done, that they should be treated kindly and no one should be obliged to work beyond his capacity, or if unwell, and that they should be furnished in a day or two with full soldiers' rations."[53]

Pierce offered an additional incentive. The word "freedom" was often on the Yankee's lips. From him, the slaves learned that although the government had not yet taken steps to liberate them, their conduct as laborers would go a long way in pushing the nation toward abolition. Their work could demonstrate that emancipated slaves would be a source of strength for the Union. Pierce explained that "we had come to suppress the rebellion, and although the object of the war was not to emancipate them . . . that might be the result." He concluded that the slaves "understood . . . perfectly" and performed the labor without protest. A newspaper correspondent on the Peninsula concurred, reporting that the contrabands "comprehend the existing state of affairs much better than could be expected. They are quite industrious." Pierce found that they did not require much urging to work. "There was a public opinion among them against idleness," he recalled, "which answered for discipline. Some days they worked with our soldiers, and it was found that they did more work, and did the nicer parts—the facings and dressings—better."[54]

As the black laborers rested during the hottest parts of the day and at night, Pierce tried to discern "their currents of thoughts and feelings" and learn about their lives. He found that most of them had not suffered severe physical punishment but always felt the threat looming. "A locust-tree in front of the jail had been used for a whipping-post," he related, "and they were desirous that it should be cut down." While most described their masters as kind, they were equally adamant about hating slavery.[55]

Pierce "obtained definite knowledge" of Virginia's increased involvement in the domestic slave trade. As he collected the names of the slaves and their dependents, a frequent response was, "Yes, I have a wife but she . . . was sold off two years ago and I have not heard of her since." In addition, the slaves often reported that their masters had sold their children. "It was no [abolitionist] that came amongst us . . . telling us we ought to be free that turned our hearts against our master," a slave man named Hanson explained to army chaplain J. J. Marks. "No, it was the sale of our fathers and mothers, our children and brothers."[56]

Almost all the laborers told Pierce that their masters claimed that "the Yankees were coming . . . only to get the land, that they would kill the

Negroes and manure the ground with them, or carry them off to Cuba or Haiti and sell them." He also discovered that masters attempted to use the Bible to coax the slaves into loyalty. Selectively quoting from the eleventh chapter of Daniel, slave owners explained how "the King of the South" victoriously attacked "the King of the North." Carrying a Bible that his mistress left behind, one slave asked Pierce to read the full context of those verses. He was no doubt heartened to hear the parts that the masters had left out. The passage explained that despite the King of the South's initial victories, the King of the North would come back in greater force and successfully lay siege to a fortified city. Pierce then read another passage from the thirty-fourth chapter of Jeremiah that described how God had become angry at the Israelites for not freeing their slaves. Consequently, the Lord had wrathfully condemned them to famine and defeat. To the slave, this passage was most astounding.[57]

Besides quoting scripture out of context and attempting to frighten slaves with tales of evil Yankees, some masters insinuated that loyalty to the Confederacy would reap benefits. Pierce learned of a slave minister who "had been something of a pet among the whites." The man learned that his daughter was soon to be sold away. "Some leading secessionist," Pierce relates, "persuaded him to offer the services of himself and his sons, in a published communication, to the cause of Virginia and the Confederate States." By publicly demonstrating "loyalty" to the South, he secured his daughter but lost his hold on his black congregation. "He felt uneasy about his betrayal, and tried to restore himself to favor by saying that he meant no harm to his people; but his protestations were in vain."[58]

This man's story reveals the dilemma facing Virginia's African American community early in the Civil War. Blacks naturally desired improved conditions for themselves and their families, but they were not sure which side offered the better prospects. The signals were mixed and complex. The enslaved community overheard whites discussing their belief that Lincoln favored emancipation, and they learned through the grapevine that Yankees welcomed runaways at Fort Monroe. Amy's testimony, the experiences of George Benjamin West, and the increasing number of runaways clearly demonstrate that many slaves already believed that the Union army was an agent of liberation. However, masters warned their slaves that Northerners would kill or sell them, that the Bible prophesied Confederate victory, and that staying loyal to the Confederacy might secure a better life. Moreover, "the negro who boasted the loudest of his desire to fight the Yankees . . . [and] to aid the Confederates," Joseph T. Wilson, a Norfolk slave who later became a Union soldier explained, "was granted the most freedom and received the approval of his master."[59]

Furthermore, even if the Yankees were friends, slaves could not be certain that the North would win the war. As the slave John Washington observed, it seemed that the vast numbers of southern soldiers arriving in Richmond could never be defeated. Slaves could easily imagine their fate if they threw their lot in with the Federals and their masters won the war. They would be in the same situation as the slaves who had supported the British during the Revolution and whose masters had reclaimed them after Yorktown. African Americans had to absorb and interpret this complex and incomplete information and make choices. Like the reluctant Aunt Lucy who carried her husband's clothes with her when he ran to the Federals, the majority of slaves chose to wait and see how the situation developed.

Many others took a gamble and picked sides. George Scott and the contrabands at Fort Monroe served the North. A few blacks such as Shep Brown may have either believed their masters or were deceptively trying to demonstrate "loyalty" and thus were firing guns at Union troops in the Battle of Big Bethel. No matter their choice, however, like the blacks who faced each other from opposite sides at Yorktown during the Revolution, these African Americans were seeking the same thing—a better life for themselves and their families.

The contrabands at Fort Monroe could not be sure they had made the right choice. Pierce talked with many who feared that a Confederate victory would leave them at the mercy of their vindictive masters. Some were not confident that the North would truly emancipate them. Johnny Johnson, for example, was a twenty-year-old slave still in mourning for his wife, Mary. Their master had murdered the slave woman by striking her in the head with a hoe, and Johnson had managed to escape just before the fight at Big Bethel. He was now living in the contraband camps near Fort Monroe and requested information from a journalist on how to get to Canada. "He would not be persuaded that it was yet safe for him in the States," the reporter explained; "he was afraid the people of the Government might yet return the contraband."[60]

Others were willing to take the risk. "They said they had prayed for this day," Pierce recalled, "and God had sent Lincoln in answer to their prayers." Despite having heard their masters use the Bible to justify slavery, "they built their hopes of freedom on scriptural examples, regarding the deliverance of Daniel from the lion's den and of the children from the furnace, as symbolic of their coming freedom."[61]

Ministering to the refugees at Fort Monroe, abolitionist minister L. C. Lockwood observed their religious practices. "The brother who led the . . . prayer meeting had a sing-song manner," he noted, "but his sentiments and expressions were very scriptural and impressive." The slaves "assured me that this was what they had been praying for. . . . They [believed] that some great thing was in store for them and their people." A slave man named Carey explained that "after Lincoln's election, and before his inauguration, his master said to him, 'You are the cause of all this.'" Since then, "there has been a general and growing expectation among the slaves that God would soon undertake for them."[62]

The slaves at Fort Monroe expressed a "universal desire" to be free. "Upon this point my inquiries were particular, and always with the same result," Pierce explained. "When we said to them, 'you don't want to be free—your masters say you don't,' they manifested much indignation, answering, 'we do want to be free—we want to be for ourselves.'" Pierce asked if all slaves felt the same. "We never heard of one who did not," they reported. They conceded that there might be some "half-crazy" ones who did not want to be free but insisted that they had never met one.[63]

Pierce's ninety-day regiment was due to disband on July 15 and return home. In his last meeting with the black laborers, Pierce thanked them and declared that "every one of them was as much entitled to his freedom as I was to mine, and I hope that they would all now secure it." The slaves returned the affection. "'Believe you, Boss,' was the general response, and each one with his rough gravelly hand grasped mine, and with tearful eyes and broken utterances said, 'God bless you!' 'May we meet in Heaven!' 'My name is Jack Allen, don't forget me.' 'Remember me, Ken Anderson' and so on."[64]

When Pierce left behind the contrabands at Fort Monroe, the Civil War was only three months old, but these African Americans had already made it difficult for Northerners to forget the activities of Virginia's black community. The Confederacy immediately began using its African American population to help defend against invasion, and hundreds of Peninsula slaves quickly demonstrated their eagerness to use the Federal army as a means of liberation. In doing so, they prompted Lincoln into the policy of sheltering slaves as "contraband of war," and his decision soon encouraged others to follow. As the Yankee presence on the lower Peninsula grew, white Virginians fled, leaving behind thousands of their slaves. When both armies took steps to prevent the other from using these abandoned slaves as laborers, it helped cause the first land battle of the war.

As in previous wars throughout history and on the Peninsula, during the small fight at Big Bethel there may have been a few slaves fighting on both sides. Masters attempted to convince their slaves that the Yankees meant them harm and hinted at rewards for remaining loyal. Since it was impossible to know who would win the war, such lies provided ample motivation for slaves to openly support their masters or remain passive. Others discounted the outlandish deceptions of their owners and gambled by fleeing to the Federals.

When the Civil War began, the vast majority of Northerners were committed to fighting to save the Union but were generally opposed to a war of emancipation. However, if the South continued to use its slave property in the fight against the Union and if slaves continued to demonstrate their desire to help the northern army, such convictions might slowly erode.

3

WAR IS A SWIFT EDUCATOR
JULY–DECEMBER 1861

"SLAVES WITH THE REBEL ARMY," both the *New York Times* and the *Chicago Tribune* boldly declared in the summer of 1861. The assertion was based on an article published by the *New Orleans Crescent* praising a slave named Tom who "took a fancy to go a soldiering, and his master willingly gratified him." His owner, James H. Phelps of New Orleans, hired out the slave as a body servant to a Confederate officer who eventually served on the Virginia Peninsula. "There are hundreds of other slaves like Tom gone to kill the Yankees," the *Crescent* claimed. The paper quoted a letter the slave supposedly wrote his mother from Yorktown explaining how he had been "scout[ing] about the woods" and in which he asked her to tell the "white folks" that he would not be home "until I kill a Yankee." This questionable evidence outraged the northern editors, but the New Orleans paper was pleased. "We hope he will be gratified in hunting up and obtaining a Yankee scalp," the paper gleefully declared.[1]

Meanwhile, the northern press praised slaves on the Virginia Peninsula who were laboring for Yankee troops. "While Congress and the Cabinet are casting about for a settlement of the question, 'What shall we do with them?'" the *Philadelphia Inquirer* reported, "the contrabands at Fort Monroe are solving the problem practically." The paper's correspondent estimated that by December 1861 there were nearly 3,000 runaways working at the fort. "Those who are employed as servants receive eight dollars a month, and those who build fortifications are paid ten dollars a month." Instead of going directly to the workers, however, the wages went into a support fund for their families.[2]

During the second half of 1861, both Union and Confederate troops increased their use of African American laborers. In northern Virginia, black workers constructed the fortifications that contributed to the North's defeat at Manassas, and rumors that blacks were fighting for the South helped spur Congress into passing the First Confiscation Act. On the Peninsula, Union general Ben Butler's contrabands became an effective labor force, and he continued to pressure the Lincoln administration into a consistent policy on runaways. Despite reluctant slave owners, Confederate general John Magruder procured more black laborers to construct defenses on the lower Peninsula. After observing the progress of these works, free black William Ringgold provided Union troops with military intelligence that played a role in the planning of the Peninsula Campaign. Whether serving the North or the South, Virginia's black population supplied abolitionists and radical Republicans with rhetorical ammunition in their struggle to shape the purposes and course of the war.

"The first step toward emancipation"

One week after Edward Pierce left the black laborers at Fort Monroe, the Civil War began in earnest at the First Battle of Bull Run. Robert E. Lee was now the chief military adviser to Confederate president Jefferson Davis, and they both recognized the importance of the railroad junction at Manassas, Virginia, as a forward line of defense. The Federals could use the rail lines there to invade the heart of the state and threaten Richmond. Davis assigned General P. G. T. Beauregard to defend the vital position. The general had earthworks constructed at the railroad juncture and just north of town along Bull Run. Almost immediately, Confederate troops complained about performing labor considered degrading to white men. As Magruder had done on the Peninsula, Beauregard asked slave owners to send "such of their negro men as they can spare" to dig entrenchments.[3]

Union troops under the command of Irvin McDowell attacked the position on July 21, 1861, and drove the Confederates from their forward lines. Stubborn resistance (particularly by Thomas J. Jackson's brigade) stalled the Union advance, buying time for the Rebels to bring up the reinforcements that eventually routed the Federals and sent them scurrying in panic back to Washington.

The defeat stunned the northern public and elicited profound joy, patriotism, and self-congratulation from Southerners. Beauregard's official report praised his soldiers and expressed gratitude to the local planters who had made their slaves available. "I regret my inability to mention the names of those patriotic gentlemen of Virginia," he wrote, "by . . . whose slaves the intrenched camp at Manassas had been mainly constructed, relieving the troops from that laborious service, and giving opportunity for their military instruction."[4]

Northerners knew that black labor had constructed the fortifications at Manassas. Before the battle, the *Philadelphia Inquirer* explained that "nearly all the work about the Rebel entrenchments and camps [at Manassas was] being executed by slaves." The *Boston Herald* reported "20,000 Negroes at Work on Entrenchments" and quoted "a wealthy Virginian residing a few miles from Manassas Junction [who was] of Northern birth and Union leanings." He told the paper that "there are upwards of 12,000 negroes employed in the entrenchments at Manassas, and about the same number at Richmond. He owned a large number of negroes, and was compelled to furnish a certain number of them to work for the rebels every day." One week after the battle, the *Chicago Tribune* credited the Union defeat to slave labor. McDowell "threaded his way though roads and defiles obstructed by negroes, plunge[d] into a honeycomb of batteries erected by negroes, suffer[ed] a stunning defeat, and los[t] his command."[5]

The fortifications may not have been the only assistance that blacks provided the Confederacy that day. As at Big Bethel, a combination of excitement and cajoling masters might possibly have swept some body servants into the combat. Almost before the smoke cleared on the battlefield, scattered reports surfaced in both northern and southern newspapers claiming that blacks were fighting for the Confederates. Just days after the battle, the *New York Times* declared that "we hear of black regiments" fighting for the South and then a week later reprinted a story from the *Richmond Enquirer* heralding an "ebony patriot" who shot a Yankee officer, clubbed another, and captured both during the thick of the fight. The *Reading (Pa.) Journal* featured an interview with a runaway slave named John Parker, who claimed to have helped work a Confederate battery during the Union assault. The *Charlotte Western Democrat* celebrated the "sable patriots" of Manassas and claimed that there were "many cases . . . of [northern] prisoners being taken by negroes." The ultraconservative *Daily Chicago Times* reported that slaves "have jeered at and insulted our troops, have readily enlisted in the rebel army and on Sunday, at Manassas, shot down our men with as much alacrity as if abolitionism had never existed." The abolitionist newspaper *Principia* passed along the story of a slave who taunted Union prisoners at Manassas "by impudently strutting up and down before them clothed in the uniform of one of the New York Fire Zouaves, proclaiming that it was the uniform of one of the d——d Yankee sons of b—— he had killed with his own hands."[6]

Some northern newspapers claimed that blacks had fought for the Confederates that day in significant numbers. "It is boasted that there are two well drilled regiments of negroes in Beauregard's army," the *Chicago Tribune* reported. The day after the battle, both the *Philadelphia Inquirer* and the *Boston Herald* ran a story about nine runaway slaves who came into Union lines in northern Virginia claiming that "all the able bodied male negroes in Essex and Middlesex counties, Va. were being armed." The next day, the *Inquirer* featured an interview with a Confederate officer captured at Bull Run, who said the southern army had had "large numbers of negroes in fine fighting order" at Manassas.[7]

"The fact that negroes fought in the battle at Bull Run is undisputed," one correspondent concluded after discussing the battle with Union soldiers who had been in it. "They were forced to do it, but they fought." By the end of 1861, the rumor mill continued to churn out stories of organized black Confederate units. The *Indianapolis Star*, for example, published a letter from a Union soldier, who declared, "We have heard of a regiment of [Confederate Negroes] at Manassas." In May 1862, *Harper's Weekly* passed along reports of "a regiment of mounted negroes, armed with sabers, at Manassas" and claimed that "a regiment of black men" had escorted about 500 captured Union soldiers to prison.[8]

Obviously there were exaggerations and fabrications in these accounts, but the evidence does suggest that early in the war at least some blacks were observed fighting in Confederate ranks. Most were probably body servants, and while some may have been caught up in the thrill of combat, it is more likely that they were forced into service, deceived by their masters' tales about the designs of evil Yankees, or motivated by a desire to demonstrate their loyalty to their owners when it was unclear who would win the war. "We wish to our hearts that the Yankees would whip," explained runaway slave John Parker. He continued: "[During the battle,] I felt bad [for firing at Union troops] . . . worse than dead. We would have run over to their side but [Confederate] officers would have shot us if we had made the attempt."[9]

These scattered reports appear to have had a significant impact on northern public opinion and Union war policy. The day before the battle at Manassas, the U.S. Senate had been debating a bill that would allow for the confiscation of Rebel property used by Confederate armies. It was abundantly clear that the South employed thousands of slaves to build fortifications and that slave labor freed up whites to fight. Nevertheless, conservative senators had quashed any attempt to confiscate slaves, and only Illinois senator Lyman Trumbull's moderate bill made it to the Senate floor. On July 20, however, Trumbull boldly offered an amendment that broadened the definition of property liable for confiscation to include slaves.[10]

The Manassas battle the next day clearly gave the bill momentum.

While slaves with shovels were troubling, slaves with guns elicited outrage. As part of a group of senators, Trumbull had gone out to watch the fight and was caught in the chaos of the retreating army. Visibly shaken and fatigued the next day in Congress, he argued in favor of his confiscation bill by referring to the South's use of slaves to build fortifications. But in pushing for the amendment, Trumbull broke with his moderate reputation by adding, "I understand that Negroes were in the fight which has recently occurred . . . . Negroes who are used to destroy the Union and to shoot down the Union men by the consent of their traitorous masters [should be confiscated]."[11]

Senator Henry Wilson of Massachusetts agreed: "The time has come," he maintained, "when we should deal with the men who are organizing negro companies and teaching them to shoot down loyal men." He hoped that "there is a public sentiment in this country that will blast men" who maintained that the government should protect Rebel property, including slaves used in the rebellion. As for himself, he declared, "I shall vote [for this proposal] with more heart than I vote for ordinary measures."[12]

While there was some objection to the amendment, most notably from Senator John C. Breckinridge of Kentucky, who feared "a loosening of all bonds" if the government began confiscating slaves, news from Manassas swayed most of the senators. Conservative senator Ten Eyck of New Jersey, for example, explained that he had previously voted against the amendment in committee because he did not believe that the Confederates would use slaves in their armies and because he "did not know what would become of these poor wretches if they were discharged. God knows we do not want them in our section of the Union." Indeed, abolitionism was not popular in New Jersey, and the free-soil senator had proclaimed back in April that "if attempts should be made to interfere with [slavery] in the states where it exists by law . . . the people of New Jersey will stand, if need be, by their brethren in the South." He now changed his mind. "Having learned and believing that these people have been used and employed with arms in their hands to shed the blood of Union-loving men of this country," he argued, "I shall vote in favor of this amendment with less regard for what will become of these people than I had."[13]

When a roll call vote was requested, Trumbull declared that he would be glad to learn "who is willing to vote that a traitorous owner of a negro shall employ him to shoot down the Union men of the country, and yet insist upon restoring him to the traitor that owns him." The amendment and the bill overwhelmingly passed the Senate. The House then scheduled the confiscation bill for debate in August. Reports that slaves were fighting for the South also circulated among the representatives and caused some outrage. Indiana's William M. Dunn, for example, aggressively insisted that southern blacks "were firing at our troops yesterday [at Manassas]" and asked Congress to pressure the secretary of war into investigating the matter.[14]

The confiscation bill had broad public support. Even those opposed to emancipation agreed that the loss at Manassas called for sterner measures. Most Northerners tentatively applauded the effort to limit the South's ability to use slave labor on fortifications and on the battlefield. Emancipationists thus rejoiced over the benefits gained from the loss at Manassas. The battle, George L. Sterns argued, was "the first step toward emancipation. If we had won a decisive victory, in less than six months the rebellious states would be back in the Union." Because most Northerners and the Lincoln administration did not yet believe that saving the Union required freeing the slaves, an end to the conflict at that time would have kept slavery intact. "All the Contraband of War would have been restored," the *National Anti-Slavery Standard* argued, "and we [would] have given [the South] guarantees for slavery."[15] Thus, from the perspective of abolitionists and the slaves, the Union defeat at Manassas had been beneficial.

Abolitionists soon tapped into the emotions aroused by the specter of slaves fighting for the Confederacy, and they used such stories and rumors to promote emancipation. In September, Frederick Douglass maintained that "it is now pretty well established, that there are at the present moment many colored men in the Confederate army doing duty . . . as real soldiers. . . . There were such soldiers at Manassas, and they are probably there still." A month after the battle, William Lloyd Garrison's *Liberator* reported that a runaway slave had arrived in Washington claiming that he "was one of a regiment of negroes that took part in the battle at Bull Run. . . . He asserts that there are in the rebel army in Virginia from two to three thousand negroes armed with . . . rifles." Lest anyone think these black Southerners held pro-Confederate sympathies, the slave was quick to point out that the blacks fighting against northern troops "have been taught [by their masters] that they would be butchered if they fell into the hands of the Unionists." He believed, however, that most slaves in Virginia did not believe these deceptions "and would run away if they could. This statement," the *Liberator* noted, "is corroborated by another negro . . . brought in by the 2nd Maine Regiment."[16]

Harriet Beecher Stowe pointed out that soldiers returning from Manassas claimed that they had fought against black Confederates, and she wondered if slaves were fighting because their masters had offered "that freedom which we had the power to give them, and did not give." Blacks in arms against the Union at Manassas were a warning. "The question is not Shall there be black regiments," Stowe maintained, "but, Shall they fight on our side or the side of the enemies?" The melodramatic author's words were provocative. "We may rest assured," Stowe argued, "if we delay till we alienate the blacks" the South would continue to use slaves effectively against the Union. If the government did not emancipate the slaves, the North would have to fight against men "whose wrongs we would not make right, and whom God will justly make our punishers."[17]

The moderate *New York Times* issued a similar warning. "Already we hear of black regiments before the first campaign is over," the paper pointed out on September 7. If the war were to drag on, the newspaper cautioned, "we shall hear of whole armies of blacks, who will receive liberty on the condition of defending the lives of their late masters." The *Chicago Tribune* shared these concerns. "The negroes have been compelled many long years to support the South by their labor," the paper noted. "Why should not the South compel them to fight her battles as well?"[18]

These fears would prove to be unwarranted. The Confederate government vehemently resisted officially enrolling black troops until the last months of the conflict. In fact, after the Manassas battle, a Rebel officer proposed the creation of black regiments, but Confederate president Jefferson Davis labeled the idea "stark madness" and claimed such an action "would revolt and disgust the whole South."[19] Nevertheless, these were legitimate northern concerns: in previous wars masters had mobilized their slaves by offering the reward of freedom.

The *Tribune* was the leading Republican newspaper in Chicago and had been influential in getting Lincoln nominated for president. In August 1861, the paper unleashed a string of passionate editorials insisting that the country should learn from Manassas. "We do wonder," the paper mused, "what will be the effect . . . on the loyal millions of the country who have tried to believe that it is both possible and proper to put down the slaveholders' rebellion and save slavery for the rebels at the same time." Northerners who opposed the confiscation bill "would have the soldiers of the Union mowed down by batteries planted and fortified by slaves working under the lash." Clearly, "the experience at Bull Run, where slave-built batteries repulsed the finest army ever organized on the American Continent, has taught its own lessons." The editors maintained that the "negroes employed to dig those entrenchments at Manassas . . . were worth to the rebels as much as that number of soldiers; and they would be worth as much to us. Those two regiments of colored men in that insurgent army would much rather fight . . . on the side of freedom." Because the battle had awakened Northerners to these facts, the paper concluded, "Bull's Run has not been without its advantages to the cause of liberty."[20]

"They seemed proud of themselves"

Despite the boost that Manassas gave to emancipation, however, the government was not ready to turn the conflict into a war of liberation. As the confiscation bill worked its way through Congress, the House and the Senate passed a resolution reaffirming that they had no intention "of overthrowing or interfering with the rights or established institutions" of the southern states.[21] More significant for the future direction of the war and events on the Peninsula, Lincoln placed General George B. McClellan in command of the newly designated Army of the Potomac. The handsome, athletic, and self-confident thirty-four-year-old officer had recently cleared the western part of Virginia of Rebel forces and was widely perceived as the only Union officer who had directed a successful operation. Lincoln needed him to whip the army back into shape, restore its morale, and calm the northern public. To the president's relief, the young officer accomplished these tasks in remarkably short time, and when Winfield Scott retired in November, Lincoln promoted McClellan to general in chief of all Union armies.

McClellan presented a potential problem for emancipationists. The Democratic general believed that a powerful slaveholding aristocracy had manipulated and cajoled the southern population into secession— a cause that most were only half-heartedly committed to when the war began. McClellan therefore suggested moving vastly overwhelming forces into the South, thereby crushing any hope that the Confederacy could overcome the matériel and military might of the North. Equally important, northern armies should maintain a "rigidly protective policy" regarding civilian property (particularly slaves), dispelling the notion that secession was necessary to maintain the institution of slavery and other civil liberties. This overwhelming display of force and respect for property rights would convince the majority of Southerners that secession was hopeless and unwarranted.[22]

The new general in chief cared little for African Americans, but down on the Peninsula one of his subordinates increasingly spoke on their behalf. Before Manassas, General Benjamin Butler had been preparing for an advance "by which I hoped to cripple the resources of the enemy at Yorktown, and especially by seizing a large quantity of Negroes who were being pressed into service in building the entrenchments there." After the defeat, however, Butler had to send several of his best regiments to bolster Washington's defenses. He therefore canceled the advance, pulled out of Hampton, and withdrew his regiments into the entrenchments closer to Fort Monroe. The families of the black laborers working on the fortifications had to abandon Hampton and seek shelter within Butler's new lines.[23]

Providing protection for these contrabands would be a burden, but the general knew that if he did not protect the slaves, the Confederates would gather them up. The gamble they had taken coming into the Federal lines would backfire. "An indescribable panic ensued among the colored population," the *National Anti-Slavery Standard* reported as Butler's men abandoned Hampton. "The streets swarmed with the terrified people." The *Baltimore American* correspondent explained that "a stampede of the colored population took place. . . . Nearly a thousand contraband men, women, and children, must have come in during the last twenty-four hours." The Confederate victory at Manassas, the *National Anti-Slavery Standard* noted, coupled with Butler's withdrawal, made them "so frightened . . . they know not what will be the next." The correspondent for *Harper's Weekly* cruelly described the rush of frightened slaves into the fort as comical but at the same time admitted that it was "the most . . . pitiable sight I ever witnessed." The journalist described a horde of African Americans "hurrying along lest their masters should finally snatch them from their newly found freedom, and again send them into the fields under the overseer's whip." Most slaves carried out the movement during the night in "agony of fear."[24] Perhaps Aunt Lucy's husband wondered if his wife and other slaves who had decided to demonstrate loyalty to their masters had made the wiser choice.

Butler did not know if he had the authority to protect the runaways who had not been working for the Confederates. Earlier, the administration allowed him to shelter these families temporarily but maintained that their final disposition would be determined later. Since then, the increasing number of refugees only worsened the problem. In addition, the government's policy was inconsistent. The administration supported other Union officers who turned away runaway slaves. Butler hoped that this would not become the administration's official stance. His fondness for and dependence on the black laborers had increased since the day he had skillfully turned Major Cary away, and he did not want to leave their families unprotected.[25]

Butler asked Secretary of War Simon Cameron about the contrabands "who had trusted to the protection of the arms of the United States, and

"Stampede of Slaves." On August 8, 1861, Harper's Weekly *depicted slaves rushing to Fort Monroe upon learning of Butler's decision to pull his troops out of Hampton.*

who aided the troops," and who might be left to the mercy of "rebel soldiery, who had threatened to shoot the men who had wrought for us." The general estimated that he had 900 slaves within his lines, "and many more are coming in." He believed that when owners abandoned their slaves while fleeing the lower Peninsula they had terminated their slaves' status as property. Butler asked the administration if he did not have a duty to protect the slaves as he would any person who had become homeless as a result of supporting the Union. The terrified slaves forced the issue on Butler, and the skillful politician was attempting to force the administration into a consistent policy.[26]

It was a week before Butler received a response from Cameron. Meanwhile, the House passed the Senate's confiscation bill. The president, concerned about how the Border States might react, reluctantly signed it. Butler's policy of seizing slaves who had worked for the Confederacy was now law. Realizing the degree to which the Confederacy relied on slave labor, Peninsula planter Edmund Ruffin condemned the law as "virtually a decree of general emancipation for all the slaves."[27] The thousands of slaves toiling on Confederate fortifications, as well as black men such as John

Parker who had manned Rebel batteries at Manassas, had unknowingly delivered a blow for freedom by pushing Congress into action. This pattern would continue on a larger scale.

On August 8, Cameron assured Butler that his problem had received "the most attentive consideration." The Confiscation Act now settled the issue of what to do about slaves who had worked for the Rebels. "A more difficult question" was the status of slaves belonging to loyal masters, "as well as fugitives from disloyal masters" who had not been working for the Confederacy. Cameron instructed Butler to use the slaves as military laborers, but his soldiers were not to encourage slaves to run away nor to interfere if they voluntarily chose to return to their masters. Butler was to continue to record the names of these slaves and their owners so that Congress could determine their status once the war was over.[28] This was essentially the same answer the general had received when he first brought up the issue. The ultimate fate of those runaways who had not been working for the Confederacy remained unresolved. Soon, Benjamin Butler was not the only one pushing for answers.

The day that Butler received Cameron's response, his belief that Confederates would gather up slaves left in Hampton was confirmed. After learning of the Federal withdrawal, Magruder ordered troops to "scour the country . . . and to capture and send up to the works at Williamsburg . . . any blacks left behind." These patrols managed to round up about 150 slaves. Under Magruder's orders, Confederate soldiers then set fire to Hampton. The general had heard a rumor that the city was to become a permanent settlement for runaway slaves, and he preferred to reduce the historic town to ashes. He justified the move as a military necessity, but the *Richmond Dispatch* concluded that "it was done by our own people, to prevent its being appropriated for a far worse end than conflagration, that is, the fall and winter abode of yankees and runaway slaves."[29]

Two days later, Butler was relieved of command at Fort Monroe. He believed it was because his "views on the Negro question were not acceptable to the government." The slaves at Fort Monroe, however, saw him as a valuable friend. Before he was relieved of command, Butler had shown a reporter from the London *Times* around camp, where hardworking contrabands were "saluting [the general] with a ludicrous mixture of awe and familiarity as he rode past. 'How-do, Massa Butler?' 'How-do, General?' accompanied by absurd bows and scrapes." Butler displayed an obvious pride in them and their work. "And," the reporter added, "they seemed proud of themselves."[30]

Despite the departure of Butler, slaves continued to come to Union

Ruins of Hampton. (Library of Congress)

lines. One of these was Robert Moody, a forty-four-year-old slave who had been Richard Eppes's body servant. The planter—whose Peninsula plantation had been at the center of the case in which the slave Amy had testified—was serving with a Confederate regiment on the lower Peninsula, and Moody took the opportunity to run away, taking two of Eppes's prized pistols with him. Many of the other runaways fled in rowboats and when chased, often received assistance from the Federal navy. The sight of Union naval artillery was enough to turn back anyone attempting to catch up with the fugitives.[31]

On November 7, a *Chicago Tribune* correspondent noted that slaves were also coming from areas well beyond the Peninsula, detailing the story of thirty-six runaways the Union navy had picked up after the fugitives had floated down the Rappahannock River into Chesapeake Bay. "They said they had left because they were to be taken to Richmond to work on the fortifications, and they did not want to help Secesh against 'Massy Lincoln.'" The black men noted that "others were preparing to leave, and there is no doubt that there will be large accessions as the cold weather approaches."[32]

The runaways were now laboring for Lincoln rather than against him. In the fall of 1861, there were perhaps a few thousand fugitive slaves in and around Fort Monroe, and they were busier than ever securing the Federal position and manning the docks. One correspondent reported that the blacks "are considered superior . . . to any other class of laborers." They were "quite as productive . . . [and] more cheerful and willing." Envious of the labor force gathered on the Peninsula, the War Department ordered Butler's replacement, General John E. Wool, to send his contrabands to work on the Washington defenses. The officer promised to share "as many as can be spared." Provisioning the families of the laborers proved difficult for Wool just as it had been for Butler. Abolitionist groups sent aid, but it was not enough. Many of Wool's men were hiring servants, and the general required such soldiers to pay into a general support fund for the slaves.[33]

That these payments did not go directly to the workers highlighted the fact that the Confiscation Act did not actually free them, and doubts about their choice to come to the Federals persisted. "Their future condition is frequently discussed among themselves," a newspaper correspondent observed; "they do not appear to have any settled idea about it." Masters' lies about Northerners lingered in some minds. A few worried that when "the Yankees . . . were through building fortifications [they] would take the negroes to Cuba."[34] Despite these concerns, however, the slaves at Fort Monroe continued to labor for Union troops and undoubtedly prayed that they had made the right choice by fleeing to their masters' enemies. As Edward Pierce had explained to them months earlier, their labor for the Union might yet help to convince Northerners to embrace emancipation.

"To press into service all of the slaves of the country"

Meanwhile, Confederate general John Magruder's biggest obstacle was not Fort Monroe's reception of runaways—it was Virginia's slave owners. Confederate secretary of war Leroy P. Walker continually grappled with a "Negro question" of his own. In August, Charles City County resident John Tyler, ex-president of the United States and member of the Confederate Congress, complained to the secretary of war about the continued impressments of his slaves. Six weeks earlier, he had patriotically delivered half of them, but he had no idea they would be gone so long. Their absence "has delayed the threshing of the wheat crop, [and] has engendered some little feeling of discontent among some of our people who begin to question the legality of it." Edmund Ruffin was equally unhappy and could not understand why the soldiers in Magruder's command could not handle the work themselves.[35]

Other planters agreed and griped about their slaves coming back in bad health due to hard work and poor medical treatment. Engineer officers found it difficult to negotiate terms with local doctors for treating slaves and free blacks working on the fortifications. For example, physicians told Thomas Talcott, a captain in the Confederate engineer corps, that they would agree to render services only if they could make paid visits once-a-day whether needed or not. These terms were unacceptable, and consequently the laborers received little medical treatment, making local slaveholders more reluctant to send their slaves to work for the Confederacy.[36]

To deal with the shortage of laborers, Magruder forced all free blacks in the region to work on the entrenchments but found that their frequent desertions created more problems. By September, the general was on the verge of having to force slave owners to send their slaves to him. He told local planters that he had "full authority . . . to press into service all of the slaves of the country." However, he preferred "to rely upon the patriotism of his fellow citizens for the needful supply of labor."[37]

The appeal did not work. On September 20, General Magruder informed the inspector general that "some wealthy men" refused to send their slaves. The fortifications were "very incomplete, and my troops have worked until they are too sick to work any longer." The general sent cavalry out to round up more slaves, but the problem persisted. In October, Magruder asked slave owners in nearby King and Queen, Gloucester, and Mathews counties to provide a third of their best slaves. The owners reluctantly complied but predictably complained about the poor treatment and diet their slaves received.[38] Among Virginia slaveholders, Magruder's name was quickly becoming as accursed as Lincoln's.

"The whole pack of Anti-Slavery, Abolition devils are at work"

As summer turned into fall, Lincoln increasingly faced his own pressures. General John C. Frémont, former Republican presidential nominee and commander of Union troops in Missouri, stunned the nation by proclaiming that all slaves owned by rebellious masters in that state were now free. Undoubtedly, Benjamin Butler would have liked to have solved his problem in the same manner, but he was too astute a politician to make such a bold move. Frémont's proclamation pleased abolitionists, but they were outraged a few days later when Lincoln publicly admonished the general and revoked the order. Frémont's measure did not conform to the Confiscation Act because it attempted to free slaves rather than confiscate them and did not limit its mandate to slaves who were actually laboring for the Confederacy.[39]

Thus far, emancipationists did not view Lincoln as a terrible hindrance. The president had supported Butler's contraband policy and signed the Confiscation Act. However, when Lincoln revoked Frémont's order, emancipationists unleashed a storm of criticism. From that point on, abolitionists and radical Republicans became increasingly wary of Lincoln and stepped up their efforts to educate the northern public about the need for emancipation.[40]

Their message, presented in pamphlets, books, speeches, sermons, and newspaper editorials, drew on the experiences of the past few months. When Benjamin Butler first contacted the government concerning the slaves coming to Fort Monroe, he had written, "As a military question it would seem a necessity to deprive their masters of their services." Now emancipationists latched on to the phrase "military necessity." They maintained that the Constitution's war powers gave the president the authority to emancipate the slaves (in this they depended heavily on arguments made by John Quincy Adams twenty years earlier). They insisted that because slavery was the chief cause of the war, the North could not triumph without eliminating the institution. They added that emancipation would ensure that the Confederacy would not secure foreign recognition.[41]

Beyond these core arguments, emancipationists also developed three lines of reasoning directly related to military matters. First, it was clear that many slaves already expected that the war would liberate them, and Butler's contraband policy only heightened and encouraged that belief. Slaves all over the South would continue to come into Union lines whether invited or not, especially after passage of the Confiscation Act. Runaway slaves, "not in scores but in hundreds and thousands," Henry Ward Beecher reminded the country, "are held by the government." Unfortunately, as Butler's correspondence with Secretary Cameron illustrated, the Confiscation Act did not specify the ultimate status of such fugitives, especially those who had not been laboring for the Confederates before fleeing. "This government is not going, I take it, to put them up at auction," Beecher sarcastically remarked; "our government has got to do something with them."[42]

Representative Martin F. Conway of Kansas offered an unsettling possibility: "Should the rebellion be suppressed tomorrow," he told Congress, "the slaves now coming within our lines, and helping us" could be reclaimed by their masters under the Fugitive Slave Law. As their numbers rose, the need to protect these individuals would become more pressing. "If it does not stare us in the face at this very moment," Senator Charles Sumner warned, "it is because unhappily we are still everywhere on the defensive." As the armies advanced, "you can not avoid it. There will be slaves in your camps or within your extensive lines whose conditions must be determined."[43]

The question of what to do with slaves who were fleeing to Union lines, however, was not the most pressing consideration. "If you ask what are you going to do with these slaves," abolitionist George B. Cheever queried the nation in a published sermon, "perhaps you had better answer another question first; what are you going to do without them?" The minister touched on the second line of emancipationist reasoning: "What are you going to do with them at command of your enemies?" Despite Magruder's struggles with Virginia's slaveholders, the South had effectively impressed slaves by the thousands to support their armies, and most shocking of all, the Confederates were apparently using them in combat. Emancipationists frequently cited Manassas and the Peninsula to prove these assertions and more broadly referred to Confederate claims that slavery remained an essential source of strength to the southern cause.[44]

If the North refused to free the slaves, emancipationists feared that more of them would voluntarily serve the South. The fugitive slaves at Fort Monroe had recounted to northern soldiers and journalists the lies their masters told about Yankees and their hints that loyalty to the South would yield rewards for slaves and free blacks. "We have certain knowledge that we have been represented to [the slaves] as their bitterest foes," Moncure Conway explained in his best-selling book of late 1861, *The Rejected Stone.* "They have been told that our plan was to slay a proportion of them and banish the rest." Because the government was only confiscating the labor of slaves and not emancipating them, Conway asserted, "we have done nothing to disabuse the slave's mind in this particular." Consequently, some might be inclined to serve the Confederacy.[45]

Echoing Harriet Beecher Stowe's comments after Manassas, emancipationists argued that as the war progressed, the South would only use African American labor more effectively, perhaps even arming the enslaved population. "There is no doubt that we shall have armed slaves against us, the *New Bedford Mercury* cautioned. "We must fight them, or free them." George B. Cheever agreed: "If we refuse to [free the slaves] the rebellious Confederacy may do it for themselves, and in that case the opportunity is not only gone from us forever, but turned against us."[46]

Butler's successful conversion of slaves into a Federal asset inspired the third line of reasoning adopted by the emancipationists. The black laborers at Fort Monroe were prime examples of what could happen on a grand scale if slaves were freed. "Why should we overlook the millions of the oppressed . . . who, by the laws of God, are our natural allies," Conway asked, "unless, by our inhumanity, we drive them to the side of the enemy?" The work that slaves were doing for the Confederacy they could do for the North, and would with more zeal and passion than whites. "So many slaves, so many enemies," Sumner quoted an ancient proverb; "there are now four millions of enemies intermingled with the rebels; being four millions of allies to the National Government. Can we afford to reject this natural alliance?" Sumner used Butler's change of heart as an example of what could happen once the entire northern population recognized the military necessity of protecting runaway slaves.[47]

Using such reasoning, emancipationists waged a propaganda campaign in the fall of 1861. They formed "Emancipation Leagues" in several northern cities, which pooled resources, shared hundreds of newspaper articles and speeches with various publications, organized lectures, lobbied politicians, and published books. One of their most successful endeavors was a series of lectures at the Smithsonian in Washington, where many members of Congress were regularly in attendance. Even Lincoln appeared to hear several of the speakers. "Such lectures in Washington," army chaplain A. M. Stewart noted, "are surely an index of the marvelous change which has been working for the past year." The overriding theme was that the events of the war had shown that emancipation was a military necessity. "War is a swift and infallible educator," Moncure Conway publicly informed the president.[48]

Abolitionists had not abandoned their commitment to emancipation as a moral imperative. They continued to demand abolition as a matter of justice and a means of securing God's blessings for the Union cause. "God is not on the side of the best battalions," Conway corrected Napoleon's famous maxim; "the best battalions are the ones on the side of God." Nevertheless, many abolitionists understood that the military necessity argument had the potential to be more persuasive than a moral one and watched as radical Republicans took the lead in publicly arguing for emancipation. Representative Martin F. Conway told Congress that "the abolition of slavery . . . has been elevated by events into . . . the overruling necessity of a nation." Former Massachusetts governor George S. Boutwell was more blunt. The war, he argued, had shown that freeing the slaves was now "a matter of necessity to ourselves; for unless it be by accident, we are not to come out of this contest as one nation, except by emancipation."[49]

Newspaper editors took up the argument. The *Chicago Tribune* continued to insist that Union armies "have been fighting both rebels and slaves. They have repelled the assistance the latter would gladly give them, and have allowed their enemies to use them in whatever way they can render the most help to the rebellion." Doing nothing to deprive the Rebels of using their slaves for military labor was a "silly and absurd course." Cincinnati's leading newspaper, the *Gazette*, agreed. "Our armies must either have these negroes as enemies or friends. They cannot be put out of the question, for they are in the hands of the enemy and are used against us. They build the fortifications which are so prominent an element in this war." The *Daily Cleveland Herald* concurred: "The Rebels get the most war 'aid and comfort' they can out of both free and slave negroes in their midst. They put shovels or guns into their hands, and compel them to use both, just as exigencies demand." The paper insisted that "Gen. [Joseph] Johnston is organizing the negroes [in Virginia] as fighting men." For the *Chicago Tribune*, it was "simply a question [of] whether it is best to oblige [the slaves] to help the rebels, or to let them assist us." Pointing out that Andrew Jackson had used black troops in New Orleans in 1814, the paper sarcastically noted: "We, of this generation, have risen superior to such examples. We are sending white men into the field to be shot down by negroes . . . pressed into the rebel service."[50]

The logic behind these arguments attracted a good deal of attention. Abolitionists such as Wendell Phillips, William Lloyd Garrison, and Frederick Douglass were now applauded in cities and other places that had previously shunned them. Newspapers gave wide circulation to statements of radical Republicans such as Charles Sumner. "Never has there been a time when Abolitionists were as much respected as at present," William Goodell claimed at the end of 1861. "Announce the presence of a competent abolition lecturer and the house is crammed." Reporting on a speech by Wendell Phillips, the Democratic *Detroit Free Press* summed up the abolitionist's argument succinctly: "The negro, he said, held the balance of power in this contest, and it was impossible to conquer without him. His doctrine, therefore, was to abolish slavery that we may save the Union."[51]

Opponents of emancipation were forced onto the defensive. "The Emancipation League is now in full blast," the *Boston Herald* lamented at the end of the year. "The furnace is heated ten times hotter than ever, and the whole pack of Anti-Slavery, Abolition devils are at work to make Bedlam appear lovely and inviting." Democrats acknowledged that fugitive slaves in the Union lines were a problem but believed the Confiscation Act was sufficient to handle it. They supported the seizure of slaves who were working for the Confederacy and the use of these men to labor for Union armies but balked at further steps toward freedom. The abolitionists, complained the staunchly Democratic *Daily Chicago Times*, "would arm the slaves. Thus armed, nine out of ten of them would probably fight for their masters. . . . It is a great pity that things cannot be so ordered that both the abolitionists and negroes should be armed and set upon each other."[52]

The *Boston Courier* declared that emancipation would only "inflame still further the minds of Southern people against the Union and the North," thus creating an even larger rebellion. The *New York Herald* concurred: "Two-thirds of the people of the Southern States are sound Unionists. . . . [But emancipation] would . . . make them as deadly enemies as the most rabid secessionists." The *Louisville Democrat* leaned on the old proslavery argument that abolition would spawn a race war and that "the two races . . . can not exist in the same country, unless the black race is in slavery. It is no question for theory, argument or discussion. It is a direct law of God, final and conclusive." The Border State paper issued an ominous warning: "We speak it plainly; the scheme for general emancipation or arming the blacks will lose every State to the Union."[53]

Many Northerners refused to accept the premise that the North could not win without the aid of the slaves. The author of a letter to the *Washington Sunday Morning Chronicle* wrote: "We are not ready to admit our incapacity to restore the Union without letting 'slip the dogs of war'" by freeing and arming the slaves. "The President relies for success in the salvation of the government, not upon slaves, but the resources and manly courage of twenty millions of free, loyal, and intelligent people, and he will not do so in vain." The *Daily Chicago Times* agreed: "The white population of the loyal states is twenty one millions against seven millions in the disloyal States. If we can not whip out the rebels with these odds in our favor, we had better abandon the contest and plead guilty to the rebel taunt that we are an inferior people." Because the armies were moving forward in "nearly every department," the *Washington Daily Intelligencer* reasoned, "we are aware of nothing in the military exigencies of the country which calls for any change of policy in the prosecution of war."[54]

Finally, the opponents of emancipation maintained that Union soldiers had enlisted to save the Union, not to free the slaves. They argued that emancipation would demoralize the army, weaken its effectiveness, and hamper future recruitment. Conservatives expressed faith in General McClellan's ability to win the war and make emancipation unnecessary. The general concurred with these sentiments and reiterated them to radical congressmen whenever he got the chance, later claiming to have told Sumner and others that he "was fighting for my country & the Union, not for abolition and the Republican party." The general was convinced that the radicals were disingenuous when they pushed for emancipation as a military necessity to save the Republic, arguing that they "only had the negro in view, & not the Union . . . & merely wished to accomplish a political move for party profit, or from sentimental motives." Writing a Democratic friend that fall, McClellan explained that emancipation would hamper his upcoming campaign to capture Richmond and begged, "Help me to dodge the nigger, we want nothing to do with him."[55]

For their part, emancipationists were not attempting to persuade McClellan, and many radicals believed that he was actually proslavery. By their logic, the president's war powers allowed him to emancipate the slaves, and therefore they sought to work on the commander in chief. They directed many of their "military necessity" arguments at Lincoln. In a public letter to the president, Moncure Conway wrote: "It is not often . . . one man is given the magnificent opportunity which . . . has [been] placed within your reach. For the first time there stands a man on the Earth empowered to break four millions of fetters."[56]

On a more personal level, Senator Charles Sumner was a powerful link to the president. The two men developed an unlikely friendship, and Sumner took every opportunity to harangue Lincoln on the slavery issue. By the end of 1861, he felt he had made considerable progress. "Well, Mr. Sumner," Lincoln reportedly said, "the only difference between you and me on this subject is a difference of a month or six weeks in time." Thus, despite the powerful opposition, emancipationists were optimistic when Congress reconvened that December. Their public and private campaign to push the military necessity argument seemed wildly successful, and they expected considerable support in Congress. There were now 105 Republican and 44 Democratic representatives in the House; and there were 31 Republican senators to only 10 Democrats in the Senate.[57]

"We should not be in haste"

Emancipationists were therefore stunned by Lincoln's opening message to Congress on December 3. The president did indicate that slaves seized under the provisions of the Confiscation Act were "liberated" but said nothing about the status of slaves who had not been working for the Confederates but were now within Union lines. He proposed colonizing confiscated slaves "at some place or places in a climate congenial to them," and he encouraged free blacks in the North to leave as well.[58]

Even more distressing was Lincoln's apparent rejection of the military necessity argument. Ever sensitive to Border State concerns, he echoed conservative fears that emancipation would elicit more southern resistance and that the result would be a war so extensive it would require the complete subjugation of the South. He asserted that the government should only do what was absolutely necessary to save the Union and believed that events had yet to demonstrate that emancipation was a necessity. "We should not be in haste to determine that radical and extreme measures . . . are indispensable," he said. The message saddened abolitionists and radical Republicans. "Mr Lincoln had his *face Southward* when he wrote this *thing*," one of Senator Trumbull's constituents complained.[59]

Most Americans had a different reaction. The country and "every loyal and conservative Union man," the *New York Herald* proclaimed, should "experience a cheering sense of relief" after the president's message. The *Boston Daily Advertiser* praised Lincoln for demonstrating "that he has not been misled by the passionate impulse[s]" of abolitionists. The Democratic *Detroit Free Press* agreed: "We are thankful that [the message] gives evidences that the reign of radicalism is over, and that henceforth a wise, conservative policy will be adopted in the administration of the government."[60]

The president's hometown *Illinois State Journal* lauded his rejection of the military necessity argument. "This is as we expected," the Republican paper claimed. "Mr. Lincoln is for the indiscriminate confiscation of all rebel property for military purposes, but questions the present expediency of a law which would go to the extent of a general emancipation measure." Quoting Lincoln's admonition that "we should not be in haste," the *Washington Daily Intelligencer* praised his "terse and simple words." On this issue, the paper believed that "Mr. Lincoln has correctly interpreted the mind and heart of the loyal population throughout the land." The *Baltimore American* concurred: "This declaration, we are convinced, will be eminently satisfactory to the country." The Border State paper believed that because he had rejected emancipation, "the President is taking the shortest course to end the war." Twelve days after the speech, the *Washington Sunday Morning Chronicle* proclaimed: "From every part of the country we hear the most enthusiastic approval."[61]

Nevertheless, emancipationists were not entirely dismayed. Lincoln's message was politically astute. He understood that the nation was not ready to embrace emancipation. Although he was sympathetic to the radicals, he could not afford to lose the support of conservatives and the Border States by advancing too far ahead of popular opinion. Although the president's message did not address the status of slaves within Union lines who had not labored for the Confederates (like those the Vermont soldiers had hidden from George Benjamin West), he did indirectly encourage Congress to take up the issue. "I have adhered to the act . . . to confiscate property," he wrote. "If a new law upon the same subject shall be proposed [it] will be duly considered."[62]

"We hope they will try him," the radical *Racine (Wis.) Weekly Journal* responded. Referring to Mary Lincoln's southern roots, the paper quipped: "[Then] we shall see whether he cares more for the rebels and the Todd family than he does for the loyal men of Union." The *Chicago Tribune* believed it knew Lincoln's true sentiments and was therefore optimistic: "The cautious language which Lincoln employs does not hide from us, who know the deep moral convictions of the man, the purpose that he has in view." The paper interpreted his statements to mean that "we must not be in haste to say that [emancipation] measures must be adopted; but when the necessity for such is apparent, let us have them."[63]

While the president waited for more proof that emancipation was a military necessity, the radical Republicans moved forward. Two days after Lincoln's message was read to Congress, Lyman Trumbull introduced another bill for the confiscation of Rebel property. Unlike the first bill, the new one proposed to confiscate all property, including slaves, of individuals in rebellion against the federal government, whether that property was being used in the war or not. Any slaves confiscated under the provisions of the bill would become free. "These measures," the *Illinois State Journal* declared, "will doubtless command much attention in Congress, and lead to protracted discussion." Indeed, the bill had many high profile enemies, not the least of which was the leader of all northern armies. "I have heard from straight authority," a well-connected ally wrote radical senator Zachariah Chandler the day after the bill was introduced, that McClellan "will sheath his sword if your confiscation policy . . . shall prevail. I hope he will . . . so that we may have war upon right principles."[64]

Once introduced, the controversial bill was sent into committee and was hotly debated by Congress and the northern public for the next eight months. Democrats and other conservatives struggled to keep the legislation tied up as long as possible, hoping that McClellan's impending campaign to capture the Rebel capital would end the war and thus kill the measure. Conversely, for the radicals to gain presidential and popular support for the bill, McClellan's campaign would need to strengthen their claims that emancipation was a military necessity.

Ringgold's Story

As radical Republicans introduced the second confiscation bill to Congress, McClellan slowly pieced together a plan to capture Richmond. The general employed famous spy Allen Pinkerton as head of his intelligence department and had him gathering information on Confederate military dispositions in the Old Dominion. On December 2, William Ringgold, the free black who had gone to work for the Confederacy eight months earlier on the steamship *Logan*, walked into Pinkerton's Washington office and told the officer a story that would shape the planning of the Peninsula Campaign.[65] Like George Scott (Butler's spy during the planning of the fight at Big Bethel), Ringgold demonstrated that African Americans could contribute more than just their labor to the Union cause.

The young African American had worked for months on the York River helping transport laborers and soldiers to the lower Peninsula, but the Confederacy discharged him when a Tidewater storm damaged his vessel. On a trip to Richmond, Ringgold noticed that there were no artillery batteries protecting the York River railroad running from West Point into Richmond and that only a handful of men guarded the bridges along the railroad line. There appeared to be few troops on the Peninsula, though many of these soldiers had body servants. Such slaves were "generally armed in full, the same as the white soldiers, with muskets and all." Ringgold explained that "they do not form into line with the white soldiers, but [they do] follow the regiment, as usual, fully armed." Nevertheless, the Peninsula slaves "generally anticipate being freed, on the triumph of the Federal arms." Ringgold did not stay long in Richmond, but while there he observed over 700 free blacks and 2,000 skilled and unskilled slaves laboring on defensive works. Everywhere Ringgold looked, the Confederates were advantageously using African Americans to protect Virginia from invasion.[66]

Having come all the way to the city to be paid, Ringgold and two of his crewmates were frustrated when Confederate authorities sent them back down the Peninsula to Gloucester. After finally receiving their wages there, they set off on the York River and crossed the enormous Chesapeake Bay in a small canoe. Upon reaching the Eastern Shore, they made their way back to Baltimore and reached their hometown in late November.[67]

Ringgold told Pinkerton everything he could remember about the Virginia Peninsula, and most of his information was quite specific. He identified southern regiments and their positions, as well as the types and locations of Confederate batteries. After interviewing Ringgold, Pinkerton concluded that the black man was well spoken and intelligent and possessed valuable information about Confederate works and troop dispositions. The officer quickly forwarded the particulars to General McClellan.[68]

Ringgold's information suggested that Virginia's powerful river batteries could prevent Union naval vessels from taking the city. An attack on Richmond from the east would have to be accomplished by infantry, but Magruder's entrenchments would significantly slow any army advancing toward the city on the Virginia Peninsula. However, the York River railroad that led from the river into the eastern side of the city was comparatively unprotected. If an army could get to West Point, Virginia (where the railroad began at the head of the York River), without having to move up the Peninsula, it could use the railroad to advance on the city. An attack on the eastern side of Richmond was exactly what was on McClellan's mind, and Ringgold's report offered the most detailed information that the general would use in formulating his strategy.[69]

The labor on Confederate fortifications that Ringgold left behind was far from complete. Magruder continued to clash with local slave owners while overseeing the construction of fortifications. Responding to pressure from Virginia planters, the Confederate government refused to support another request by Magruder for more slaves. Nevertheless, the general found a temporary solution at the end of the year. "I am informed," he wrote the Confederate War Department, "that negroes can be hired by the year for $100 each. Without this I am sure the works . . . will not be completed and made safe. No time can be lost, as the day of hiring is the first of January next."[70] The department authorized the expenditure, and Magruder dispatched agents to hire the slaves.

The summer and fall of 1861 was a time of little actual combat in Virginia, but before the Peninsula Campaign even began, the activity of the region's slaves and free blacks had already begun to shape the ways in which it would be fought. McClellan's army would have to fight its way to Richmond through fortifications built by Virginia's blacks, and as it marched deeper into Rebel territory, it would be greeted by slaves eager to be "confiscated" and to help in any way they could.

Although previous events helped abolitionists and radical Republicans promote their agenda, much of the northern public was not yet ready to embrace emancipation.[71] However, Northerners would pay close attention to the upcoming attempt to capture the Rebel capital, and thus the Peninsula Campaign could potentially strengthen the military necessity argument in several ways. If slaves beyond the mandate of the Confiscation Act (those who had not necessarily been laboring for the Confederates) continued to enter Union lines, the government would have to determine the status of such runaways. By expanding their aid to the northern army, fugitives could further demonstrate their potential as a source of strength to the Union. If Magruder and the Confederacy continued using slave labor to build fortifications that significantly hindered the advance of Federal troops, this too would demonstrate that slave labor was a powerful southern military asset. And if more slaves were observed fighting with the Confederates, it would stir the same passions that had resulted in the passage of the First Confiscation Act after the Battle of Manassas.

Even so, another formidable obstacle to emancipation remained. If George B. McClellan's strategy of using overwhelming force and protecting southern property worked, the war would end without emancipation. The Union general's plans, therefore, would need to be frustrated and defeated. "If it be found that the power of the loyal States is insufficient to quell the rebellion," the moderate Republican *Indianapolis Journal* declared at the end of 1861, "and that the Government must have some other help than its own strength, then, and not before, will it be time to summon slaves to the rescue. That extremity we have not yet reached. We do not believe that we shall ever reach it." The paper believed Northerners were in favor of winning the war "by our power *if we can*" and believed emancipation and black troops "should be the last resort of desperation. . . . [If] it becomes manifest that we can't end the rebellion without calling upon slave help, the whole country will say 'amen' to the call."[72]

As it turned out, the black laborers at Fort Monroe, Magruder's labor gangs, runaway slaves, William Ringgold, and other African Americans working for both armies were voluntarily or involuntarily engaged in activities that would help to shape the Peninsula Campaign to their advantage.

THE BEST INFORMED RESIDENTS IN VIRGINIA DECEMBER 1861– APRIL 1862

On a dank and frigid night in January 1862, William Davis, a slave from Hampton, Virginia, nervously awaited introduction on a stage at New York City's Cooper Institute. The opening speaker, the Reverend L. C. Lockwood, an abolitionist, had asked the forty-seven-year-old African American to come north on a speaking tour to solicit donations for the contrabands. That night at the Cooper Institute, Lockwood gave a brief description of the slaves at Fort Monroe, and then he struggled to find a proper phrase to describe Davis's status. Because the slave had not worked on the Confederate works before coming into Union lines, he did not meet the criteria of the Confiscation Act and was technically not free. Lockwood settled for calling him "one of Uncle Sam's slaves." The minister jokingly assured the audience that William Davis had no connection to Confederate president Jefferson Davis, "except the relation of antagonist." With that, the Peninsula slave stood up before the podium and told his story.[1]

The crowd was smaller than expected due to the bad weather, but Davis impressed those in attendance with an emotional description of his slave life, which included being sold several times as a child, instances of whipping, and his rise to slave foreman on his master's small Virginia Peninsula farm. His owner had sold five of Davis's seven children away, including a son auctioned off the previous New Year's Day.[2]

Davis explained that upon the arrival of the Union army on the peninsula, his widowed owner had fled Hampton and left her slaves behind. Davis, his wife, and two of their children then entered Federal lines at Fort Monroe. While he labored for the government, his children received an education from the abolitionist missionaries, something the young blacks described as "getting white." That his progeny were going to school filled Davis with profound joy, and according to the *New York Times*, he discussed it "in terms not only of impressive feeling, but in many cases, of real eloquence."

Turning to the war, Davis confirmed reports that some slaves were armed and fighting for the South, but he assured his audience that it "was done solely on compulsion." Having been a slave foreman, he perceptively compared their plight to that of slaves who "were often made to fill the place of whipping-master." He maintained that the best way to prevent the South from continually taking military advantage of the enslaved community was to free the slaves so they could "go forth conquering." Davis compared his mission to that of Moses before Pharaoh. He had come from the Virginia Peninsula to ask the government to "let the people go."[3]

As the New Yorkers applauded William Davis in the early days of 1862, other members of Virginia's African American community were also helping to shape the future direction of the Peninsula Campaign and the war. For the Federals, African Americans proved to be an important source of not only labor but also military intelligence. In northern Virginia, slaves demonstrated for McClellan the usefulness of information gleaned from runaways, and their reports played a small role in where the general began his campaign to capture Richmond. To increase the likelihood that the Union army would liberate them, blacks may have also given deceptive and exaggerated statements to the Federals concerning the South's military use of slaves. The statements of runaways and other reports from the Peninsula continued to bolster emancipationists' warnings that Southerners were arming their slaves. Meanwhile, Confederate general John Magruder considered slave labor indispensable for defending the Peninsula, and he continued to clash with local slaveholders over the impressment of their slaves. Nevertheless, he effectively used black labor to build fortifications that delayed the Union offensive.

"Many colored men were in the enemy's ranks"
William Davis was not the only black Virginian telling his story to Northerners in January 1862. John Parker, the runaway slave who claimed to have manned a Confederate battery during the Battle of Manassas, was also in New York meeting with abolitionists and granting interviews. "We ourselves have seen and conversed with Parker," the editors of *Principia* declared. "He was carefully questioned and left no doubts in the minds of those who heard him of the truth of his statements." The *New York Evening Post* ran his account of Manassas, including his claim that many African Americans were fighting for the Confederacy. Parker assured Northerners that blacks in Confederate armies had no desire to kill Union soldiers and

fired over their heads during battle. In fact, they ostracized anyone who purposely killed a Yankee. As an example, Parker claimed that one particular Alabama regiment used one of its slaves as a sharpshooter and that he had killed several Federal picket guards. The other slaves in Confederate ranks universally despised him, and they rejoiced when Union sharpshooters eventually killed him.[4]

Other reports added weight to the statements of Parker and Davis. Back on December 22, approximately 700 Confederate soldiers had attacked several companies of the 20th New York at New Market Bridge during a routine reconnaissance up the Peninsula. The Yankees had six men wounded in this small skirmish and claimed that among their assailants was one full company of armed blacks (about 100 men). "Many colored men were in the enemy's ranks," Chaplain Richard F. Fuller recorded in his diary, "the rebels having no tender scruples about arming the slaves." The African Americans reportedly wounded several of the Union soldiers.[5]

"Mention has been made of such companies in the Southern papers heretofore," the *Philadelphia Inquirer* correspondent noted at the end of December, "but the reports were not credited. The facts of the matter are now established beyond contradiction." When other soldiers in the 20th New York heard that blacks had apparently attacked their comrades, "they were literally frantic to advance." But the Confederate troops had already retreated. "A wounded Rebel was taken prisoner," the *Inquirer* continued. "He acknowledges that there was a company of negroes in action."[6]

These accounts infuriated Union troops, and a day after the small skirmish, the rumor mill wildly inflated the numbers of blacks engaged. In a letter to the *Indianapolis Journal*, a Hoosier soldier made the outrageous claim that the New Yorkers came upon "a body of 700 negro infantry, all armed with muskets, who opened fire." The wounded soldiers "testify positively that they were shot by negroes." Knowing that many people would doubt such a story, the soldier reiterated that there was "no mistake about it. The [Union soldiers] were actually attacked and fired on, and wounded by negroes." The "dastardly act" of using blacks against them incensed the men of the 20th Indiana, and they swore to "kill any negro they see." The soldier maintained that people had for too long disbelieved stories of blacks fighting for the Confederates and that "it is time that this thing was understood." The letter called on the government to act: "If they fight us with negroes, why should not we fight them with negroes too?"[7]

Many emancipationist newspapers reprinted and discussed the Hoosier soldier's claims.[8] The *Chicago Tribune* believed that the news would be a "dose [that] will cure" those who opposed freeing and arming the slaves. The *Indianapolis Journal*, the *Chicago Tribune* pointed out, "has been a stout defender of the conservative" policy. The Indiana soldier's letter, however, "has completely 'knocked into pi' all the arguments [they have] employed, and brought [the *Journal*] over to the *Tribune*'s ground." The conservative paper's position on emancipation "gave way before the charge of the [southern] negro regiment."[9]

As John Parker and William Davis had explained, however, the *Tribune* reminded its readers that "one thing should be borne into mind" when discussing evidence of blacks fighting with the South. "The negroes employed against us, are pressed into that service. Every man of them would desert to our side, if opportunity offered." The *Tribune*'s editors were certain that slaves had "no love for the rebels, and they feel no allegiance to 'Jeffdom.'" Subsequent news from the *Philadelphia Inquirer* bolstered that opinion. A correspondent reported on a group of runaways that included a slave who claimed he had "fought for the Rebels at New Market Bridge before escaping to the Union army."[10]

In the early months of 1862, allegations that Southerners were coercing African Americans into combat continued to be a regular feature in the speeches and editorials of emancipationists. In pushing for both emancipation and the recruitment of black troops, the abolitionist newspaper *Principia* maintained that the Confederates "have been fighting in close companionship with negroes, from the beginning!" Southern blacks, the paper claimed, "are regularly drilled for the service. And the proportion of negro soldiers is increasing." Anywhere from 800,000 to 1 million male slaves were of fighting age, Indiana representative George Julian warned Congress on January 14, and "they cannot be neutral. As laborers, if not as soldiers, they will be the allies of the rebels, or of the Union. . . . The rebels organize regiments of black men, who shoot down our loyal soldiers."[11]

Two famous abolitionists shared these concerns. At the Cooper Institute, William Lloyd Garrison repeated the assertion that 800,000 male slaves were capable of fighting. "They are at the service of the country whenever we accept them. But the Government will not accept them, and the rebel slaveholders are mustering them in companies, and in regiments, and they are shooting down Northern men." Wendell Phillips presciently observed in February 1862 that if the Confederacy started to lose the war, the arming of their slaves would only become more widespread. They would play their "last card" by calling "the negroes to their aid [and] offering liberation in return." Thus, immediate emancipation was required. A month later, Phillips reiterated the point while lecturing at the

Smithsonian. "If Abraham Lincoln does not have the negro on his side," he told the audience, "Jefferson Davis will have him on his."[12]

In the face of such assertions, some Northerners came to believe that Southerners were arming their slaves and would continue to do so in growing numbers. In March, the popular *Frank Leslie's Illustrated Newspaper* informed its readers, "Not only have the slaves of the Southern rebels been extensively employed against us in the erection of fortifications . . . but the free negroes, and it is also believed many slaves, have been enrolled in the rebel army and made to fight as soldiers." The *North American and United States Gazette* labeled it a "well established fact that there are companies and whole regiments of negroes in the military service of Jeff Davis's confederacy." The editors marveled at those who still refused to believe it, when "the proof that such is the fact accumulates daily."[13]

"They look as if they could take care of themselves"

Although the abolitionists' attentions began to shift in January away from Fort Monroe to the thousands of slaves behind Union lines farther south in Port Royal, South Carolina, they continued to monitor the situation on the Peninsula.[14] Northern newspaper correspondents assigned to Fort Monroe reported on the runaways still coming to the Federals. The *Boston Journal*, for example, told of a slave who had twice been caught trying to escape before he finally managed to get away with a group of blacks who had been working on Confederate batteries. During the night, the band of fugitives stole a small boat while the Rebel sentry slept, carried it two miles on their backs, and then launched it on the York River. The next morning, the reporter related, "they were glad to get on board of . . . [a Union boat], after much fatigue and cold." Investigating a similar escape, a *New York Times* correspondent asked a group of runaways why they had come to Union camps. "We wanted to do better, sir," the self-emancipated slaves responded. "They look as if they could take care of themselves," the correspondent opined.[15]

"A census . . . is now being taken," the *Philadelphia Inquirer* reported from Fort Monroe on February 4, "and it appears to indicate that there are about 5,000 persons . . . here who were formerly held in bondage." The correspondent praised the black laborers and insisted that "if they are not independent themselves, their posterity will be." The *Chicago Tribune* described the black workers' daily routine. The able-bodied men were mustered in groups of fifty and marched off to build the outer works

"Morning Mustering of the Contrabands." (Frank Leslie's Illustrated Newspaper, November 2, 1861)

of the fort. The laborers shouldered their spades and pickaxes and followed a "lively refrain" of songs to keep in "regular step." The *Tribune* correspondent lamented that in other places "similar measures have not been taken" to use black labor. Because of their work, he argued, "Fortress Monroe may safely be set down as impregnable." The runaway slaves also spent much of their day eagerly learning from abolitionist missionaries. "Spelling books and primers" were delivered to the fort, the *Philadelphia Inquirer* reported, "and 'sich a spellin' and 'sich a readin' as is in progress is really astonishing."[16]

The black laborers were earning ten dollars a month for their work, but eight dollars of it went into a fund the government used to feed, clothe, and house their families. The laborers received the other two dollars in four weekly installments of fifty cents each. Such an arrangement was short of independence, and the status of slaves who had not been laboring for the Confederacy was still uncertain. From his headquarters on the Peninsula, U.S. general Joseph Mansfield weighed in on the issue in a letter published by the *New York Times* on February 9. He argued that the slaves at Fort Monroe should be able "to go where they please" and urged the government to start directly paying the workers their full wages.[17]

Each day brought more runaways into Union lines, and officers closely questioned them about Rebel troop strength on the Peninsula. Fugitive slaves soon became notorious for overestimating numbers. Nevertheless, some of their reports were somewhat accurate, such as that given by a group of black men in late January, who estimated that the Confederates had 1,500 men across the York River at Gloucester and 6,000 to 7,000 at Yorktown.[18]

The African Americans on the Virginia Peninsula were gaining allies among soldiers who had previously been opposed to any form of emancipation. Lieutenant Charles B. Haydon, for example, noted the effect the runaways had on a fellow officer in the 2nd Michigan. "Major Underwood has always been very bitter on the Abolitionists," Haydon explained in his journal on March 24, "but to night he worked more than 3 hours in water up to his waist to help 20 contrabands across the river & on their way to their Paradise at Fortress Monroe." The runaways had come all the way from Richmond. "He said they looked so frightened that he had to help them."[19]

The fugitives had also begun to reshape northern opinion more generally. The *Chicago Tribune* announced the "TOKENS OF PROGRESS" they gleaned from the pages of the *Philadelphia Ledger*. "That constant organ of the Democratic party," the editors noted, had consistently argued against the "wholesale confiscation of property" in the southern states. However, they quoted the *Ledger* as now making "one grand exception to this, and that is the confiscation of 'contrabands.'" The *Ledger* claimed that such runaways at Fort Monroe and elsewhere "know the country and can bring underground information." Acting as "scouts and spies," they helped keep Union troops informed of enemy activity. "Without them," the paper claimed, "we are without information or friends in a hostile or unknown land." The *Tribune*'s editors concurred: "This is sound doctrine, and when it is uttered by such a journal as the *Ledger*, the friends of the Republic may well be encouraged. The world moves, after all; and there is reason to hope that the people of the United States may see the means of their salvation from national destruction before it is too late."[20]

"I . . . found the Negroes of invaluable assistance"

As the nation debated the contributions blacks were making to both armies in early 1862, the biggest question was whether George McClellan would fight. The general brought organization and discipline to the Army of the Potomac and quickly turned the men who had been soundly defeated and demoralized at Bull Run into a proud army. As the nation cried out "on to Richmond," however, it appeared that McClellan intended to do anything but take his men into combat.

Reacting to what they perceived to be a failed war effort, radical Republicans and much of the northern public increasingly clamored for aggressive action to put down the southern rebellion. Particularly troubling was that the Army of the Potomac (which was stationed in and around Washington) had seemingly done nothing of importance since McClellan assumed command. Recent military disasters, and the radicals' conviction that there were not enough antislavery officers in the army, spurred Congress into creating the infamous Joint Committee on the Conduct of the War in December 1861. The panel summoned officers to Capitol Hill and aggressively interrogated them about why McClellan was taking so long to put the army into motion.[21]

Congress was not alone in attempting to pressure McClellan. Early in the year, Lincoln named Edwin M. Stanton as the new secretary of war, and the energetic cabinet member quickly cleaned up the mess left by his predecessor, Simon Cameron, brought efficiency to the War Department, and lost patience with McClellan. He met frequently with the general to prod him into moving sooner rather than later. Preferring a direct advance on Richmond, Stanton and the president issued an order directing the Army of the Potomac to begin moving by February 22.[22]

Despite these pressures, however, information collected from African Americans and other sources helped convince McClellan that the Rebel positions south of Washington were too formidable to assault. After bravely fleeing their Confederate masters, resourceful northern Virginia slaves played a role in determining where McClellan would begin his campaign against the Confederate capital. On a daily basis, runaways near Washington followed the example of those on the Peninsula and poured into Union camps. Many soldiers considered them a nuisance, but Allen Pinkerton, the army's intelligence chief, felt otherwise. "From the commencement of the war," he later maintained, "I . . . found the Negroes of invaluable assistance."[23]

Pinkerton understood the wealth of information he could gather from fugitive slaves and ordered that in addition to Rebel deserters and white refugees, his operatives should interview all runaways coming into Union lines. Interrogators asked about the numerical strength of southern armies, where and when the Confederates expected the Federals to move, the types of Rebel weaponry, and the general health conditions within their camps. Pinkerton's men also asked about the horses and mules, soldier and civilian morale, roads and railways, and the local economy.[24]

Although Pinkerton's best informants were Rebel deserters, runaway slaves were the most numerous and most cooperative.[25] Among the blacks, those who had been impressed into working for the southern army were the best sources of information. Runaways who had not served in Confederate labor gangs could hardly be expected to know much about southern camps, but they might know about the condition of roads and railways and the morale of their masters. Pinkerton feared, however, that the Confederates might be using some of these blacks to disseminate misleading information. To validate their claims, he required the African Americans to tell how and why they had escaped.[26]

Most of the slaves interviewed by Pinkerton and his staff during the first three months of 1862 explained their fears of being sent to other parts of Virginia. Just like General Magruder on the Peninsula, Confederate authorities near Manassas were aggressively impressing slaves and free blacks to labor on fortifications throughout the state. Escaped slave Henry Ball said that he had seen slaves impressed on his plantation and had overheard a Confederate cavalry officer tell his master that they would be back later in the week "to take every Negro off the farm."[27] Sixty-three-year-old Henry Smith reported that "slaves are rapidly being sent south" and believed that "expense [is] the only impediment to such removals being universal."[28]

Another reason for sending the slaves farther south was to prevent them from going off to the Federals. Runaways claimed that owners in the area were locking their slaves up at night or sending their property south "for fear that the damned Yankees would get them." One runaway overheard white Southerners say that "they would rather put their slaves in barns and burn them than that the Yankees should have them."[29] James Lucas related that "the colored folks are now worse treated in the south than they have ever been before [and] . . . they universally want to get away."[30] According to Pinkerton's reports, the runaways all agreed that owners were repeating the rumor that Yankees would ship confiscated slaves to Cuba to pay for the war. Most of them, however, claimed that they did not "believe the story enough to prevent them from running away if they could get the chance."[31]

Soldiers in the Army of the Potomac were not in agreement concerning the arrival of these runaways. "The whole regiment is almost in a state of mutiny on the Nigger question," Union officer Charles Harvey Brewster wrote from northern Virginia on March 4. The enlisted men of the 10th Massachusetts were angry with officers who allowed slave catchers into camp and who were attempting to chase out the black men who were working as body servants for members of the regiment. Brewster witnessed "strong [black] men crying like children" from fear of being returned to their owners. He agreed with the enlisted men; they "did not come down here to oppress Niggers and they are not quite brutes yet, as some of their officers are." As for himself, "I never will be instrumental in returning a slave to his master in any way shape or manner, I'll die first."[32]

Congress shared Brewster's outrage. The First Confiscation Act allowed for the protection of runaways who had been laboring for the Confederates but did not necessarily force officers to do so. Moreover, with the new confiscation bill tied up in committee, there was still no legislation concerning slaves who had not been laboring for the South. Down on the Peninsula, and in other commands across the South, many Union officers were sheltering all runaways regardless of the limitations imposed by the First Confiscation Act. Nevertheless, the actions of the officers of the 10th Massachusetts were common. On March 10, Congress attempted to put an end to the inconsistency by issuing an article of war prohibiting officers from returning runaway slaves.[33]

Yet the status of slaves behind Union lines in northern Virginia remained precarious, and it was therefore all the more important for runaways to claim they held valuable information about the Confederate army. In interviewing these runaways, as well as Rebel deserters and prisoners, Pinkerton and his staff had to wade through a considerable amount of useless and fabricated information, but the efforts paid off. He amassed important information about Confederate positions in northern Virginia. Although his estimates of Confederate numbers were notoriously inflated, he gleaned somewhat accurate (although incomplete) descriptions of the deployment of Confederate troops, pinpointed the location of fortifications and heavy artillery, and produced maps of the southern positions.[34]

McClellan did not rely solely on Pinkerton's evaluation of the raw data, however. He also employed two Frenchmen, Louis Philippe d'Orleans and his brother Robert, to analyze the evidence. Using many of the same sources (slave runaways, deserters, and prisoners), the brothers provided McClellan with detailed descriptions of Confederate positions. In contrast to Pinkerton, however, they concluded that "we have in front of us much fewer troops than is generally believed." That McClellan chose to accept Pinkerton's inflated numbers rather than the lower estimates demonstrates more about the cautious mind of McClellan than it does the weakness of the evidence supplied by the runaways.[35]

In any case, the Confederate fortifications at Manassas seemed formidable. McClellan refused to send his soldiers to attack an entrenched enemy across the same fields where they had been repulsed in July 1861, and he steadfastly argued against the idea with Lincoln and Stanton. In doing so, he used an understanding of Confederate positions in northern Virginia supplied to him by Pinkerton and the French brothers—information they had collected from several sources, including runaway slaves. It cannot be asserted that McClellan's decision to forgo an attack on the Confederate works at Manassas and to shift his force to the Peninsula was primarily the result of the intelligence Pinkerton gathered from slave runaways. However, the eyewitness testimony of fugitive slaves definitely strengthened the general's conviction that the Confederate works needed to be outflanked rather than assaulted. "I am well assured," he wrote his superiors, "that the [Confederate] army of Manassas remains intact & that it is composed of the best armed & best disciplined troops the rebels have."[36]

Rather than attack in northern Virginia, McClellan planned to transport the army down the Potomac into the Chesapeake Bay and then land at Urbanna on the Rappahannock River. This would place the Army of the Potomac in the rear and on the flank of the large Confederate army at Manassas and yet avoid the entrenchments Magruder was known to be constructing on the Peninsula. The Federals would then march to West Point, Virginia. From there, they could use the railroad line into Richmond that free black William Ringgold had previously reported the Confederates were only lightly defending. In the event that Confederate forces fell back from their Manassas lines before McClellan reached Urbanna, a backup plan called for a landing farther south at Fort Monroe and a long march up the Virginia Peninsula using the York and James Rivers as supply lines. While this would necessitate a longer march and having to contend with Magruder's defenses, it would still place the Federals well south of the main Confederate army and enable them to use the railroad to advance on Richmond. McClellan was not moving as quickly as the White House wanted, but he would soon put his plan into motion.[37]

"The people must yield their Negroes or submit to Yankees"

Once McClellan made the decision to float his army down the Potomac River, Pinkerton continued to gather useful military intelligence. After interviewing one group of runaways near Manassas, Pinkerton was especially impressed with the intelligence of a man named John Scobell. The slave's master had recently freed him and his wife, and, looking for employment, Scobell had made his way to Federal lines. According to Pinkerton, "He had a manly and intelligent bearing and his straightforward answers . . . impressed me favorably." The recently freed slave provided "an intelligent account of his travels through the country, and appeared to be well informed about the localities through which he passed, and the roads and streams round about." Scobell's intelligence challenged Pinkerton's racial assumptions, but he still described the former slave as "remarkably gifted for one of his race."[38]

Two weeks later, Pinkerton decided to use Scobell as a spy and eventually sent him to Richmond with a white female operative named Hattie Lawton. Scobell posed as Lawton's servant, and the two worked closely with Pinkerton's most productive spy in the Confederate capital, Timothy Webster. The group gathered information concerning Richmond's fortifications and armaments in the early months of 1862.[39]

While Pinkerton's spies were in Richmond, the city government was struggling to procure enough laborers to strengthen the capital's defenses. By the end of 1861, many owners refused to send their slaves to work on the fortifications, and free blacks were now avoiding the work. The *Richmond Dispatch* bemoaned "the large number of idle men daily seen in our streets" who should either be in the army or working on the city's entrenchments. The editors hoped that patriotism would be a sufficient inducement but warned that if enough men did not start volunteering to work on the fortifications, the government "will be forced to compulsory measures."[40]

In December 1861, the Richmond city government began forcing free blacks to labor on the entrenchments. To collect the workers, the city's chief engineer employed a street boss named John Hagan, who was infamous as a harsh Negro driver and, according to the *Richmond Examiner*, was the "best bully in town." His ability to deliver election votes from the seedier parts of the city gave Hagan the political connections to procure the appointment. On December 31, he placed a notice in the city's papers, warning free blacks that on January 2 "you shall all be prepared and appear at the City Hall, in the city of Richmond, to execute your part in the service of the Southern Confederacy. In failure whereof you shall be dealt with as the law directs."[41]

Hagan and his thugs in fact ran an extortion racket. They allegedly gave free blacks the option of either paying forty dollars to get out of the work or being whipped and then placed on the fortifications. On payday, Hagan mandated that to receive wages each man had to be identified by someone who had supervised his labor. These supervisors were Hagan's bullies, and they charged for their identification services. Hagan's overseers also allegedly whipped the workers mercilessly. Sympathetic whites revealed these abuses when they took Hagan to court for extorting forty dollars from a free black named James Evans. "In the name of God," Edward A. Pollard of the *Richmond Examiner* editorialized, "is there no justice to be found in the courts of human justice for iniquities like this?" Unfortunately, Evans's case was eventually thrown out.[42]

While Richmond's free blacks were cruelly forced to labor on the South's fortifications, down on the lower Peninsula Confederate general John Magruder continued to strengthen his defenses. He believed the Federals would soon reinforce their positions in his front, but he assured his superiors that he was using "not only the best, but the only way of successfully defending this Peninsula with the means at my disposal." As in Richmond, the continual procurement of black labor was a crucial component of his efforts. Due to what he called "the sickly season," Magruder had "substituted negro labor almost entirely for that of Soldiers." However, the hiring of slaves had not gone as smoothly as he had hoped. "I found it occupied more time and was attended with more difficulty than had been represented to me," he informed Confederate authorities.[43]

He sent agents into the various counties of the Peninsula to hire slaves, but they were coming in slowly. Magruder also used the Richmond newspapers to advertise for at least 800 slave laborers, teamsters, and mechanics. Owners interested in hiring out their slaves were requested to contact the quartermaster general's agent in the city by January 8. Response to the ad was apparently light, because on January 10 longer and more descriptive notices appeared. They included the fees masters would be paid (fifteen dollars per month for laborers, twenty dollars for mechanics and teamsters) and guaranteed that the slaves would be given ample rations, comfortable housing and clothes, and medical attention. The advertisements also promised, "The Government will be responsible for the value of the negroes, if captured by the enemy or allowed to escape to them or killed in action."[44]

While awaiting the arrival of hired slaves, Magruder deemed it necessary to resort to impressments once again. He knew, however, that Peninsula owners would bitterly resist another effort to grab more of their slaves. Under heavy pressure, he had released all but 160 of their bondsmen, and he felt it would be more "prudent" to impress slaves from other counties. He targeted counties near Richmond, such as Hanover, King William, Dinwiddie, and Chesterfield.[45]

As on the Peninsula, however, many owners proved reluctant to hand over their property. "Magruder is after the slaves of King William County again to work on the fortifications," Confederate colonel Roane Aylett informed his wife from the Peninsula in February. He thought the army would likely require as many as half of the county's slaves and instructed her to refuse to send any showing signs of illness. He speculated that one slave in particular, a man named Joe, "from his habitualation to camp life and his acquired knowledge of how to take care of himself, will have to be sent." Other than Joe, Aylett advised his wife, "whatever may be the number required, get off with sending as few as is possible."[46]

Other owners shared Aylett's reluctance, and some even hired lawyers to argue their cases. Magruder claimed that while "nine-tenths" of Chesterfield slaveholders were cooperative, "four or five" others objected and refused to hand over their slaves. In response, he reduced his demands on Chesterfield County and informed his agent in Dinwiddie to take only those slaves whose owners would willingly consent. He soon received notice that President Jefferson Davis sympathized with the Chesterfield slave owners and would not back him up. Magruder insisted that he could not meet the demands made upon him by General Lee unless he had the power to impress slaves. The War Department responded that slave impressments were not the issue—the problem was that he had overstepped his authority. It admonished him to "confine the exercise of the power of impressment to the geographical limits of [his] own command."[47]

Magruder could not let it go at that. On February 1, he told the War Department that he had "impressed the negroes of the counties composing my department so often, that it would be oppressive and unjust in the extreme to call upon them again to do the work in which all are interested." He preferred to get the labor from counties such as Chesterfield and Dinwiddie. "The quantity of labor necessary in this department," he continued, "is greater, perhaps, than that required in all the departments in Virginia put together." He was convinced that the Federals would soon be moving up the Peninsula and that time was therefore "precious." He pleaded for the government to allow him to continue the slave impressments unimpeded.[48]

Magruder was not the only Confederate official pleading for more slave laborers on the Peninsula. Virginia governor John Letcher, responding to the complaints of one slaveholder in late February, argued, "The public necessity demands and the people must yield their Negroes or submit to Yankees." Benjamin Ewell, who served under Magruder, informed the War Department that "not less than 1,000 or 1,500 negroes ought to be at work," and that with them the works could be "rendered well-nigh impregnable." The counties around Richmond "can well afford to furnish this labor." The shortage in slave labor, Ewell bemoaned, had brought the work on the fortifications to a "stand still."[49]

The War Department could not help Magruder and Ewell, but the Virginia legislature took steps to alleviate the problem. Fearing the wrath of white slave owners, the state followed Richmond's lead and targeted blacks who had no owners. In February, Virginia passed a law requiring all male free blacks between the ages of eighteen and fifty to register with local courts. When a commander needed labor, he could submit a requisition to the local judges, who would select free blacks from the registration lists. Perhaps learning from the Hagan case, the state assigned the task of rounding up the laborers to local sheriffs.[50] One element of the "Black Confederate" legend is an insistence that many southern free blacks voluntarily and patriotically offered their services to the Confederacy. However, Magruder's difficulties procuring laborers, the Hagan case, and this law all seem to demonstrate that free blacks were not a reliable source of support for the South unless they were forced.

One result of this law was that Pinkerton saw an increasing number of free blacks coming into the Federal lines at Manassas. A fifteen-year-old free black named John Lewis told Pinkerton that his Unionist employer informed him that "all the colored people" would be forced to work for the southern army and that when the work was done they would probably be required to bear arms. He had advised Lewis to head for the Federal camps. Nevertheless, the law did increase the number of African Americans laboring for the Confederacy. The legislation, along with slave hiring, helped ease Magruder's labor shortage. He was able to report on March 6 that "the negroes are coming in pretty rapidly."[51]

"I am aware of none more meritorious"

Three days later, the famous battle between the USS *Monitor* and the CSS *Virginia* (*Merrimac*) took place at Hampton Roads in the Chesapeake Bay. The *Virginia* was the Confederacy's secret weapon: an ironclad ship that unless challenged by another ironclad might break the Federal blockade of the Virginia coast. Should that occur, Union troops and fugitive slaves at Fort Monroe would become isolated, and Federal reinforcements would be unable to land on the Peninsula.

The Confederacy had taken possession of the wooden frigate USS *Merrimac* when the Federals abandoned the Gosport Navy Yard during the secession crisis of 1861. The South renamed the ship the CSS *Virginia* and began to repair the damage done to it when the evacuating Federals put the vessel to the torch. Besides making several structural changes, the

Rebels planned to transform the *Virginia* into an ironclad.[52] The U.S. navy was aware of what was going on in the Gosport Navy Yard and was therefore busy constructing its own ironclad, the USS *Monitor*. Secretary of the Navy Gideon Welles hoped the navy could complete the ship before the CSS *Virginia* got out of dry dock. If so, the *Monitor* could steam up the Elizabeth River and destroy the mighty Confederate ironclad before it even hit water.

While North and South raced to complete these ships, Gideon Welles recalled, the Rebels were taking "extraordinary pains" to keep their work secret. In this, they "were not wholly successful, for we contrived to get occasional vague intelligence of the work as it progressed." Spies, local Unionists, and blacks kept Welles informed about the status of the Confederate ironclad. In January, for example, a Union vessel in the Chesapeake Bay picked up seven fugitive slaves, who warned that the *Virginia* was near completion and would soon try to break the Federal blockade.[53]

A black woman, Mary Louveste, brought Welles the most complete and useful information he received from Virginia's black population. She was an employee of the Gosport Navy Yard and, along with several other white and black Unionist employees, had been closely observing the ironclad's progress. Once the ship neared completion and the Confederates took it out of dry dock, the spies decided that the time had come to inform the federal government. The group chose Louveste for the dangerous mission of crossing Confederate lines and entrusted her with a letter written by a Unionist mechanic in the Navy Yard. She concealed the document in her dress and journeyed to Washington.[54]

Late in February, Louveste came to the Navy Department and asked to speak to Welles in private. She described the condition of the *Virginia* "and other facts." As Welles later recalled, Louveste presented the letter from the mechanic, which revealed technical information about the ironclad. "This news, of course," Welles continued, "put an end to the test, which had been originally designed, of destroying the 'Merrimac' in the dry dock."[55]

Thanks to Louveste's letter and other sources of information, Welles learned enough about the *Virginia* to know that the *Monitor* could stand up against it. Some members of Lincoln's cabinet panicked when the *Virginia* made its first appearance in the Chesapeake Bay and made short work of two wooden vessels, but thanks to his information, Welles remained unruffled. The secretary calmed the frenzied cabinet members and the president, explaining that the *Monitor* could neutralize the Confederate ship and that "our information of the Merrimac . . . was that she could not, with her heavy and ill-adjusted armor, penetrate the [Potomac] river nor venture outside [the Chesapeake Bay]." Secretary Seward then remarked that this news "gave him the first moment's relief he had experienced" since hearing of the Confederate ironclad, a sentiment that most of the cabinet and the president shared. After the war, Welles helped Mary Louveste get a federal pension, writing, "I am aware of none more meritorious than this poor colored woman whose zeal and fidelity I remember and acknowledge with gratitude."[56]

When the two ships finally clashed in Hampton Roads on March 9, they created a grand spectacle that ex-slaves vividly recalled many years later. "I kin 'member de battle of de Merrimac and de Monitor," said Matilda Carter. "Took place twix here an Newport News. We was all standin' on de show watching. I 'member my mother she hel' me up in her arms so dat I could see." Robert Ellet remembered the big crowds as well: "The shores was lined thick with people watching that strange fight. All I could see was the flash of the guns." The guns impressed Charles Grandy: "I was way up 'bove Norfolk 'bout ten miles away. I didn' see a bit o' de battle, but I could heah de guns a roarin.'"[57] When it was all over, the *Monitor* had fought the *Virginia* to a draw. Nevertheless, as Welles had predicted, the Confederate ironclad was neutralized, leaving the bay, Fort Monroe, and its runaway slaves securely in Federal control and the Peninsula a viable route for McClellan's advance on Richmond.

"We know what's gwine on"

Federal control of the Chesapeake Bay became all the more important when, on the same day the ironclads clashed, a runaway slave came into Federal lines west of Washington with astounding news. He claimed that during the past two days the Confederates had begun leaving their entrenchments around Manassas. Dispatches and slave reports from other areas soon confirmed the news: the Confederates were falling back.[58]

McClellan marched troops out the next day and was embarrassed when newspapers reported that many of the formidable Confederate artillery emplacements were phony. The Rebels had fashioned logs to look like cannon by painting them black. This news further angered those in the North who had clamored for action and now increased the political pressure on the Lincoln administration to force McClellan to use his army. The president's arbitrary February 22 deadline had come and gone with no movement from the Army of the Potomac, and it now appeared to many that the nation's largest army had been held in check by "Quaker guns." In fact, because of information collected from runaway slaves and Confederate deserters, McClellan had already known for the past six weeks that many of the artillery positions were just logs.[59]

Nevertheless, this all was a major embarrassment for both the general and the administration. The Joint Committee on the Conduct of the War openly called for McClellan's dismissal, and northern newspapers increased their criticism of the war effort. The general had to begin his campaign immediately. The northern public, radical Republicans, and Lincoln himself would now accept nothing less.[60]

Because the Confederates had fallen back from Manassas and because McClellan had to move quickly, the general depended on the backup plan that he had designed for "the worst coming to worse." Moving the army to Urbanna would no longer place them well south and on the flank of the Confederates. To reach the railroad line running from West Point to the Rebel capital, the Army of the Potomac would now need to sail farther south, land at Fort Monroe, and march up the Virginia Peninsula. McClellan's massive army began to sail down the Potomac at the end of March.[61]

Confederate general Joe Johnston, commander of the soon-to-be-named Army of Northern Virginia, had made the strategic decision to pull back from his Manassas lines and to reconcentrate south of the Rappahannock River.[62] "By retreating when he [does]," the *Boston Herald* explained on March 18, "he saves his entire army, all his artillery, and baggage, and falls back to a position equally" as defensible as Manassas. The Republican paper was sure that Johnston would fortify behind the Rappahannock and reminded its readers that, "as he has the labor of many thousand slaves, it will not require that much time."[63]

After the departure of the Rebel army, the number of slaves coming to Pinkerton increased, and many of them arrived with shocking stories. On March 14, for example, Pinkerton's staff interviewed a group of fifteen slaves, which included men, women, and children. "The principal motive for leaving," Pinkerton reported, "was that arrangements had been made to send them all south without delay." Furthermore, "the rebel army took with them all the colored persons they could find when it retreated." Edward Paine, a slave from Fauquier County, had heard his master say that "if it came to the last they would shoot their slaves before the yankees should get them."[64]

The panic of these Rebel slave owners in early 1862 is understandable. Since the victory at Manassas, the news from all fronts had been bad. Western Virginia had fallen into Federal hands. Northern troops had captured coastal forts in North Carolina and gained a foothold on the Sea Islands in South Carolina. Worst of all, a little-known Federal general by the name of Ulysses S. Grant had won fame by capturing Forts Henry and Donelson in northern Tennessee, forcing the evacuation of the city of Nashville. "Everybody here seems to have had a gloom over them ever since our defeat at Fort Donelson," Roberta Page Saunders wrote from the Peninsula. Dr. John Minson Galt agreed, confiding in his diary that in Williamsburg there was "great despondency hereabout [after] news reached us that Fort Donelson was captured by the villainous Yankees."[65]

Making matters worse, the USS *Monitor* had neutralized the South's mightiest naval weapon, the CSS *Virginia*, in the Chesapeake Bay. Now Johnston's army was destroying the supplies at Manassas and falling back into the interior of the state. "Dangers thicken around us," Confederate attorney general Thomas Bragg wrote from Richmond in early 1862, reflecting the sentiments of many Southerners. "Our people are disheartened," he said, "and do what I will, I cannot drive the horrid picture [of defeat] from my mind."[66]

Such feelings of impending doom and the fear of losing their slaves may have led some northern Virginians into rash action. When Peninsula masters fled the advance of the Federals, they had left their slaves behind to take care of their property, only to learn that their bondsmen showed no loyalty and that northern troops had "confiscated" their slaves. Now many slaveholders in northern Virginia were apparently determined not to make the same mistake. Toward the end of March, Pinkerton's staff interviewed runaways who insisted that the retreating Confederates were driving hordes of slaves south. Some claimed that white citizens who followed the retreating Confederates had hired slave catchers to round up the slaves left behind and to shoot any who refused to go. "Several were shot accordingly," Pinkerton's staff reported to McClellan.[67]

Whether or not such a large movement of slaves to the south was actually occurring, it is clear that the runaways either believed that it was or wanted to convince the Federals that it was in the North's best interest to "confiscate" slaves before the South took even greater advantage of their black laborers. As one runaway had earlier explained to a Yankee reporter, "We know what's gwine on. Darkey not so blind as white folks think. . . . [Slaves] will say anything, depends on who he talks to." According to the correspondent, "This [statement] was got off with great glee," and the slave concluded, "Black people knows what they're about, these times."[68]

The most provocative claims, as runaway Edward Paine explained, was that his master had informed him that "the rebels would compel their Negroes to fight."[69] Such allegations were not new. A runaway named Abraham Brown had previously told Pinkerton's staff that he had seen "20 colored men from South Carolina" being drilled as soldiers.[70] James Bowman had reported that "some of the slaves brought from Mississippi, when passing from one place to another, are armed with pistols, guns, knives etc."[71] Another runaway in Bowman's group maintained that "he saw about 30 colored men belonging to a Mississippi regiment drilling in a field near Fort Evans, all of whom were uniformed like the white soldiers in their regiment." Furthermore, "about 25 of them were armed with shot guns and bayonets." The northern population was generally aware of such claims. Back in February, for example, the *Lowell (Mass.) Daily Citizen and News* had reported, "Some contrabands who have lately reached our lines on the Potomac say that the Confederate officers at Richmond are forming the colored people into regiments, for the defense of Richmond."[72]

With the Rebels in retreat from Manassas, these reports of armed blacks became more specific. On March 17, Pinkerton's staff interviewed Richard Kirkendall, a body servant who had escaped from the 17th Mississippi. The fugitive claimed that three days before the Confederate withdrawal, the colonel gathered all the regiment's body servants and told them that "the colored men would have to take up arms and help fight their battles." Many of the blacks, the runaway maintained, were then "armed with muskets and ordered to . . . be drilled." Pinkerton's staff reported that Kirkendall was still carrying the musket and ammunition he claimed the Confederate regiment had issued to him.[73]

Kirkendall also explained that his master, Jacob Kirkendall, had asked "if he was willing to fight against the yankees" and declared that "if the colored people did not help whip the damned yankees the rebels would be taken for sure." The Mississippi slave owner was feeling pessimistic about the Confederacy's fate, and he told his slave that they had "no chance of succeeding but to put arms in the hands of both black and white." The other body servant in this group of runaways, Chad Singleton of the 18th Mississippi, reported a similar conversation with his master. His owner asked him "if in case he was shot down, whether he would be willing to take a gun and shoot the man that did it." Singleton hesitantly told his owner that he was afraid to fight; the captain "called him a coward and dropped the subject."[74]

Alfred Radlock, however, brought in the most alarming story. The runaway claimed that his master, who owned eighty male slaves, had "armed and uniformed [them] as soldiers." Other masters had done the same, and together they had created a company of black soldiers numbering about 216. Radlock claimed to have escaped from this company as it marched toward Richmond, and he provided the names of all the owners who had contributed slaves as well as the number of slaves that each had enrolled.[75] If this "company" of black soldiers ever did exist, Confederate authorities definitely rejected it. The government refused to enlist blacks as combat forces until the very end of the war.

Considered alone, these statements to Pinkerton's staff that some Southerners were arming their slaves and encouraging them to fight seem impossibly overblown. Nevertheless, similar claims had been coming in from both southern and northern sources ever since the start of the war. However exaggerated these stories were, they do suggest that in some cases masters attempted to cajole or force their slaves into fighting for them.

A more intriguing possibility, however, is that these African Americans were aware of the propaganda-like warnings from abolitionists that some southern civilians were trying to use their slaves in combat. Perhaps Kirkendall, Radlock, and the others exaggerated or fabricated their accounts to add weight to the abolitionists' argument about the military necessity for emancipation. Slaves had long specialized in deceiving whites, and they may have put that skill to use to convince the Yankees of the military value of emancipation.

Pinkerton was not the only Northerner encountering runaway slaves once the Confederates abandoned Manassas. The *Cincinnati Commercial* explained that "most of them fled from the regions of the Rappahannock and entered our lines by various routes, some by highways, some from the jungle. . . . Most of them were under forty years of age, stout, muscular, intelligent fellows, not field hands, but household servants—the class so boastfully assumed to be faithful to their masters." When asked where they were headed, the joyous slaves typically responded with "Gwine to be free, massa; gwine North, bin waiting long while." Even the Democratic *New York World*'s correspondent claimed to have seen "hundreds—I think I could truthfully say thousands—of both sexes and all ages, bound toward Washington." Just as Pinkerton had learned, the fugitives told reporters that they left their masters because they feared the Confederates were going to send them south to work on the fortifications around Richmond.[76]

Like Pinkerton, the correspondents were impressed with the fugitives. "I talked to many of the negroes," the *World* reporter related, "and I must say, in all justice, that they are decidedly the most intelligent and best informed residents I found in Virginia." Notwithstanding its praise of the runaways, this statement was likely meant mainly as an insult to white Virginians, but the *Cincinnati Commercial* correspondent claimed, "Not one [black Virginian] was unconscious of the issue which sets so many bondsmen free." Correspondents discovered that the African Americans had detailed and interesting information and queried them about why the Confederates abandoned their positions, where they might be going, the mood of their army, and what they had done to their supplies before leaving.[77]

One fugitive struck the *World* correspondent as particularly wise. When asked what he thought had caused the war, the black man "replied without hesitation; 'I 'spose its to make ebery man earn dere own feed by de swet ob dere own brow!'" However, the reporter continued, "there was a perceptible difference of opinion on this question. One or two feared they would be sent back, and questioned me suspiciously as to their status." The *New York Times* also discovered this uncertainty among the runaway slaves. "They all manifested considerable anxiety in reference to their future disposition," the paper reported.[78]

With the northern public bitterly divided over the issue of emancipation and some officers attempting to turn fugitives away, blacks could still not be completely certain of Yankee intentions. This uncertainty provided plenty of motivation for these runaways to point out how the South used black labor on fortifications and to claim that the Confederacy was in the process of compelling its slaves to fight. Surely, northern troops would not fail to confiscate slaves who worked on Rebel fortifications and who might soon bear arms against them.

As their owners retreated deeper into the interior, most of these northern Virginia slaves felt optimistic. "They leaned sunning themselves against the side of [a] house," the *National Anti-Slavery Standard* reported about one group of runaways. As correspondents gathered around them, the blacks enjoyed answering questions. They were also "laughing gleefully at the expense of their recent owners." When talking to a group of fugitives, a *New York Times* correspondent asked them "how they had managed to get away when it seemed natural that a most vigilant watch would be kept on them." The answer provided a glimpse into the deceptions that slaves used against their masters. "We talked sweet and pretty to 'em," one man explained. "Told 'em we wasn't such people [who would run away]—wouldn't do it for the world." The correspondent was amused: "So much for the professions of attachment between master and slave," he wrote. "Undoubtedly the former has some feeling in the matter, but it is scarcely reciprocated."[79]

One newspaper correspondent "observed several in Confederate uniforms" who explained that they had served as body servants to Rebel officers. Another reporter, however, noticed "in a few cases [the blacks] were actually carrying muskets." Just as Jacob Kirkendall explained to Pinkerton's staff, some masters had apparently armed their slaves. "Did you drill and help fight with your master?" the reporter asked one fugitive. "Dars just whar we and him fall out," the black man responded; "he wanted us to fight, and we couldn't bear it."[80]

"All that . . . several hundred negroes could do . . . has been done"

As slaves poured into Union lines, they were protected by Congress's recently passed article of war forbidding the military from returning fugitive slaves to their masters. The legislation was just one of several successful emancipationist efforts that took place while McClellan's army shifted to the Virginia Peninsula. Indeed, abolitionists had begun their most extensive petition drive in over a decade, inundating Congress with demands for emancipation. Earlier in March, the president asked Congress to offer federal compensation to any state that voluntarily enacted a gradual emancipation statute, and the measure was approved on April 10, 1862.[81]

Members of the Joint Committee on the Conduct of the War could even rejoice that their criticism of McClellan had apparently borne fruit. On March 11, Lincoln informed the general that he would no longer hold the position of general in chief of all Union armies and would only command the Army of the Potomac. The president explained that he took the step so that McClellan could focus all his attention on his campaign in Virginia, but the radicals exalted in the apparent demotion of one of their chief obstacles. Although Congress was still bitterly debating the second confiscation bill, emancipationists were generally optimistic as the Peninsula Campaign began.[82]

When Confederate forces retreated from Manassas and moved south of the Rappahannock River, the soldiers, slaves, and laborers under the command of John B. Magruder were still working on the fortifications. The works that free black William Ringgold had observed in November were now much stronger and easier to defend with fewer men, and they now stretched across the length of the Peninsula. McClellan and Pinkerton failed to get up-to-date intelligence on the Confederate fortifications because the original plan had been to land at Urbanna, not Fort Monroe. McClellan had to act quickly when he decided to shift the campaign to the Peninsula. He had no time to gather much intelligence beyond Ringgold's now-dated observations.[83]

During the last week of March, Federal forces began landing at Fort Monroe. Within two weeks, McClellan would advance up the Peninsula with close to 70,000 troops, and many thousands more were arriving daily. Meanwhile, Magruder informed Richmond that he had "not more than 10,000" troops at his disposal, and in response, the Confederacy barely managed to send around 3,600 reinforcements at the end of the month.[84] No matter how strong Magruder's Peninsula defenses were, the overwhelming Federal numbers would have allowed an aggressive commander to quickly overrun his works. McClellan, however, was anything but aggressive.

When the Army of the Potomac appeared in his front, Magruder realized the precariousness of his situation and sent to Richmond for reinforcements, ammunition, and, as usual, more slaves. His immediate superior, General Joseph E. Johnston, agreed that slaves were "indispensable" to the Confederacy's defense. However, Confederate president Jefferson Davis's military adviser, General Robert E. Lee, was worried about sending more slaves to Magruder. That so many slaves were running off to the Federals made it dangerous to place them so close to such a large Union army, and in the case of combat they would be "much in the way." Lee instructed Magruder instead to start making the soldiers do more of the labor. Besides, complaints continued to come into Richmond that Magruder was mistreating his slave laborers. While defending himself, he nonetheless admitted, "It is quite true that much hardship has been endured by the negroes in the recent prosecution of the defensive works on our lines; but this has been unavoidable, owing to the constant and long-continued wet weather." He insisted that the slaves fared better than the soldiers because they had better shelters.[85]

Despite Lee's apprehensions, Magruder kept pleading for more slaves and turned again to local slaveholders. "McClellan, at the head of 100,000 men," Magruder informed Peninsula citizens, "is threatening our whole line." To hold the Yankees off, he argued, they would need to keep improving the Peninsula's fortifications. Because "soldiers cannot be expected to work night and day and fight besides," he needed each master to send at least one male slave equipped with an ax or a spade. "I am sure that no patriotic citizen," he pleaded, "would hesitate to respond most cheerfully to the call which I now make." Without the additional slave laborers, he warned, "we cannot hope to succeed, and the Northern army will be in possession of your farms in a few days." Soon Magruder received 1,300 slaves from fourteen different Virginia counties.[86]

As Magruder cajoled local slaveholders, on April 4 McClellan's troops finally began their advance toward the Confederate lines. McClellan intended to quickly overwhelm the Rebel defenses on the lower Peninsula, but the poor condition of the Peninsula's roads slowed the march of his large army, and the troops unexpectedly encountered Confederate defenses stretching across the entire length of the Peninsula. In the face of these obstacles, the Army of the Potomac halted only one day after beginning its advance. That night, McClellan began to carefully plan siege operations against Magruder's fortifications.[87]

McClellan was in for a shock. He received a telegram stating that Secretary Stanton and President Lincoln were worried that he had left for the Peninsula without adequately providing for the defense of Washington. Therefore, one entire corps (about 35,000 men) under the command of Irvin McDowell would not be arriving to reinforce his army, as McClellan had expected. The general wanted to assign McDowell's corps the task of capturing the Confederate works across the York River at Gloucester, and the loss of these troops thwarted his plans.[88]

McClellan characteristically detected a conspiracy in the president's orders. The general most certainly knew that abolitionists were aggressively petitioning Congress, crisscrossing the country delivering speeches calling for emancipation as a "military necessity," and touting the fidelity and services of the contrabands in order to sway public opinion. He knew that the Republicans had managed to pass antislavery legislation in the last couple of weeks and that they were pushing hard for a new confiscation act. He was also acutely aware that his own views on emancipation were unacceptable to the radicals and suspected that Lincoln and Stanton tended to side with the Joint Committee on the Conduct of the War. McClellan therefore erroneously concluded that the withholding of McDowell's men was an emancipationist plot to ruin his plans.[89]

"The administration did not intend the Peninsular campaign to be successful," McClellan later argued. He was convinced that Lincoln and Stanton believed that "to end the war before the nation was ready for [emancipation] would be a failure." Until the Lincoln administration could get the public to support emancipation, McClellan maintained, it intended to prolong the war and "would not permit me to succeed." Complaining about the situation in a letter to his wife on April 11, McClellan predicted, "History will present a sad record of these traitors who are willing to sacrifice the country & its army for personal spite & personal aims."[90]

The truth, of course, was quite different. Before McClellan left Washington, Lincoln had expressed his concerns for the safety of the capital and was reluctant to let the general take the army to the Peninsula. McClellan managed to persuade Lincoln only after detailing the number of men he would leave behind. Once the army moved, however, Lincoln discovered that McClellan had been less than candid in presenting his calculations. It was this discovery that caused Lincoln to withhold McDowell's command.[91]

Even without McDowell, however, McClellan heavily outnumbered the Confederates, with even more troops in reserve. "You now have over one hundred thousand troops," Lincoln estimated on April 6 in response to the general's complaints. "I think you better break the enemies' line . . . at once." Still McClellan refused to move. He, of course, overestimated Magruder's numbers, and the southern fortifications clearly intimidated him. Relying on his own reconnaissance, McClellan repeatedly described the Rebel works as "truly formidable" and informed Secretary Stanton that "were I in possession of their entrenchments and assailed by double my numbers I would have no fears as to the result." Magruder's defensive positions, the general maintained, were so well prepared with cleared fields of fire, flooded approaches, extensive fortifications, and heavy artillery, that attacking them would be "an act of madness." Given his natural caution and confidence in his abilities to direct a siege, it is unlikely that McClellan would have attacked Magruder's forces even if the president had sent along McDowell.[92]

Magruder's exploitation of slave labor had paid off. There was no radical conspiracy to defeat General McClellan. The only hindrance to his advance was his exaggeration of Magruder's strength, and especially the effect on his overly cautious mind of seeing the elaborate fortifications that Magruder's "indispensable" slave and free black laborers had helped to construct. "All that ten engineers & several hundred negroes could do to day has been done," Confederate brigadier general Howell Cobb wrote his superiors on April 9, bemoaning the lack of laborers but revealing his reliance on slaves to maintain his section of Magruder's defenses.[93] Contrary to McClellan's belief, it was not Lincoln, Stanton, and the radicals who had stalled his advance and prolonged the war; it was the South's successful use of African American laborers.

The delay allowed the Confederates to move most of the forces available in the Department of Northern Virginia to the Peninsula and to strengthen Magruder's defenses. During the first weeks of the campaign, the Confederate Congress adopted and began to implement a conscription law. The opportunity that McClellan had had for quickly overwhelming the Confederates was gone.

However mistaken McClellan had been, the strong fortifications largely constructed by slaves and free blacks shaped the Peninsula Campaign into one of slow advances and lengthy sieges. The Federals hoped that Virginia's slaves would continue to flee their masters and provide military intelligence as the army crawled toward Richmond. With McClellan now stalled before slave-built fortifications, evidence was mounting that the Confederacy was gaining significant military advantage from its slaves, and an increasing amount of information encouraged the belief that the South was arming them. Growing ever more impatient and pressing for quicker results from the Army of the Potomac, Northerners paid close attention to the situation developing on the Peninsula and would likely seek to eliminate anything that contributed to the slow progress of their army. The longer Magruder's fortifications impeded McClellan's army, the more the war endangered the institution of slavery.

5

THE MONUMENTS TO NEGRO LABOR

APRIL–MAY 1862

As more of McClellan's army landed on the Virginia Peninsula, three male slaves entered Union lines at Newport News after hiding out for two months near Mulberry Island. A northern newspaper correspondent asked them why they ran to the Federals, and the runaways explained that they escaped after each had received fifty lashes for being off their plantation without a pass. In addition, they claimed that another slave had been shot and killed after authorities caught him a second time trying to visit his wife on a neighboring plantation. The First Confiscation Act ensured that such horrific experiences were now over for the three runaways. Because the men claimed that the Confederate government had previously forced them to labor on fortifications, upon reaching the Union army the federal law liberated them. They were not alone: "Runaway slaves continue to come into our army almost every day," the correspondent noted. One Union soldier described the area near Fort Monroe as "crammed full of contrabands."[1]

During the siege of Yorktown, soldiers in the Army of the Potomac received important military information from runaway slaves, and many came to appreciate their presence in camp. At the same time, Yankees grew frustrated that the southern army was effectively using black laborers to strengthen the entrenchments that stalled Union efforts on the lower Peninsula. Even more infuriating were the multiplying reports that the Confederates were coercing slaves into combat, and such claims were becoming more specific and potentially explosive during the siege. The contributions that African Americans made to both armies bought time for congressional radicals to patiently debate the second confiscation bill and provided them with compelling evidence in their fight against the moderates and conservatives of both parties.

"Set adrift as free men"

By the start of the Peninsula Campaign, the military had loosened its contraband regulations at Fort Monroe. "They seem to be allowed to go where they choose . . . the Government retaining no exclusive control over them," the *Baltimore American* correspondent explained. Many of the black laborers hired themselves out to officers in the Army of the Potomac, advancing with the soldiers to Yorktown. Others took jobs on naval vessels or as teamsters. Those skilled at unloading cargo with rope and tackle were "making their own bargains and acting as free men." They "now receive their pay weekly, and seem much more contented and more active in their labors than under the former system."[2]

Stalled before the Confederate lines at Yorktown, General McClellan began siege operations and planned to break the Rebel fortifications with a massive artillery bombardment. "I . . . hope we will not be seriously interfered with until I can open an overwhelming fire," he wrote the president. Every day ships brought more matériel and men into Fort Monroe. "They have been landing troops and provisions all day and are [still] at it," Pennsylvania soldier James H. Mitchell wrote home on April 6, "and the river is full of all kinds of vessels." After disembarking and regrouping in Hampton, regiments optimistically marched up the Peninsula. "Yorktown is not far from here," Mitchell explained. "It will be taken in a day or two I suppose."[3]

As they advanced, many Yankees admired the natural beauty of the area but were generally not impressed with the lower Peninsula. The burned-out town of Hampton seemed particularly desolate. "Not one of the former inhabitants remains," Massachusetts soldier Walter J. Eames explained to his wife, "except a few negroes who lounge about the ruins and appear fit . . . to preside over such a scene." Farther up the road, the correspondent for the *Philadelphia Inquirer* noted that homes seemed beneath the standards of the "poorest farm-houses found in the North." The men were ignorant, and the "women are not very attractive. Most of them 'rub snuff.' If these are the first families [of Virginia]," the correspondent quipped, "where are the second?" As for the black population, Eames contemptuously noted that they "lounged lazily in the sun and stared stupidly at us as we passed."[4]

Nevertheless, other soldiers had different experiences and gained a new appreciation for the Peninsula's black community. As the army approached farmhouses, they frequently noticed slaves "stretched at full length on the lawn," the *Inquirer* noted. However, blacks "jumped to their feet the moment [Union troops] came in sight," secured the officers' horses, offered encouragement, and brought pails of water to the parched men. The living conditions shocked the Yankees: "The negro cabins," the *Inquirer* correspondent explained, "without exception are more like smoke-houses in the inside. . . . As to the furniture, an old table and a broken chair or two, with an old shelf, and a 'shake-down' to sleep on."[5]

When troops arrived in front of the Confederate entrenchments at Yorktown, slaves streamed into Union lines and offered their services. Officers hired body servants, and blacks labored for the commissary department unloading ships on the York River. "[This] work is all done by negroes," the *Inquirer* correspondent wrote, "though a number of soldiers are scattered all along the shore and wharf, lying lazily." Enterprising blacks obtained northern newspapers at Fort Monroe and brought them to Yorktown, where soldiers eagerly snapped them up at ten cents apiece. The *Inquirer* told of a young African American entrepreneur who raised the price to twenty-five cents when his supplies got low. The runaways also sold food to the soldiers. The *New York Herald* reported on one particular group of black fugitives that brought oysters: "They had been told [by their masters] that every negro coming within our lines would be hung to the nearest tree; but, not withstanding this announcement, they were willing to take the yawl boat and the chance." They were now safely in Union lines and turning a tidy profit from the famished Yankees.[6]

Massachusetts soldier John L. Parker recalled two Richmond slaves who had left the city three weeks earlier and made their way down the Peninsula to the Union army. They "sprang from the weeds in a field where they had been [hiding out], and came bounding toward our column like frightened rabbits. They cleared the fence as if it had been only a foot high and jumped into the midst of the soldiers with every expression of joy." One of the officers hired them as servants, and they "made themselves at home at once."[7]

Many of the runaways came from Magruder's lines, and correspondents for the *Philadelphia Inquirer* explained how they escaped. Using their well-honed "laying out" skills, slaves drifted off at night and hid in the woods and swamps before coming into Union camps. They also took advantage of spring storms: "The darkness of the night and amid the howling of the winds, seems the favorite time for the slaves to start. Past the Rebel pickets, they lay down upon the damp ground until daylight, and then approach our pickets with a feeling of safety that shows they are not entirely deluded by the stories . . . that we are going to sell them to Cuba." Not all the runaways were so certain, however. The *Philadelphia Press* correspondent claimed that the newly arriving fugitives "anxiously inquire about the truth of the report that they are to be sold by the Yankees to the West India planters, as they have been led to believe by the owners." Nevertheless, the *Inquirer* described the flow of runaways as "a stream . . . and unless we are deceived, it will not stop soon; they are now kindly treated, well fed, given work at good wages or sent to Fortress Monroe."[8]

Despite these arrivals, Union soldiers remained the primary laborers on the entrenchments. "We ought to have [more] of those fat 'contrabands' up here from Fort Monroe to dig trenches and to do the heavy work," Private Robert Knox Sneden complained. "What with picket duty and digging trenches, [our] men . . . are grumbling very much."[9] The soldiers prepared for the installation of the heavy artillery, dug trenches and artillery positions, went on reconnaissance raids to gather information about the Confederate works, and dodged the deadly fire of Rebel sharpshooters.

Conversations with African Americans helped relieve the drudgery. "We called on the slaves," Bell Halsey Miller recorded in his diary, "and were both amused and edified by their stories; stories about themselves and the war." Soldiers enjoyed the jokes and joyful antics of the newly liberated slaves, appreciating the injection of humor into the deadly business of war. "I don't dislike the animals so bad as I used to," Charles B. Haydon wrote condescendingly. "They are very convenient to have around & I have more hearty laughs out of mine than from all other sources." George Williamson Balloch wrote his children that he did not "see many little boys out here except black boys. There are lots of them." One young African American reminded Balloch of his youngest son, and he explained to his children that the boy "wants to come home with Papa so he can be free. Mother will tell you how they buy and sell little black boys and girls for slaves."[10]

The developing relationship between fugitive slaves and the Army of the Potomac during the Yorktown siege was mutually beneficial. Miller complained in his diary that rations were low when the Army of the Potomac first disembarked on the Peninsula, "and we have to do the best we can. That is to buy . . . off the darkys." But while the runaways used the army to escape the cruelties of their masters and earn money, they also brought "a good deal of valuable information about the fortifications at and around Williamsburg and Yorktown," the *New York Herald* explained.[11]

That Union troops and Peninsula blacks were cooperating with one another did not escape the attention of local whites. As one company of Federals arrived at Big Bethel on its way to the Yorktown lines, the *New York Times* reported that the men entered a house where "an Irishman was dis-

Allen's farmhouse, near Yorktown, Virginia. Slaves and soldiers gather at the headquarters of Union general Fitz John Porter. In the background can be seen an encampment of the Fifth Corps. (Library of Congress)

covered secreted under a bed." After forcing him to crawl out, the soldiers howled with laughter to find that "he had blackened his face, hoping by this means to pass himself off as a negro." While this episode most likely did not transpire exactly in the manner the newspaper claimed, soldiers did frequently discover whites living inside slave shanties and cabins because they feared the northern army would direct artillery fire at their own houses.[12]

On April 5, the *Baltimore American* noted the irony of the situation developing on the Peninsula. "The war was got up on the pretext of being for the interest of the slaveholder," the border state paper remarked, "and [instead] is proving his ruin." Slaves were being "set adrift as free men, without master or overseer. This is one of the inevitable results of this rebellion, and the longer the war lasts the more destructive will it be to the slave owner."[13]

"His army and his trench digging negroes"

Since the fall of Forts Henry and Donelson back in February, Northerners had been highly encouraged by the news from other military fronts. The navy had reclaimed much of the Mississippi River; Nashville and Memphis had fallen; and Union troops were strengthening their hold on the coastal islands of South Carolina. Most recent, while McClellan sat immobile, General Grant had used aggressive tactics to win a costly but important victory at Shiloh in Tennessee that forced Rebel troops to retreat southward toward Corinth, Mississippi. It appeared to Northerners that the only obstacle in the way of crushing the rebellion was the Confederate army on the Virginia Peninsula. "All the eyes in the nation," the *Detroit Free Press* proclaimed, "will now be centered upon Yorktown."[14]

McClellan, the *New York Herald* optimistically claimed, was poised to deliver "the coup de grace to this rebellion," and "the issues of the war are reduced to this single siege." Consequently, Northerners thirsted for every scrap of information from the Peninsula. "I suppose the papers keep you informed of the progress of the siege," Union captain Richard Tylden Auchmuty wrote his mother on April 13, "which seems here to be slow." It seemed slow to northern citizens as well, and they scrutinized news from the Peninsula closely. "The curiosity & anxiety about Yorktown is feverish," the managing editor of the *New York Tribune* informed one of his correspondents on the Peninsula. "There is no progress at Yorktown," New Yorker George Templeton Strong recorded in his diary on April 12. "We are in great ferment and fever, looking for news from that place. Broadway is full of people . . . collecting in knots on corners, from which one is sure to hear in passing the words . . . Fortress Monroe."[15]

Much of the news coming from the Peninsula concerned Magruder's defenses. "There seems to be an obstacle in the way of this Army," Union brigadier general William T. H. Brooks wrote home. "We have been against this obstacle some two weeks without much progress." Federal officers understood that blacks had performed most of the labor on the lines that now stood between the Army of the Potomac and Richmond.

Confederate fortifications at Yorktown. (Library of Congress)

"Our knowledge [of the Confederate works] is yet far from perfect," Brigadier General Erasmus Keyes reported. "[But] enough has been ascertained to be certain they are exceedingly strong, and . . . that thousands of slaves have been long occupied in their construction." The enlisted men understood this as well: "The Confederates," Massachusetts private Warren Less Goss bitterly noted, were using "negro servants from different plantations to work upon the fortifications . . . thus leaving their soldiers fresh for other military duties." The result, Michigan soldier John Berry noted, was trench works "on a very extensive & formidable scale."[16]

That slaves had done much of the work on the Rebel fortifications was not lost on northern newspaper correspondents. "The inquisitive reader," the *New York Herald* asserted the day after publishing a detailed map of the Confederate works, "may here interpose the question, 'How does it happen that General McClellan finds himself near Yorktown in front of such a labyrinth of rifle pits, forts and batteries?'" The paper explained that since the Battle of Big Bethel, Magruder had overseen the construction of the Confederate defenses on the Peninsula, "with his army and his trench digging negroes." Making the same point, the *National Anti-Slavery Standard* maintained that "it was the sweat, and the muscle, and the blood of the black men that rendered these breastworks." The paper featured an interview with "an aged negress," who explained that "hundreds and hundreds" of slaves had been "goaded on like so many mules in this service."[17]

The *New York Herald* pointed out that as the Army of the Potomac built its own defenses, Magruder's troops continued to "render [their] fortifications still more impregnable. Thousands of rebel soldiers and thousands of negro slaves, have been working night and day. From before sunrise till after sunset we can see them . . . and when the darkness renders them invisible we can hear them." The *Philadelphia Public Ledger* claimed that "all the slaves in the entire [area] have been collected" to work on the lines, and the *Philadelphia Press* reported that "Negroes [can] be seen swarming around certain points like bees." The paper explained that when laborers had to work in areas where they were easy targets for Union troops, "the negroes . . . [are] forced into [the] exposed places." The *New York Times* reported an incident in which Federal artillery fired on black laborers to hinder their work on the Rebel lines. "Three of our shells fell directly in their midst, causing a panic among the woolly heads. Many of them jumped off the parapets to the ground, in their haste to get out of range."[18]

Despite the dangers and the difficult labor, some African Americans found Confederate camps to be a convenient hiding place from their masters or were drawn to them because of the opportunities they afforded for ultimately fleeing from bondage. During the Yorktown siege, L. H. Minor of Hanover County complained to the Confederate secretary of war about a practice he described as "habitual and extensive." Just like their Union counterparts, Confederate soldiers were hiring slaves as body servants or cooks. "The consequence," Minor asserted, "is that negroes are encouraged to run away, finding a safe harbor in the [southern] army. Two of my neighbors have recovered runaway negroes within the last few weeks. . . . [They were] found in the employment of the soldiers on the Peninsula." Minor pointed out that he had not complained about the impressment of half of his male slaves to work on the fortifications. "I, for one rendered this tribute cheerfully to a cause which is dear to my heart. . . . I think however, we ought to be protected . . . from the abuses mentioned."[19] Owners like Minor were annoyed because the increased number of slaves working for Confederate armies deprived masters of laborers at home, trampled on owner property rights, and provided opportunities for their slaves to escape to Union lines.[20]

Due to the continual complaints of slave owners and the increasing number of runaways, the Confederate army was unable to procure enough laborers to relieve white soldiers completely from working on the fortifications. Rebels continued to complain about performing labor considered fit only for blacks. "We were ordered to go & work 2 hours on the breastworks," Thomas Ware of the 15th Georgia recorded in his diary. "This indeed was a hard, and rather bitter pill, but go we must. We worked like negroes hard for 2 hours."[21]

Because his soldiers resisted the difficult labor, Confederate general D. H. Hill explained to army commander Joseph E. Johnston that he had "withdrawn all the negro force from the outworks and will try to [use them] to relieve the troops here. Fifty more negroes here would give a great relief." Due to the high demand for black laborers along the line, Magruder once again needed to impress slaves, but he knew that Peninsula masters would resist. He explained to General Lee that he had sent an officer to "Richmond to bring down a thousand additional negroes. I find the time too short to get the negroes from the neighboring counties, which would require two or three weeks." Because he knew his defenses could not hold back the Army of the Potomac for long, Magruder wanted the additional slaves "to erect works in the rear, which may enable me to save this army in case of being overpowered by numbers and forced to retreat from my present position."[22]

As a result, Richmond and Petersburg newspapers published calls for half the male slaves in the counties of Prince George and Surrey to work on the works near Williamsburg. Copies of these newspapers made it into the hands of northern correspondents at Yorktown. Passing along the news of slave impressments to their readers, the *New York Herald* commented, "We think that the facts . . . are sufficient to show that the task . . . of passing up to Richmond by way of Yorktown, has been anticipated and amply provided for by the rebels, and that the siege . . . can only be ended by a terrible and sanguinary struggle." That the Confederacy was gathering more slaves to strengthen their lines, the *Illinois State Journal* noted, "is commended to the notice of such patriots [who] are stricken with horror whenever it is proposed that we make use of the negroes in whatever capacity they may be serviceable."[23]

Making the same point, the *New York Tribune*'s Yorktown correspondent recounted a conversation he claimed to have had with a Union soldier. The two men observed a Rebel steamer bringing troops down the York River and the "swarms" of laborers "at work upon the Yorktown entrenchments," which included "very many slaves." In disgust, the correspondent rammed the joints of his telescope together harder than necessary, attracting the soldier's attention. "Pretty hard, Sir," the soldier allegedly said, "that President Lincoln won't let us use the Negroes against them while they use negroes against us!" The correspondent agreed. "When I saw . . . negroes in Yorktown throwing earth with long-handed shovels on top of the enemy's breastworks—making them higher and higher for our troops to scale, preparing . . . death and wounds for [Union soldiers] . . . I felt that it was high time the nigger was fighting for the Union."[24]

"The matter can be put beyond room for doubt"

As both sides worked on their entrenchments, sharpshooters continually added to the war's death toll. "There is no glory in being shot by a picket behind a tree," one Union soldier complained; "it is regular Indian fighting." At least one Confederate sharpshooter was a black man, and his accurate fire terrorized the Yankees. "[He] has had it all his own way for some days," Union officer Charles Wainwright wrote in his diary, "keeping everything clear from his perch in a tree over near the peach orchard." One day, however, the marksman climbed out of his tree to stretch his legs. A Union soldier lined him up in his telescopic site, and, as Union private Alfred Bellard witnessed, he "suddenly flopped on his face before taking six steps. Two white men . . . tried to haul him back, but a few doses of leaden pills being thrown their way, he was left alone until darkness gave them a chance to take him away."[25]

Wainwright and Bellard were not the only Northerners who witnessed the Confederates using black sharpshooters at Yorktown. George Alfred Townsend, a *New York Herald* correspondent, later recalled that blacks were "excellent sharpshooters" within the southern lines at Yorktown. While on the Peninsula, he exaggeratedly informed his readers that "there are among the rebel sharpshooters a large number of Negroes who show a good bit of ability in the use of the rifle—in fact, our pickets declare that the best shot among them is a stalwart darkey who climbs up into the chimney of a recently burnt house." Union sharpshooters, Townsend reported, "watch him very closely." The correspondent for the *Baltimore American* claimed that before the black sharpshooter was killed, his "accurate firing made him the dread as well as the admiration of our own crack marksmen. . . . At any practical range, and with the least site on one of our men, he seemed to know no such thing as failing to hit."[26]

Union sharpshooter Harrison DeLong labeled one black marksman "a pretty good shot" and explained that he "had a loop hole through a big hallow tree from which he fired at our pickets." Eventually, however, he "was shot by one of our boys." On a brief visit to the army on the Peninsula, U.S. Sanitary Commission treasurer George Templeton Strong noted, "The best rebel sharp-shooters are niggers. One of them seems to bear a charmed life and has been very successful. He is known as the 'irrepressible nigger' and . . . [Union sharp-shooters] have thus far failed to touch him."[27]

The Army of the Potomac encountered more than black sharpshooters on the Peninsula. On April 22, Brigadier General John W. Davidson reported to his division commander that 100 to 200 Confederates had attacked his pickets before dawn. The Rebels were quickly repulsed, but the general reported "quite a number of negroes among the enemy in their advance."[28]

Massachusetts officer Charles Harvey Brewster also witnessed the small fight and provided graphic details that exaggerated the number of blacks involved. "We yesterday forenoon [saw] two regiments of Niggers come out from the rebels," he explained, "and [they] drove [in] the Pickets of the seventh Maine Regt." He watched as the black men managed to surround one Union soldier who tried to surrender. "They shot him through the head and bayoneted him half a dozen times." Seeing this, a squad of Maine soldiers "sallied out upon this party right in the face of the enemy and securing . . . a big nigger they chopped him all to pieces."[29]

Because this was a predawn fight occurring in what General Davidson described as "dense woods," these claims are suspect. Nevertheless, added to previous sightings of blacks fighting in Confederate ranks, to William Ringgold's testimony that body servants were "armed in full," and to information gathered by Pinkerton near Manassas, these reports offer more evidence that suggests that early in the war the Confederates coerced at least some blacks into combat.

These instances of slaves apparently fighting in the southern army definitely caught the Federals' attention. Earlier in April, Brewster had informed his mother, "I saw a number of men who had been wounded on Picket [duty]. . . . They all agree that lots of the enemys Pickets are negroes. Probably the chivalry do not like to expose themselves to such dangerous business." Harrison Delong explained that the Confederates "keep their darkies busily employed. Negroes can be seen with the aid of [telescopes], carrying bags, working the guns, and they also do picket duty." Brewster added, "It is a notorious fact that the rebels have any quantity of niggers in their service [;] our pickets have seen them and shot them. They not only have them to work Fortifications but they are organized into Regts and are armed and do the most dangerous part of the fighting." Just as the Indiana soldier had indicated back in December, Brewster maintained that the use of blacks against them was "rousing a spirit of revenge in our boys."[30]

More important, these claims were widely disseminated in the North. The *New York Times*, the *Philadelphia Inquirer*, and several other papers published a correspondent's report of the small fight of April 22, pointing out that General Davidson reported that "his men were fired upon in the skirmish yesterday by negroes uniformed and armed." Claiming the information was received from "undeniable authority," the correspondent opined, "Now let the order go forth—no quarter to men fighting with . . . negroes!" A few days later, both the *Baltimore American* and the *Lowell (Mass.) Daily Citizen* reprinted a dispatch from one of the *Inquirer*'s correspondents that reported, "The enemy have a large number of armed negroes with them, who are plainly visible keeping guard as other soldiers. This exasperates our own soldiers very much."[31]

As at Manassas the previous summer, soldiers and correspondents at Yorktown also observed Confederates using African Americans to operate their batteries. "The rebel guns, especially those on the heavy works," the *New York Times* reported on April 22, "are manned altogether by negroes, or at least all the work of swabbing, loading, and shifting is done by them, with white men to oversee and direct them." The reason for this, Michigan officer Charles B. Haydon explained, was that Union sharpshooters "make such warm work for the [Rebel] gunners . . . that they now compel the darkies to do all the loading [of cannon]." The *Philadelphia Inquirer* pointed out that such instances "could be plainly seen by our troops," and the *Boston Daily Journal* correspondent saw Confederates force blacks to work the guns by "driving them up to it with clubs." Escaping dangerous duty by making blacks do it, the *Journal* declared, was "a display of Southern chivalry, very characteristic, if not complimentary, to their spirit."[32]

A *New York Times* correspondent assured his readers, however, that when opposing Confederate batteries, "our marksmen choose a white mark . . . in preference to a black one." On April 22, the *Cincinnati Gazette* reported on a particularly effective Union sharpshooter nicknamed "California" and detailed the havoc he played on Rebel artillerists. One day during the siege, a Confederate battery had a ramrod lodged in the barrel of a cannon, and the Union marksman wounded or killed several Rebel soldiers while they attempted to remove it. "At last," the *Gazette* correspondent related, "the rebels forced a negro on the parapet, and [since] California said 'he did not like to shoot the poor darkey,' the rammer was removed."[33]

"Southern Chivalry." During the siege of Yorktown, Union troops all too frequently witnessed incidents such as this one depicted in the May 10, 1862, Harper's Weekly.

Unfortunately, sharpshooters could not always practice such mercy. A *Harper's Weekly* correspondent observed an artillery barrage in which Yankee sharpshooters managed to chase Confederate gunners away from their artillery pieces. Peering through binoculars, the correspondent watched as a Rebel officer forced two blacks at gunpoint to leave their cover and man the guns. With Confederate pistols at their backs and Federal rifles in their front, the black men loaded the cannon. They were promptly felled by Union sharpshooters. The correspondent recorded the sad story and sketched a drawing of the event, which *Harper*'s soon published.[34]

Such reports were commonplace during the Yorktown siege. Michigan officer Charles Harvey Brewster wrote: "There was one big nigger the day before yesterday [who] got up on a parapet to swab out a gun. Crack went a rifle, and he fell outside of their works." After witnessing another sharpshooter kill a black man who was forced to load a cannon, the *Philadelphia Inquirer* labeled it "a 'justifiable homicide,' as the gun might have killed several of our men." The *Boston Daily Journal* claimed, "Four of the poor fellows [who were] forced to the post of danger were shot in one day." On April 25, Pennsylvanian James H. Mitchell wrote to his mother: "Yesterday a Rebel officer was pointing a pistol at a nigger trying to make him work a gun. One of the sharpshooters in a tree saw him [and] fired and killed the officer and nigger both." One sharpshooter asserted that when the Confederates forced blacks to man their cannon, "they soon found we could kill niggers as fast as we could white artillerymen, though we did not like it as well. It was hard to see these poor darkeys shoved out to be shot in places which should have been occupied by white men." Vermont colonel Edwin H. Stoughton reportedly declared that such sights "had made an abolitionist of him."[35]

"The rebels possess a certain kind of common sense which some other people lack," the *National Anti-Slavery Standard* declared after reporting stories of blacks manning Confederate artillery batteries at Yorktown. "They never make a point of color, when they have work or fighting to be done." When the Democratic *Baltimore American* ran an account of black Rebel artillerists on the Peninsula, the *Standard* pointed out that "this is not an 'abolition' story, as the *Baltimore American* detests 'abolitionists,' much more cordially than it does secessionists."[36]

On April 26, the *Philadelphia Inquirer* correspondent was exasperated by the Confederate army's use of African Americans but was also angry with Northerners who refused to believe they were being forced into combat. He wrote an impassioned dispatch that several northern newspapers reprinted, including the radical *Chicago Tribune*, the border state *Baltimore American*, and the moderate *Boston Daily Advertiser*. "Two miles and a quarter below Yorktown," he asserted, "are three Rebel forts on the west side of Warwick river. . . . In the centre can be seen, every day, from two to three hundred negroes, with red coats, grey pants, and slouch hats," laboring on the Confederate lines. Whenever Rebel troops fired their artillery, "these negroes ram home the balls which white men fire at the hearts of our soldiers. Any one who doubts that the Rebels are fighting side by side with their slaves can be convinced at any hour of the day by going up to the edge of the woods, about twelve hundred yards in front of their works. With the aid of an ordinary glass the matter can be put beyond room for doubt."[37]

"It is a matter of necessity to deprive them of these auxiliaries"

As Northerners learned about the activities of African Americans during the Yorktown siege, they also closely monitored political events in Washington. "The decisive battle in behalf of human rights and Divine law," abolitionist minister Levi L. Paine told his Farmington, Connecticut, congregation on April 18, "will not be fought at Yorktown or Richmond . . . but on the floor of the American Congress." Just before the Army of the Potomac shifted from northern Virginia to the Peninsula, the Senate Judiciary Committee reported out Senator Lyman Trumbull's confiscation bill. The measure providing for confiscation of all slaves owned by those in rebellion was hotly debated in April while the army settled into its Yorktown lines. Nearly every congressmen spoke on the bill while the House considered its own version.[38]

Congress could only confiscate slaves as a military measure. Because the president and most Northerners maintained that the war's primary objective was restoration of the Union, if the North prevailed before Congress passed the bill the opportunity to liberate slaves would be lost. Despite recent Union victories, however, and with the Army of the Potomac stalled at Yorktown, there seemed to be no pressing need for radical Republicans to push for immediate passage. After speaking with a Swiss military officer, Senator Charles Sumner believed that Union troops could not take Yorktown without a siege lasting up to two months. Despite a Republican majority in the Senate, and to Trumbull's increasing chagrin, the Senate repeatedly delayed a vote as the senators debated and amended the bill.[39]

Attempting to stall as long as possible, Democrats raised their typical economic and racial alarms about freed slaves flooding northern communities and questioned the constitutionality and necessity of the measure. Kentucky senator Charles Crittenden, for example, argued that with recent military successes, slave confiscation seemed unwarranted. "If we have the means [to win the war]," he maintained, "why should gentlemen insist on prosecuting other measures about which we differ, measures of doubtful constitutionality, and doubtful policy?"[40]

As they had done with the First Confiscation Act, many Democrats and some conservative Republicans asserted that slave confiscation would only cause more Southerners to join the rebellion and would alienate the Border States. Radical Republican senator Henry Wilson of Massachusetts had little patience for such arguments. "Last summer," he reminded the senators, "when it was proposed to free the slaves who had been actually employed by their masters with arms in their hands to smite down our brethren," the same objections were made. "Well sir, we passed the act in spite of these doubts, and it is the law of the land today." Despite Democratic warnings then, the Border States had not joined the rebellion, and there was no reason to believe they would do so now.[41]

Besides Democratic resistance, however, emerging divisions within the Republican Party also slowed the bill's passage. Some conservative members agreed with the Democrats that the proposed legislation was unconstitutional or would set a dangerous precedent by making all property liable to Federal seizure. Moderates pushed for a confiscation bill that did not include slaves. Other Republicans, even including such radicals as Charles Sumner, supported the measure but initially assumed that the president could more effectively confiscate the slaves using his war powers. Sumner knew Lincoln disliked Trumbull's bill, and the senator still had faith that Lincoln would soon move to emancipate the slaves.[42]

While most debate centered on constitutionality and over the relative powers of Congress and the president, the legislative branch could only liberate slaves as a war measure, and thus many congressmen continued to remind their colleagues of the military necessity for doing so. It was time to put aside constitutional arguments, Iowa senator James Grimes maintained: "It is the undoubted right and duty of every nation . . . to avail itself of every legitimate means known to civilized warfare to overcome its enemies."[43]

As the discussions proceeded, congressmen paid close attention to the situation on the Peninsula. "'What's the news from Yorktown?' is the question here, *par excellence*," the *Boston Daily Journal*'s Washington correspondent reported in late April. "During the most exciting portions of the debates on confiscation now going on in the Senate and the House, the appearance of anyone from the [military] departments who may have the coveted intelligence is sufficient to divert attention from the ablest speakers."[44]

Those in favor of the new confiscation bill fortified their arguments with news from the Peninsula. "The rebels have this day thousands of slaves," Grimes reminded his colleagues, "throwing up entrenchments and redoubts at Yorktown, and thousands performing military duty elsewhere; and yet we hesitate [to confiscate the slaves]. . . . How long shall we hesitate?" Former Democrat-turned-Republican representative John Hickman of Pennsylvania echoed Grimes's frustrations. "Does not every man see," he asked, "that when [the Confederates] . . . are at liberty to employ their slaves, not only in the erection of fortifications, but in the formation of companies and regiments, and in the defense of military works, it is a matter of necessity to deprive them of these auxiliaries?"[45]

"Slavery . . . is an element of strength to the rebels," New York representative Rodolphus Holland Duell added. The Confederacy used slaves to "build their fortifications, strengthen their columns, perform the menial service of the camps, and in a thousand ways contribute to their power, comfort, and success." Indiana representative Schuyler Colfax represented constituents who feared the economic consequences of freed slaves migrating into the region; nevertheless, he favored the new confiscation bill. "The [South's] slaves work on their fortifications," he pointed out, "from cannon behind which our soldiers are mercilessly slain; they perform [the South's] camp drudgery, thus increasing the power of their army." Radical Ohio senator Benjamin Wade was more blunt: "They have used . . . slaves to murder your brethren and mine," he argued. The Confederacy had "made use of these very slaves as the fulcrum by which to overturn the Constitution of the country."[46]

Colfax concluded that the time for adopting a new confiscation act had arrived. "If we wish to break the power of the rebellion," he maintained, "let us strike it wherever we can weaken it, and strike it boldly and fearlessly." In pushing the new legislation, Ohio four-term incumbent representative John A. Bingham explained: "We propose to disarm [the South] by taking from them the means by which and through which they would accomplish their destructive purposes. . . . The terrible slaughter of battle is not the only means by which this great rebellion is to be suppressed—it must be suppressed by law as well as by arms."[47]

Throughout April, newspapers provided extensive coverage and editorial comment on the debate. The *Indianapolis Daily Sentinel* shared General McClellan's belief that there was a radical conspiracy to ruin his campaign. The confiscation bill, the *Sentinel* argued, was "calculated to *exasperate* the South into still further resistance to the Union" so that the war would go on until Lincoln freed the slaves. Moreover, those opposed to emancipation argued that the recent military advances in almost every theater of war proved it was unwarranted and were confident that McClellan was about to end the war at Yorktown. "It cannot now be argued that there is any military necessity for this or any similar measure," the *Boston Daily Advertiser* asserted. "The army is . . . making very respectable progress without it" and was close to winning the war. "Military necessity is, in the present state of affairs, the last argument which any one would now venture to rely upon in urging a change of policy."[48]

Emancipationists interpreted the ongoing events on the Peninsula quite differently. "In all probability," the *North American and United States Gazette* argued, "fifteen or twenty thousand combatants against us on the Peninsula have already been drawn from the slave population of eastern Virginia, who have been doing work in the trenches, manning the guns the chivalry dare not man, and otherwise aiding the rebellion as so many full able-bodied men." The *Daily Cleveland Herald* concurred: "The rebels employ their slaves upon their fortifications not only to build them, but to load and fire upon white freemen engaged in defense of the Union flag." John W. Forney, secretary of the Senate and close friend of President Lincoln, criticized Democrats in a letter to the *Philadelphia Press*. While they opposed the use of blacks in the military, he asserted, "the Union soldiers see the negroes marshaled by the thousands in the rebel service."[49]

The *Illinois State Journal* pushed for not only emancipation but also the organization of black troops. "The rebels have set the example in this respect," the editors argued on April 15. "Regiments of well drilled and capable negroes have been formed in different parts of the South since the war began, and although slaves have been held to the practice of arms against their will and under immediate terrors of coercion . . . the fact that they have been so employed shows that they can be used as soldiers." The Democratic *Baltimore American* issued a warning that was familiar to emancipationists: "The rebels have a hardy negro population of four million to draw soldiers from, and they will make use of them in that way, more and more, as the war progresses."[50]

"All our reliable information . . . is brought in by them"

As the debate raged, runaway slaves continued to come into Federal lines at Yorktown, demonstrating their value by providing detailed information about the Peninsula's roads and geography, as well as about Confederate positions. In fact, African Americans were the most reliable sources of information. "We talked to quite a number of citizens," Union soldier Benjamin C. Stevens noted, "but couldn't get much out of them. I don't think there is one Union citizen in this part of the country." There was "one man who pretended to be sort of a national man, but at the next place we stopped there was a free colored man who told us all about him." The black man warned the Federals that they had been talking to a Rebel soldier who could not be trusted. "He said that the same man had tried to force him into [Confederate] service as a cook and had threatened his life [but] he would not go."[51]

"The deception practiced by white spies," a letter published by the *Philadelphia Press* asserted, "has become so common and so chronic" that Union officers could not trust white southern civilians. "It is different with the slaves," the writer observed. "They have repeatedly shown, and are repeatedly showing, how entirely they may be confided in." Although the *Cincinnati Gazette* opposed the new confiscation bill and maintained that the Union army was often hostile to runaways, it admitted that "it is a remarkable fact . . . [that] nearly all our reliable information of the enemy is brought in by them." The *Philadelphia Press* claimed, "There is not a general officer in the Union service who will not testify that his best intel-

ligence of the movements of the enemy, and of the topography of the seceded country has come from blacks."[52]

Fourth Corps commander Erasmus Keyes would have agreed; he depended on information from three runaway slaves in placing his troops in
front of the Rebel works at Yorktown. Union soldier George Stevens witnessed Keyes's meeting with the three slave women, who spoke "with an
earnestness that proved their sympathies were not with their late masters." The general questioned the slaves about the Confederate forces in
his front and "listened eagerly to their words." The runaways explained
that the Confederates had a strong position just ahead, and if the Union
soldiers advanced any farther they would come under Rebel fire. One of
the slaves added that the Confederates had a substantial number of men
there but then pointed at the Federal troops and remarked, "But . . . noting like all dese yer."[53]

The slave woman noticed what General McClellan had not figured out:
the Army of the Potomac greatly outnumbered the Confederates on the
Peninsula. Due to the erroneous information supplied to him by Pinkerton about Rebel troop strength and his own cautious nature, McClellan
refused to believe that he held a two-to-one advantage over the Rebels.
After assessing the situation at Yorktown, Confederate army commander
Joe Johnston remarked to General Lee, "No one but McClellan could have
hesitated to attack." Magruder himself knew his lines were strong but
worried that in the end, "numbers must prevail."[54]

With his heaviest guns finally in place, McClellan at last planned a
grand bombardment of the Confederate lines for the first week of May.
One Yankee soldier predicted that the Confederates would not be there
for the artillery barrage. A runaway slave had assured him that the southern army would soon abandon the lines and pull back to more defensible
ground closer to Richmond. Other runaways offered similar assessments.
The *Philadelphia Public Ledger* reported that on April 22 a slave came in
claiming to have been a cook for high-ranking Confederate officers. "The
colored man describes Gens. Johnson and Magruder so accurately that he
must know them," the correspondent added. According to the black in-
formant, Rebel officers had instructed the southern army "to hold itself
in readiness to evacuate its present position and fall back to Richmond."
The *New York Times* reported that on April 30 two runaways came into the
lines and said that "the rebels [were] moving their stores, baggage and
personal property back to Williamsburgh. For the last three nights, they
say, the road from Yorktown to Williamsburgh has been filled with wagons transporting goods."[55]

On the far left of Union lines on May 2, New York colonel Regis de Tro-briand grew suspicious of Confederate activity across the Warwick River in front of his 55th New York. A black man swam the river for the colonel and returned with confirmation that the Rebels were evacuating. Trobri-and later recalled that he immediately sent the slave to his division com-mander "but heard nothing from it." The 33rd New York passed similar reports to the Fourth Corps headquarters of Erasmus Keyes, and the gen-eral later confirmed that he "learned from a negro" that "the enemy had been for a day or two making preparations to retreat." Nevertheless, Colo-nel Trobriand suspected that General Keyes did not send the black man's information to army headquarters.[56]

Black informants continued to give reports of Rebel evacuation to newspaper correspondents as well. Unlike Trobriand however, *Philadel-phia Inquirer* correspondent Uriah H. Painter spoke directly to army head-quarters, explaining to Chief of Staff Randolph Marcy that a Confederate officer's runaway body servant told him that Rebel supply wagons were moving matériel away from the lines. McClellan's staff was receiving mixed reports, however, as other information did not seem to indicate the Rebels were evacuating. Consequently, McClellan continued to methodi-cally prepare for a bombardment.[57]

In the predawn hours of May 4, members of the 2nd Massachusetts and the 13th New York went out on picket duty. "On the way," John L. Parker recalled, "we met a contraband who said 'Dem rebs done gone run away.'" The word rapidly spread through Federal lines. After aerial reconnais-sance from balloons confirmed the news, Union soldiers advanced into the vacated fortifications. Most of the soldiers in the Army of the Potomac were disappointed because they anticipated gloriously storming the Con-federate works and avenging Bull Run. Colonel Trobriand, however, was angry. "I state this fact," he recalled, "which is not without some impor-tance . . . that upon the left of our lines we had been held motionless two days before abandoned positions and works evacuated by the enemy." If army headquarters had heeded the news brought in by African Ameri-cans, the colonel implied, the Army of the Potomac might have been able to pounce on the retreating Rebels.[58]

Nevertheless, the army had captured Yorktown, and the Union soldiers examined with curiosity the earthworks that had stalled their advance on Richmond for a month. Michigan soldier John Berry was impressed, noting in his diary that the Confederate works were "on a very extensive & formidable scale." James Mitchell described them as "immense," and the men of his 81st Pennsylvania "concluded that the enemy is a cowardly

Union troops examine portions of the abandoned Confederate works at Yorktown. (Library of Congress)

set to leave such a strong place without a struggle." The soldiers of the 49th New York agreed: "We were greatly surprised that [the Rebels] should have left," adjutant George Selkirk wrote home after walking through the Confederate defenses. "Their works were very strong, forts and rifle pits one behind the other for quite a distance. . . . On these a great deal of labor had been expended." But while most soldiers thought only of the Confederates who had gotten away, at least one Yankee saw something more. George Townsend, a correspondent traveling with the army, remarked that "the fine works at Yorktown are the monuments to Negro labor. For *they* were the hewers and the diggers."[59]

Despite the strength of the Rebel defenses on the lower Peninsula, Confederate army commander Joe Johnston wanted to rely upon Richmond's stronger fortifications. He believed that the superior Union navy would ultimately gain complete control of the York and James Rivers, allowing the Yankees to outflank his Yorktown lines. A position closer to the Confederate capital, he advised Jefferson Davis and Robert E. Lee, would stretch Union supply lines, protect the Confederate flanks, and bog the Union army down in the Chickahominy swamps. They initially disagreed and forced Johnston to hold his lines at Yorktown as long as practical. By the start of May, however, Johnston got his way, and his troops evacuated the lower Peninsula.[60]

The withdrawal ruined McClellan's plans to destroy the southern army and crushed northern hopes that the Army of the Potomac would win the decisive battle of the war at Yorktown, as the Patriots had done during the Revolution. McClellan's monthlong stall in front of the "monuments to Negro labor" only gave the Confederates time to strengthen their army and their fortifications around Richmond.

As the Confederates withdrew, the effect the war was having on the institution of slavery annoyed the Border State *Baltimore American*: "Scornfully abandoning the shelter of the Constitution," the editors opined on May 6, "the Seceding States have appealed to the sword in order to protect slavery, and are palpably getting the worst of it." Moreover, Confederate military practices had set in motion a process that was breaking down slavery. "Right upon our borders, within sight of almost our territory, the irrepressible negro is made to work to his 'own hurt' literally, as well as in a political sense. . . . General Lee, as commander in chief of the rebel forces at Yorktown, puts the 'institution' to building redoubts and manning guns to destroy those who are in the field to maintain the Constitution and laws." That the Rebels were using the enslaved community for these military purposes justified the Union army's confiscation of slaves, and in fact only encouraged runaways. "Nay, putting the negro himself into the field as a constituent of the strife, as the Confederates have done almost from the first, boasting of him as a direct aide in organizing a means of resistance, . . . what can they expect?" The editors urged slaveholding Marylanders to prepare themselves for complete emancipation. "In view of all that is thus occurring everyday, can any sensible mind suppose that the revolution begun is going suddenly to end?"[61]

Despite the *Baltimore American*'s concerns, most Northerners were still not ready to advocate emancipation at the start of May 1862. In the west, northern forces had captured many of the South's larger cities, and Grant's army had won an important victory at Shiloh. In Virginia, the Army of the Potomac had not yet destroyed the southern army, but the Rebels did appear to be falling back to the last ditch. Northerners were confident that Richmond would soon fall, and thus the military necessity argument was still highly debatable.[62] Nevertheless, the Baltimore paper sensed the true direction of things. The Yorktown siege had demonstrated that the Union army could rely on black Southerners, had frustrated Northerners with the South's use of blacks as laborers and combatants, had bought time for radical Republicans to fight the moderates and conservatives of both parties, and had supplied emancipationists with more evidence to argue that freeing the slaves was becoming a military necessity.

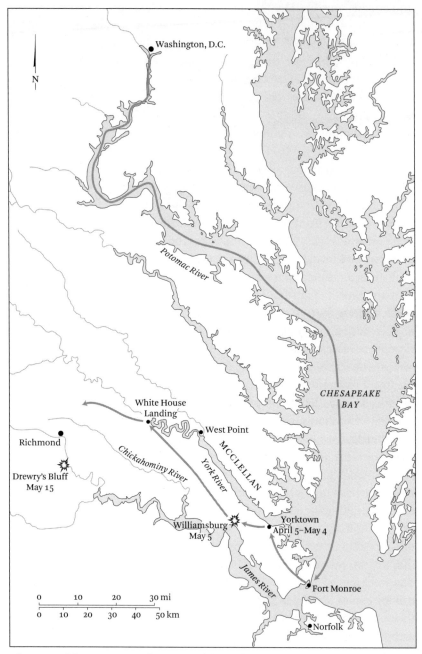

The Army of the Potomac's advance on Richmond during the Peninsula Campaign

6

THOSE BY WHOM THESE RELATIONS ARE BROKEN MAY 1862

When Union troops entered Yorktown, they found it deserted by all but a few slaves, who claimed their advanced age had prevented them from running to the Federals. Soldiers gathered around these gentlemen and aggressively sought information. The correspondent for the *Philadelphia Press* told of one slave who "might have [had] a thousand tongues . . . and [yet] fail to answer half the questions that [were] propounded to him in chorus." The soldiers asked where the Rebels had gone, when and why they left, how many soldiers they had, and the mood of their army. "Each of these interrogatories was propounded a dozen times at least in my hearing," the reporter claimed, "and appeared to afford unspeakable gratification" to the slave. With their masters in flight, the joyous slaves relished the attention. When asked about the siege, one black sage asserted "dat he seed dat ting before," claiming to have been alive when Cornwallis surrendered at Yorktown during the Revolution. He "always has a band of eager listeners around him," the paper noted, "when, in an amusing way, he tells the incidents of two sieges."[1]

The Confederate withdrawal and subsequent Federal advance up the Peninsula had the potential to bring even more slaves into Union lines, a fact well understood by Confederate artillerist James DeWitt Hankins. The day before his regiment withdrew from its fortifications on the lower Peninsula, he wrote his father, "God only knows what will happen within the next two weeks. . . . I expect to learn that many of your negroes have deserted. If the Yankees take occupation [of more areas of the Peninsula] it is impossible to keep the negroes from running away."[2] The Rebel soldier's prediction was accurate, and the runaways soon provided the Union army with valuable assistance.

As McClellan approached the Confederate capital, the debates surrounding the second confiscation bill entered a new phase. Coupled with Union military success in other theaters of war, the Army of the Potomac's advance made the military necessity argument increasingly questionable, and thus emancipationists suddenly faced the specter of the war ending with slavery intact. In reaction, congressional radicals became more aggressive, and the Peninsula provided them with an increasing amount of rhetorical ammunition for their debates with moderates and conservatives. Many African Americans were reliable guides as the army advanced toward Richmond in May 1862, and their military intelligence significantly influenced events during the Battle of Williamsburg. Meanwhile, Peninsula masters were surprised and angered that many in the enslaved community showed no loyalty and fled to the Yankees. Although the relationship between blacks and northern soldiers was hardly free from racial animosity, the slaves were overjoyed to see the Confederates in retreat and eagerly cooperated with the Federals. Many Yankees repaid the kindnesses and sometimes even threatened and intimidated southern civilians who tried to control their slaves. As a result, the mostly positive contacts between the Army of the Potomac and Peninsula blacks dramatically increased the number of runaways willing to aid the Union cause.

"They encouraged the belief that some of the enemy's works . . . were not occupied"

As the Confederates retreated from Yorktown, General Joseph Johnston learned that his supply trains and artillery had bogged down on their way to Richmond. To buy time, he sent General James Longstreet's division to guard the army's rear. Longstreet quickly set up a defensive line centered on Fort Magruder, a work that covered the junction of two roads east of Williamsburg. Peninsula blacks had in fact predicted Johnston's deployment of Longstreet. "Those [slaves] remaining here [at Yorktown]," the *New York Herald* correspondent wrote on the day the Confederates abandoned the lower Peninsula, "say that the rebels have started for Richmond; but will halt at Williamsburg just long enough to annoy us." Elements of the Army of the Potomac were in swift pursuit of the Rebels and forming lines in Longstreet's front.[3]

General Winfield Scott Hancock commanded one of the Union brigades opposite Longstreet's lines. Like many other Federal commanders on the morning of May 4, he first learned of the Confederate withdrawal from runaway slaves. Pursuing the Rebels, Hancock's brigade had halted when it received fire from Longstreet's rear guard. Division commander William Smith then placed Hancock's brigade on the far right of the Union line facing Longstreet. As darkness fell, the soldiers prepared to assault the Rebel lines in the morning.[4]

"Intelligent Contraband." France's Prince de Joinville created this watercolor when he accompanied the Army of the Potomac during the Peninsula Campaign. It depicts a scene he witnessed just after the Federals began their advance from Yorktown. His original handwritten caption: "An intelligent contraband provides highly important information." (Courtesy of Réunion des Musées Nationaux/Art Resource, N.Y.)

The next day, Smith observed the Confederate works facing his division. It appeared to him that the enemy's lines stretched to his right "as far as the eye could see." To confirm this, he sent an engineer officer to reconnoiter. This officer reported to Smith that because of the Rebel forts, there appeared to be no suitable spot to launch a frontal assault on Longstreet's defenses. Fortunately for the Federals, however, Magruder's southern troops were not the only people who knew the Confederate trenches and forts well. African Americans in the area possessed detailed knowledge of the fortifications they had labored on for almost a year. The day before, for example, *Philadelphia Inquirer* correspondent Uriah H. Painter had aggressively followed the Rebel retreat, had ridden his horse through the advancing Federal soldiers, and had gotten "within a mile and a half of Williamsburg." At that point, he learned "from a contraband . . . where all [the Confederate] works were."[5]

As Smith searched for a place to attack, sixteen slaves from various farms came into the headquarters of the two highest-ranking Union officers on the scene, corps commanders Erasmus Keyes and Edwin "Bull" Sumner. "I questioned one of them," Keyes reported, "and General Sumner ordered the examination of the others. Their reports did not agree, but they encouraged the belief that some of the enemy's works on his left were not occupied." Based on this information, Keyes began his own reconnaissance to determine if the information was accurate.[6]

Around the same time, General Smith's engineer reported that he too had spoken with a slave who insisted that the two small forts on the Confederate left were unoccupied. If this were true, troops filling the empty works would be in a protected position on the flank of the Confederate army. Attacking from that point would make the entire Rebel line untenable, and the Federals might rout and capture a substantial portion of the enemy forces. Furthermore, this black man knew of a hidden path that led, under cover, right to the empty works. Upon hearing this, General Smith ordered the engineer to take four companies from his command and verify the information. They discovered that what the blacks had told them was true: the left of the Confederate line was completely unguarded, and the Federals could turn the Rebel flank by using the concealed route.[7]

Smith passed this intelligence along to his corps commander, General Sumner, and begged to take his division up the path "and do some good work." By this time, Keyes and other officers had also confirmed the black men's information. Unfortunately, Bull Sumner (who outranked Keyes) failed to appreciate the tactical advantage the unguarded Rebel forts provided. With the Confederates in his front and already opening fire, he insisted that a movement to the right was too dangerous. The enemy was in his front, and there the battle would be fought.[8] This type of unimaginative generalship hindered the Army of the Potomac in the early years of the war. At this point, many of the officers with real talent for quickly evaluating a situation and making bold and effective tactical decisions did not have sufficient rank to take the initiative. All they needed was a chance to prove their leadership abilities. Thanks to the information gleaned from runaway slaves, Winfield Hancock's chance came on May 5.

By eleven that morning, Sumner's attack on the Confederate defenses in his front had already bogged down, and it became increasingly apparent that success in that direction was unlikely. Smith finally persuaded Sumner to let him send at least one brigade on the secret trail pointed out by the black men. He chose Hancock for the task and instructed him to occupy the abandoned Confederate works but not to move his brigade any further without orders.[9]

The approach was an obscure and narrow path, and at times Hancock's men had to cut through dense foliage. For the last leg, the black guides led the soldiers across a mill dam as well as into a gorge that pond water had sliced into a hillside. Eventually the brigade emerged from the wooded labyrinth and found the works abandoned, just as the slaves said they would be.[10]

Looking across an open field, Hancock saw other empty Confederate works. Slaves in the area explained that the Rebels had been in the forts the day before but were now gone. Approximately two miles away, Hancock could see Fort Magruder and Longstreet's men fending off the Union attacks in their front. No Confederate troops faced Hancock, and the Rebels appeared to be unaware of his arrival on their flank. The general quickly grasped the tactical advantage: a quick and determined assault by a larger force could easily turn the Confederates out of Fort Magruder.[11]

But still Hancock could not get Sumner to send reinforcements and approve an assault. He sent several dispatches pleading for permission to attack but received only orders to withdraw. Risking a charge of insubordination, he delayed carrying the order out as long as possible, but at shortly past five o'clock he realized he had to follow Sumner's directives and began to abandon the position.[12]

Just then, however, Hancock noticed that the Confederates were moving in his direction. Because the fighting in his front had died down, Confederate general Longstreet finally noticed the threat on his left and dispatched a Confederate brigade toward Hancock. Sumner's obstinacy had squandered the opportunity to make a surprise attack on the Rebel flank, but now Hancock saw the chance to repulse a Confederate assault. As the Rebels filed into the open field in his front, Hancock shouted to his men, "You must hold this ground, or I'm ruined!"[13]

The Rebels rashly charged and tauntingly shouted, "Bull Run!" at the Federals. Colonel Hiram Burnham of the 6th Maine reported that "the rebels . . . reached the rail fence in our front, not 15 rods from us. On they came, evidently feeling sure of their success." Hancock's men were not intimidated and were determined to avoid another Bull Run. "It was our turn now," Burnham boasted. "We poured a volley into them which thinned their ranks terribly. Blinded and dismayed they still pressed on, firing wildly at random." From their protected position, Hancock's men reloaded, and "again our forces poured into them, sending death and destruction in their midst. They wavered, they faltered, [and] they halted."[14]

Recognizing the critical moment in the fight, Hancock shouted to his men, "Gentlemen, charge with the bayonet!" Rushing forward, the soldiers bayoneted a few Rebels in the front ranks, and then the other Southerners broke for the rear. "The force which had attacked us was transformed into a mob and fled wildly across the field," Burnham recalled. Hancock's men completely routed the Confederates and brought in the first enemy flag captured by the Army of the Potomac in the Civil War.[15] The Peninsula's enslaved community had made the brigade's success possible by pointing out the tactical advantage that placed the Yankees in a protected position on the enemy's flank.

The Battle of Williamsburg established Winfield Hancock's reputation. In a telegram to Lincoln, McClellan claimed, "Hancock was superb today." Because the Confederates repulsed the Union's frontal assaults, the northern press focused on Hancock's success and exaggerated its significance. "The battle was undoubtedly decided by the magnificent charge made by the troops under General Hancock," the *New York Herald* reported. "This is the most important victory of the war." The North had discovered a hero. "The conduct of General Hancock and his Brigade . . . has excited universal admiration," the *New York Times* maintained. "A standard of colors . . . was captured and is now on its way to Washington." The *Philadelphia Inquirer* believed that "the country . . . will have an eye open for the deeds of Superb Hancock."[16] The officer quickly moved up the chain of command and became the hero of Gettysburg by defending against Pickett's charge. By the end of the war, he was arguably the army's best corps commander. The military intelligence delivered by runaway slaves had helped to launch Hancock's illustrious career. Surely, they too were "superb" that day.

Unfortunately, the role of Peninsula blacks was largely lost in the hero making. The *New York Herald*, for example, reported only that Union officers had gathered the information about the abandoned forts and the concealed path from "a native" of Virginia. The staunchly Republican *Chicago Tribune* was one of only a few papers that reported that black guides had led the soldiers to the battlefield.[17]

Nevertheless, as the Army of the Potomac advanced up what one correspondent eloquently described as "the most atrocious mudroads that can disgrace the barbarism of a slave state," northern papers broadly recognized the aid of African Americans. "Our armies have hardly taken a step," the moderate *New York Times* claimed, "without reliance upon the reports of the faithful black fellows, whose accuracy has been remarkable." Lincoln confidant John W. Forney agreed: "Let us admit," he argued in the *Philadelphia Press* as the army made its way up the Peninsula, "that it is from the contrabands that we receive our most accurate information. It was a contraband who gave the first notice of the evacuation of Manassas to General McClellan, [and others] that brought news of the flight from Yorktown," and they continued to supply more information as the army advanced. Connecting the services of blacks on the Peninsula to the abo-

"The Reliable Contraband," by Edwin Forbes. This postwar illustration celebrates African Americans who provided military intelligence to Union troops during the war. (Library of Congress)

lition question, the *New York Times* asserted, "The country will owe much to its Africa allies by the time the war is ended. Shall it pay the debt by giving them up to their vindictive masters and [leave them] in hopeless slavery?"[18]

"Very different beings"

In compliance with McClellan's original strategy for advancing on Richmond, after the Battle of Williamsburg, the Army of the Potomac set out to secure West Point, the terminus of the railroad that ran from the head of the York River into Richmond. McClellan also hoped that by landing there the Federals might cut off some of the retreating Confederates. Accordingly, Union general William Franklin's division sailed up the York and landed across the river from West Point near Eltham Plantation. From there, his instructions were to move his division southward to gain possession of the main road that a portion of the Rebel army was using as its escape route from the lower Peninsula. Typically, however, the aggressive Union movement was already two days behind schedule when Franklin's men came ashore at Brick House Point during the night of May 6. The next morning, "we scarcely got some coffee ready and dry biscuits," Patrick McGlenn of the 96th Pennsylvania wrote, "when two or three negroes came in to us. They informed us that the whole Rebel army was marching on us." Francis Boland also recalled the black informants who "told us the Rebel army was advancing in full force to take us prisoners or shoot us down if we resisted." Because of these and similar reports during the night, Franklin decided that instead of advancing he would set up a defensive position covering the heavy woods west and south of the landing.[19]

The "whole Rebel army" had not arrived, but what the blacks had seen was the famed Texas Brigade and a few other southern regiments that the aggressive John Bell Hood was leading to the river landing. The confederate general's orders were simply to "feel the enemy gently and fall back," but instead he characteristically slammed full force into the Federals, despite what one Union soldier described as "one of the closest growth of pine trees and underbrush I ever saw." The resulting skirmish swayed confusingly through the tangled woods, with both sides advancing and retreating. Pennsylvania colonel John M. Gosline reported that the "denseness of the foliage . . . render[ed] it impossible to ascertain" exactly what the Rebels were assaulting them with. Hood's men finally managed to push the Federals into the clearing near the landing, but there the Yankees were able to hold their ground. Hood then withdrew, having gotten a good "feel" for the enemy.[20]

Francis Boland was convinced that his 96th Pennsylvania had fought against two Alabama regiments of black Confederate troops at Eltham's Landing. "They advanced against us," the soldier maintained. "They mutilated our dead and stripped them naked. They bayoneted our wounded and cut their throats in cold blood. It is wrong to bring Negroes into battlefields." Because Boland's claims go beyond the sighting of a handful of black sharpshooters or artillerymen, exactly what the soldier saw is puzzling. As previously noted, contrary to abolitionist warnings, the statements made to Pinkerton by runaway slaves near Manassas, and similar claims by Union soldiers at Yorktown, the Confederacy never seriously considered the creation of black regiments until the war's final days. The dense woods in which the fight took place made the fight confusing for everyone involved, and Boland obviously greatly embellished the number of blacks he may have observed.[21]

Nevertheless, it is possible that what he saw and exaggerated about were the body servants of Confederate soldiers. When they left for war, many wealthy Southerners brought a slave with them to make camp life more comfortable. "On the march," Mississippian Ruffin Thomson claimed while on the Peninsula, "the man with a boy fares best, by far."

Thomson envied other soldiers who were attended by slaves and wrote his father, "I have been thinking lately that if you could spare me Preston, or hire me a boy, it would save me a good deal of suffering." He wanted a body servant "to work for me, wash for me, carry some things for me, get something to eat for me, etc." Thomson's father sent Preston to Virginia, and he worked beside his master until dying of illness outside of Fredericksburg later that year.[22]

Although written after the Peninsula Campaign, letters composed by the slave Jack Foster to his master's son offer a rare first-person account of a body servant's wartime experiences. The slave's letters were in many ways typical of soldier letters. He complained about camp life, referred to the Federals as "blue bellies," confessed "getting tired of the Army," and seemed more concerned about the woman he had left behind than the war. Foster revealed some of his duties as a body servant when discussing attempts "to get your pa some butter" and took pride in his cooking. The body servant also came under fire: "I went on the battlefield to get the . . . [colonel's] horse and the Yankys liked to kill me . . . the balls came so fast."[23]

Foster was not the only body servant exposed to fire; others were often seen on battlefields searching for wounded masters. According to historian Benjamin Quarles, "On the battle fronts the body servant who had grown up in the family [often] proved [trustworthy]," and some may have developed compassion for masters "whose personal effects [they] handled . . . and for whom [they] foraged, cooked, barbered and nursed." Confederate soldier Thomas Caffey would have agreed: "Their devotion to dead or wounded masters has been exhibited on many trying occasions," he wrote in 1864. Body servants often came to the aid of wounded masters during the thick of a battle. "I have seen several instances where the poor boys have been wounded while dragging their masters out of action."[24] One understandable motive for such devotion was that a servant who cared for a severely wounded master or who bore a slain owner's body home for burial might well receive some form of reward or better treatment.

It is possible that what Francis Boland observed in the dense woods and battle smoke around Eltham's Landing were these body servants who made their way on to the battlefields. After all, William Ringgold claimed that the body servants he saw while on the Peninsula were "armed in full." Boland may have viewed them through the thick underbrush stripping dead Federal soldiers or assisting wounded masters off the field, and it is possible that a few were fighting as others had seen blacks doing at

Big Bethel, Manassas, and Yorktown. However, the battlefield conditions around Eltham's Landing were perfect for creating confusion and false impressions. Moreover, after the battle, a Federal surgeon reported encountering one Union soldier with his throat slashed, and several officers noted that the Rebels had stripped the dead for valuables.[25] Such emotionally charged reports and any sighting of blacks within Confederate lines were sure to stir passions and thus to be conflated and exaggerated by the soldier rumor mill as Rebel atrocities. Although not corroborated by any officers, embellished claims like those of Francis Boland helped fuel the perception, then as well as now, that many blacks fought for the Confederacy.

The reality, of course, was much different, and many white Southerners learned the true sentiments of their slaves as the Union army advanced up the Peninsula. During and after the Confederate retreat, the city of Williamsburg became increasingly chaotic. Seventeen-year-old Victoria Lee later recalled that the town "was overrun with refugees from the lower end of the Peninsula." Another resident, Charles S. Jones, found "every house . . . filled to its capacity due to the refugees." On the night of the Williamsburg battle, the town's overcrowding worsened as wounded Confederate soldiers found their way into homes and churches in search of comfort. Cynthia Coleman remembered that her "mother's house was full" of needy soldiers, and, making matters worse for Williamsburg's white residents, "the servants had already begun to show their sense of freedom" and some were refusing to take orders. "[We] had come to regard [them] no longer as friends, Coleman maintained, "but as bitterest foes."[26]

The next day, lead elements of the Army of the Potomac marched into town. "It was one of the most magnificent sights I have ever seen," Victoria Lee recalled. "Countless thousands of blue-clad troops, all in new uniforms." Coleman described how Union bands were "playing Dixie, Yankee Doodle, Hail Columbia and John Brown's Body." She was not pleased: "Indignant faces [looked] out from behind closed blinds upon the desecration . . . of our beautiful old town." Besides nasty looks, white citizens hurled insults such as "nigger worshipers" at Union troops.[27]

Williamsburg's African Americans reacted much differently. "The Negroes . . . were smiling," recalled the Prince de Joinville, a French nobleman traveling with the army; "many of them put on the most grotesquely victorious airs." A *Philadelphia Inquirer* correspondent observed, "At the corners of the streets were congregated groups of darkeys, male and female, who showed their white ivories and grinned and bowed to almost

"A View in Williamsburg, Va." This 1862 watercolor by William McIlvaine depicts Union soldiers and supply wagons on Williamsburg's Duke of Gloucester Street. (Library of Congress)

every soldier passing that way." The Comte de Paris, another French observer traveling with the army, noted that as Union soldiers entered Williamsburg, "a large crowd of Negroes rushe[d] toward us from all sides."[28]

During the months before the campaign, most blacks on the Peninsula had not made their way to Fort Monroe because they were unsure if throwing their lot in with the Federals was a safe gamble. With the Confederate army in retreat and the Union army advancing up the Peninsula, going to the Yankees began to look like a safer decision. They "decamped in the direction of Fortress Monroe," Joinville noted, "that is to say, of freedom, carrying their wives and children with them in small carts." The black fugitives discovered a bounty of goods left behind by the retreating Confederates, including small weapons, knapsacks, blankets, and overcoats. "The blacks of Williamsburg are rich in 'portable property' to-day," the *Boston Daily Journal* correspondent observed.[29]

Union soldier Thomas Hyde recalled the "crowds of contrabands [who] passed to our rear, looking like so many old clothes-bags, but in great joy, as they believed the millennium had come." Gilbert Adams Hayes vividly remembered the exodus as well. "Following the Battle of Williamsburg our camps began to fill up with Negroes . . . aged aunties with great bundles on their heads, old gray-haired uncles, lively youngsters, all came flocking in with the confidence and trust of children, believing that when they reached the 'unions' they were safe from future trouble." In a highly ironic statement, Confederate engineer John A. Williams believed that as the Rebels withdrew up the Peninsula and the slaves fled to Union lines, "I reckon they will regret their leaving as I understand the Yankees make them work very hard on their fortifications."[30]

In fact, the enslaved community gladly offered their services to the Union soldiers and even discovered new forms of relaxation. "The old servants wait [on some officers] just as they did their old masters," Union officer Charles Wainwright noted while in Williamsburg. "Many of our officers have picked up servants here." The blacks took special joy in the furniture left behind by owners who fled up the Peninsula. "Our headquarters tents are pitched in the door yard of a small abandoned house," Wainwright explained; "most of the furniture was gone . . . [because] the Negroes on the place . . . appropriated much of it to their own use and were indulging in all the luxury of cushioned rocking chairs."[31]

Such happy experiences and the positive reactions of blacks came despite, or perhaps because of, the fact that Williamsburg's white residents had warned their slaves about evil Yankees. "The negroes have been told the most absurd stories about our designs against them," a newspaper correspondent claimed, "that we would put them into wagons and drive them, and the like." The *Boston Daily Journal* noted that masters told their slaves that "the object of the war on the part of the North is to steal the slaves of the South and sell them."[32]

The *Philadelphia Inquirer* reported from Williamsburg that "the slaves in this vicinity were told to beware of the 'horrible Yankees, who had very small bodies, but with great large heads, with front teeth like horses, and were known to eat human flesh." Union private Wilbur Fisk encountered a free black who said that "the rebels told him to burn his house and follow them, for the Yankees would destroy him, and all he had." Farther up the Peninsula, at Eltham's Landing, Massachusetts soldier Walter Eames talked with a black man who claimed that his master had sent "droves" of his slaves to work on the fortifications at Yorktown and that they were told "that if the Yankees came here they would be beaten by them, have their throats cut, be sold to Cuba and ill treated in every possible way." Eames also encountered a female slave who told him "that her master used to show the slaves pictures of the Yankees harnessing the negroes to wagons, and when they failed to work, cutting off their ears, etc." The *Philadelphia Press* correspondent encountered a slave owner named Parsley who used stories of cruel Yankees to successfully convince his slaves to hide from Union troops. When one Union soldier asked Williamsburg slave Eliza Baker how she liked the Yankees, she replied, "I don't know, sir, I ain't seen none." When the soldier pointed out that he was a Northerner, she replied, "You can't be, cause Mrs. Whiting told us the Yankees have horns." The soldier had Baker take him to her mistress, and he scolded the owner for spreading such lies.[33]

Parsley's frightened slaves and Eliza Baker's response to the Union soldier suggest that owners may have had success at creating negative preconceptions of Yankees in the minds of some blacks, but many claimed to have never believed such tales. They "appeared confident," the *National Anti-Slavery Standard* reported, that blacks would not "suffer from us, and might possibly benefit." An elderly women interviewed by the *Principia* assured the Northerners "that she never had any fears that the Yankees would harm her." Fisk recalled that the free black who was told the Union soldiers would kill him "manifested as much inward satisfaction at seeing us, as if he had suddenly recognized an old friend."[34]

As Williamsburg's African Americans tried to form new alliances with the Federals, their actions shocked patriarchal owners who had long deluded themselves into believing that their slaves were loyal and contented friends. Cynthia Coleman, for example, attempted to protect the large library of one of her neighbors who had fled the town. She asked the man's slave butler to help carry the books away and hide them from Union soldiers, "but he declined." He claimed to be "afraid to meddle." Coleman was not deceived, and the experience made her bitter. She concluded that the slave was "a good-for-nothing, ungrateful wretch." Revealing the depths of her anger, Coleman continued, "I never shall believe that negroes have souls, I know they have no heart." She was unable to save the books. "Day by day I see them carried away by the armful."[35]

This was no isolated event. "Negroes are presuming very much under the present administration," another Williamsburg resident, Harriette Cary, remarked two weeks after Union troops took over the town. The slaves, Cynthia Coleman claimed, "did not immediately leave ... but went off by degrees as they made their arrangements." Before leaving their masters, however, "they were very different beings from the trusted and faithful friends we had supposed them to be. Every house that contained one of them sheltered a traitor, every secret was conveyed to the enemy. The hiding place of every valuable was in time betrayed."[36]

The actions of Coleman's own slaves pained her the most. "I used to think of my Mamy the perfection of a Mamy," she recalled, "so gentle and quiet in her manners. Such a lovely countenance. . . . Could she betray the child she raised, or forsake the friendship who had always been good to her, her children, and her children's children?" Coleman recalled that when the Union army arrived in Williamsburg, her mother begged the slave mammy to stay and help the family, saying, "Patty if you will only stay with me until this dreadful war is over and my children are back, I will gladly give you your freedom as a reward for your fidelity." Nevertheless, "the day came when she left [Coleman's family] without a servant, alone in the [same] house which had always given [the slave] her shelter." The slave mammy was not the only family servant to leave. "They all went," Coleman noted sadly.[37]

Decades after the war, Coleman still could not understand the true nature of slavery, accrediting the flight of her slaves solely to what she perceived as the deceptions of the Union army. "Who was to blame?" she wrote. "The . . . creature who had never had a harsh word from master or mistress, who had always been loved, trusted and venerated by the children of the family—or those who made her think it a fine thing to be free, a fine thing to abandon the mistess who had always been her friend—a fine thing to [get] freedom?" Conveniently forgetting her wartime characterization of slaves as having no hearts or souls, Coleman romanticized the Old South by describing blacks as a "bright, happy race—they loved us, and we trusted them. Those by whom these tender relations are broken have done them, and us, a great wrong."[38] A lifetime of proslavery indoctrination had obviously skewed Coleman's perspective, but she was on to something when she noted the importance of the developing relationship between the Union army and the enslaved community in the process of emancipation.

"They knew and felt they were among friends"

Nevertheless, some evidence suggests that at least a few Peninsula slaves may have shared Cynthia Coleman's hostility for Union troops. The Democratic *Detroit Free Press*, for example, reported that the lower Peninsula's roads were dangerous to be on at night because roving bands of black men were attacking and robbing Federal soldiers. Pushing an anti-emancipation agenda, the editors added, "The Negroes as a mass have shown no friendship to the Union. . . . The truth is that there was never a greater humbug than the talk about Negro loyalty. Abolition has asserted it from the beginning of the war, but every fact of the times proves that it is a mere assertion."[39]

Democratic papers were not alone in remarking on violence directed at Union troops by blacks. The moderate *New York Times*, for example, reported that the roads on the lower Peninsula were unsafe after dark, placing most of the blame on white deserters from the Confederate army. Nevertheless, the paper maintained, "many of the depredations and outrages are also committed by runaway contrabands who roam all over the countryside and do pretty much as they please." Even the radical Republican *Chicago Tribune* reported on "two negroes brought into Yorktown . . . charged with shooting Union soldiers." The correspondent was quick to add, however, "I heard of no other cases where we had received [anything] but kindness and good cheer from the colored people."[40]

Regardless, in the aftermath of the Battle of Williamsburg, the belief that some blacks were fighting against Union troops persisted. "The Ambulance Corps are burying the dead," Union corporal Timothy J. Regan observed on May 10. "They find some . . . with their throats cut, which is supposed to be the work of some negro soldiers who were seen in the rebel ranks. I would as soon [believe] that the white rebels did it." Reporting on the battle, the *Albany (N.Y.) Evening Journal* featured an interview with "a colored Confederate soldier" named George Jackson. "The poor fellow's hands were frightfully burnt in the handling of hot shot," the paper claimed. "He informs us that a large number of negroes were employed on the different batteries [at Yorktown]." Shortly after the Williamsburg fight, a *Philadelphia Inquirer* correspondent told of a black man who was "uniformed and armed" and taken prisoner by the soldiers of the 5th Maine. The slave claimed "he belonged to a [Confederate] company of about one hundred."[41]

Army chaplain James Marks encountered a group of African Americans confined in Yorktown by Union military officials. "I spoke to the [black] leader, and asked him why they were in prison." The man informed Marks that Federal authorities had arrested several of the men for allegedly shooting at Union soldiers in ambush "on the roads and in the forests between Yorktown to Williamsburg." A citizen had informed the Federals that this particular group of blacks was responsible for the attack, and when soldiers searched their homes they found weapons. The slaves professed innocence, explaining that they had picked up the weapons, along with clothing, blankets, and shovels, from the dead left on the Williamsburg battlefield. Shifting the blame to white Southerners, the slaves further claimed that it was "de oberseers dey kill your men; they lie in bush to shoot de soldier."[42]

Marks assured the accused blacks that the army would release them if they proved to be innocent. Not surprisingly, the slaves expressed little confidence in white justice. "White man bery uncertain," the leader told Marks. "And here the poor, ignorant creatures," remarked the chaplain, "thinking they had no defenders, and concluding that some morning they would all be led forth to be shot or hung, were making deliberate preparations to die." Marks never heard what happened to the arrested slaves but felt sure they were acquitted.[43]

Perhaps the army did release these slaves, but others were not as fortunate. "Two negroes were hung here today," Corporal Timothy J. Regan recorded in his diary on May 10, "being found guilty of murdering and robbing two soldiers while asleep." In this particular case, vigilante justice was swift. "The soldiers of the company to which the murdered men belong," Regan continued, "caught the blacks, tried them, found them guilty, and hanged them before the proper authorities could interfere. Good."[44]

Many soldiers in the Army of the Potomac loathed abolitionism, the vast majority held racist opinions, and some treated African Americans harshly. Joel Cook, a correspondent for the *Philadelphia Press*, recalled that while on the Peninsula, northern troops found the slaves to be "a most amusing set of people, and the soldiers plagued them terribly to get more fun out of them." Cook recalled that Union soldiers would try to confuse the slaves by arguing "secession up and Union down" until they were completely "befogged." The correspondent claimed, "This was a process through which nearly every negro boy entering the camps was made to pass."[45] Cook considered this treatment to be "playful" fun, but for slaves still not completely sure of Yankee intentions it was nothing short of cruel.

Unfortunately, in many instances soldiers went well beyond such treatments. While cruelty directed at southern blacks was perhaps slightly more common in the western armies, eastern soldiers often stole from African Americans, physically abused slave children, and sometimes raped enslaved women. Such incidents were especially typical behind the lines at Fort Monroe or Norfolk. Army quartermasters there frequently sold the provisions the government allocated for the contrabands, and soldiers cruelly took over the humble shelters that runaways had built for themselves at Hampton. Some Federals allegedly returned runaway slaves for reward money. Two years after the campaign ended, an abolitionist missionary called for more aid for the blacks sheltered behind the lines on the Peninsula. He strengthened the plea by reporting on the numerous examples of soldier cruelty and hyperbolically claimed, "Many negroes who had had kind masters preferred to return to slavery rather than be driven to the [contraband] camps."[46]

Moreover, soldiers who did not participate in cruel treatment of blacks nevertheless often displayed little emancipationist sentiment. Michigan officer Robert A. Everett became dangerously ill while marching through New Kent County and was more than grateful when a white family took him in and provided "a little darkey to wait on me." While occupying Williamsburg, the men of the 5th Pennsylvania Cavalry published a newspaper and made sure that the inclusion of the word "Freedom" in their motto in no way "even insinuated that we have any sympathy with abolitionism" (although they took satisfaction in pointing out that slaves on the Peninsula were becoming free because their masters had "skiddadle[d]"). Increasingly angry from reading emancipationist criticism of McClellan's slow movement, Walter Eames wrote home while marching up the Peninsula that he had "lost about all the abolition sentiment I ever possessed."[47]

Additionally, although most slaves claimed to not believe their masters' lies, many feared that the Yankees only intended to harm them. Furthermore, while there were now hundreds of blacks laboring for the Union army, the federal government had yet to officially emancipate those slaves who had not labored on Confederate fortifications, and they were not always receiving the full pay the army had promised them. There were ample reasons for slaves to distrust the white soldiers of the Union army, and it should not be surprising that a few Peninsula blacks may have been involved in these alleged assaults on Union troops.

Regardless, as the Union army advanced toward Richmond, the interactions between African Americans and Federal troops continued to influence the debate over emancipation. As they had done for months, in May 1862 radicals touted the services that blacks provided for the Federals and pushed for emancipation by pointing to the stories of Confederate troops forcing blacks into combat. "Of course the . . . Democrats and the 'conservatives,'" the *Chicago Tribune* editorialized as Union troops converged on Richmond, "see nothing wrong [with the Confederates] training the black man to cut up our troops, but let the proposition be made for a negro regiment in the Union service, and they start back in terror at the idea." The editors were outraged that "slaves may build forts and carry muskets for our Southern brethren" and "shoot down our soldiers under the fear of their master's lash" but were not allowed to fight for the Union cause. Furthermore, the *Tribune* complained, "they . . . escape through incredible hardships to give important information to our generals" but were not rewarded with emancipation.[48]

Democratic newspapers responded by downplaying the assistance that blacks gave to the army, labeled such reports "humbug," and argued that fugitive slaves were in fact lazy and unwilling to work for the Federals. They insisted that the reports of blacks attacking Union troops on the Peninsula demonstrated that the slaves were actually hostile to the Union cause. If the preponderance of news from Virginia seemed to confirm that an antagonistic relationship existed between the slaves and the Army of the Potomac, it is unlikely that Northerners would ever come to embrace emancipation as a military necessity.

But if some blacks were guilty of attacking Union troops, their actions were isolated incidents during the Federal advance up the Peninsula and certainly did not prove the Democratic contention that "the Negroes as a mass have shown no friendship to the Union." Behind the lines, blacks undeniably suffered from the cruel treatments of perhaps overly bored, frustrated, and racist occupation troops. On the front lines, as the army advanced up the Peninsula, however, blacks overwhelmingly and joyously welcomed the Yankees. Union soldier Bell Halsey Miller described the Peninsula's blacks as being "in ecstasy" because they believed the advance of the Union army brought freedom. U.S. Signal Corps officer Luther C. Furst shared this opinion. "The darkies," he noted, "are always glad to see us and all wish to be free." As the soldiers marched by, Union soldier George Stevens recalled, the slaves yelled such things as "bress de Lord! I'se been praying for yous all to come all dis time; and now I'se glad yous got so far." Charles Harvey Brewster wrote his sister, "I wish you could see the darkies. They range themselves along the side of the road as we go along and then stand and bow, hat in hand, and they keep abobbing until all have passed."[49]

Slaves laughed with the Federals about the behavior of their masters and how they expected the blacks to remain loyal. According to Miller, the slaves said the Rebels left "drefful quick, dat dey stop none for nobody, dey tell us nigs 'you stay home dar, and keep da pigs and cows from dem Yankees.'" Such remarks drew howls of laughter from the slaves as well as the soldiers. "They amuse us much," Miller noted. Walter Eames wrote his wife about a similar conversation he had had with a slave at Eltham Plantation. The black man was "a bright, intelligent fellow," Eames claimed, and "it was amusing to hear him tell how the rebels used to boast of their strength and invincibility." According to the slave, his owner was always "telling what a slaughter they would make among the Yankees, and wishing they would come." Nevertheless, when Union troops finally did arrive, "golly boss, how dey runned," the slave related with glee.[50]

While complaining to his wife about Southerners who dishonestly claimed to be loyal to the Union, Eames noted another humorous conversation with a slave who laughed at his owner's expense. The black man was asked sarcastically if his master had been "a good Union man." He certainly was, the slave responded, "been so these two days." When asked to elaborate, the black man replied that his master had "belonged to the Southern army, [but had come] back home to tend to his planting." When he attempted to rejoin his regiment, Union soldiers "wouldn't let him pass and he had to stay. But he's a good Union man now," the slave jovially delivered the punch line.[51]

"The Negroes are delighted to see us," Union soldier Elisha Hunt Rhodes claimed, "but the whites look as if they would like to kill us." Peninsula slaveholders blamed the loss of their slaves on pillaging Yankees. "Town and country are infested [with Northerners]," Williamsburg's Harriette Cary wrote. "Daily complaints are learned of their theft. . . . Negroes, horses, mules, sheep, bacon and grain are the booty of these marauding parties which scour the Country in every direction." Sarah Dandridge Cooke Duval of New Kent County later recalled that her slave-owning family was "disturbed by the announcement from several of our servants—with unmistakably jubilant countenance—'De Yankees is Comin.'" She delusionally believed, however, that these happy expressions only came from the "two or three [slaves] of recent purchase from the more Southern states, on whose affections we had no hold." Union soldier George Stevens held a different view. "Those who had hitherto regarded the relation of master and slave as one of mutual affection," he argued, "had only to witness these unique demonstrations of rejoicing at our approach . . . to be convinced that the happiness and contentment claimed for those in servitude was but a worthless fiction." Peninsula slaves, he recalled, gathered "in crowds along the wayside [and] would grasp the hands of the Union soldiers . . . leaping and dancing in their frantic delight."[52]

In addition, the soldiers received a more tangible welcome from the slaves. Charles H. Bane, an officer in the Philadelphia Brigade, recalled that as the soldiers rapidly advanced, the army struggled to keep the men fed. However, "when the haversacks were nearly empty," slaves frequently came to the rescue. "Their knowledge of the country . . . enabled them to replenish [the] scanty stock." *Philadelphia Press* correspondent Joel Cook claimed that "the inmates of every negro-hut were besought for hoecakes [by the soldiers]," and that "plaguing the negroes" for food was the extent of the army's plundering. Most soldiers did not have to go looking for food from the slaves. As they marched up the Peninsula, William Beach of the 1st New York Cavalry remembered the "crowds of colored people [that] came to the roadside to see us. They brought . . . an abundance of corn bread and hoe cake with jugs of buttermilk."[53]

Soldiers repaid the enthusiastic outpouring in large and small ways. Ex-slave Elizabeth Sparks recalled a Union cavalryman who stopped for directions and noticed her baby. "Den he lean't over an' patted de baby on de haid an ast . . . its name," she related. "I tole him it was Charlie, like his father." The soldier asked for the child's last name and learned that it was Sparks. He then drew money from his pocket, thanked her for the directions, and told her to buy something for the baby. Before riding off he said, "Goodbye, Mrs. Sparks." Elizabeth was shocked: "Now what you think of dat? Dey call me '*Mrs.* Sparks.'" She was not the only slave to receive money from benevolent Union soldiers. Although McClellan had ordered his men to respect the private property of southern civilians and to pay for what they took, William Beach claimed that in his regiment, "provisions taken were generally paid for, but the pay went into the hands of the colored people."[54]

Camped on the road "between Williamsburg and West Point," Pennsylvania soldier Joseph Baker reflected on all he had seen so far in Virginia. "This country has fine soil," he wrote his sister, "but the curse of slavery is in the middle of it." Marching up the Peninsula exposed Baker and the other northern soldiers to the physical punishment blacks had endured under southern slavery. Passing through the village at New Kent Courthouse, Walter Eames was disturbed by the sight of "a sort of 'nigger' jail, a low, dark dungeon, for confining runaway or refractory slaves" awaiting corporal punishment. At one plantation, William Beach came upon "a secessionist mistress" who had forbidden her slaves to aid the Union soldiers. "To enforce discipline," he recalled, "she had resorted to the free use of the lash on one of her women." Soldiers in Beach's 1st New York Cavalry regiment brought the slave before their officers and showed "the swollen marks of the lashing." The officers, Beach claimed, "warned the mistress that such things would not be allowed." Soldiers gave the same warning to the overseer on another plantation when he complained that he had lost all control of his slaves and that "the black people were doing about as they pleased." Luther C. Furst told of the fate of a white Southerner named Wickerts, who had a history of whipping slaves and was suspected of being a Rebel spy. "He was the overseer, & when the darkies learned we had taken him prisoner, they danced with joy."[55]

Lieutenant J. S. Brown described how his regiment prevented a slave whipping. Union soldiers had asked three older slave women to bake bread for them, but the cooks were reluctant because their mistress warned she would whip them if they aided the Federals. Nevertheless, the soldiers coaxed the slaves into it. "Sure enough," Brown related, "the lady of the house sent her son, a boy of ten years of age, to whip those three women. That is a fine business to set a boy at. Whipping women 60 years old." The soldiers quickly grabbed "the little varmint" and spanked him until he "was quite satisfied to run into the house. Fine effect such education must have on children," Brown derisively noted. Oliver Wilcox Norton, Pennsylvania soldier and future officer in the U.S. Colored Troops, recalled another slave owner "who had inhumanly whipped" his slave and who came into camp looking for the runaway. Even had the Pennsylvanians wanted to return the slave, the recent military order of Congress forbade it. The soldiers protected the fugitive, and Norton noted that the slaveholder "came near losing his life in the operation." The Federals only allowed the Southerner to leave once he took the oath of allegiance to the United States, "but he lost his nigger."[56]

Such positive front line interactions between slaves and soldiers in the Army of the Potomac helped to ensure that the flow of runaways did not slow, and in fact, they only increased it. With masters telling outrageous and graphic lies about the intentions of Union soldiers, if slaves had encountered overwhelmingly cruel treatment from Union soldiers, the word would have quickly spread on the slave grapevine that Union soldiers were not "Moses" and were in fact more akin to the evil people that their masters claimed them to be. Thus, the stream of slaves to Union lines would likely have slowed considerably. But this was not the case.

Some historians have asserted the "self-emancipation thesis," as if Union troops could not have significantly curtailed the flow of runaways. In fact, the Yankees could have consistently turned the first few Peninsula fugitives away, uniformly treated them as harshly as their masters claimed they would, and generally been less receptive than they were. Such actions could have shut off the initial trickle of Peninsula runaways who were "testing the waters," especially with the northern government disavowing a war of emancipation. Therefore, the Union army's attitude toward slaves was crucial in encouraging, or at least not slowing, the surge of fugitives into Union lines on the Peninsula. Moreover, in the historiographical debate over "who freed the slaves," historians who tout the Federal army's importance correctly assert that Union military advances were crucial in the process of emancipation because they provided slaves with their best opportunities for liberation.[57] Frequently overlooked, however, is the importance of positive interactions between Yankee soldiers and the enslaved community.

"They were well received and treated kindly by the soldiers," Massachusetts officer Daniel G. Macnamara claimed, with some degree of exaggeration. "The confidence the poor innocent blacks placed in the Union soldiers was quite touching. That they knew and felt they were among friends and on the road to freedom was freely expressed and sincerely shown." A *Philadelphia Inquirer* correspondent reported, "The Soldiers told them that if their owners had entered into Rebel service, or had abandoned them, they were free, and now could go wherever they liked." In Williamsburg, even slaveholder Harriette Cary disdainfully noted that "there seemed to be much congeniality" between Union soldiers and the slaves.[58]

As a result, Oliver Wilcox Norton noted, "contrabands are pouring in on us every day. . . . They hardly know what to do with themselves on learning that they will never be returned to their masters." Soldiers found that elderly slaves were often reluctant to leave their plantations because of declining health and long attachment to their homes. "The younger fry, however," a *Philadelphia Inquirer* correspondent noted, "caper along like young colts just escaped from the halter, willingly to live any life in preference to their former ones." As word spread about how well Union troops received the runways, slaves arrived from all over the region. The *Inquirer* told of a slave who had rowed thirty miles down the Pamunkey River to reach Union troops. "He says he had heard the Yankees were down the river and were setting all the slaves free, so off he came."[59]

Many of the runaways had used their "laying out" skills and were waiting for Union troops to arrive. The *Inquirer* reported that before the Confederates retreated from Yorktown, slave laborers there had fled and "have been in the swamps and woods secreted, some of them for ten days." Others came from the environs of Richmond: "This morning, the *Philadelphia Press* correspondent related on May 18, "I met a party of five [walking] in on the railroad, who said they had left Hanover, eight miles this side of Richmond, two days ago, traveling at night, and lurking in the woods by day."[60]

Federal officer Daniel Macnamara claimed that the fugitives "were ready to go anywhere except back to their old servitude" and were willing

Union soldiers and slaves interact at Foller's farm. This remarkable 1862 photograph was taken in New Kent County during the Peninsula Campaign. Note the shy child sheltered comfortably between the soldier's legs. (Library of Congress)

to work for the military. Slaves understood that their freedom depended on the success of the Union army. "They profess themselves willing to work, fight, or do anything for us," a correspondent for the *Philadelphia Inquirer* noted, "if, when we 'whip out de Suthern army,' they will be allowed to work for themselves."[61]

Correspondents for emancipationist newspapers traveling with the Union army reported the collapse of slavery on the Peninsula with great satisfaction. On May 21, the *National Anti-Slavery Standard* published a letter from an army chaplain traveling with a New Jersey regiment, who described the slaves as thrilled by the "ignoble retreat of . . . [their] vainglorious and boasting lords. . . . There is a universal desire for freedom expressed by these down-trodden victims of oppression." A correspondent's dispatch published by the *Principia* was more ebullient. "Those at home," he wrote, "though they may read continually the writings of those who wield the pen, . . . know but little about the great work being done here." He found it difficult to describe the joyous "feelings of those who are careful observers of the work as it progresses."[62]

"That is not the way to Richmond"

While the Army of the Potomac advanced up the Peninsula helping to shatter the institution of slavery, Federal naval forces were also making progress toward the Rebel capital. When Joseph Johnston's Confederate army withdrew toward Richmond, southern forces in Norfolk were isolated and had no choice but to evacuate and join the troops gathering to defend the Confederate capital. Because the CSS *Virginia*'s draft was too deep for the vessel to retreat up the James River, the Rebels destroyed their prize ironclad. As a result, Union forces gained control of Norfolk, the Chesapeake Bay, and the James River all the way up to a point seven miles below Richmond.[63]

From there, the Confederate fortifications at Drewry's Bluff prevented the U.S navy from getting any closer to the city. Situated on the south bank of the James River, the bluff was part of Richmond's last and best line of defenses. Overlooking a sharp bend in the river, the Rebels had a large redoubt 110 feet above the water, which boasted three heavy cannon and five naval guns. The fortification dominated a mile-long stretch of the James.[64]

Here, too, slaves had done much of the work. From March to May 1862, approximately 250 slaves from King George, Henrico, Hanover, James City, Charles City, Surry, Prince George, Frederick, and Nottoway counties toiled at the site alongside white troops. In deep mud and constant rain, the laborers hauled planks, constructed cribs, dug the works, and assisted in the mounting of the guns. To obstruct the river, workers filled the water with logs, stones, and iron, drove piles into the river bottom, sunk several sloops and schooners into the channel, and left only a small opening, which passed directly under the guns on the bluff.[65]

The Federal navy's ability to operate on the James River caused a panic in Richmond, especially in light of the recent capture of New Orleans. For a time it seemed likely that the navy rather than McClellan's army would capture Richmond. "The gunboat fever ran high all day yesterday," the *Charleston Mercury*'s Richmond correspondent reported. "Many citizens and negroes, and several companies of soldiers, went down the river to assist in completing the blockade." A week later, the correspondent was not optimistic. "Richmond is likely to share the fate of New Orleans," he wrote. "The gunboats are [near], and the obstructions will not be complete for a week. Very many negroes and others are at work trying to push ahead the . . . work."[66]

While impressed slaves helped prepare the Rebel defenses and obstruct the river, other African Americans helped the U.S. navy advance up the river. Several free blacks, who, according to one disgruntled Confederate officer, "lived by fishing and . . . are good river pilots," directed Yankee gunboats along the river. They also helped the fleet mark the channel and noted the river landings.[67]

On May 15, the U.S. ironclads *Monitor*, *Galena*, and *Naugatuck* and two wooden gunboats attacked Drewry's Bluff. Entering a virtual shooting gallery as they approached the river obstructions, they received artillery fire from the bluff and musketry fire from sharpshooters along the bank. After three and a half hours of severe pounding, the ships backed off and headed downstream as a Confederate sharpshooter on the riverbank shouted to the Federal navy, "Tell the captain that is not the way to Richmond!" The defenses that impressed slaves had helped prepare assured that naval forces would not be able to capture the Rebel capital. McClellan's Army of the Potomac would have to take the city.[68]

"They will keep messing in the white man's war!"

Despite the Federal setback at Drewry's Bluff, the North cheered news from the Peninsula that seemed to indicate that the war was coming to a glorious conclusion. "I am happy to announce to you that the rebellion will soon be played out," East Tennessee Unionist William G. "Parson" Brownlow exclaimed to the enthusiastic cheers of a standing-room-only crowd at New York City's Academy of Music. "Richmond will be obliged to fall very soon, for that noble fellow, McClellan, will capture the whole of them." The *New York Herald* agreed. "Having routed the rebel forces from their defenses at Yorktown [and] Williamsburg on the James and York river peninsula," the paper commented on May 11, "and having thus secured a comparatively unobstructed road to Richmond, we dare say that before the expiration of the present week the victorious army of General McClellan will be resting in that city." Once that occurred, "it will be such a blow as will require only the rout of the army of Beauregard at Corinth [Mississippi], or wherever it may be, to close up the rough work of this war." For once, the *Herald* and the *New York Times* concurred. "McClellan's policy is yielding its excellent fruits," the paper declared on May 19. "Richmond is doomed, and everybody knows it. . . . This week, it is thought, will open the last seal, and pour utter ruin on the Confederacy."[69]

Like most Northerners, abolitionists were paying close attention to the advance of the Army of the Potomac. On May 9, William Lloyd Garrison opened the annual meeting of the American Antislavery Society by heralding the news of the Confederate withdrawal up the Peninsula. "I congratulate you upon the tidings which have come to us from Yorktown," he proclaimed. As good as the news was, however, Garrison and other speakers reminded the abolitionist audience that their work remained unfinished. In fact, with the Union army closing in on Richmond, there was a new sense of urgency lest the war end without emancipation. "There is [yet] to be something more glorious than any retreat of the enemy either from Yorktown or any part of our country," Garrison proclaimed, "and that is the retreat of slavery from our country and the world."[70]

Famed abolitionist and runaway slave William Wells Brown reminded the convention audience that when the war began Northerners tried to keep blacks out of the fight. "Yet scarcely had you got into conflict with the South, when you were glad to receive the news that contrabands brought." Brown pointed out that newspapers frequently credited the enslaved community with the information in their dispatches. The moment runaways came into camp, they were asked for information, "and the news is greedily taken in, from the lowest officer or soldier in the army, up to the Secretary of War." What was more, "the black man welcomes your armies and your fleets, takes care of your sick, [and] is ready to do anything" to help.

Wendell Phillips agreed: "Yes, [the black man] has shown in every way that he recognizes the Union is indefeasibly on his side." From the start, "they saw, with the instinctive sagacity of self-interest . . . that this quarrel on our part could mean nothing but liberty to them." Making the same point, the *Chicago Tribune*'s Peninsula correspondent maintained that slaves "all along the route" of the Union army had been helping wounded Union soldiers and demonstrated "unceasing readiness" to aid the troops. Directing sharp criticism at Democrats who wished to fight the war without the aid of blacks, the correspondent sarcastically mocked their sentiments. "Them pesky niggers again, they will keep messing in the white man's war!"[71]

To ensure that the war would not end before the slaves were emancipated, congressional radicals continued to push for the passage of the second confiscation bill. Most of the debate continued to revolve around constitutional questions. Challenges by Democrats and other conservatives forced the radicals to repeatedly argue that the Constitution granted Congress the ability to liberate the slaves as a war measure. After nearly two months of debate, nearly every congressman in the House and Senate had explained his interpretation of the Constitution.

"This never ending gabble about the sacredness of the Constitution is becoming intolerable," Indiana representative George Julian declared on May 23, arguing that the legal debate was a mask. "I must regard much of this clamor about the violation of the Constitution on our part as the sickly higgling of pro-slavery fanatics, or the poorly disguised rebel sympathy of sniveling hypocrites." The antislavery Hoosier had won his seat in an 1860 election landslide, giving him a mandate to boldly proclaim that Republicans would continue to "seek earnestly to use the present opportunity to get rid of [slavery] forever."[72]

By the end of May, Massachusetts senator Charles Sumner, who for months had harangued the president about the military necessity for emancipation, was quickly losing hope that Lincoln would act. With McClellan apparently poised to win the war, Sumner became one of the staunchest supporters of Congress using its war powers to eliminate slavery. Unfortunately, with Union armies advancing on all fronts, time appeared to be running out. "When claiming these powers for Congress," Sumner told the Senate, "it must not be forgotten that there is a limitation of time with regard to their exercise. Whatever is done against the rebels in our character as belligerents under the Rights of War, must be done during war, and not after its close. Naturally, the Rights of War end with the war." God, he maintained, "offers to nations, as to individuals, opportunity, *opportunity*, OPPORTUNITY. . . . Do not fail to seize it."[73]

Reminding senators that war and slavery had a long and complex relationship, Sumner proclaimed, "By the old Rights of War . . . freemen were made slaves; but by the Rights of War which I ask you to declare, slaves will be made freemen." Over in the House, Charles B. Sedgwick represented a strongly antislavery New York district, and like Sumner, he called attention to the historic relationship between war and slavery. "The negro has never failed to respond with alacrity and bravery to a call to arms when the proffered reward was freedom," he asserted. "I might cite abundant historical examples to show that no civilized nation ever failed, when entering upon hostilities with a State having the institution of slavery, as a first step toward weakening the enemy to proclaim the freedom of the slaves."[74]

With the war apparently won, however, Democrats and conservatives deplored any effort to pass a confiscation bill, which now seemed unwarranted. The Democratic *Boston Herald* argued that Sumner's new sense of urgency had startled Congress, and "it is evident that the radical element is growing desperate, at least in the Senate." Radical Republicans, the *New York Herald* argued on May 22, "are still devoted to the . . . purpose of pushing this war into an abolition crusade, because they fully understand that, with the restoration of the revolted States as they were in the Union, there is an end of the political power of abolitionism. . . . The radical anti-slavery element in both houses would be pretty effectually silenced. This is the special danger which just now threatens this abolition faction."[75]

There was no need for emancipation, Massachusetts Unionist representative Benjamin F. Thomas told Congress: "Our armies and navies are victorious. The war seems to be drawing to a close. There is reasonable ground to hope that before the next session of Congress, the power of this rebellion will be broken, and the sword have substantially done its work." Ohio Democrat representative Samuel S. Cox agreed: "Are we to be deceived by the prevarications of this Congress in regards to extreme measures. . . . Are these extreme measures to be taken as the Army advances with its triumphant flag?" After Union successes at Yorktown and Williamsburg, the Democratic *Detroit Free Press* condescendingly asserted: "Let the small abolition fry stop their barking, and turn in and try to act as decent as possible."[76]

The prospect of the war ending without emancipation thoroughly alarmed the radicals, and thus they argued that any peace with the South would be short lived if the government left slavery intact. "Late victories give assurance that ere long the rebellion will be crushed," Minnesota representative William Windom conceded. "It will then be for us to say whether we shall have enduring peace, or a mere armed truce, to be followed by another war, more bloody and terrible than the present." Windom was considered a moderate, but he now sounded more radical. If proslavery Southerners returned to Congress, he warned, their "political demands will be renewed and resisted, and a never-ending controversy will be the result." George Julian agreed, maintaining that "the mere suppression of this rebellion will be an empty mockery of our sufferings and sacrifices, if slavery shall be spared to canker the heart of the nation anew, and repeat its diabolical deeds." Those who still opposed emancipation, he warned, "would put back the chains upon every slave made free by our Army [and] would completely re-establish the slave power over the national Government as in the evil days of the past."[77]

Other Republicans doubted that McClellan was about to win the war. Even with the loss of Richmond, they maintained, Southerners would continue to resist and would win European recognition. "I see a cloud in the East—from foreign nations," Sumner wrote to Orestes A. Brownson, a conservative Catholic who had become a strong critic of slavery. "Nothing but great triumphs, & a positive policy on Slavery can save us from some form of intervention." Ohio representative John A. Gurley agreed, maintaining that emancipation was still a military necessity. "The truth is," he told Congress, "the delay of our army . . . to strike decisive blows against the rebels was . . . erroneously interpreted [by European countries] as an indication that we had not the power or the skill to crush them out; and now, unless we close the contest substantially within a few months . . . I feel confident . . . we may look for foreign intervention in some form."[78]

Despite the fear of a prolonged war and foreign intervention, when Republicans shifted from legal and moral arguments to focus on the military necessity of emancipation, they most often did so by pointing out the military activities of African Americans. In a letter to the *Philadelphia Press*, Secretary of the Senate John W. Forney insisted that Democrats who opposed emancipation were not of the same mind as Democrats in the army. "They almost universally concede that [escaped slaves] have been faithful and useful." An ex-Democrat, Forney claimed that he had recently happened upon a former colleague and Union officer and that they had discussed the confiscation bill. "Do not these legislators know," Forney quoted his unnamed friend, "that our best information comes from the contraband blacks? Do they not know that this intelligence, often conveyed at risk of life, has saved thousands of our Union soldiers?" Pushing for both emancipation and the use of black troops, Forney pointed out that "France employs the Algerines, England the natives of India and the blacks, and the rebels of this country their own slaves . . . for military purposes. Thus, not only the custom of other nations, but the example of traitors on our own soil."[79]

News from the Peninsula continued to strengthen such arguments. "It is by the hands of slaves," New York representative Alfred Ely claimed, "that these multiplied entrenchments are erected, which meet us at every point of our progress. It is slaves who perform all the duties of the enemy's camp, and in instances not in a few, it is by slaves that his artillery is worked against our brave soldiers."[80]

Reports that the Confederates were not only using slaves to build fortifications but were also forcing them to act as sharpshooters, artillerymen, and soldiers continued to be a mainstay in speeches by congressmen who favored the confiscation and liberation of southern slaves. "A vital element of the strength of the rebels consists in their slaves, California representative Aaron Sargent observed. Bondsmen "dig their entrenchments, drag and load cannon, and as has been known in several recent instances, use as soldiers to shoot down the defenders of the Union." Abolitionist New Hampshire representative Edward H. Rollins reminded Congress that "thousands of negro slaves are forced to dig trenches before our lines, exposed . . . to shot and shell, or to stand upon the ramparts and man the guns, while their masters skulk behind the works." Referring to one widely reported episode during the Yorktown siege, Rollins claimed that "at the bayonet's point they are thrust forward to meet the unerring bullets of our sharpshooters. . . . The revolver glares at them . . . behind, and the telescopic rifle fixes its steady glare upon them before." Rollins blamed Congress for allowing such cruelties and for letting the South use slaves to its advantage. "This we do because we are so scrupulous of the constitutional rights of slave owners," he maintained.[81]

"They build fortifications for the rebels, why not for us?" Minnesota's newly radical William Windom asked. "They relieve rebel soldiers of nearly all the fatigue duties of war. Why should they not aid ours? They man rebel batteries. Why not ours?" Michigan representative F. C. Beamen agreed. Emancipate the slaves "and you end the struggle. Release them from their fetters, and allow them to dig your trenches and your fortifications, and you save the lives of your soldiers by the same act that weakens your enemies. It seems to me that a proposition so plain as this needs little argument or illustration to enforce it."[82]

Beamen considered emancipation not only a military necessity but an act of justice for people who had demonstrated their desire to help the North win the war. "It is too late to [argue] that [slaves] are satisfied with their condition," he maintained. "The constant arrival of deserters into our camps . . . sufficiently refute such pretenses. . . . Freedom to the slaves of rebel masters would be but simple justice, because they are faithful [to the Union]." Referring to the military intelligence brought to army commanders by runaways, Beamen maintained that slaves were "waiting patiently for an opportunity to serve their country, and have repeatedly communicated to the Government information of the highest importance." Unless they had worked on Confederate fortifications, Windom pointed out, the First Confiscation Act did not liberate all the "slaves who have come within our lines and brought valuable intelligence of the designs and movements of the enemy." Even more slaves "would have gladly built our fortifications, saved our soldiers many a weary day's labor, and rendered us the most efficient aid" if they had been offered emancipation as the reward. Because the government was technically only freeing slaves who had labored for the Confederate army, the others "have been told by our actions, if not our words, 'you must stay with your rebel masters and support them while they madly strive to overthrow the government.'"[83]

Should Congress continue to stall, New Hampshire's Edward H. Rollins warned, the slaves might return to the service of their masters. "These slaves have hearts, they feel; they have minds, they think. They know what all this war is about," he explained. If Congress did not pass the confiscation bill, even though slaves repeatedly aided the Union army, southern blacks might become disillusioned with the North. "If you force this despair upon them, they will seek to make their servitude endurable by faithful devotion to their masters, and by their lives and their labors they will hope to gain some favor at the hand of those whom they serve."[84]

The slaves understood why their masters seceded, Rollins claimed, and had demonstrated that "they know [the war] is waged to perpetuate the dismal night of their servitude." Therefore, "they offer us aid and [are] grateful . . . [for] the privilege of serving us." And yet the government had not rewarded them with emancipation. "Disguise it as you may," Beamen maintained, "you have thus far, in effect, compelled that unfortunate people to be disloyal. You have compelled them to be traitors. You have compelled them to dig trenches and erect fortifications for the enemy. You have compelled them to [man artillery] that has sent death and destruction into the midst of our own people. Is this course sound policy?" the Michigan representative demanded to know. "Is it justice? Is it humanity? Is it statesmanship?"[85]

By the last week of May, the Senate had debated and amended Lyman Trumbull's confiscation bill to the point of exhaustion. It became clear to the radicals that they were unlikely to get a version comprehensive enough to emancipate most slaves. Meanwhile, the House neared a vote on its version of the bill. Republican leaders in the Senate, therefore, decided on May 21 to take up debate on a new tax bill, put aside their confiscation bill, and wait to vote on whatever version the House was able to pass. The strategy failed. Although the House passed a bill allowing for the confiscation of Rebel property, it did not apply to slaves. On May 26, by a mere four votes, the House rejected the bill that would have emancipated all slaves whose masters were in rebellion.[86]

The legislation did not die, however. Republican leaders sent it back into committee. With Union armies successfully advancing on almost all fronts, and with McClellan's army preparing to assault the Confederate capital, supporters of the confiscation bill apparently needed more proof that emancipation was a military necessity. "We find in the press the wildest discrepancy of opinion as to the effect the war is going to have on the security of slavery and on the public estimate of that institution," the *Boston Daily Journal* observed as the Army of the Potomac settled in front of Richmond. While "one class of papers persist on putting abolition and secession" in the same abhorrent category, "others maintain that a sweeping edict of emancipation is absolutely necessary to the work of suppressing the rebellion and that the loyal community will soon see and recognize this fact. Between these views are all shades of differences, and continually changing at that." The military successes out west and McClellan's advance on the Peninsula seemed to weaken the military necessity argument. On the other hand, the activity of blacks during the campaign was also providing emancipationists with arguments to the contrary. The editors of the *Boston Daily Journal* wondered if "the number of those who consider slavery as a prop to the rebellion, which ought to be . . . remedied, [has] increased, or diminished during the war?"[87]

The results of the Peninsula Campaign would likely help to settle the debate. Together with Union military successes elsewhere, if McClellan captured the city he could conceivably end the war, or at the very least legitimize the strategy of winning by respecting southern property rights, including slavery. If so, emancipation legislation would die, President Lincoln would not strike against slavery, and, as Charles Sumner feared, the opportunity to free the slaves as a war measure would be lost. As for how the progress of the war would influence the emancipation question, the *Boston Daily Journal* asserted, "We can only state what has been done, what is going on, and leave the rest for the future."[88]

"Their own responsibility"

As Congress debated, McClellan established his headquarters at White House, the plantation home of General Robert E. Lee's son, William H. F. "Rooney" Lee, and the site of George Washington's courtship of the widow Custis. It was located on the Pamunkey River, astride the Richmond—West Point railroad. After the Battle of Eltham's Landing, the Army of the Potomac secured West Point, where the railroad began and the Pamunkey flowed into the York River. Union supplies now moved smoothly up the York and Pamunkey Rivers to White House Landing, where laborers unloaded them, placed them on railroad cars, and delivered them to Union troops establishing their lines in front of Richmond.[89]

When Union soldiers had first arrived at the site two weeks earlier, they found a tranquil farm with about one hundred slaves left behind by General Lee's family. "There has been about a dozen of families of slaves lived here," Pennsylvania soldier James Graham wrote home from White House, noting that it was mostly "the women and children [who] still remain." According to the *Baltimore American* correspondent, the venerable Virginia family had "told [their slaves] the usual stories about what the Yankees would do with them . . . but all these stories had no effect." The overseer, a man named Jedo, was still on the plantation trying to retain control. He "told the darkies not to cook anything for the Yankies," Luther Furst recorded in his diary. Nevertheless, the slaves "were very kind to us & [gave] us corn cake, eggs, fresh herring, & salmon. They catch any [amount] of fish here in large sums."[90]

Referring to the infamous character in *Uncle Tom's Cabin*, a *Philadelphia Inquirer* correspondent described Jedo as having "the look of Legree" and reported that he told the slaves "he would cut them to pieces" for aiding the Federals. In response, the slaves informed the northern troops. "A corporal [then] went to him, and . . . threaten[ed] to drown him," the *Inquirer* claimed. The action won over the slaves, who now "all obey everything a soldier tells them, and seem very grateful for kind words spoken." They "refuse any longer to recognize [the overseer's] authority." The *New York World* correspondent noted that if Jedo kept trying to punish the slaves, "there will be one less slavedriver."[91]

The living conditions on the Lee family plantation appalled Luther Furst. "The more I see of slavery, the more I think it should be abolished," he remarked. Oliver Wilcox Norton described the "long rows of 'quarters,'" which were nothing more than "log huts with no windows but holes in the walls and only a mud floor." New York officer Richard Tylden Auchmuty noted, "Their quarters look like a village of pigsties." An *Inquirer* correspondent claimed that Rooney Lee's slaves were "ragged, dirty, and the smallest [were] nearly naked." Most had never been off the plantation their entire lives. "There were all sorts of darkies there," Norton wrote home, "stalwart field hands, old worn out men, laughing, careless 'Topsies' carrying buckets of water on their heads, strong-limbed boys, and little toddlers running around [barely clothed]." Norton added that they "were a happy set of darkies when they learned that they were free."[92]

Rhode Island soldier Elisha Hunt Rhodes attended "an outdoor jubilee meeting held by the Negroes" at White House. Rhodes noted how the slave preacher delivered a sermon that was "not exactly Scripture, but it came near the truth. Our chaplain addressed the slaves, and the scene was a wild one." The *Inquirer* correspondent added: "The contrabands gather around the camps and listen to the music and drill with as much interest as a boy when he pays his first visit to a menagerie. They already look upon the soldiers with a kind of veneration and fear." The *Principia* correspondent described a joyous scene at White House: "We found most of the negroes in a high state of glee. They felt, on the arrival of the Union Army, that their chains were broken."[93]

These positive interactions between the Army of the Potomac and Peninsula slaves once again encouraged more runaways, and it did not take long for the number of African Americans at White House Landing to multiply exponentially. The *New York Herald* correspondent reported that fugitives "come through the enemy lines from Richmond constantly, and give much information as to the designs, force and spirit of the rebels." One claimed to be General Magruder's slave. He supposedly "got disgusted with working for the rebel commander, and thought he would try Union service for a change."[94]

Other slaves coming into Union lines in May 1862 also claimed that their owners were high-ranking Confederates. The *Boston Herald* correspondent told of a runaway who provided military intelligence and who claimed General Lee owned him. When he arrived, "he was driving a four-horse team containing a trunk and some private property belonging to Gen. Lee," the paper noted. Another fugitive, William A. Jackson, claimed to be a coachman for Confederate president Jefferson Davis. Jackson came into Federal lines near Fredericksburg while the southern army was abandoning Yorktown. He provided information about Rebel troop dispositions around Richmond and quickly became something of a celebrity. Many northern papers told his story and reveled in his assessment of the Davis family as distraught with recent Confederate losses. At the annual meeting of the American Antislavery Society, Williams Wells Brown received a hearty laugh from the audience when he quipped about the fact that Northerners now knew "so much about Jefferson Davis and Mrs. Davis and the little Davises." Eventually Jackson traveled as an abolitionist speaker, including a visit to Britain in late 1862.[95]

As the Federals finished their march up the Peninsula, the once-quaint White House plantation underwent a transformation. "The visit of our army here," the *Boston Herald* reported at the end of May, "and the establishment of the grand depot . . . has changed it, as if by magic, into a temporary village. . . . Hundreds of contraband negroes assist in the discharging of vessels." As at Fort Monroe, able-bodied men were put to work unloading ships and performing other manual labor. Union soldier Edward A. Acton claimed that "nearly all" the laborers were escaped slaves and that there were "hundreds of them." He vividly described "the contraband women and children in their camp flitting from tent to tent and their clear ringing laugh falling musically upon my ear."[96]

Within five miles of White House, Michigan soldier John Berry's regiment arrived on another large plantation, which held over one hundred slaves. The owner was a man named Garlick, and he had fled before the arrival of Yankee troops. "Part of the males he took with him," Berry noted in his diary; "the rest with all the female slaves he left behind." The officer and his comrades were curious about the slaves, so they "roamed all over the plantation to the different cabins occupied by the familys & different specimens of the negro race." Berry observed "a number of slaves of mixed blood. Indeed I saw but few of the younger slaves but showed considerable mixture with the anglo saxon race." They were "in the best of spirits & . . . highly pleased to see the Union soldiers."

However, before Garlick left, he had made sure to tell his slaves the common lie that the Federals "would cut their ears off and then send them off to Cuba" to labor. "On the first arrival of the Yankees the negroes here fully expected this was to be done," Berry noted, but the developing relationship with Union soldiers was again critical in erasing those perceptions. "They soon found out the delusion they had been laboring under," Berry continued. "They were now regaling these same ear cutting Yankees with the cakes & cooked chickens of their late masters which the soldiers readily pay in large price for. . . . In fact these negroes were now making more money than they have ever seen before."

This exposure to southern slaves impressed the Michigan soldier. Throwing off their slave garments, Berry observed, "the negroes have appropriated to themselves their late masters wardrobes" and were now act-

Group of contrabands at Allen's farmhouse. Union soldiers and slaves during the Peninsula Campaign. (Library of Congress)

ing on their newfound freedom. "Many of the younger folks were getting married, while a great many of the young males were hiring out to Northern officers as cooks and servants." Some of the older slaves had decided to stay on the plantation to harvest the wheat. "Whether the negro is capable of self government or not," Berry mused, they seemed to be acting "on their own responsibility, not only here but [also] . . . on all the neighboring plantations."[97]

"Breathless with anxiety"

McClellan had begun his campaign over a month and a half earlier with the goal of getting to West Point and White House Landing before the Confederates had a chance to concentrate in his front. He had failed to do so, thanks in part to his own timid generalship and in part to the fortifications, largely constructed by slave labor. The general hoped to restore the Union by respecting slave property, "dodg[ing] the nigger," and "hav[ing] nothing to do with" blacks.[98] If he had pushed rapidly up the Peninsula and captured Richmond, it is possible that he could have done so and made emancipation highly unlikely.

However, McClellan's halting campaign was providing yet more evidence that emancipation was a military necessity. In May 1862, Northerners continued to read about slave-built fortifications that hindered the progress of their army as well as reports that Confederates were using slaves in combat. Despite the racist sentiments of northern soldiers, as well as the frequently cruel treatment of African Americans behind the lines, the developing relationship between slaves and the Army of the Potomac was increasingly positive. Because of this, runaways continued to flow into Union lines. Slaves understood that their freedom was dependent on the Federal army, and thus they eagerly offered their services. Soldiers and newspaper correspondents informed the northern population about the valuable assistance and morale-building support that slaves were providing the army. The activities of African Americans on the Peninsula were advancing the cause of their freedom.

Nevertheless, with Union armies marching victoriously in nearly every theater of war, McClellan and his anti-emancipationist military strategy might still prevail if he captured Richmond just now as the confiscation bill was defeated and was stuck in congressional committee again. With the church bells of Richmond close enough for Union soldiers to hear in their camps, such a possibility appeared increasingly likely. "The army has been rapidly advanced within the past two days," the *New York Herald* reported on May 24; "we are on the eve of our greatest struggle."[99]

The nation closely observed the situation, and newspaper editors continued to tie the campaign to the emancipation debate. "A few more days," the Democratic *Boston Herald* argued, "and we may expect that Gen. McClellan will have driven the enemy from their strongholds. . . . Disturbing questions should be allowed to subside," and the country should unite to see the work finished. "All extreme men and measures," the paper insisted, "should be avoided." The *Philadelphia Public Ledger* maintained that the impending doom of the Confederacy should make even "the South itself . . . never again believe in 'slavery as a source of power.'"[100] If McClellan could quickly capture Richmond, emancipation would prove to be militarily unnecessary and the war might terminate with slavery intact.

However, as the *New York Herald* also reported from White House Landing, "contraband intelligence represents . . . that Richmond itself is all fortifications." The *Philadelphia Inquirer* concurred: "[The runaways] continue to come within our lines, represent the [southern] force in Richmond to be a large one, and [insist] that they certainly intend fighting us. Their fortifications are said to be extensive ones, and the current impression among [the slaves] is that a hard battle is before us." Other Peninsula correspondents made the same observation and noted that blacks predicted a Rebel attack near the Chickahominy River. "The nation," the *Boston Daily Advertiser* maintained on May 23, "is breathless with anxiety to hear the story which Richmond is soon to tell."[101]

AN INVALUABLE ALLY

LATE MAY–JULY 1862

7

"Robert Meekum and his wife Diana are the leading colored people on this plantation," the *New York Times* reported on May 25, 1862, from White House, Virginia. Robert served as slave "advisor . . . in both spiritual and temporal affairs" on the property, and military officials engaged him to help organize the slaves to work for the U.S. army. The elderly couple (Diana was eighty-three) lived in a cabin crammed with "several children, grandchildren, and hens and chickens" and claimed to have never heard of abolitionism. Diana "did not know what the word meant," the *Times* reporter noted. Years earlier, she had had a child sold away from her, and a captain on a northern vessel plying the Pamunkey River tried to ease her pain by telling her "that I should lib to see de day when all would be free; but it nebber come." In fact, Diana had never even been away from White House Plantation. With her husband assisting the Army of the Potomac as it prepared to assault the Confederate capital, she happily exclaimed, "Now I know I hab a Lord and Savior, and I thank him." Her master, General Robert E. Lee's son, Rooney Lee, was serving in the Confederate army, and when the correspondent asked if she was worried that he might be killed, she indifferently replied, "De Lord['s] will must be done unto him."[1]

As the Peninsula Campaign neared its climax, the Meekums were just two of thousands of slaves providing invaluable services to both armies. General Robert E. Lee's strategy for driving the Federals away from Richmond remained dependent on the continued impressment of slaves to work on fortifications, and black workers staffed the Confederacy's overburdened hospitals. Yet slaves also continued to vex their owners by running away and aiding the Yankees. Blacks labored to keep McClellan's supply line running smoothly, offered valuable military intelligence to the Federals, and helped prevent the destruction of the Army of the Potomac's Fifth Corps.

"Who are our friends?"

While the Army of the Potomac sat outside of Richmond, the U.S. Navy operated freely on the James River east of Drewry's Bluff. Yankee ships shelled plantations on either side of the river, driving off the white inhabitants but attracting great interest from the slaves. "Hundreds of slaves could be seen in the vicinity of City Point, begging for deliverance with white flags," the *Philadelphia Press* reported. The warships did their best, but many slaves "could not be rescued for the want of means of transportation." Some slaves were fortunate enough to secure passage to Hampton and Fort Monroe. Peninsula master Edmund Ruffin, who had been so surprised at "the readiness of the slaves to flee" back in 1861, now conceded that "the number, & general spreading of such abscondings of slaves are far beyond any previous conceptions."[2]

Richard Eppes's James River plantations were especially hard hit by the Federal navy. His City Point "estate was broken up, the negroes leaving en masse, immediately after the first bombardment." On his various plantations, Eppes lost field hands, skilled slaves, and "excellent" house servants ranging in ages from one to seventy. They were all "able bodied and in excellent health," Eppes bemoaned, "and taken as a whole, were as likely and valuable as is to be found on any estate on James River."[3]

One slave who ran away from Eppes was thirteen-year-old Richard Slaughter, whom the owner described as "well grown for his years." Slaughter, who eventually served in the U.S. army during and after the Civil War, recalled the day his family escaped. "It happened this a-way," he explained; "the gunboats would fire on the towns and plantations and run the white folks off." His father "and three or four men left in the darkness and got aboard." Their success proved that it was safe to go to the Federal boats, and soon thereafter, Slaughter and his mother and cousins fled as well. "After that they would carry all the colored folks [away] . . . and put 'em behind the Union lines." Slaughter served as a water boy until he joined the army in 1864.[4]

Slaughter's family was fortunate to have escaped together. Eventually, the navy had to give priority to those who were most able bodied. Male slaves, Eppes recalled, "were mostly taken aboard the gunboats" to be used as laborers. Women and children left behind awaited transport on the James, turning Eppes's estate into "a depot" for escaped slaves. By the end of May, Edmund Ruffin soberly concluded, "We may expect that we shall thus lose all the slaves that can have access to the enemy's army or out-post."[5]

The situation was much the same on the north side of the Peninsula.

Richard Slaughter. This photograph was taken when the Works Progress Administration interviewed the elderly gentleman in 1936. The size and robustness that Richard Eppes noticed in the thirteen-year-old enslaved child is still noticeably apparent in the eighty-seven-year-old army veteran. Today the former runaway slave rests in Hampton National Cemetery alongside fellow U.S. veterans. (Courtesy of Hampton University Archives)

So many slaves were now at White House Landing that a correspondent observed runaways and free blacks unloading all the transports. "These negroes would commence at daylight and work until dark," he related, "everyone arguing, ordering, singing, or shouting." The *Philadelphia Press* correspondent noticed that many of the slaves were replacing their slave rags with Union uniforms, "some of them completely, others partially. . . . I apprehend the slaves of the rebel Lee are much better clothed now than when he was here to look after their wants." The army divided the laborers into groups of twenty or thirty and placed them under the direction of a black overseer, whose pay was determined by how much labor his gang performed. The men spent their day rolling barrels and carrying boxes, and at night they slept on the barges they had unloaded. The *Philadelphia Press* correspondent considered the black laborers a "useful appendage to our army" and claimed that "every one to whom I have spoken would fight for 'Lincum,' if he was called upon."[6]

Thus hundreds of fugitive slaves had come to the Army of the Potomac, but they were not the reinforcements McClellan desired. Stalled before Richmond, the general grew increasingly frustrated by Lincoln's refusal to send more troops. In particular, McClellan coveted the roughly 35,000

Supply vessels at anchor, White House, Virginia, 1862. Young men congregate at the riverbank, while in the background a crew of black laborers is clearly visible resting on the deck of a recently unloaded cargo ship. (Library of Congress)

men stationed at Manassas under the command of Irvin McDowell, as well as the 8,000 soldiers serving with Nathaniel Banks in the Shenandoah Valley. Lincoln, however, continued to worry about the safety of Washington, and Confederate general Robert E. Lee had sent General Thomas J. "Stonewall" Jackson into the Shenandoah Valley to exploit those fears. After a series of successful engagements, Jackson managed to drive General Banks's command across the Potomac River and appeared to threaten the U.S. capital. Lincoln was alarmed, especially with his largest army sitting in front of Richmond doing little more than collecting runaway slaves. He refused to send McClellan reinforcements and encouraged him to "either attack Richmond or give up the job and come to the defense of Washington."[7]

Lee and Jackson brilliantly manipulated Lincoln's fears, but McClellan, for once, understood the situation. All his military intelligence indicated that Jackson's campaign was merely a decoy. He explained to the president, "The object of the movement is probably to prevent reinforcements being sent to me. All the information obtained from balloons, deserters, prisoners, and contraband agrees in the statement that the mass of the rebel troops are still in the immediate vicinity of Richmond, ready to defend it." Unworried by Stonewall Jackson's movements, McClellan continued to follow his own timetable.[8]

McClellan had identified for the president the sources of his military intelligence: deserters, prisoners, and especially runaway slaves. Fugitives provided details about road conditions around Richmond, offered directions, scouted for the Federals, and pinpointed the locations of Confederate troops.[9] "It is well known that these negroes have a more thorough knowledge of the enemy's country than any white men," the *New York Evening Post* told its readers as McClellan's army approached Richmond. The paper insisted that runaways provided more reliable information than Confederate deserters. "Their means of getting information are certainly better than those of the average privates in the rebel army." Besides, white Southerners who offered assistance to Union troops could not be trusted. Massachusetts officer Charles Harvey Brewster asserted that he "would no more take the word of a white man [who was] a native of Virginia than I would the greatest [liar] I ever knew, if he claimed to be in favor of the Union."[10]

As McClellan developed plans for laying siege to Richmond, he sent various commands to reconnoiter Confederate forces on the roads, streams, and rivers around the city. These squads repeatedly relied on blacks for directions, to scout ahead, and to warn of Confederate forces nearby. On May 18, for example, a Union sailor informed a small detachment of Federal infantry that a body of Confederate troops was forming in line of battle near them on the south side of the Pamunkey River. "I had left a small picket on that side," Major George D. Willard of the 19th U.S. Infantry reported, "and the non-commissioned officer in command sent a negro to ascertain if the report of troops was correct." Stealthily making his way through familiar woods, the slave returned and warned of "a large force

Allen Pinkerton and staff converse with an African American man. This 1862 photograph was taken in New Kent County during the Peninsula Campaign. The Union spy chief sits in the background smoking a pipe. (Library of Congress)

of soldiers drawn up in the road." Willard withdrew his small detachment on the opposite side of the river and retreated safely.[11]

One of McClellan's immediate priorities was to establish communication with naval forces operating on the James. On May 25, Lieutenant Frank C. Davis led a group of eleven hand-picked men from the 3rd Pennsylvania Cavalry to link up with the gunboats. Surrounded by Confederates as they made their way through Charles City County, the troopers came within 300 yards of southern cavalry before a slave steered them safely away from the Rebels. A slave owned by Hill Carter of Shirley Plantation then guided the soldiers to the river landing on his master's property. As they traversed the plantation, Carter himself confronted the soldiers and demanded to know whether they were Confederate or Union troops. Carter claimed that he did not allow Rebel troops on his property because the Union gunboats shelled them and he feared an errant shot would destroy his house. Upon reaching the landing, two slaves rowed Lieutenant Davis out to the USS *Galena*. Once aboard, the cavalryman pinpointed for naval officers the position of the Army of the Potomac. When the men returned to McClellan's headquarters, they informed the general that the navy was unable to penetrate the river beyond Drewry's Bluff. Reporting on this episode and the assistance from the Peninsula's black community, the *Daily Cleveland Herald* told its readers that Lieutenant Davis "never could have performed [the] mission without such aid," and asked rhetorically, "Who are our friends?"[12]

Soon McClellan sent out another expedition led by signal corps officer Franklin Ellis to locate a position for signal flags to communicate with the navy. This time, the soldiers were unable to reach the river because Confederate cavalry, including forces led by Hill Carter Jr., aggressively patrolled the area. While the Union troopers were at Charles City Courthouse, a free black warned Ellis that the Confederates were aware of his operations and that they were coordinating efforts to capture his command. Hearing this, Ellis aborted the mission and returned to Union lines. He reported that he did not believe signal corps operations could be set up "by the usual methods" but advised establishing communications with the navy through use of balloons. "I am also convinced," he informed headquarters, "that many free negroes can be found who could be fully trusted with the transmission of messages in cipher."[13]

"Negroes should be employed night and day"

While McClellan tried to establish his lines and communications, the Confederates were determined to prevent the Army of the Potomac from beginning siege operations against Richmond as they had at Yorktown. McClellan had his army positioned on both sides of the Chickahominy River, and Confederate general Joe Johnston developed an elaborate plan for attacking the Union forces on the south side of the swampy waterway. The assault began on May 31 at Seven Pines, but the tactical orders were too complicated for Johnson's largely inexperienced soldiers to execute. During the two-day fight, McClellan shifted troops from the north side of the river to reinforce those on the south. The Union army held its ground, and the battle ended in stalemate. Aside from the realignment of McClellan's army, the most important result was that General Johnston was wounded. After the battle, McClellan learned from runaway slaves and rebel deserters that General Robert E. Lee had assumed command of the Confederate army.[14]

Soon after the battle, a *Boston Journal* correspondent reported how a Confederate sharpshooter near Seven Pines had shot at him and Union soldiers several times. "So last night," he explained, "about a dozen sharpshooters went down to the railroad and laid a trap for him." They managed to get him to expose his position, and the Yankees killed him. "So glad were the boys that they had got him (for it had become dangerous for a man to show himself) that the whole company turned out to receive the body, which proved to be a nigger's."[15]

This black sharpshooter was one of over 1,100 southern causalities suffered at the Battle of Seven Pines. Before the fight, sick and wounded Confederate soldiers had already overwhelmed Richmond's hospitals, and the impending battle for the Confederate capital promised to exhaust resources. Just as Southerners depended on slaves to do much of the labor on the city's fortifications, they also relied upon them to staff hospitals and care for wounded soldiers.

The laundresses, cooks, and nurses in Richmond's hospitals were mostly black, and as McClellan's army neared, doctors feared losing the services of their enslaved staffers. Hospital officials worried that the black laborers might flee to Union lines, but a larger concern was that their owners might remove them. On May 17, Dr. James B. McCaw, commander of Chimborazo (the largest military hospital in the Confederacy), explained to the Confederate surgeon general that he "only had two hundred and fifty-six cooks & nurses in my Hospitals, to take care of nearly four thousand sick soldiers." Making a desperate situation worse, he reported, "the owners of these slaves are threatening to remove them to the interior of the country to avoid losing them."[16]

Dr. McCaw could not allow the slaves to leave. "I am confident a large number will be removed in a few days unless measures are taken to prevent it." He wanted the government to impress the slaves he already had working, as well "as many others as may be needed." He warned officials, "This subject requires immediate action." Pressing the issue, McCaw claimed that "it will be entirely impossible to continue the hospital without them." The Confederate surgeon general agreed, arguing to officials, "If these negroes are permitted to leave, the hospitals will be abandoned & the sick left destitute of nurses." The dire warnings worked, and the slaves were impressed into Confederate service.[17]

Chimborazo had been highly dependent on slave labor since its creation. The facility covered forty acres and included 105 buildings constructed by slaves hired from Richmond's tobacco warehouses. Slaves also built the beds, tables, and other furnishings, and two slave well diggers named Morley and Cornelius provided the hospital's fresh water. On a daily basis, the enslaved workers at Chimborazo made soap, attended to the dairy, baked bread, raised crops, and herded cows and goats. The hospital had its own trading boat that plied the James River between Richmond and Lynchburg bartering cotton, yarn, shoes, and other items to obtain fresh vegetables and provisions for hospital patients. The crew consisted of eight slaves and one free black. Many of the disabled soldiers who worked as nurses at the facility could do little heavy work. For that reason, able-bodied black males were the most sought-after nurses in the hospital. The hospital's survival rate attests to its efficiency. At the end of the war, the facility had cared for 77,889 patients, of whom approximately 89 percent lived.[18]

Dr. McCaw was not the only Confederate officer in desperate need of laborers as the Union army prepared to assault Richmond. Upon taking command, General Lee ordered his army to improve the fortifications and build new ones around the city. "McClellan will make this a battle of posts," he explained to President Jefferson Davis. "It will require 100,000 men to resist the regular siege of Richmond, which would perhaps only prolong not save it." Lee wanted to prepare "a line that I can hold with part of our forces in front" and use the rest of his troops to attack McClellan's rear and flanks. However, Lee understood that white soldiers were unwilling to dig. "Our people are opposed to work," he told Davis. "Our troops, officers, community & press. All ridicule & resist it." Jefferson Davis agreed with the assessment. Explaining Lee's plans to his wife, the president remarked, "Politicians, newspapers, and uneducated officers have created such a prejudice in our Army against labor that it will be difficult" to get the soldiers to work until they learn the necessity from "sad experience."[19]

Lee and Davis hoped their soldiers would adapt and do the work, but General Magruder believed that blacks were the most skilled at building fortifications. "From the experience of a year," he explained, "I know that no defensive works of any strength can be expected of troops. It is as much as they will do to throw up such temporary field works as may be absolutely necessary in the presence of the enemy." In line with Lee's strategy, Magruder suggested that having fewer soldiers working on the lines would allow more troops to "operate in the rear and on the enemy's flanks." Magruder believed that "negroes should be employed night and day" on the fortifications because they "could render them really formidable." Furthermore, he offered the services of "one of my agents, a most efficient and effective man, who impressed for me a large number of negroes [while on the lower Peninsula] . . . and who knows all about [it]." He estimated that "several thousand negroes would be necessary" to work on Richmond's defenses.[20]

Two days after Magruder offered these suggestions, the Confederate secretary of war took action. Owners in several counties south of Richmond were notified that one-fourth of their slaves between the ages of sixteen and fifty would be impressed to work on the fortifications protecting the capital. Masters would receive twenty dollars a month per slave, the slaves would get "an ample supply of provisions," and the government would pay for their transportation. In addition, the Confederate government would be fully responsible for the full value of the slaves "should they escape to, or be injured by, the enemy." The War Department immediately dispatched agents to collect the laborers.[21]

As the Confederacy strengthened Richmond's fortifications, Northerners wondered why McClellan once again delayed an attack, and they grew anxious about the fate of the campaign. "No news from the Army near Richmond," the *Principia* reported on June 12, "excepting that a 'contraband' from that city, asserts that the rebels are making preparations for resistance." "Of course," the abolitionist paper quipped, "General McClellan will kindly wait till they are fully prepared." George Templeton Strong noted that no significant news had come from Richmond since the fight at Seven Pines. "We are not at all jolly today," he admitted. "People complain of McClellan's slow progress and wonder if he is not overmatched."[22]

As at Yorktown, Northerners learned that the Confederates were effectively using black labor to hold off the Army of the Potomac. The *New York Times* reported on June 1 that many "intelligent" runaway slaves claimed that the Confederate capital's defenses were incomplete, "but strenuous efforts were being put forth to render them sufficiently strong to resist our progress." The *Philadelphia Inquirer* noted: "The whole Rebel army and a large number of negroes are now working day and night digging ditches. They now are at work as busy as though their last ditch had not yet been dug." The paper's correspondent was confident that the city would soon fall but admitted that "the series of earthworks, rifle pits, forts &c., that the darkies have turned out for them are truly formidable."[23]

Meanwhile, Union forces were busy constructing their own fortifications. Because the northern army used black laborers to unload transports and keep supply lines open, white soldiers performed most of the work on Union defenses. As the summer wore on, northern soldiers unaccustomed to the unrelenting Virginia heat and humidity began to falter. As early as May 29, Pennsylvanian James Mitchell wrote home to warn his brother "not to enlist for it is hard to come down in this hot climate." It was difficult enough for soldiers who were growing "acclimated" to the conditions, "but for men to come here now and have to undergo the hardships we have it will kill half of them off." In June, Massachusetts officer Charles Harvey Brewster pointed out that "diarrhea and other sickness" had already weakened many men, and they struggled "to go out and pick and shovel 2 hours in the broiling sun." Brewster admitted to feeling the effects himself: "I have just got strength enough to walk [to the front] with the Company and sit down and broil for two hours and then come back again." The situation promised to only worsen. Pennsylvania officer George H. Selkirk informed his mother on June 23 that his black servant warned him that it was "a great [deal] warmer in August."[24]

Northern citizens wondered if Congress could not spare their soldiers from such duty in the harsh weather if they passed the confiscation bill. In a letter to the *Chicago Tribune* published on June 6, one Wisconsinite argued, "Thousands and thousands of [black] men are anxious to aid our army in making entrenchments . . . and yet, while every division of the army is suffering, and rendered comparatively inefficient" by the hard labor on the fortifications, the government still had not passed the confiscation bill. The *Cincinnati Gazette* added that when the South used their slaves to dig trenches, "they are as completely instruments of war as guns, spades, and wagons" and thus liable for confiscation as a necessity to win the war. Such sentiments were shared not only by the Republican Party but by "nearly all the supporters of the Government in the North." Many soldiers agreed: Pennsylvanian J. R. Sypher later recalled that the men grew frustrated with digging "knee-deep in the mud after exhausting marches and sleepless watchings, while all around them" were slaves willing to labor on the lines. Refusing to employ them on the trenches, Sypher maintained, was an "absurdity."[25]

With the army stalled yet again before Confederate fortifications largely constructed by slave labor, on June 17 the *New York World* published an editorial entitled "The Prolongation of the War as Affecting Slavery," arguing that as Northerners grew impatient they embraced increasingly radical sentiments. One indication of this, the paper maintained, was the "unprecedentedly strong anti-slavery deliverances" coming from many of the North's religious pulpits. Even more telling, the editor argued, was the change coming over northern soldiers. An anonymous officer in the Army of the Potomac reported that the "daily evidence of what I see before me" had changed his mind with regard to slavery. "I now think," the *World* quoted the officer, "if we wish to bring this rebellion to a speedy and successful close, that the sooner we adopt the most severe measures the better. I want to see Congress pass the confiscation bill, slavery abolished," and traitors punished. The *World* believed "these feelings are acquiring strength daily." The *Washington Sunday Morning Chronicle* agreed, asserting on June 22 that those who continued to battle against the confiscation bill were fighting a losing cause. "It will be rather hard to convince the masses," the editor asserted, that the government should do nothing to stop the South from using slaves to build fortifications which would inflict "carnage and death" on Union soldiers.[26]

"Long denied manhood"

With the Union army camped within eight miles of Richmond, Peninsula slaves continued to happily greet the soldiers. "We are now steaming up the Pamunkey," Union soldier Jacob Heffelfinger recorded. "The band has been on the deck all evening discoursing its best pieces, which affords infinite satisfaction to the large crowds of negro slaves . . . [who] congregate on the banks as we pass, attracted by the music." The slaves joyously welcomed every Union troop transport. "Their antics are curious and laughable," Heffelfinger condescendingly remarked. J. R. Sypher recalled that as his troop transport made its way to White House, slaves gathered on the riverbanks and "cheered each vessel as it passed by, swinging their hats and handkerchiefs in the air and sending forth exclamations of joy."[27]

On one Union vessel anchored near White House, another Yankee used racist caricatures to claim that blacks aboard were "always jolly and grinning." He noted a particular verbal "ejaculation" of the runaways. "'Yah! Yah!' says [one slave to another], 'dis yer's a heap better than Massa Coleman's'; whereupon [the other slave] performs an affirmative comedy of 'yah yahs,' and looks all teeth." Perhaps such joyous expressions were what led Union soldier Elisha Hunt Rhodes to describe the slaves as "queer people," but he also believed that blacks "seem to understand the war. They leave for Fortress Monroe as soon as they can get to our rear." The *New York Times* confirmed this assessment: "The contrabands in this neighborhood evidently appreciate the present state of things and are quite anxious to proceed with us to Richmond, or to any other point rather than return to the masters."[28]

Coming from a generation raised on virulently racist black minstrel shows, Union soldiers condescendingly viewed the fugitive slaves as a ready source of entertainment. "The negro quarters were always a popular place of resort after nightfall for all who wished to be amused," *Philadelphia Press* correspondent Joel Cook recalled. The hardworking African Americans at White House relaxed with songs and dances—but also challenged the racist assumptions of many soldiers by engaging in perceptive "stump speeches and arguments," which were not weakened by their improper grammar. "A negro is an exhaustless wit," Cook claimed, "and [the runaways were] brim-full of every kind of fun, [and they] talked politics, discussed the war, gave characters to their former masters, and settled the fate of Richmond nightly."[29]

Soldiers particularly enjoyed listening to older African Americans tell their stories. *New York Times* correspondent David W. Judd recalled a "grey haired toothless negro [who claimed to be] 102 years of age," who kept the men of the 33rd New York entertained as they sat outside of Richmond. Southern civilian Henry Clinton Sydnor later recalled that when he was a young boy a family slave, Uncle Americus, was believed to be over 100 years old and told the "most remarkable stories" about the Revolution. "I looked up to him with awe and admiration," Sydnor recalled, and "when the Yankees came, he was in all his glory." Looking back, the white Southerner realized that Americus largely embellished the tales and was a "master" at taking advantage of white credulity to survive. "He would always ask for alms when his story was ended."[30]

Virginia's slave owners could not understand why their slaves welcomed Union troops. "The delusion of the negroes is astonishing," Edmund Ruffin wrote. He concluded that the Yankees must have deceived them with promises of "enormous wages, plenty to eat and no work to do." The *Richmond Dispatch* also rhetorically emasculated the slaves by maintaining that those who ran away were only seeking freedom from work. "The Yankees have never understood the negro," the paper argued. Northerners assumed at the start of the war that slaves would participate in a "general insurrection." Because that did not happen, Union troops resorted "to the enticement of contrabands from their homes, in which they have been successful, simply on account of the contraband's childish love of novelty and his favorite idea that liberty means nothing to do." The *Dispatch* claimed that when the infantile runaways realized the northern army wanted them to work they would return to their masters.[31]

Many Yankees who observed African Americans on the Peninsula dismissed claims that runaways were simply avoiding work. The *New York Herald* correspondent reported that slaves near Richmond "escape as soon as the army arrives, and generally attach themselves to some of the officers in the capacity of servants." Union officer George H. Selkirk wrote his mother about "our little contraband" and claimed that "most every officer has a darkey" working for him. Cyrus S. Halderman, assistant to the Union military governor on the lower Peninsula, sounded even more enthusiastic: "No sooner was Yorktown in possession of our troops . . . than the 'contrabands' were set to work. . . . And from that time to the present a more desirable class of laborers has not been at our disposal." The blacks, he promised, "perform their duties with commendable alacrity. They are in almost every case willing, contented and happy." Blacks were replacing white laborers in the quartermaster's, commissary, harbormaster's, and medical director's departments and were working ten-hour days. While the *Richmond Dispatch* claimed that slaves fled to Union troops because of a "childish love of novelty," one Yankee commented on a black man at White House who was thrilled that he would receive wages. The expectation of "just recompense of his free labor" filled the runaway slave with optimism and an "exuberant glee upon attaining . . . his long denied manhood."[32]

"They were scared clear through and through"

In mid-June, as both armies made extensive use of black laborers to prepare for the coming battle, Lee discovered that McClellan's right flank (which was situated north of the Chickahominy River) was vulnerable. Rebel cavalry officer J. E. B. Stuart had led 1,200 troopers on a 150-mile reconnaissance around the Army of the Potomac. The daring officer destroyed Union supplies, gathered intelligence about McClellan's right flank, and captured over 200 Yankee prisoners. Based on Stuart's information, Lee decided that once his fortifications were strong enough, his first target would be the isolated Federal troops north of the Chickahominy and the Richmond–West Point railroad that served as McClellan's supply line.[33]

During J. E. B. Stuart's raid, a small detachment of troopers under Robert E. Lee's son, Rooney Lee (the owner of White House Plantation), was sent to Garlick's Landing on the Pamunkey River, approximately five miles northwest of White House. The raiders captured a handful of Union soldiers there, burned two Federal schooners, set a third one adrift, and destroyed twenty wagons loaded with food. The *New York Times* correspondent reported that "some negroes" were fighting in Lee's command when they attacked the Yankees at Garlick's, a statement that went unchallenged by the *Richmond Dispatch* when the paper reprinted the story a few weeks later.[34]

Stuart's raid is one of the most celebrated exploits of the Civil War, but *Philadelphia Press* correspondent Joel Cook recalled that "the enemy were particularly harsh toward negroes. Every one found was compelled to go along with them." Indeed, J. E. B. Stuart's official report listed the recapture of slaves as one of the successes of his expedition, and the raid caused considerable alarm among the runaways at White House Landing. "When they learned that the Confederates were likely to arrive," Union soldier Gilbert Adams Hayes recalled, "they were scared clear through and through." The soldier claimed that the fugitives immediately gathered their belongings and "filled the air with dismal groans." Some "prayed loudly and fervently, others, too badly scared to pray, uttered wild and incoherent ejaculations."[35]

In this vivid recollection, the gamble that African Americans took when they fled to the Federals becomes clear. If the Confederates were to destroy McClellan's army, the blacks would fall back into the hands of vindictive owners who felt betrayed by their slaves. Any paternalistic sentiments that masters may have held before the Peninsula Campaign were long shattered, and one can imagine that owners such as Cynthia Coleman, Richard Eppes, and Edmund Ruffin would have been particularly harsh on any recaptured slaves. Hayes's description of the terror-stricken community at White House demonstrates that the blacks understood their insecure and precarious status.

Nevertheless, while some blacks trembled in fear of Stuart and a handful may have fought with him, others were busy helping to stop him. At this point in the war, the Federal cavalry was vastly inferior to the Confederate cavalry and proved incapable of thwarting Stuart's bold raid. However, Union troopers stayed on Stuart's trail, forcing him to flee at breakneck speed. White citizens were unwilling to assist the Yankee cavalry track the Rebel horsemen and in fact they gave deceptive information to the Federals. As a result, Union troopers sought the aid of several blacks, who acted as guides through the Virginia countryside and supplied reliable information about the route of Stuart's men.[36]

The fear that Stuart's raid provoked did not reduce the number of slaves escaping to the Federals. Late in June, Edmund Ruffin was still complaining about runaways from both sides of the James River. He now believed that the Federals were collecting runaways not only to liberate slaves but also to "cause the loss of the growing crops, & of the wheat now ready for reaping, by taking away the needed laborers." Ruffin had heard about owners who had lost all or most of their bondsmen, and he concluded that the slaves' "credulity & disposition to abscond are epidemic— & I think it not unlikely . . . that every negro now remaining will follow." Just as Chimborazo's Dr. McCaw had feared, Ruffin and other planters decided to stop their losses by selling slaves who had not yet fled.[37]

White Virginians suspected another reason why the Army of the Potomac enticed slaves to run away. Observing the Federals using slaves as laborers and hearing some Northerners advocate more use of blacks in U.S. military service, the *Richmond Dispatch* warned that McClellan was arming runaway slaves. Abolitionists had long argued that emancipation was necessary because the South would arm its slaves on a larger scale; now the *Dispatch* turned the same argument against the Federals. Reporting unfounded rumors that the Yankees had organized a "battalion of negroes" in Williamsburg, the paper criticized McClellan for inciting servile insurrection. Demonstrating an ignorance of the history of slavery and warfare, the paper stated: "In no other war of modern times did the invading party ever arm the slave against the master." Waging war in such an "inhuman" fashion only reduced McClellan to the level of "captain of a huge horde of pirates." The use of blacks as troops, the paper threatened, "would indeed lead to the abolition of slavery; but it would be by the extermination of the slaves."[38] With southern defeats mounting in nearly every theater of war, the Army of the Potomac poised to strike at Richmond— and, with their slaves absconding in large numbers, white Virginians were clearly on edge over the fate of the Confederacy and the security of their slave property.

"That contingency will soon arrive"

Virginia's slave owners had ample reason to believe that the U.S. government would keep encouraging runaways. With Stonewall Jackson seemingly threatening Washington, J. E. B. Stuart riding a ring around the Union army, and McClellan's forces yet again stalled before slave-built fortifications, emancipationist sentiment in the North reached new heights. "In proportion to [the South's] continued resistance is Slavery endangered," Charles Sumner noted. He did not expect Southerners to surrender, and "the war, therefore must go on, & unless the slave states submit, Slavery will be directly abolished by military decree." The *New York Times* agreed. "The necessity of some action [against slavery] is admitted on all hands," the paper declared on June 5. "Probably not less than a hundred thousand slaves have been directly engaged in forwarding this rebellion. . . . It is very doubtful whether, in a military point of view, it could have attained anything like its present proportions without the labor and the aid of Southern slaves."[39]

Two days after Stuart's raid, the House of Representatives, led by the "abolition negro brigade of Congress," as the *New York Herald* derisively termed the radicals, finally passed a bill to emancipate slaves owned by Rebels. However, instead of voting on that legislation, the Senate attempted to amend the House's previously passed confiscation bill by including slaves as property liable for seizure. The senators had long exhausted the arguments over the necessity of the measure and the constitutionality of confiscation. Now, Illinois senator (and Lincoln confidant) Orville Hickman Browning focused the debate on whether the war powers claimed by the radical members of Congress more properly belonged to the president. "These necessities can be determined only by the military commander," he maintained. "It is not a legislative, but an executive function, and Congress has nothing to do with it." Browning considered it a matter of the proper balance of power in the federal government and deemed it "heresy" to believe otherwise. In response, Senator Charles Sumner insisted that Congress had the power to confiscate and liberate slaves and pointed out that the bill could not become law without executive approval, thus maintaining the balance of powers.[40] Unfortunately for the radicals, however, as McClellan stood on Richmond's doorstep, President Lincoln showed no outward signs of moving toward their position.

Even so, Lincoln's antipathy to slavery was not in doubt. Although he insisted that the war's objective was to maintain the Union, he had long denounced slavery on moral grounds. In recent months, he had supported several antislavery measures, including the prohibition of slavery in the District of Columbia as well as in the western territories. The president had pushed for compensated emancipation in the Border States and agreed to a treaty with Britain for the suppression of the international slave trade.[41] None of these actions, however, encouraged emancipationists to believe that he had changed his mind on the constitutionality of moving against slavery in the southern states.

In fact, his cautious stance on the whole slavery question infuriated abolitionists. In May, Lincoln publicly overruled General David Hunter, commander of a military district that included coastal areas of South Carolina, Georgia, and Florida, when that officer issued a military order proclaiming emancipation in his jurisdiction. In addition, despite the fact that Congress had prohibited the army from returning fugitive slaves, newspapers widely reported instances in which officers turned them away. Worse still, although slavery was now illegal in Washington, Lincoln approved of the rigid enforcement of the Fugitive Slave Law within the city.[42]

More important, the president had recently shown that he was apparently not yet convinced that emancipation was a military necessity. When he overruled Hunter on May 19, Lincoln declared it his responsibility to determine "whether at any time . . . it shall have become a necessity indispensable to the maintenance of the government" to liberate the slaves. That time had not yet arrived. On June 20, a small delegation of Quakers met with Lincoln in the White House to argue that emancipation was "indispensable to your success." The group presented the president with a memorial (written by William Lloyd Garrison) requesting him to use his war powers to emancipate the slaves. Lincoln agreed that slavery was immoral and hoped God would direct him but noted that the use of war powers might not be the best way to liberate the slaves.[43]

"Whenever the question of emancipation or the mitigation of slavery had been in any way alluded to," Secretary of the Navy Gideon Welles remarked, "[Lincoln] had been emphatic in denouncing any interference by the General Government with the subject." As Congress engaged in a final round of debates over the confiscation bill, Senator Browning met with the president to discuss the legislation. Lincoln and his old friend agreed that "Congress has no power over slavery in the states, and so much of it as remains after the war is over, will be in precisely the same condition that it was before the war began." Lincoln maintained that the army would never return slaves who were already behind Union lines, but the government should not encourage others to follow their lead. "They come now faster than we can provide for them," Browning paraphrased Lincoln's opinion, "and are becoming an embarrassment to the government."[44] Clearly, Lincoln did not approve of the new confiscation bill and was not ready to concede that emancipation was necessary to win the war.

In large measure, Lincoln's reluctance was rooted in his belief that the government could not take the radical step of emancipation without broad public support. Events were moving in that direction, but it was not yet clear that emancipation had become a military necessity, especially in light of Union successes in the war's Western Theater. Nevertheless, Treasury Secretary Salmon Chase sensed that the president's position was flexible and that Lincoln was still grappling with the problem in his own mind. On June 24, Chase suspected that a "contingency" could force the president to see that the time was right for recognizing the military necessity for emancipation. Writing to the general who had first confiscated slaves on the Peninsula, Benjamin Butler, Chase explained, "My conviction is that that contingency will soon arrive."[45]

"They performed their mission faithfully"

Only two days later, the climactic battles of the Peninsula Campaign would begin. Although the Army of the Potomac outnumbered the Confederates, General Robert E. Lee felt secure enough behind his strengthened fortifications to use most of his army to strike at the detachment of the Army of the Potomac that was north of the Chickahominy River. Lee recalled Stonewall Jackson from the Shenandoah Valley to hit this smaller portion of McClellan's army from the north, while Lee himself struck it from the west. Because McClellan's supply line, the Richmond–West Point railroad, lay north of the river, if Lee's planned assault could dislodge the Union troops there, McClellan would be cut off from his base at White House Landing.[46]

McClellan had only 26,000 men north of the river under Fifth Corps commander Fitz John Porter—in Hanover County near the village of Mechanicsville and a crossroads tavern known as Cold Harbor. "I have not seen in all this country a professed Unionist," the *New York Herald* correspondent noted. The reporter's assessment was accurate; back in 1861 there had been no votes cast against secession in the Cold Harbor precinct. The *Herald* noted that every family in the neighborhood had men fighting in the Rebel army, "and they leave their farms in charge of slaves, who escape as soon as the army arrives." Hanover County plantation owner William Fanning Wickham noted that "multitudes of negroes are leaving the neighborhood and going to the Northern army." His corn crop looked particularly impressive that spring, but "it is uncertain how we shall put in with the harvest, from the number of hands . . . who are gone—and others may yet go." Masters could not even rely on slaves who did not run away. "Upon arrival of the Union troops," Henry Clinton Sydnor recalled, "all work ceased with the negroes."[47]

Another resident, H. B. White, returned from a visit to Richmond and found seven of his slaves missing. "Of course they are in Yankee land," he bitterly noted. Most of his slaves had not yet fled, "but how long they remain, can't say, should not be surprised any morning to find that most . . . had gone." One of the missing was a young girl named Betsy whose mother was still on the farm. White told the mother that he had "a mind to take a pole and whip her off the plantation" for letting Betsy go. The mother insisted that she did not know where her young daughter had gone but claimed the other slaves had seized Betsy only to entice her to run away too. With the Yankee army all around, White wanted to leave his farm again but felt if he did "my negroes will be more apt to go off." Everyone in the community had lost slaves, but one neighbor suggested that White's bondsmen fled only because he had been away in Richmond. "I don't know that that made any difference. I hope they have a jolly time of it," he sarcastically noted, "as I have no doubt they will."[48]

The Army of the Potomac's Fifth Corps camped around a large and attractive plantation near Cold Harbor owned by a Dr. Gaines. The wealthy Virginian held close to 100 slaves, which one Massachusetts soldier described as "a smart looking set." According to the *New York Times*, the slaves were "more willing to serve the Union soldiers than obey [Dr

Gaines's] commands." The newspaper's correspondent was adamant that the owner was "the most unblushing, undaunted and defiant rebel that we have yet encountered." Gaines's wealth and heavy investment in slaves no doubt caused him to be such a "rank secessionist," as the *Principia* described him. Although Union troops were ordered to protect his buildings, the *Times* maintained that Gaines "is exceedingly ungrateful and indulges in the most insulting expressions, not hesitating to proclaim that we are vandals and vampires, and cherishes the hope that not a man of us will ever leave Virginia alive." The defiant Virginian's slaves shared horror stories with reporters and soldiers. "I have had 'Uncle Tom's Cabin' from their lips," Massachusetts soldier T. E. Chase wrote home. An older black man told *Principia* that the doctor had promised to shoot his disobedient slaves as soon as the Union army left. The correspondent was glad that "the old [slave] gentlemen that has worked all his life under the lash [will] spend the remainder of his life a free man."[49]

Gaines, White, and Wickham would have been pleased to know that Lee's army was soon to strike the Federal Fifth Corps and that Stonewall Jackson's troops would join the attack. As Lee prepared to cross the Chickahominy River, the location of Jackson's troops remained a mystery to the Federal command. The War Department informed McClellan that they had no reliable intelligence indicating where Stonewall was or where he was heading.[50] If the Confederates could keep their locations and plans secret, Jackson would be able to launch a surprise attack on General Porter's right flank and rear while Lee attacked in Porter's front. If so, the Rebels had a chance to destroy the Fifth Corps.

Fortunately for McClellan, many slaves around Richmond knew Jackson's whereabouts. A day or two before the Confederates planned to strike, Fanny Gaines Tinsley, Dr. Gaines's daughter, overheard the family's slave cook, Mary, calmly ask Mrs. Gaines: "Miss Jane, did you know that Jackson's men are up here at Mechanicsville?" The black woman apparently had picked the information up along the slave "grapevine," but Gaines discounted it, telling the slave, "You haven't your share of sense."[51]

Union troops took such reports much more seriously. One runaway warned the Yankees that the Confederates were about to cross the Chickahominy River near Mechanicsville. A fugitive from Richmond reported hearing that Jackson was about to attack the Federal rear. Another runaway claimed to have seen an "almighty lot" of troops, supposedly Jackson's, near Hanover Courthouse, and several other slaves repeated the report. Finally, a body servant from the 12th Georgia came into Union lines and in "a remarkable manner" confirmed that Jackson was about to attack the army's right flank and rear.[52]

Piecing the information together, McClellan correctly interpreted Lee's intentions. On June 25, he telegraphed the secretary of war: "Several contrabands just in, give information confirming supposition that Jackson's advance is at or near Hanover Court-House.... I incline to think that Jackson will attack my right and rear." Because McClellan himself would never contemplate such a bold attack unless he outnumbered his opponent, the timid general concluded that his worst fears were true and that Lee enjoyed a large numerical advantage. Although he in fact outnumbered Lee, McClellan felt sure the Rebels were about to attack him with no less than 180,000 to 200,000 men. His immediate concern was to save the Fifth Corps, and he crossed to the north side of the Chickahominy River to arrange a defense.[53]

On the morning of June 26, having spent the night preparing his forces north of the river, McClellan informed the War Department that "there is no doubt in my mind that Jackson is coming upon us, and with such great odds against us we shall have our hands full." The Union general had overseen the placement of a division behind a strong defensive position at Beaver Dam Creek. General Porter had also sent cavalry off to the north and west to look for Jackson and detailed axmen to fell trees and obstruct the southern advance.[54] Thanks in part to intelligence received from slaves, there would be no surprise attack on the Fifth Corps. That afternoon, Lee began his offensive.

Even before it had started, the information gleaned from blacks helped Union troops win the Battle of Mechanicsville. As Lee's men charged across Beaver Dam Creek and into the strong Federal position, Stonewall Jackson failed to attack Fitz John Porter's flank and rear. There are many reasons for the famed commander's failures that day, not the least of which was extreme fatigue. However, chief among Jackson's problems were the obstructions placed in his path, which slowed his movement considerably. For example, he was delayed nearly an hour at a stream because the bridge had been burned and the path obstructed. Union cavalry also harassed Jackson's troops, and he insisted on deploying skirmishers each time he encountered them.[55]

Back at Beaver Dam Creek, in the absence of a support flank attack by Jackson, the Confederates stood little chance of carrying the well-planned and selected defensive line, and they were bloodily repulsed. At least one Confederate body servant may have participated in the assault.

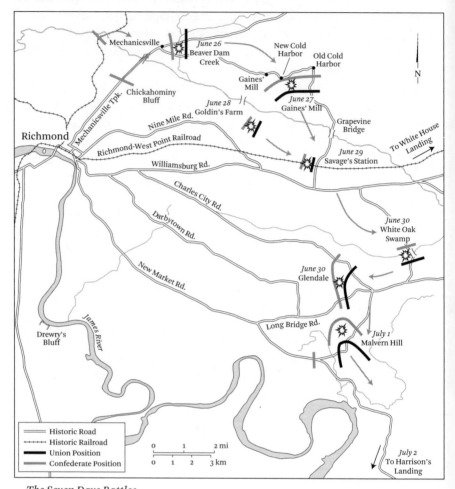

Mechanicsville

June 26
Beaver Dam
Creek

New Cold
Harbor

Old Cold
Harbor

N

Chickahominy
Bluff

Gaines'
Mill

June 28
Goldin's Farm

June 27
Gaines' Mill

Nine Mile Rd.

Mechanicsville Tpk.

Grapevine
Bridge

To White House
Landing

Richmond

0

Richmond–West Point Railroad

Williamsburg Rd.

June 29
Savage's Station

Charles City Rd.

Darbytown Rd.

June 30
White Oak
Swamp

New Market Rd.

June 30
Glendale

James River

Long Bridge Rd.

Drewry's
Bluff

July 1
Malvern Hill

Historic Road
Historic Railroad
Union Position
Confederate Position

0   1   2 mi

0   1   2   3 km

July 2
To Harrison's
Landing

The Seven Days Battles

When one slave-owning Rebel backed out of the combat, his body servant, Westley, reportedly asked to fight in his stead. Another Confederate soldier claimed in 1864 that the slave "followed the company into action, and though the shells and minie balls were falling thick and fast, Westley never wavered and brought down a Yankee with every fire."[56]

Despite Westley's aid, the Federals inflicted heavy losses on the attackers, but McClellan was convinced that he could no longer maintain a position north of the Chickahominy River. Retreating from that side of the river meant abandoning the Richmond–York River railroad as a supply line, as well as White House Landing as a base. McClellan determined to shift his entire army to the James River and to use it as a supply line instead. The Union commander had completely surrendered the initiative to Lee.

As they moved toward the bridges in order to cross to the south side of the Chickahominy River, the Fifth Corps had to take a defensive position near Dr. Gaines's plantation to fight off the combined attacks of Lee and Jackson. The Battle of Gaines' Mill on June 27 was the largest battle that either army had fought up to that time, with Lee hurling nearly 60,000 men in frontal assaults on the Union Fifth Corps. Porter's outnumbered men skillfully held their ground for most of the day, until a coordinated Rebel attack along the entire length of the nearly two-mile front (and largely spearheaded by the Texas Brigade) forced the Federals from the field and across the river. Years later, former slave Henry Smith, who had been a body servant with the Texas Brigade, provided an accurate account of the battle. Most interesting, he claimed that when officers instructed the slaves to remain behind he refused and insisted on entering the fight alongside the Texans. Smith justified his action by claiming that he feared that if his owner were killed he would be unable to locate the white man's body. As southern troops advanced, his master teased him for showing fear when Yankee shells began bursting in the ranks, but while "us black boys didn't [have] no guns," Smith claimed he went into combat with "a razor an' a big club."[57]

Like many civilians that day, the family and slaves of Fanny Gaines Tinsley were caught in the chaos of battle. Mary, the slave, had earlier warned that Jackson was coming, but it was not until the Confederates were attacking Union troops on their property that the family felt the need to flee. Tinsley, her infant, Hattie, her mother, the slave cook Mary, and the baby's young slave nurse fled on foot toward Confederate lines. Returning home after the battle, Tinsley found that "everything on the place was destroyed, and all the negroes left except some old ones who could not get away."[58]

Apparently, other slaves were also unable to escape the area with Union troops. After two straight days of combat, soldiers in the 33rd New York discovered that several black fugitives who had been with them since Yorktown were missing. It is possible that they fell into Confederate hands. John S. Tucker of the 5th Alabama claimed that after Union troops retreated from Gaines's farm, the regiment benefited from a "quantity of goods & chattels captured from the enemy."[59]

Miles away, at White House Landing, the thousands of black laborers faced a similar prospect. With the first rumors that McClellan would retreat, "there was . . . a great commotion among the crowds of contrabands," the *Philadelphia Inquirer* reported. "They soon understood that danger was apprehended." Pennsylvania soldier Benjamin E. Ashenfelter described it as "a panic" that infected not just the black laborers but also the "Suttlers, and hangers on of the Army. It was difficult to get the crowd calmed down and the Labourers to work." The *New York Times* added that "the contrabands discussed the subject, and finally made up their minds to prepare their [belongings], and get on board some boat, ready to go, 'if de Union folks was going.'" Some 3,000 slave women and children piled onto canal boats, but their husbands and fathers were held back in order to assist with the evacuation. An army band attempted to boost the morale of these black laborers, but their mood did not brighten until officers assured the runaways "that they would not be left behind to meet the vengeance of their masters." Relieved, the black laborers diligently loaded Union vessels, clamored aboard the canal boats, and floated away from the land of their bondage. "Every one of them seemed delighted to think they could go where they were to be free," the *Times* reported.[60]

On the same day that McClellan began his retreat, the U.S. Senate was still trying to amend the House's confiscation bill to include slaves. Although Senator Browning continued to insist that the war powers belonged exclusively to the president, Minnesota senator Morton Wilkinson pointed out that if Lincoln denied that Congress could confiscate and liberate slaves, such a position would be inconsistent with his approval of the First Confiscation Act. Charles Sumner agreed and stated for the record one last time that emancipation was "now, in the course of events, a necessity of war. Only through liberation can we obtain . . . complete triumph." To liberate the slaves, he maintained, was to deprive the Rebels "of an invaluable ally, whether in labor, or in battle."[61]

Two days after Sumner spoke, a group of black laborers demonstrated the kind of aid the senator remarked upon when they proved instrumental to Lee's effort to keep pressure on the retreating Federals. Confederate soldiers were repairing a destroyed bridge across the Chickahominy and doing a "shilly-shally [job] . . . as usual," the foreman admitted. The soldiers were relieved of the duty when Captain C. R. Mason and a gang of skilled black laborers arrived. The crew likely included slaves and free blacks who had been impressed into service. Stonewall Jackson, disgusted by the delay, told Mason that he wanted the bridge built "so soon as the engineers could prepare the plan and specifications." Mason replied: "Never mind the pictures General! . . . I will have the bridge ready by the time the engineers can prepare the pictures." The blacks, according to one soldier, completed the work "in a marvelously short time," allowing Jackson's men to continue their pursuit of the retreating Federals.[62]

Other incidents during the Union army's retreat seemed to validate Sumner's other assertion that some slaves may have been aiding the Confederates in battle. After the Battle of Gaines' Mill, the Yankees ran for the James River and the Rebels aggressively attempted to destroy the Army of the Potomac before it reached safety. Over the next few days, Lee forced the Federals to repeatedly fend off Confederate attacks and in the process captured large amounts of supplies and prisoners. After a battle on June 29, Thomas Ware of the 15th Georgia wrote: "Here again . . . more prisoners [were] brought in. One case I must mention, a negro was seen bringing a Yankee to Gen'l Toombs." Apparently, this was rare enough for the southern soldier to consider it notable, but it was not an isolated event. Georgia soldier Ivy W. Duggan recalled that during the pursuit, "a negro belonging to our brigade marched up a prisoner whom he alone captured. . . . The negro had taken the Yankee's gun and was walking quite independently by his side." Ware and Duggan recorded these incidents within days of witnessing them.[63]

Nevertheless, whatever aid slaves may have willingly or unwillingly provided the southern army during the retreat, African Americans once again provided assistance to the Federals. Not all of it was given voluntarily. Separated from his regiment during the chaotic retreat, New Yorker William Westervelt stumbled upon a black man who was about to eat some humble scraps of pork that he had struggled to procure. The famished soldier "persuaded" the slave to hand over the meat, "after threatening to shoot him if he did not." Despite such cruel incidents, most blacks did not have to be forced to aid the retreating Yankees. Before leaving White House, the *Philadelphia Inquirer* correspondent noted that black labor proved essential in removing the army's supplies so that they would not fall into

Confederate hands. "Stores and munitions everywhere disappeared from the landings with great rapidity," the newspaper reported, "and were being packed on the wharf boats and vessels contiguous." More important, as the army moved south into increasingly unfamiliar territory, it was stretched thin and extremely vulnerable to Rebel assaults. Thankfully, Private Robert Knox Sneden observed, "negro guides [were] employed to show the roads to the advance, and they performed their mission faithfully."[64]

Lee's best chance to destroy the Army of the Potomac came on June 30 at a crossroads known as Glendale, but he could not get his dispersed units to cooperate properly (particularly vexing was Stonewall Jackson's lack of aggression at White Oak Swamp). After desperate fighting, the Yankees slipped away and set up a powerful defensive position on the gentle slopes of Malvern Hill. The next day, the Federals repulsed repeated and uncoordinated Rebel frontal assaults and won what turned out to be the last of seven consecutive days of combat.[65] Many Union officers felt that the army should have followed up the victory at Malvern Hill with an offensive of its own, but McClellan had already decided to reach the safety of naval gunboats on the James River. He ordered the army to continue its retreat.

Just days before, Captain William G. Le Duc, quartermaster for the Army of the Potomac's Second Corps, was frantically trying to locate the best roads to get the army safely to the James River. His staff sought assistance from white civilians but only met with "unfriendly replies." At a fork in the road, Le Duc happened upon "a Negro who gave us information readily." The slave explained where each road led and pointed out the quickest route to the James River. Shortly thereafter, Le Duc came upon the army's chief of staff, General Randolph B. Marcy (McClellan's father-in-law), who expressed concern that the army was making such a large movement with "no maps [and] no knowledge of the country or its roads." Le Duc calmly dismounted and used a stick to draw a map in the dirt based on the roads that the slave had shown him. While they talked, General McClellan himself rode up, "looked over the dirt map, and asked questions." Le Duc then guided the army's commander back to the fork: "Here I pointed out the different roads, as explained by the negro, and he directed the movement of transportation to be made down the road."[66]

By July 3, the bulk of the Army of the Potomac had safely reached Harrison's Landing on the James River. Naval guns protected them from further assaults by General Lee, but McClellan had failed to capture Richmond. During the climactic weeks of McClellan's Peninsula Campaign,

African Americans had once again proven to be an "invaluable ally" to both armies. They constructed the Confederacy's defenses, staffed hospitals, and continued to be seen armed and fighting with Rebel troops. Conversely, blacks labored mightily at White House Landing to keep the Army of the Potomac supplied and provided military intelligence and other aid to Yankee soldiers operating in unfamiliar and hostile territory. The information they brought in played a role in saving the Union's Fifth Corps from being destroyed by the combined attacks of Lee and Jackson, and they helped guide the entire Union army safely to Harrison's Landing.

During the retreat, northern soldiers, civilians, and politicians endured a harrowing week of anxiety for the fate of the Army of the Potomac, and the defeat stunned the country. Once it became clear that the army was safe, Northerners wondered if the campaign's outcome could have been different had the government embraced emancipation as a military necessity. The result of this public discussion would soon radically change the course of the Civil War.

"Very bad," New Yorker George Templeton Strong remarked as the first word of McClellan's retreat appeared. "What news will come tonight no man can tell, but just now . . . things look disastrous." During the first days of July, Northerners clamored for more information about the Army of the Potomac's fate. The latest from the Virginia Peninsula was "the all-absorbing theme of public conversation," according to the *Philadelphia Inquirer*. "Scarcely any other topic is heard on the street." Northerners were soon relieved to learn that the army had at least fought well in its retreat and was now safe at Harrison's Landing on the James River. As reports trickled in, however, it became clear that after months of ever-rising expectations, McClellan had failed to capture the Confederate capital. "The details fell . . . with the most disheartening effect," the *New York Times* noted, "and produced a shock which has never before been felt." Lincoln shared the public's despair: "I was as nearly inconsolable as I could be and live," the president reportedly declared.[1]

As Northerners sifted through the newspapers for more information, the *Cleveland Herald* published a letter from a correspondent with the Army of the Potomac. "History will record that the only friends found by this army in Eastern Virginia are among the slaves," he claimed just before the climactic battles began. Maintaining that he had spoken to many officers in the topographical department, the correspondent noted that most of the army's faulty maps had been "corrected by contrabands," that various reconnaissance missions had been greatly aided by the slaves, and that "the best maps were drafted upon information communicated by negroes." The fact that politicians and military officers were not giving blacks an even larger role in the war struck the correspondent as "stupidity and heartlessness."[2]

As they reflected on the failed campaign over the next few weeks, Northerners of varying political stripes would come to agree with the correspondent's assessment. The contributions that African Americans had made to both armies, coupled with the failure of McClellan's Peninsula Campaign, played a role in turning many Northerners in favor of emancipation. "It is one of the grand characteristics of our people that every new danger calls from them new courage," Lincoln confidant and secretary of the Senate John W. Forney anonymously wrote in the *Philadelphia Press*. Claiming that "defeat madden[ed]" the people, he viewed the reverses before Richmond as a lesson. "God, in his providence, may send us disaster to chasten as well as to crystallize us."[3]

"The prevalent opinion in the army"

"I am sick, tired and disgusted," Charles Harvey Brewster wrote his sister from Harrison's Landing on July 9, "and how I ever got through the retreat is more than I can account for." Nearly every soldier in the Army of the Potomac felt the same as they collapsed from fatigue upon reaching the James River. "You can't conceive the wear & tear," Massachusetts officer Oliver Wendell Holmes Jr. told his family. Months of hard labor had preceded the fighting and marching of the previous week, but there was little rest for the weary. Soldiers were quickly put to work digging new defensive works and cutting away timber to improve the artillery's range of fire. "We are in a sickly climate," army surgeon Benjamin Roher somberly wrote his wife. The camp was "devoid of all comforts," and there was "nothing but hard work before us." After a long night of working on the trenches, Pennsylvanian Clement D. Potts bitterly complained, "I think our regiment is getting enough work." Making matters even worse, Massachusetts soldier Jonathon P. Stowe observed, the men were required to drill. "More than half our men are sick," he contemptuously noted in his diary on July 8. "Nevertheless, "Reg[iment] ordered to drill!!"[4]

In letters written during their first weeks at Harrison's Landing, most soldiers discussed being "worked down and worn out." They recalled the "drudgery" of their lives, described "spirits . . . at very low ebb," and maintained that the troops were "completely demoralized." Army surgeon Robert A. Everett described the army as a "pitiful lot of human beings," and Charles Becker claimed that "to look at our decimated Regiments and Companies moves you to tears." Further making conditions unbearable, Michigan soldier John Berry pointed out, "We are now sweltering under an almost tropical sun." As if all this were not enough, "Flies have arrived here in armies," Becker explained, "and are being heavily reinforced by all the flies from Richmond and the Rebel camps." The flies "have smelled our sugar and have come to fight for it," the soldier eloquently complained. "Besides [all] this," Berry noted just as the army arrived at the camp, "we are all hungry & have nothing to eat."[5]

"There's a lack of patriotism here," Jonathon Stowe observed. The army's "state of demoralization," as William Burns described it, seemed to have sapped many of the soldiers of their ardor for the cause. On the Fourth of July, Berry simply noted in his diary, "We are completely worn out, what there is left of us." Benjamin Roher claimed, "Those whose Patriotism was only skin deep sweated it out running from Mechanicsville to Harrison's Landing." Even many of the officers were "poor miserable specimens of humanity—they mope about camp whining and telling of their suffering until they succeed in getting their resignation accepted." Sergeant Charles E. Perkins spoke for many of the enlisted men when he moaned that "we have been out here now 13 months and over and I cant see as this War is eney near to a close nor so near as it was the day I enlisted, and now here we are pened up by the side of the James river twenty miles from Richmond and no place to git out." New Yorker Henry Gerrish agreed: "I can assure you [the retreat] was mournful and discouraging to all the boys."[6]

The depressed and overworked soldiers pondered why they had failed to capture Richmond, but there was little agreement. Those with Democratic leanings blamed the War Department and the White House for not sending McClellan's requested reinforcements. Some agreed with their commander that the failure to reinforce the Army of the Potomac was part of an abolitionist plot to ensure that the war would not end until the government saw the necessity of freeing the slaves.[7] At the other extreme, some soldiers blamed "proslavery" generals who had been reluctant to damage southern civilian property and seemed to care more for slave owners than they did for Union soldiers.[8]

Without choosing sides between the White House and McClellan, George Selkirk opined, "It seems to me that what plans we have had were drawn by a very poor architect, whoever he may be." The Pennsylvania officer continued, "We have been worked pretty hard, there has been a heavy loss of life, and it seems as though little or nothing has been accomplished toward the desired end." Politics aside, "One thing is certain," Selkirk argued, "since we crossed the Chickahominy we have had little rest." He believed that "it is about time" that the army was given a respite "if such a thing is allowable. . . . Our regiments are getting worn down, a great many are sick at present, many have died, or been discharged." When fellow Pennsylvanian Joseph D. Becker received a letter from his sister claiming that many Republicans at home were placing the blame on McClellan, the soldier lectured her on the sentiments of the men. Most did not blame their commander and felt that perhaps too much was expected of a fatigued army. "Do you think us to be iron clad soldiers both in constitution and invulnerability?"[9]

Regardless of their political beliefs, soldiers agreed that they had been required to perform labor from which their southern counterparts were seemingly exempt. From the siege lines of Yorktown, to the Chickahominy swamps outside of Richmond, to their new base at Harrison's Landing, the soldiers had toiled on fortifications, as Massachusetts officer Daniel G. Macnamara recalled, while "the same kind of work in the Southern army was performed by negro labor almost wholly." To Pennsylvania soldier J. R. Sypher, it seemed "insane absurdity" that Union soldiers had been worn down doing manual labor while black men acclimated to doing hard labor in the Virginia heat and humidity were more than willing to help. Many Union soldiers concluded that the spirited Rebel attacks had succeeded in driving the army away from Richmond because southern soldiers were better rested.[10]

The *Indianapolis Journal* published a letter from the same soldier who back in December had informed readers about blacks fighting with Confederate troops at New Market Bridge, maintaining that the soldiers were so angry about it that they wanted to "kill any negro they see." Months of campaigning had apparently changed his mind. The soldier now believed that the war could not be brought to a successful conclusion until the army assigned "a regiment of negroes in every brigade to do the fatigue duty." In his view, "Fighting and marching does not wear the soldiers half so fast as ditching and fatigue duty, and the prevalent opinion in the army is in favor of negroes doing that kind of work." Furthermore, such a policy would boost recruiting. The Hoosier claimed that other soldiers were writing letters to friends encouraging them "not to [enlist] as long as this state of things exists. And I have seen letters from [back home in] Indiana stating that reason for our men holding back" from enlisting.[11]

The soldier concluded by asking, "The Rebels use them for such purposes, why should not we?" The *Journal* concurred and added, "There is neither justice nor mercy" in not using willing black laborers on the fortifications so that "our men [may] have the rest and comfort they so much need. . . . This is the language of soldiers everywhere, and in every rank." The staunchly Democratic *New York World* agreed: "The fact is notorious," the editors maintained, "that the prolongation of the war operates almost everywhere to deepen the hatred of slavery. It is even more manifest in the army than among the people."[12]

"There is no resisting such an argument as this"

In early July, abolitionists echoed these sentiments and blamed the campaign's failure on the nation's refusal to liberate the slaves. Henry Ward Beecher and Theodore Tilton published widely quoted editorials calling for emancipation. Susan B. Anthony went on a speaking tour in upstate New York, and Angelina Grimké Weld received hundreds of signatures in a Democratic neighborhood in New Jersey on a petition calling for a "Declaration of War on Slavery." Frederick Douglass told a Fourth of July gathering that recent "calamities" made it "never more palpable than at the present moment, that the only choice left to the nation, is abolition or destruction." One abolitionist preacher proclaimed that McClellan's loss occurred because "God has bound up our interests in the same bundle with those of his oppressed people." The *National Anti-Slavery Standard*'s Washington correspondent argued even more strongly that "men who are accustomed to see the finger of Providence in every event . . . will not fail to see the hand of God in these disasters."[13]

These expressions left the abolitionists vulnerable to the accusation of actually being pleased to see the campaign fail. The Democratic *Detroit Free Press* maintained that abolitionists "rejoiced as openly as they dared" when news of the defeat reached the North. "The fact is . . . these crazy fanatics would rather see the whole Army of the Potomac defeated and destroyed than that McClellan" should be successful. The moderate Republican *Boston Daily Advertiser* warned abolitionists that the results of the campaign should not be seen as bolstering the military necessity argument. "Reverse, it has been said, would bring abolition. But this is not so," because the real reason for the defeat, the paper argued, was the administration's failure to reinforce McClellan.[14]

Nevertheless, abolitionists were not alone in insisting that the failed campaign revealed the need for a new policy regarding slavery. "Our old Conservative solid men are ready for the most radical measures," an abolitionist friend assured Charles Sumner. One example was New York political boss Thurlow Weed: "I want to 'strike while the iron is hot,'" the conservative Republican proclaimed in an editorial that appeared in many northern papers. "The public mind is now taking the right direction with regard to the 'contrabands.'" If the government had only emancipated the slaves when the war started, Weed asserted, "at least half a million of slaves who have been at work in the rebel armies, would have been relieving our worn-out troops from exhausting drudgery—thus *weakening* the enemy, and *strengthening* ourselves in corresponding degree." Reprinting Weed's letter, the *Washington Chronicle* added, "There is no resisting such an argument as this."[15]

Conservatives and even some Democrats agreed with what many soldiers offered as the best explanation for the army's failure to capture Richmond. "Our troops have been overworked on the Peninsula and elsewhere by their military labors," the Democratic *Philadelphia Public Ledger* explained. "It is this excessive labor down in the swamps of Virginia which has decimated the ranks of McClellan's army and left it in a condition inviting attack." The Democratic *Boston Herald* concurred: "We were not beaten by the arms of the enemy, but by the picks and spades in the hands of our own soldiers, with which they have wasted their vigor."[16]

The editor of the *Ledger* was opposed to enlisting black soldiers but fully believed that they would be useful as laborers. Racial assumptions fortified the argument: the *Ledger*, like many northern newspapers, maintained that African Americans were naturally acclimated to the humid conditions in the South and thus more suited for hard labor than white soldiers. The moderate *Cincinnati Daily Commercial* agreed that "any measure authorizing their employment in digging trenches, throwing up fortifications, doing camp and hospital duty, would meet the approval of the country." The editor even favored emancipating those who labored and joked that the government could colonize the freed slaves in South Carolina.[17]

Although the Democratic editors of the *New York World* maintained that they would rather see the war "strike clear of the peculiar institution," they nevertheless argued that "if rebel slaves can impart information, they will be welcomed. If they can be turned to account by relieving our soldiers of manual labor, they will be put to work; if, in certain localities, they can best perform military service, they will be armed and put into service." The *New York Times*, probably the best indicator of moderate Republican sentiment, was not ready to support a general emancipation either but proclaimed on July 17: "There is a very loud demand just now, on the part of the public, for the employment of slave labor in our camps. This is perfectly natural and proper."[18]

Radical Republican newspapers were of course even more adamant on this score. The *Bangor (Maine) Daily Whig and Courier* pointed out that the Confederacy used its slaves to perform the manual labor in camp "as well as in the building of bridges, entrenchments, &c., and in consequence of this their soldiers are fresh for the fight. The paper then asked whether there was "any reason why every able bodied negro who comes into our lines" should not work for the Union cause. From the Peninsula, *New York Tribune* correspondent Samuel Wilkeson reported that the campaign had demonstrated "that it is utterly impossible for us to subdue the rebels without an alliance with their slaves." Making the same argument, the *Chicago Tribune* described the South's use of its black laborers as an "immense advantage" which "cannot be longer resisted." A letter to the editor of the *Racine (Wis.) Weekly Journal* simplified the point: "This struggle for national life is reduced to this: *Who shall have the Nigger?* Shall it be [Jefferson] Davis, Barbarism," and the Confederacy, where they are compelled to serve the Rebels and are "even forced [in]to shooting Union soldiers? Or, shall it be Lincoln, Civilization & Co., whom he is eager to serve in any capacity?"[19]

Shortly after the Army of the Potomac's arrival at Harrison's Landing, Richard Yates, the antislavery governor of Lincoln's home state of Illinois, sent the president a letter, which newspapers soon published. The governor called for "more decisive measures" and an end to the "conciliatory policy" toward Southerners, especially since the Confederates "armed negroes . . . in their behalf." Yates also encouraged Lincoln to make more use of blacks in the military. The *Chicago Tribune* heralded the letter as "bold, energetic, manly" and was sure "it will meet with cordial reception among all classes of truly loyal men no matter what party they may belong to. . . . Well done, Governor Yates," the editors proclaimed. "You lead the van." The *Illinois State Journal* believed that the letter reflected "the overwhelming current of loyal public opinion in favor" of using black labor to relieve white soldiers from working on the trenches.[20]

But while Northerners of varying political affiliations were uniting in the belief that the military needed to take greater advantage of African American labor, they remained divided over the questions of raising black troops and emancipating the slaves. Radicals, however, saw signs of progress in the wake of the failed Peninsula Campaign. Noting that even the staunchly Democratic *Illinois State Register* was now in favor of using more black laborers, the Republican *Illinois State Journal* crowed: "The world moves. . . . There is only one step between organizing the blacks for the purpose of building fortifications, [and] digging entrenchments . . . and that of using them after they are organized to assist in defending those forts and trenches." In the middle of July, the *Bangor (Maine) Daily Whig and Courier* went a step further by predicting that Lincoln would soon declare emancipation as a military necessity.[21]

"With us or against us"

A week after the Army of the Potomac staggered to Harrison's Landing, the second confiscation bill neared passage. At the beginning of July, President Lincoln had called for the enlistment of 300,000 more troops, and now radicals in the Senate decided to couple the confiscation bill with legislation authorizing the president to enroll African Americans in the military. Because blacks were already laboring for the Federals, some congressmen felt that such an action was unnecessary. Others insisted that the legislation would strongly demonstrate to the people that the government would no longer sit idly by while Rebels used slaves to their advantage; moreover, it would encourage the president to begin the recruitment of black soldiers to help meet his new enlistment request.[22]

The radicals aggressively used their interpretations of the campaign's failures to criticize McClellan and to push for an expanded role in the war for African Americans. Michigan senator Zachariah Chandler, for example, had no patience with the argument that the government had failed to adequately reinforce the Army of the Potomac. He maintained that while McClellan sat outside of Richmond calling for more men, the ones he already had were "rapidly wasting away." Indeed, he insisted, "we have lost more men by the spade than the bullet—five to one since the army started from Yorktown under McClellan. Had the soldiers been relieved from digging and menial labor by the substitution of negro laborers, the army of the Potomac would to-day, in my estimation, contain thirty thousand more brave and efficient soldiers than it does." Writing to his wife on July 11, Chandler promised that he would steadfastly promote this message and expressed even more outrage at the recent turn of events. McClellan "will not take negroes to dig ditches, cut down timber & do hard work, but will force [soldiers] to do this menial work & die in doing it. Rather than take negro slaves belonging to rebels & who only ask freedom in return, 40,000 brave men have been sacrificed." The passionate senator believed that McClellan's actions had amounted to "treason" and promised, "I will no longer keep quiet."[23]

More significant, Chandler and his fellow congressional radicals were no longer alone in pushing for the legislation that would increase the military use of African Americans. Calling the proposal "one of the most important" measures yet considered, conservative Ohio senator John Sherman told Congress: "The question must be decided whether the negro population of the United States shall be employed only to aid the rebels." The opposition maintained that using slaves as laborers in camp and on entrenchments was perfectly acceptable, but that arming the slaves would only incite more southern resistance, and Union soldiers would likely refuse to fight alongside blacks. Sherman responded to such arguments by pointing out that in the South, slaves not only performed all the army's hardest labor, but the "rebels fight side by side with them. . . . Now, shall we avail ourselves of their services, or shall the enemy alone use them?" Sherman had previously opposed the use of blacks in the military, but recent events had changed his mind.[24]

"How far emancipation should be extended to those slaves who render faithful service to the country is a more difficult question," the conservative senator admitted. Nevertheless, Sherman argued that justice required the government to free any slave who performed labor for the military. "I am willing to affirm for myself," he argued, "that never will I consent to surrender a slave [to his master] who has rendered any service, however menial, to our Army." The fact that such sentiments should come from such an unexpected source, the *Philadelphia Press* commented, "gives much force" to his opinion "on this vexed question."[25]

Reporting the debates, the *Illinois State Journal* noted the "remarkable indications of the rapid change in sentiment now taking place in the most conservative minds." The paper maintained, however, that "without a doubt the most remarkable speech was made by" Democratic senator Henry Rice. Like Sherman, the Minnesotan admitted that he had once opposed the use of blacks in the military. Now he "would not hesitate for a moment." The senator insisted that the South had "brought the slave into the service" and had "forced the free negro in to the fight against us." There was no reason why the North should not more fully avail itself of these men, who would voluntarily and passionately serve the Union cause. The senator pointed out that the British had long enrolled blacks in the military, and that George Washington and Andrew Jackson had as well. "If it be right for them," the senator asked, "why was it wrong for us?" New York senator and former Democrat Preston King agreed, confidently declaring that the legislation only reflected "the sentiments and opinions of this country."[26]

As debate progressed, more evidence accumulated of blacks fighting within Confederate ranks. Some Democrats insisted that the northern public's concern over the South's military use of its slaves was simply an emotional response to the Union's recent failures and that it should not dictate congressional policy. To counter such assertions, Michigan senator Jacob Howard sought to prove that the South was using slaves not only as laborers but also in combat. He produced a letter from Benjamin B.

Luce, a sutler with the 3rd Michigan. Luce insisted that during the York-town siege he had met with several runaway slaves who were wearing Confederate uniforms and they claimed to have served as Rebel soldiers. Luce recounted speaking to several Union officers and soldiers who confirmed encountering a black Confederate sharpshooter at Yorktown. After the Battle of Williamsburg, he heard a couple of officers remark that they came across "three or four dead negroes in rebel uniforms" on the battle-field. Luce also claimed to have spoken to soldiers who had been attacked at Garlick's Landing by J. E. B. Stuart's raiders, and they maintained that the soldiers who had killed their sergeant there were black. After reading Luce's letter into the record, Senator Howard added, "In every word of this, I have the utmost confidence."[27] Whether or not Luce's information was trustworthy, it shows how in pursuing emancipation, congressmen continued to assert that the South was using blacks in combat.

"I think we can not be mistaken," Wisconsin's moderate Republican senator James Doolittle argued, "the traitors in arms against us have employed negroes not only upon intrenchements and in camp service, but have organized and put arms in their hands to shoot down our sons and our brothers on the field of battle." Because of this "fact," the senator maintained, the government should authorize the president "to employ them, and even to arm them."[28]

Like senators Sherman and Rice, Doolittle was a recent convert to such convictions. A staunch free-soil Democrat before the war, he had long detested the abolitionists. By 1862 he had come to favor some form of emancipation but was an ardent champion of a particularly odious colonization scheme to deport all female blacks of childbearing years. Back in May, the *Racine (Wis.) Weekly Journal* blasted the senator for not only failing to support the second confiscation bill but also because "he hampers, embarrasses, prolongs, protracts, delays, and uses every means known to tricky legislators to prevent" passage of the bill. The editor believed that "Wisconsin, the most thoroughly anti-slavery state in the Union, is not fairly represented" by Doolittle. When the senator worked against passage again in June, the paper sarcastically predicted that "the Confederate Congress will vote him a medal, and run him on their next ticket for Vice President or Attorney General." Because of such attacks, Doolittle believed he stood little chance of reelection that fall.[29]

Apparently, a combination of this political pressure and military reality altered Senator Doolittle's opinions. Some of those opposed to the use of blacks in the military argued that such a measure was barbaric because it would incite servile insurrection. In response, Doolittle suddenly sounded much more like a radical by declaring, "We cannot be condemned by our own consciences, nor before the civilized world, if we employ the same class of persons to fight against the rebels which they employ against us. If it be wrong, they alone are guilty." By using slaves in combat, the senator passionately insisted, Southerners "have sown the wind; they may reap the whirlwind."[30]

That such radical sentiments were coming from unexpected sources thrilled the editors of the *Chicago Tribune*, and they believed that the Peninsula Campaign had caused the change. "That a body which only recently stumbled and boggled at the confiscation bill," they noted, "should have become so transformed in sentiment as to debate all day on a measure for actually enabling blacks to win their freedom by bearing arms in the service, is a decided, and startling response to the recent reverse to our arms before Richmond." A letter to the editor of the Border State *Baltimore American* complained that there was "no disguising the fact" that slaves had been a "pillar of strength to the Confederates" and that Union soldiers had been worn down by labor that Southern soldiers avoided by using their slaves. The Washington correspondent for the Democratic *Boston Herald* agreed and after observing the Senate debates was positive that legislation was forthcoming that would alter the government's policy toward slaves.[31]

Commenting on the debates, the conservative *New York Commercial Advertiser* noted that the Confederates had used their slaves in three ways: "As builders of intrenchments, as gunners on fortifications, and as picket guards. These are ascertained facts. It is also said they have some negroes enrolled in regiments." Just as abolitionists had been arguing for almost a year, the paper warned that if the government did not take the initiative to offer blacks their freedom, the Confederates "as sure as destiny itself" would free their slaves as a last resort if they were ever losing the war. The *Commercial*'s editors found it "refreshing" that "the recent debates in Congress indicate a definite policy" that would begin to deprive the South of their black laborers. Such sentiments, the editors believed, have "made a greater advance since the Army of the Potomac found its new base on the James, than during the whole fifteen months since [Fort] Sumter fell."[32]

As the debates raged in Congress, General Lew Wallace was visiting Washington from the battlefields of the war's Western Theater, where he had recently commanded an army division at Shiloh. On the night of July 9, a band and a large serenading crowd gathered at the National Hotel calling for a speech from the Indiana war hero. The future author of *Ben Hur* did not disappoint and gave a rousing address calling for a reinvigorated war effort in response to the recent defeat at Richmond. After Wallace indicated that he had been in the Senate earlier that day listening to the debates, members of the crowd asked to hear "a soldier's opinion" on the slavery question. Wallace, a known Democrat, responded, "[It] would be a poor soldier . . . who would fail to use every element of war which God Almighty gave him, if he could use it to his advantage." The crowd reacted to this opinion, according to the *Philadelphia Inquirer*'s Washington correspondent, with "prolonged and enthusiastic cheering."[33]

With the crowd's encouragement, Wallace elaborated on this point. If slaves were available and willing to labor for the army, he maintained, using them would relieve white soldiers "of onerous duties and hard work." Once again loud cheers came from the crowd, and a voice was heard to shout, "Soldiers will follow you to the death for that!" The general was then asked whether the military should arm black laborers. "If I accept the services of a negro," Wallace asserted, "and he works well and faithfully . . . would it be human, would it be cruel, to put him into the army, in the way of shot, and yet give him nothing with which to defend himself?" The crowd responded with shouts of "that's so!" The general was careful to maintain that he was no abolitionist and remained "as much opposed to slavery agitation as any of you can be." Nevertheless, he insisted that the time had come when leaders must view the issue militarily, not politically. Wallace did not favor placing black soldiers on the front lines, but "to each one who did good service, I would at the end of the war give him or her freedom." This comment was reportedly followed by substantial cheering.[34]

General Wallace's speech was widely reported in newspapers across the country while Congress engaged in its final round of debate on the second confiscation bill. Lincoln confidant John W. Forney heard the speech in person and noted anonymously in the *Philadelphia Press* that "Wallace was a leading [Stephen] Douglas Democrat in 1860 . . . and has always been known for his moderation and conservatism. His speech created a great impression, and was received with repeated cheers." The *Indianapolis Journal* praised the speech and remarked that the general "is a Democrat, as everybody knows, but he is more of a patriot than a Democrat." The Democratic *Boston Herald* remarked on the general's "sound doctrine," and the *New York World* maintained that Wallace's sentiments, "beyond any manner of doubt, express the feeling now dominant among the people and in the army."[35]

Lew Wallace's experiences in Tennessee fostered the opinions he had expressed that night in Washington, and other officers in the war's Western Theater shared his sentiments. Dr. William Caldwell of the 72nd Ohio, for example, wrote to his father from Mississippi on July 15, noting "the utter folly of being so over sensitive about the means to be employed in the prosecution of the war on our side, while our enemies scruple not to employ any and every means against us that can be made available."[36] As in the Army of the Potomac, Western Theater soldiers also dealt with the practical, legal, and moral dilemmas involved with runaway slaves entering Federal lines, officers received valuable directions and advice from slaves, and the armies were slowed by slave-built fortifications.[37] "Ever since the war commenced," Caldwell pointed out, blacks had been "employed to do the drudgery and hard work of the Army of the South. Their fortifications are built by the niggers. Their niggers drive their teams and cut wood and build the bridges." Meanwhile, he bemoaned, after long marches, the soldiers "were compelled to shoulder the spade and work hour after hour." As a result, the doctor noted, the Army of the Tennessee had been "decimated" by sickness.[38]

The slave issue bitterly divided Union soldiers in every theater of war, and substantial numbers of the men continued to oppose emancipation until the end of the conflict. Like William Caldwell and Lew Wallace, however, by July 1862 increasing numbers of Federals had come to embrace emancipationist views. Exposure to the cruelties of southern slavery shocked many soldiers, and the experience frequently heightened emancipation sentiments.[39] More numerous were soldiers who maintained that emancipation was becoming a military necessity to save the Union. "Let every man be branded as a traitor," Caldwell insisted from Mississippi, "who is not in favor of using any and every measure necessary to the successful and speedy crushing out of this Rebellion."[40]

Nevertheless, Union victories in the Deep South and elsewhere seemingly weakened the argument that emancipation was a military necessity. Had the Army of the Potomac achieved the same level of success as other Federal armies, it would have been exceedingly difficult to convince the northern public that freeing the slaves was vital to winning the war. Combined with the Western Theater triumphs, the capture of Richmond in July 1862 would likely have ended the war with slavery essentially intact. Despite the Army of the Tennessee's victory at Shiloh and successful advance on Corinth, Mississippi, William Caldwell took note of the Peninsula Campaign's lessons. "The fortifications at Richmond were built while there were no troops there," he surmised. "And the very works against which our brave troops dashed themselves, and from which they were repulsed so disastrously, were built by the omnipresent nigger."[41]

The intense interest, news coverage, and disheartening failure of the Peninsula Campaign offset the victories in the war's Western Theater. Thus, the military events in Virginia played a crucial role in the increasing support for emancipation during the summer of 1862.

From his camp on the James River, General George McClellan sensed the shift in public opinion. He refused to consider his retreat as anything more than a "change of base," and like many Democrats, blamed the administration for failing to reinforce him. He continued to believe that the Confederates heavily outnumbered the Army of the Potomac and that the radicals had sabotaged his campaign so they could increase their political power to achieve emancipation. Nevertheless, he understood that his failure to capture Richmond made it likely that the government would abandon a conciliatory policy toward the South and strike against slavery.[42]

Other factors promoted this shift in northern opinion, not the least of which was the desire to wage a more aggressive war against the South. Like General McClellan, many believed at the start of the war that northern armies respecting southern property rights would nurture and encourage southern unionism. Fifteen months of war had proven otherwise. Federal soldiers in almost every theater of war found no large groundswell of unionism in the South, dealt with hostile and bushwhacking civilians, and thus grew weary of protecting southern property. The South's continued resistance despite the Union's conciliatory policies increased calls for more punitive measures against Rebels. McClellan's failure on the Peninsula multiplied these demands, and such sentiments combined with the military necessity argument to strengthen calls for both the passage of the new confiscation bill and emancipation.[43]

When Lincoln had visited the Army of the Potomac on July 8, McClellan had lectured the president on the need to resist these increasing demands for emancipation. He had handed Lincoln the famous "Harrison's Landing letter" in which he advised that the "abolition of slavery should [not] be contemplated for a moment."[44] The irony is that McClellan's failure was the "contingency" that Salmon Chase hoped would finally help convince Lincoln that emancipation was a military necessity.

Lincoln offered no response to McClellan's letter, but over the next week he revealed his thinking. As newspapers across the North were calling for "harder war," giving extensive coverage to the debates in Congress, and praising General Lew Wallace's speech, and on the same day that Illinois governor Richard Yates's letter to Lincoln was made public, the president met with representatives and senators from the Border States. Back in May, the president had unsuccessfully tried to goad them into adopting a program of compensated emancipation, and he now renewed the plea. Lincoln told the men that pressure to liberate the slaves was "still upon me, and is increasing," and that he could not afford to lose the support of the radicals.[45]

Reporting on the meeting, the moderate *Boston Daily Advertiser* argued, "It is very clear to our apprehension . . . that the present state of the campaign has been largely influential in leading him to urge his scheme afresh." Lincoln himself later recalled, "I believed the indispensable necessity for military emancipation, and arming the blacks would come," unless the Border States would agree to compensated emancipation." When they did not, "I was, in my best judgment, driven to the alternative of either surrendering the Union . . . or laying a strong hand upon the colored element. I chose the later."[46]

The day after the meeting, Lincoln informed Secretary of the Navy Gideon Welles and Secretary of State William Seward that after much thought, he "had about come to the conclusion that it was a military necessity absolutely essential for the salvation of the Union, that we must free the slaves or be ourselves subdued." Lincoln explained that this was the first time he had mentioned the subject to anyone, and he desired their opinions. Both were in favor of emancipation. Welles believed that the "reverses before Richmond" had swayed the president into this new course of action. In addition, it was now clear that "slaves were undeniably an element of strength" to the Confederacy, not only because they worked the land but also because "thousands of them were in attendance upon the armies in the field . . . and the fortifications and intrenchments were constructed by them." Lincoln concluded: "We must decide whether that element should be with us or against us."[47]

In succinct form, this was precisely the line of reasoning that abolitionists had begun to develop after the Battle of Manassas a year earlier and that the radicals and the newly converted conservatives in Congress had advanced while debating the second confiscation bill. The president, spurned by the Border State representatives and aware that recent events had apparently swayed northern public opinion, had come to agree. Lincoln later described emancipation as a "lever" for winning the war, and when critics subsequently condemned the Emancipation Proclamation, he defended the measure with the military necessity argument. "Let them prove . . . that we can restore the Union without it," he contended. By mid-July 1862, Abraham Lincoln's lifelong moral objections to slavery, indications that Northerners increasingly supported sterner measures against the South, and the growing acceptance of the military necessity of emancipation all came together to doom the South's peculiar institution.[48]

"They demand this . . . in every manner of public expression"

As Lincoln weighed his options, on July 17, Congress finally passed the Second Confiscation Act, as well as the Militia Act, authorizing the president to enlist blacks into military service to help meet the new 300,000-man quota. The Militia Act allowed the military to employ blacks on entrenchments and in "camp service" but did not specifically mention placing them in combat. However, it left the door open for such a possibility by calling for their use in any job "for which they may be found competent." On July 22, Lincoln issued an executive order instructing military commanders to begin enlisting African Americans as laborers. However, the president's order (unlike the Militia Act) did not expressly acknowledge that the slaves of Rebel masters would be freed upon entering Union service, something that annoyed the radicals. "This order," the *New York Tribune* complained, "does not supply the slaves . . . with an adequate reason for braving peril, privation, and death" to flee to Northern troops. "Of course," the editor admitted, "we do not know that the President will stop here. We trust that he will not."[49]

As for the Confiscation Act, Orville Hickman Browning encouraged Lincoln to veto the legislation on constitutional grounds and told the president that his decision on the bill would "determine whether he was to control the abolitionists and radicals, or whether they were to control him." Despite Browning's admonitions, the president felt he could not lose the support of the radicals (as he had explained to the Border State representatives), and he was now much closer to agreement with them on the necessity for emancipation and more punitive measures against the South. Nevertheless, Lincoln had serious reservations about Congress's bill. Mainly he was concerned about the constitutionality of seizing a traitor's property beyond their natural life. He threatened a veto if Congress did not add a resolution that would allow a convicted traitor's descendants to reclaim confiscated property. Congress reluctantly agreed, and on July 17, Lincoln signed the bill into law.[50]

"The army hails with great satisfaction the prospect of being relieved in the trenches, in the bridge-building, &c., by negroes," the *Philadelphia Inquirer* correspondent reported from Fort Monroe just before the passage of the Second Confiscation Act and the Militia Act. There were now more black laborers at the fort than were needed, and thus the correspondent thought they should "be sent up James river [to Harrison's Landing] at once." Soldiers in the Army of the Potomac welcomed the sterner measures in the legislation as well. "That bill to confiscate the rebel property is just what we want," Sergeant Charles E. Perkins asserted, "and it aught to have been done in the first place." Nevertheless, it was the prospect of being relieved from hard labor that most excited the Rhode Islander, not the prospect of seizing Rebel property, emancipation, and black troops. Perkins maintained that the government should send blacks "out here and set them to work on the trenches and let our Soldiers rest. And that is all that we soldiers want them to do. Let them work and we will do the fighting." Dr. Alfred L. Castleman, a surgeon with the 5th Wisconsin at Harrison's Landing, was also pleased that the government was apparently ready to stop "playing war" and would utilize blacks to relieve "the soldiers of much hard work and depressing labor."[51]

"When men volunteer to become soldiers," the *Boston Herald* commented, "they do not intend to dig trenches." Men in the city's streets had reportedly declared they would be damned "before they will become trench diggers in the Chickahominy swamps [outside of Richmond] for thirteen dollars a month." At the end of July, the radical *Cincinnati Gazette* maintained that "volunteering will be greatly encouraged" by the new Confiscation and Militia Acts. The editors of the Democratic *Detroit Press* concurred and declared they were "glad" that Lincoln had asked for the enrollment of black laborers. The editor had no doubt "that every volunteer who now enlists will feel the same way." The *Boston Daily Journal* trumpeted "A New Era for Recruits," because enlistees were now assured they would "handle [their] gun, [and] the spade will be in other hands. Is this not an immense improvement over the old practice?"[52]

The radicals, however, were dissatisfied with the final version of the confiscation bill. The act did allow for the seizure of Rebel property and did declare that all slaves owned by individuals "engaged in rebellion" were free, regardless of whether they had been impressed into Confederate service. However, to get the legislation passed, the radicals had had to compromise with moderates, conservatives, and Democrats, who wanted to ensure that southern Unionists would not have their property confiscated. As a result, the final version was convoluted, filled with loopholes, and open to interpretation. The biggest weakness was that the government could apparently free slaves only after a federal court found a master to have committed "the crime of treason" on a case-by-case basis. This provision might well have been unworkable and it threatened to clog up the court system.[53]

Given constitutional limitations, however, the legislation was as close as the radicals could come to emancipation. Although the Second Confiscation Act punished Rebels by confiscating all forms of property, for most radicals the primary goal was to ensure that the war would not end with slavery intact. The bill, according to Sumner, was passed "under pressure from our reverses at Richmond" and was "a practical Act of Emancipation. It was only in this respect that I [valued] it." Yet because of the weaknesses purposely imposed by moderates and conservatives, the act failed to liberate many slaves.[54]

In the end, however, the debates surrounding the measure were far more important than its limitations because they helped prepare the country to accept emancipation. After Benjamin Butler first declared slaves to be "contraband of war" and newspapers reported that blacks were fighting with the Rebels at Manassas, abolitionists had begun to craft the military necessity argument. The only way Congress could liberate slaves was to exercise its war powers. When pushing for the second confiscation bill, radicals in Congress took up the basic themes expounded by the abolitionists. They strengthened constitutional and legal arguments by noting the activities of African Americans on the Virginia Peninsula in order to portray emancipation as a legitimate and necessary measure to win the war.[55]

Three weeks after the Army of the Potomac's retreat, these efforts had clearly paid off. At the end of July, Northerners of varying political backgrounds not only called for punitive measures against the South but they also embraced an expanded role for African Americans in the war and were more willing to accept emancipation. "The conviction, we think, is nearly universal," the Boston Daily Journal noted, "that the time has gone by when loyal men can safely be squeamish about using the same means to save the Government which traitors employ to ruin it, although a slave become a free man in the process." The Philadelphia Inquirer endorsed Lincoln's order to enlist black laborers "without a particle of that sentimental negro philism known as Abolitionism" and wondered how anyone who had observed the disappointing results of the Peninsula Campaign could conclude otherwise.[56]

Such sentiments echoed from the pulpit. On July 20, Henry C. Fish told his New Jersey Baptist congregation that the South "had four million . . . human chattels, growing the food, digging the trenches, and doing nearly all the rude muscular work." The minister wondered if McClellan's campaign would have turned out differently "had all the negroes, at the entrance of our army upon the Peninsula, been invited, on promise of freedom, to join our camps, and been employed in digging [our] entrenchments."[57]

Reviewing the campaign, the *Philadelphia Inquirer* noted that in its last days the Army of the Potomac had endured an ordeal of "fighting, repelling the enemy, and retreating" every day for an entire week. Upon reaching the James River, "wearied and exhausted," soldiers faced the prospect of having to labor yet again on fortifications. "Now who will say that even one of those worn-out and battle-wearied men should be forced to labor" when there were blacks willing to do the work? "And who is to say that if these works were then attacked . . . that the men who made them should not have arms to defend them? And having made and fought for them, who will then say that these useful auxiliaries should be returned to their traitor masters?"[58]

Speaking before the state convention of the Pennsylvania Republican Party, Secretary of the Senate John W. Forney claimed that even moderates and "some of the most distinguished Democrats" had come to see the need for calling on the assistance of African Americans. Forney encouraged Republican politicians not to worry about being labeled as an abolitionist for embracing the recent acts of Congress. "What voter who has lost his relative or friend in the army will not" accept the military necessity argument? Making another familiar point, Forney also maintained that George Washington used blacks in the Revolution, and Andrew Jackson did so in the War of 1812. "Has the colored race deteriorated since the Revolution and second struggle for Independence?"[59]

In the *Philadelphia Press*, Forney reiterated his belief that even many moderates and Democrats were now embracing the use of blacks in the military. "They demand this in public meetings and private papers, and in every manner of public expression." Indeed, while they steadfastly continued to resist universal emancipation, the strongly Democratic *Detroit Free Press* admitted that "it would be mere fractiousness to find fault with" Lincoln's executive order calling for the enlistment of black laborers. The *Boston Daily Advertiser* conceded that the new Confiscation Act "may prove to be productive of good." While not endorsing either measure, the *Washington Daily Intelligencer* acknowledged that they were "demanded by the exigencies of war," and that military commanders who did not employ black laborers would be "justly suspected of postponing the interest of the nation . . . to the interest of slaveholders."[60]

In New York City, a mass meeting of "loyal citizens" gathered to promote recruiting and a reinvigorated war effort. Industrialist and political activist Peter Cooper told the crowd that slaves provided "the Rebels [with] the power on which they depend for digging the trenches [and] ploughing the field, . . . leaving them at liberty to play upon us the game of war. Should it be so any longer?" The crowd responded with a chorus of "no!" The meeting ultimately passed several resolutions, one of which called on Lincoln to issue a "proclamation . . . declaring the provisions of the recent law of Congress to be the sentiments of the Government." Presidential enforcement of the Second Confiscation Act, the citizens argued, "will take from the rebels their great source of strength."[61]

Lincoln was ready to do just that. On July 25, the president issued a proclamation warning Southerners that unless they "cease[d] participating in, abiding, countenancing, or abetting" the rebellion, they would suffer the penalties of the Second Confiscation Act. This declaration met with little criticism, an indication that Northerners were ready to accept emancipation as a military necessity. "The President has crossed the Rubicon," the Democratic *New York World* proclaimed. The paper was one of Lincoln's biggest critics, but it conceded: "It is worse than useless now to discuss either the justice or the expediency of the confiscation measure. It is the law of the land, and . . . must be supported by every loyal man." The effect upon slavery "must be nigh fatal." The moderate Republican *Boston Advertiser* carefully noted: "A year ago men might have faltered at the thought of proceeding to this extremity in any event. The majority do not now seek it, but, we say advisedly, they are in great measure prepared for it."[62]

Indeed, Lincoln's proclamation actually received hearty praise from moderate and some Democratic quarters. The Border State *Baltimore American* argued that the policy was "precisely what is needed in dealing with the rebellion." The South had boasted that their slaves were an element of strength, and the leaders in the South "do not hesitate to use them wherever available, even to the working of their artillery, thus proving that they have no scruples at all." As a result, "they must accept the result, whatever that is, even to the freeing of every slave in the South." In Missouri, former Democratic state representative (and future U.S. senator) Charles D. Drake was passionately cheered by a St. Louis crowd when he heralded the fact that the South would no longer be able to exploit black laborers to the Confederacy's advantage. "Our brave men must be spared," he maintained; "the negro shall dig the trenches, and by and by the musket will be put in his hand." The Democratic *Boston Herald* praised the administration for adhering to the "independent course" the paper had advocated "since the reverses before Richmond." The editors insisted that their positive position on the new measure "truly represented the people" and believed that "the country rejoices to-day in the changes of national policy."[63]

Concurring with this opinion was Robert Dale Owen, retired Democratic politician and son of the founder of the ill-fated New Harmony utopian community in Indiana. In late July, he wrote a letter to Secretary of War Edwin Stanton that soon appeared in newspapers. The eccentric Democrat had always been antislavery but was careful to distance himself from abolitionism. Nevertheless, he told Stanton that as the war went on he "very gradually" became convinced that emancipation was the speediest means to end the conflict. "The recent reverse under General McClellan," he wrote, increases "the probability that we must deprive the South" of their slaves "before we can succeed against their masters." Furthermore, he told Stanton, "I think the people are ready. I believe that [Northerners] . . . are to-day prepared for emancipation."[64]

Evidence supporting Owen's assessment came in public meetings toward the end of July. Because of Lincoln's call for 300,000 additional troops, New York's war rally was just one of many that took place to boost recruiting. Across the country, thousands met in parks, town squares, city halls, and all manner of public spaces to hear bands and patriotic speeches. While encouraging citizens to renew their commitment to preserving the Union, speakers frequently explained and praised the recent acts of Congress. In Lynn, Massachusetts, for example, Senator Henry Wilson justified his support for the Confiscation Act, maintaining that the legislation would make it so that the military could utilize blacks to "dig the trenches, to build fortifications, and, if need be, to handle the musket." The crowd responded to these comments from Wilson with enthusiastic cheers.[65]

In Baltimore, a rally attended by approximately 20,000 citizens passed several resolutions. One declared that confiscation and emancipation were "essential to cripple the power" of the Confederacy. In Cincinnati, according to the *Gazette*, the rally was "the largest ever held" in the city and "indeed the largest we have seen anywhere." Many in attendance heard Democratic mayor George Hatch declare, "All honor to Congress for its noble act of confiscation" and that all should give special praise to "the President for having so promptly declared that its benign provisions should be carried into effect. It is a large stride in the right direction to crush out this rebellion."[66]

"We must carry Africa into the war," retired naval commodore William

Nicholson told a cheering crowd at Independence Square in Philadelphia. Many in the throng of thousands heard him proclaim, "The people of the North, who, but a few months ago, would have scoffed at the proposition, are now in favor of it." In Concord, New Hampshire, U.S. representative Edward H. Rollins garnered loud applause when he said, "In prosecuting this war, we must use every means God has given us." Soldiers would be given rest when blacks were "set to digging in the trenches. Let us use the black man whenever we can use him to advantage." In Chicago, Governor Richard Yates conceded that Southerners had been correct when they asserted at the start of the war that slavery would be an element of their strength. Yates told the large crowd that Rebels were now "shooting down your brave and gallant men, from behind . . . fortifications built by negroes." When the governor asked if this should be allowed any longer, he was met with shouts of "No, no, no!"[67]

Colonel John F. Farnsworth of the 8th Illinois Cavalry explained the military activities of the Peninsula's blacks to a Chicago crowd. Slaves were working on Rebel defenses, but, Farnsworth insisted, "I speak from my knowledge, [they are] ready to act and work and fight for you." The officer insisted that blacks proved to be "the only reliable, truthful men from whom we obtain information about the rebel armies, their roads and the scouts." Many times, he explained, after seeking information from southern civilians, "some old negro . . . would nod to me to meet him behind the barn and would tell me 'massa lied,' and would impart to me information which subsequent experience proved true." The soldier concluded, "I want to see an expression go forth from the meeting" praising the president for acting to use "every agency we can lay our hands upon."[68]

In Philadelphia, Colonel William F. Small of the 26th Pennsylvania was also up from the Peninsula addressing a war rally and praising the new Confiscation Act. "If the nigger is property," he explained to the crowd, "and his owners are in rebellion, we will take their property—and will make the very best use of it in the world." Blacks would now build fortifications for the Union, "and we will put muskets in the hands of the property and send them in pursuit of their runaway masters, and let them meet their masters at long range." Hopefully, he asserted, his soldiers would not have to "dig any more in ditches. That is to be the work of the darkies." In Concord, New Hampshire, Captain Tileston A. Barker of the 2nd New Hampshire expressed similar views and was loudly applauded when he maintained, "I think the black man can dig trenches better than the white man, and when I go back [to the Peninsula] I'm going to set him about it."[69]

Such sentiments, of course, dehumanized the slaves, depicting them as mere brutes for the North to use in suppressing the rebellion. Nevertheless, when the war began, few other than abolitionists and radicals wanted to involve slaves in the conflict at all. Now many Northerners viewed the labor of African Americans as essential to winning the war and tended to argue that saving the Union warranted emancipation. "A notable feature" of the war rally in Chicago, the *Tribune* observed, "was the hearty approval of every sentiment endorsing or advocating the freedom of slaves." In Philadelphia, moderate former Pennsylvania governor James Pollock was applauded when he maintained, "I make no war on institutions, peculiar or otherwise," but when the nation was fighting the rebellion, "whatever crosses her path, institutions peculiar or not, let them be overthrown." Reverend J. Walker Jackson agreed and received loud approbation from the crowd when he declared, "If American slavery stands in the way of the Union—and I believe that it does—I would seize the slaves and use them. I would free the slaves forever and ever."[70]

The *National Anti-Slavery Standard* drew the appropriate conclusion. "Our reverses have taught us something," they declared. There had been a "revolution" on the question of slavery and the war. Even "Democrats admit that we must make use of the slave." Pastor Fish also sensed the change in public opinion. "Men most opposed to anti-slavery sentiments are compelled to favor them," he argued. "We see it in the late debates in Congress, and in the utterances of the pulpit and the press." As a result of the Peninsula Campaign, "the mass of the Northern people are now ready for the use of the most extreme measures. Emancipation, so far as it can be effected, is now so plainly a necessity that neglecting it would" disappoint the country.[71]

"There is light then, breaking through the clouds that rose from the swamps of the Chickahominy," the radical *Cincinnati Gazette* proclaimed just three weeks after McClellan's failure on the Peninsula. John W. Forney agreed. "Reading our reverses in this light, we must accept them as admonitions and instructions," he proclaimed at the end of July 1862. "Every day educates us for a higher destiny."[72]

Indeed, President Lincoln was now determined to do more than just enforce the Second Confiscation Act. Declaring it "a fit and necessary military measure" for restoring the Union, he had already presented the first draft of the Emancipation Proclamation to his cabinet. Maintaining that he had already "resolved upon this step," Lincoln had indicated that he welcomed suggestions but would not be swayed from the decision. However, Secretary of State William H. Seward convinced the president that

"A Consistent Negrophobist." On August 16, 1862, Harper's Weekly *ridiculed Northerners who, despite recent events, continued to resist the military necessity argument for emancipation.* "Take that Rope away, you darned Nigger!" *the caption reads.* "What decent White Man, do you suppose, is going to allow himself to be saved by a confounded Nig." *As a result, the stubborn man* "goes down, consistent to the last."

the proclamation should not be issued until after a Union victory, so that it did not appear as "our last *shriek*, on the retreat."[73] That victory eventually came on September 17, 1862, at the Battle of Antietam. For that reason, historians have far more closely linked emancipation to the pivotal battle near Sharpsburg, Maryland, than to the Peninsula Campaign.

However, Lincoln firmly resolved to issue the Emancipation Proclamation long before Antietam. By the end of July 1862, a broad spectrum of Northerners was ready to accept such a measure. They understood that slave labor was invaluable to the Southern army and that slave-built entrenchments had effectively stalled McClellan's advance and allowed Lee's army to attack his flank. Many were convinced that the Army of the Potomac had been exhausted by fatigue duty that Southern soldiers had seemingly avoided because of their slaves. They learned that slaves had provided important military information to Union forces and had demonstrated their potential to give more. Blacks had reportedly fought alongside of Rebel troops, creating the fear that the South might soon make more use of them in combat. Without such evidence, and had McClellan captured Richmond, Congress and the president would have been hard pressed to argue that emancipation was a military necessity.

When Lincoln finally announced his decision, he still received considerable criticism from those who were stubbornly unwilling to accept the military necessity argument, and the backlash helped to cause the loss of some Republican congressional seats in the fall elections.[74] Nevertheless, in the summer of 1862 many moderates and conservatives of both parties joined abolitionists and radicals in lobbying for an expanded role for blacks in the conflict, and some even insisted upon freeing the slaves as a war measure. Before, during, and after the Peninsula Campaign, the military contributions of African Americans to both the Union and the Confederacy had played a significant role in promoting emancipation as a military necessity.

On August 2, 1862, "while public enthusiasm is at low ebb," the *New York Times* heralded the "silver lining" in the Army of the Potomac's disheartening failure to capture Richmond. The editors believed that McClellan had clearly been "out-generaled," but the defeat demonstrated that the South had mustered all its resources to hold off Union forces, and thus it had convinced Northerners that they needed to make a similar all-out effort to win the war. A major component of that commitment was to put "negro labor to our own use in digging intrenchments, &c." Doing so would "add new heart and muscle to our overtaxed soldiers" and would subtract strength from the Confederacy. Senator John Sherman wrote from Ohio, "You can form no conception at the change of opinion here as to the Negro Question." The senator explained to his brother, General Sherman, "Men of all parties [now understand] the magnitude of the contest" and "agree that we must seek the aid and make it the interests of the negroes to help us."[1]

The public's growing acceptance of the military necessity argument and Lincoln's intention to enforce the Second Confiscation Act thrilled abolitionists. "A year has wrought great changes, even among those whose prejudices were most inveterate," Horace Greeley optimistically claimed. William Lloyd Garrison agreed: "The war is shaping itself, as a matter of necessity on the part of the government, into an Anti-Slavery War."[2]

Down on the Peninsula, the Army of the Potomac's presence at Harrison's Landing continued to be a means of liberation for Virginia slaves. At the expense of local slaveholders, McClellan increased his use of black laborers to strengthen his position and to keep the army supplied. When the Union army finally retreated, it caused a labor shortage that plagued the region for the rest of the war. But McClellan's campaign did not simply undermine the master-slave relationship on the Peninsula, it helped to cause the destruction of the institution of slavery itself.

"Most will make good their escape"

Unaware that Lincoln had already decided to issue the Emancipation Proclamation and that he was only waiting for a Union victory to release it, abolitionists continued to lecture him on the military necessity for emancipation. To Moncure Conway, for example, Lincoln seemed like an

Harrison's Landing during the Union occupation. On August 9, 1862, Frank Leslie's Illustrated Newspaper *depicted one segment of the Federal camp on the James River. Note the black laborers gathered in the lower right corner.*

"automaton, waiting for months until the people . . . shall force him to do what he ought to have done long before." The most famous criticism of the president at this time was Horace Greeley's "Prayer of Twenty Millions." In part, Lincoln crafted his famous public response—"If I could save the Union without freeing any slave I would do it, and if I could save it by freeing all the slaves I would do it. . . . What I do about slavery and the colored race, I do because I believe it helps to save the Union"—so that when he issued the Emancipation Proclamation, Northerners would understand that he did so as a military necessity.[3]

While his fatigued and dispirited army rested, McClellan followed Lincoln's mandate to enlist black laborers, relying on them to help construct defensive works and unload supplies at Harrison's Landing. Soldiers referred to the black laborers as "Company Q," and hundreds of runaways from Fort Monroe soon joined them. "They were mostly fine, healthy, strong-looking fellows," the *New York Tribune* correspondent noted. "They do all the drudgery, the unloading of the vessels, making roads, etc. etc." Horace Greeley took it as a sign of progress that a staunch Democrat such as McClellan "is employing all the blacks he can get, and only wishes he had more of them."[4]

In assembling his labor force, McClellan sheltered runaways and sent patrols to bring other slaves in from surrounding plantations. The Union general essentially acted as Magruder had done, but unlike the Confederate general, he could take all the slaves he wanted and ignore any complaints from their owners. On the same day that Lincoln issued his executive order instructing commanders to enroll black laborers, Union soldiers descended on Edmund Ruffin's plantation and according to the slave owner, "took off forcibly every slave on the farm, between 60 and 70 in number. The system of supplying their armies by plundering has been acted on generally," he complained.[5]

Ruffin was not the only Peninsula slave owner to suffer. Massachusetts soldier John L. Parker described Hill Carter's Shirley Plantation as "the best by great odds I saw in Virginia," but that did not stop Union soldiers from grabbing sheep, hogs, and poultry as they crossed the property during their retreat. Carter's slaves were "kept busy baking hoe cakes for the boys," Parker recalled. When the Union army moved on, many slaves followed. Carter's overseer noted the depletion of the plantation's slaves: "The negroes [are] all running off . . . to the Yankee army," he complained as the Federals were making their way to Harrison's Landing.[6]

The Union army's new base was situated around Berkeley Plantation, birthplace of former president William Henry Harrison. When Federal soldiers first arrived, they discovered that the current owner had fled, taking along his most valuable slaves. Pennsylvania soldier Joseph Baker learned from free blacks that other owners in the area had done the same. He "had a chat for a long while" with two free mulattoes, who also claimed that local slave owners had even warned free blacks that "they [too] would be sold by the Yankees to the folks who live in Cuba" if they did not leave. The owner at Berkeley had instructed those slaves left behind to burn the house when Union troops arrived (he was apparently willing to destroy the beautiful colonial-era house rather than to have it inhabited by Yankees), but they failed to carry out his orders. The *Boston Daily Journal* correspondent claimed that in an attempt to keep his slaves from being confiscated, the master had further instructed the slaves that if Union soldiers asked "whether they wished to be free," they were to claim that they had always been free. "That order too, they have failed to obey," the correspondent noted, but they shouted "hallelujahs over their deliverance from bondage."[7]

Westover House. The beautiful colonial mansion established by William Byrd II is seen here during the Civil War. (Library of Congress)

During the last week of July, a *Philadelphia Inquirer* correspondent encountered several Virginia slave owners who were grumbling about their property losses. He boarded a Union boat that went up the James River to retrieve wounded Union prisoners the Confederacy had agreed to release. Meeting soldiers at City Point under flag of truce, the correspondent spoke with a boastful Rebel corporal who maintained that he "was fighting for Southern rights." However, when pressed to pinpoint specific rights that were jeopardized, "he was not quite prepared to say." Nevertheless, "one thing he did know, we were stealing their negroes, and this was unpardonable." The journalist talked to other Southerners on the James River and found them "bitter at our government. Nigger was their only cry." The situation seemed amusing: "The fact is, they do not think we ought to use the negro at all. It is enough for them to get their aid and assistance." The correspondent concluded that the angry men he spoke to must "have lost a lot of slaves."[8]

Makeshift camps were set up for the army's slave laborers at Harrison's Landing and at nearby Westover Plantation. The *Philadelphia Inquirer* correspondent estimated that there were 2,000 blacks encamped at Westover alone. At both locations, African American women started successful laundry businesses to supplement their income. "The negro women seem to have more energy than the men," the correspondent observed, "and are very expert at carrying heavy loads upon their heads." He was impressed with their skills: "I have seen them daily carry[ing] buckets of water on their heads up the side of the bluff without spilling a drop of water." On Sundays, the correspondent related, the laborers were allowed to rest, and the "colored lasses . . . do immense promenading with [the black men] around the various camps." Entire families were also present. "There are lots of black folks here," Union soldier George Williamson Balloch noted in a letter to his children. The Yankee explained to the youngsters the importance of the relationship between the runaways and the Federal army: "[They] have left their masters to live with us because we treat them better," he surmised. "They live in a little village of tents on the bank of the river. . . . There are a great many children and they look just as cunning as can be."[9]

Nestled on the bank of the James River with the Union army, these slave refugees were not completely out of harm's way. Around midnight on July 31, the Confederates bombarded the Union camps from small batteries on the south bank of the river. One soldier noted that Union gunboats sparred with the Rebel artillery "for about two hours," and another added that "they made things pretty lively for awhile." For most of the soldiers, the event was nothing more than a disruption of sleep, but watching the navy find the range on the southern guns and eventually silence them proved interesting for some. George Selkirk noted that before returning to bed, one officer casually quipped that he was "anxious to get the New York papers to learn what [the fight] was [all about]." Sadly, the fugitive slave camps, which were along the riverbank, were the most vulnerable to the Rebel fire. William J. Burns noted that "there were several niggers killed and wounded as they laid nearer the river." Selkirk believed the number to be only three or four killed, but William Westervelt estimated that twenty were killed and another forty were wounded.[10]

Despite such hazards, the New York Tribune correspondent noted that the runaway slaves were "cheerful" and that they "labor willingly, diligently, gratefully, and to the entire satisfaction of those who have them in charge." Regardless of the dangers and the difficult labor, one Union officer expected that the number of laborers would continue to increase. "Where the army actually is," he reported, almost every slave in the region came to their lines.[11]

During their stay at Harrison's Landing, soldiers and northern correspondents recorded temperatures that climbed into the upper nineties and sometimes over one hundred degrees. While white northern soldiers faltered in the heat, racial assumptions held that blacks would not. "The Peninsula is sickly here," an officer in the U.S. quartermaster department noted. "White laborers cannot stand the climate. . . . We depend on contrabands chiefly." When black laborers began to show signs of fatigue in the unbearable conditions, some took it as an indication of laziness. These assessments appeared in some northern newspapers (especially those of Democratic or conservative bent), challenging the popular notion that slaves would relieve the soldiers of the most difficult labor. The *Philadelphia Inquirer* correspondent went so far as to claim that "the fear of the whip would act like a charm" on the black laborers at Harrison's Landing.[12]

Such statements did not go unchallenged. The *Chicago Tribune* correspondent insisted that he had closely observed the black laborers and found them to be "steady, faithful workers, quite as good if not better than the same number of whites." After the *Bangor (Maine) Daily Whig and Courier* published an article in which a *Boston Journal* correspondent denigrated the stamina of the black laborers at Harrison's Landing, a rebuttal was printed the next day. The writer asserted that he had been with the army on the Peninsula, "and being strongly conservative, [I] took some pains to learn whether [the runaway slaves] were the lazy, thieving cowardly creatures represented." He emerged "fully satisfied" that such stereotypes were inaccurate. "I am convinced by observation," he concluded, "that negroes are not to be classed with a brute." The *Baltimore American* correspondent concurred, maintaining that the black laborers "are now doing the country excellent service."[13]

"It is unnecessary to add," the *Baltimore American* correspondent continued, that the employment of black laborers "is gratifying to our soldiers" because it allowed them to rest. At the end of July, George Selkirk was happy to report home that "we have not had much fatigue work to do lately, so that the men are getting rested and healthier than when we first came." By early August, the *Boston Herald* claimed that the spirit of the Army of the Potomac was slowly reviving as it recuperated at Harrison's Landing. The use of black laborers had "materially aided" the army's recovery. The Democratic paper praised the new policy because it was sparing white soldiers from difficult labor and "enabled [blacks] to contribute to the support of themselves and their families." The editors again touted the benefits for recruiting, because new enlistees would be assured that they would be used as soldiers and not as "sappers and miners."[14]

Ironically, the *Richmond Dispatch* criticized the Federals for relying on the blacks: "It appears . . . that McClellan proposes to employ negroes to perform the hard labor on his fortifications, with a view to save his troops the perils of sunstroke. This is the sort of freedom the deluded slaves enjoy when they get into the clutches of the abolitionists." The editor encouraged Confederate officials to reclaim some of the slaves the Union army had "stolen" by trading Yankee prisoners for them. Conveniently unaware of their own soldiers' complaints about fatigue duty, the southern paper ridiculed the Union army's laziness and dependence on slaves: "It seems that one nigger [is] equal to two Yankees."[15]

Although many Virginians claimed to believe their runaways would become disenchanted with laboring for the Yankees and would return or be recaptured, others disagreed. "My opinion," slave owner William Sydnor sadly noted, "is [that] most will make good their escape." Sydnor claimed that every slaveholder near Cold Harbor had lost slaves. "Dr. Gaines lost more than any one else," he noted of the notoriously ruthless owner who had been so uncooperative with Yankee troops. Confederate engineer John A. Williams discussed the subject of runaways with a friend. "He does not think he will ever get his [back]," Williams noted. The soldier revealed the extent to which some slave owners deluded themselves about the nature of slavery, as well as how they felt personally betrayed by their runaway slaves. "He says he thinks his [slaves] would come back to him if the Yankees had stolen them," Williams recorded, "but as they went of their own accord they cannot make up their mind to face him again." Sydnor did not know how he was going to be able to get his harvest in. He hoped that Southerners far removed from Union occupation would "make all the crops in their power," or, he concluded, "suffering and starvation will soon meet us face to face."[16] Northern advocates for emancipation would have been pleased to hear Sydnor's assessment.

The economic situation in the middle of the Peninsula was worse. "I have been trying for three or four weeks, to hire hands for your harvest," Charles City County resident Judge John M. Gregory wrote to a friend, "but I have not gotten one, nor do I believe I shall be able to get any." The problem, he explained, was that free blacks refused to work, "almost everybody" had lost slaves, "and those that [remain] do little or nothing." Gregory claimed that many farmers were offering half of their crops to anyone who would assist in the harvest, "but no one will undertake [the work]." Slaves in Williamsburg were also reluctant to assist their owners. One woman claimed that although Union soldiers in town were "attended by darkies," the slaves treated their masters as though the blacks were "monarchs of all they survey."[17]

Gregory estimated that "nearly, if not fully one-half, of the negro men have gone." With the Union army encamped to the west at nearby Harrison's Landing and to the east at Williamsburg, Yorktown, and Fort Monroe, the white residents of Charles City County felt trapped in between. "We are cut off from every means of getting out of this Peninsula even if we wanted to go," Gregory lamented, "and unless something is done . . . we must suffer greatly for the indespensables of life."[18]

Something was done, but the order came from Washington. Despite the Army of the Potomac's secure position at Harrison's Landing, Lincoln had run out of patience with McClellan. The administration attempted to prod the general into another advance on Richmond, but he delayed and kept claiming that Lee outnumbered him and that he needed reinforcements. By the beginning of August, Lincoln had long since tired of McClellan's inaction. When General Lee's army drove north and appeared to threaten the city of Washington, General in Chief Henry Halleck ordered the Army of the Potomac to abandon the Peninsula to provide reinforcements in northern Virginia.[19]

As the Yankees retreated, the *National Anti-Slavery Standard* noted that "the negroes of the whole region joined the army on its march." In Williamsburg, Massachusetts soldier Charles C. Perkins found "very few white people[;] most [were] . . . niggers." However, as the soldiers filed through town, the *New York Times* claimed that "the slaves . . . immediately took the alarm. The Union army, they said, was going the wrong way for them, and before night scores of the black population . . . packed up and prepared to leave." White resident Charles S. Jones recalled that "at the first sound of the bugle" from McClellan's retreat, blacks concluded that the "good times was getting scarce," and they "hastily made tracks" for the lower Peninsula.[20]

Union private Robert Knox Sneden found it amusing that as the army retreated it was met "on all sides with sullen and defiant remarks by the women, who complained of the loss of their slaves." Sneden concluded that the southern belles were disheartened because they were now "forced to do their own work." The *New York Times* noted that while some Williamsburg owners made "promises of protection and good usage" if the slaves would stay, others gave angry warnings. Army surgeon Thomas T. Ellis observed this as well, claiming that some whites in Williamsburg "indulged in violent threats of what should be done to the negroes when the Yankees were gone." The tactic was foolhardy, only ensuring that even more slaves would depart with the Union army. Ellis believed the town would soon be "relieved of near all of them, but a very few will remain to experience the tender mercies of their secesh friends."[21]

African Americans did more than just follow along. As the army's massive wagon train lumbered down the Peninsula, many of the drivers were black. Moreover, slaves once again demonstrated their knowledge of the terrain. "In a region of almost impervious swamps and forests," Union chaplain J. J. Marks observed, the Federals were vulnerable to "ambuscade" while they retreated. However, "invaluable aid was given by the negroes. They were our only guides in the entangled mazes." As the Yankees passed by the Yorktown fortifications again, New York soldier William E. Dunn could not help but recall how much time and energy the army had wasted there. The historic town, he quipped, was "where Magruder ran away and left [McClellan] a digging." Soon thereafter, the Army of the Potomac arrived safely at Fort Monroe, and the black laborers helped load the vessels that carried the army and its supplies away from the Peninsula. Reflecting on the rapid retreat, Dunn expressed dismay that it had been carried out "at a rate of speed that, in my opinion, had we went up [the Peninsula] we should now have held possession of Richmond instead of the rebels menacing our own capitol."[22]

Yet the army's extended time on the Virginia Peninsula had dramatically altered the region and the course of the war. Besides the number of slaves who fled to the Federals, there were many other reasons for the sharp reduction in the black population. Immediately after the campaign, General Lee ordered officials to round up all available black labor to strengthen the lines around the cities of Richmond and Petersburg. As at Berkeley Plantation, many refugee masters had taken their slaves with them. Ruffin and other owners had sold some of their slaves before they could escape to the Federals. As a consequence, Union surgeon Thomas Ellis concluded, "the Peninsula has been cleared of the more valuable portion of the slave property, those who are left behind being generally either of an ancient or very tender and juvenile age." "Practical emancipation has taken place."[23]

The Peninsula Campaign devastated the region and caused a significant labor shortage for the rest of the war. Most Peninsula masters lost their slaves after the passage of the Second Confiscation Act and Lincoln's order to enroll black laborers, and they suffered considerable damage to their homes, farms, and crops. Just before leaving the Peninsula, Michigan soldier John Berry observed that "some of the finest estates in Virginia lie in this neighborhood" and that they "extend in every direction."

However, he unsympathetically noted that they were now "desolated by the war [and] show how much has been sacrificed & lost by the Virginians." As for Berkeley Plantation, Massachusetts soldier George E. Hagar remarked that it "was once a wheat field, but is now a mud hole." When John M. Gregory estimated that half of the region's slaves were gone, he may have been close to the mark. A U.S. army census in 1863 reported 26,110 blacks behind Union lines on the Peninsula and in Norfolk. Traveling on the Peninsula in 1864, Cynthia Coleman described the lingering impact of McClellan's campaign: "The country . . . was one of . . . desolation and lifelessness," she noted. "The farms seemed never to have been cultivated, fences down and gone, houses deserted . . . waving fields of grain supplanted by the brier and noxious weeds."[24]

"Right results from this great contest"

The economic and social change wrought by the Peninsula Campaign illustrated how warfare tended to transform and undermine slavery. Throughout history, slaves had seized the opportunities that war presented for liberation. Invaders often offered slaves freedom as a reward for joining the fight against their owners, while other slaves chose to improve their conditions by demonstrating loyalty to their masters. During the Revolutionary War and the War of 1812, the British promised Peninsula slaves their freedom as reward for military service, but a few slaves created better lives for themselves by serving their masters. Some actually gained their freedom that way.

The Peninsula's economy made antebellum slave life in the region relatively less harsh than in the Deep South, but it was far from idyllic. Bondsmen there suffered most of the familiar evils of slavery and craved freedom. Yet slaves and free blacks on the Peninsula and in Richmond were intelligent and resourceful, possessing skills that became invaluable to both northern and southern armies. Slaves also developed critical survival instincts to avoid complete domination by their owners. A talent for manipulating masters, gaining information through eavesdropping and spreading it through the "grapevine," sneaking off into the woods to hold secret meetings, evading patrols, and learning all the hidden trails and paths that the woods offered—all served the slaves well during the Civil War.

From the start of the war, African American labor became essential to the basic defensive strategy of the South. Hundreds of slaves and free blacks were impressed into service by the Confederacy and put to work on the Peninsula's fortifications. Many of these laborers suspected that the presence of the Union army might somehow lead to their emancipation and decided to explore what Union troops would do if they escaped into their lines. They found a friend in General Benjamin F. Butler when he refused to return them to their masters and established the policy of treating slaves as "contraband" of war.

Abolitionist New England soldiers such as Edward Pierce greeted the slaves and further encouraged them in the belief that the war would lead to their liberation if they demonstrated their value to the Union cause. Despite the racist beliefs of most northern soldiers and their often inhumane treatment of runaway slaves, the interactions between the Union army and the Peninsula's enslaved community were increasingly positive. This developing relationship was instrumental in dispelling the lies that masters had worked so hard to implant in slave minds, and it helped encourage more African Americans to flee to and assist the Army of the Potomac.

The Federals greatly benefited from the aid of Virginia's blacks during the Peninsula Campaign. African Americans worked on the docks at the tip of the Peninsula, Yorktown, White House, and Harrison's Landing. As Union troops advanced, slaves eagerly greeted the soldiers and flocked to Federal lines by the thousands, offering their labor and providing generally reliable intelligence. Such information launched General Hancock's illustrious career, steered Union patrols safely away from Rebel soldiers, helped prevent the destruction of the Fifth Corps, and guided the entire army safely to Harrison's Landing.

However, some blacks may have believed their masters when they warned that Yankees were evil men intent on capturing the slaves, working them hard, and then shipping them off to Cuba. Hearing such falsehoods, observing the many Confederate soldiers gathering to defend the state, and perhaps hearing that the northern government had renounced a war of liberation, many slaves understandably decided it was best to stay with their masters. Some may have even demonstrated this "loyalty" on the battlefield. Nevertheless, the vast majority of slaves and free blacks who provided services for the South were either coerced by masters or impressed by Confederate authorities. Although General John Magruder constantly had to battle with slave owners to obtain a sufficient labor force, his trenches across the Peninsula slowed McClellan's advance. The extensive fortifications around Richmond protected the city from naval attack and also allowed General Lee to seize the initiative by aggressively attacking the Army of the Potomac's flank. Southerners were fighting to protect their "peculiar institution," and to the increasing chagrin of Northerners, during the Peninsula Campaign they used their slaves effectively.

Ironically, the African Americans who were forced to aid the Rebel army struck a blow for freedom. Northerners often observed and spread rumors about blacks fighting beside their masters and complained about slave-built fortifications. Abolitionists and radicals warned that if the North did not emancipate the slaves, the Confederacy would use them on a larger scale. Such fears helped Congress to pass the First Confiscation Act and fortified the radicals' promotion of the military necessity argument in favor of the Second Confiscation Act and emancipation.

So, who won the Peninsula Campaign? Certainly, it was not the Union. McClellan's invasion began with high expectations at a time when Federal troops were succeeding in nearly every theater of the war. It seemed that the Federals were on the verge of saving the Union if McClellan could capture Richmond. However, Confederate fortifications gave the Rebels precious time to strengthen their forces. General Lee boldly and aggressively attacked McClellan's army and forced it to retreat. The Army of the Potomac failed to achieve its primary objective, and northern morale plummeted. Union armies would not be this close to the capital of the Confederacy again for two long and bloody years.

The Confederates had a stronger claim to having won the campaign. Reeling from defeats in the Western Theater and with the Army of the Potomac camped just eight miles outside of Richmond, the Confederacy's future appeared bleak. But in a series of desperate battles, Lee's army saved Richmond and restored southern morale. Nevertheless, the Rebels were thwarted in their attempt to wipe out the Federal Fifth Corps; they could not cut off the Union retreat; and they wasted the chance to administer a crippling blow to the entire Army of the Potomac at the Glendale crossroads. The campaign ended with a stunning Rebel defeat at Malvern Hill, and the Confederates were unable to inflict any more damage on McClellan once he established his base on the James River. The Confederates saved their capital, but General Lee understood that they had squandered an opportunity to severely damage the Army of the Potomac.

But if both armies failed to achieve their goals, the Peninsula Campaign was something of a triumph for African Americans. At the start of the war, few Northerners wanted to liberate the slaves in a war to save the Union. Radicals in Congress and abolitionists hoped the war might result in emancipation, but public opinion was not on their side. Although President Lincoln loathed slavery on moral grounds and felt that limiting its expansion would put it on a path toward extinction, he believed that the Constitution protected it in the southern states. In addition, he did not want to risk losing public support or alienate the Border States. If the North could win the war without freeing the slaves, so be it.

Abolitionists and radical Republicans therefore attempted to convince Northerners and the president that the only way to win the war was through emancipation. Declaring it a "military necessity," they insisted that the Constitution provided the president with the war powers necessary to free the slaves. Emancipationists argued that the government must determine the status of the thousands of runaway slaves within Union lines. They pointed out that slaves were a Confederate asset and that the South might use them more extensively in combat. Freeing the slaves, they insisted, would strengthen the North while correspondingly weakening the South. Nevertheless, after months of abolitionist pressure, Lincoln's December 1861 address to Congress demonstrated that he did not yet believe that the time was right for such a radical step.

The radicals, therefore, asserted that the Constitution also granted war powers to Congress that could bring about emancipation. Although the debates surrounding the Second Confiscation Act primarily focused on property rights, how to protect southern Unionists while punishing Rebels, and the nature of legislative war powers, the radicals had to convince Congress that emancipation was a military necessity. To do so, they fortified their arguments by trumpeting the activities of blacks during the Peninsula Campaign, pointing out their value to both sides in the conflict. Without this evidence, the military necessity argument would have been far less persuasive.

When McClellan was defeated, many Northerners noted that slave labor had allowed Rebel soldiers to be fresher and better rested than Union soldiers, and they wondered whether their army could have accomplished more if it had not been fatigued from labor duty and had not been slowed by slave-built fortifications. Therefore, the outcome of the campaign strengthened the argument that emancipation would deprive the South of an important military asset while simultaneously bringing that asset over to the Union side of the ledger. By the end of July 1862, even many moderates and conservatives were passionately making this very point. Additionally, the shock of the campaign's failure offset Union victories in the west and increased northern demands for more radical measures to win the war. By laboring for the South and playing an important role in defeating McClellan, slaves had inadvertently helped bring about the contingency that finally convinced a broad spectrum of Northerners that freeing the slaves was a military necessity and prepared people to accept the Emancipation Proclamation.

While the Army of the Potomac was still at Harrison's Landing, Pennsylvania chaplain A. M. Stewart reflected on the anniversary of the First Battle of Bull Run. "Sad as that defeat was deemed," he commented, "it was nevertheless the greatest mercy God has ever conferred on our nation." Stewart believed that God had allowed the conflict to occur so that it would destroy slavery, but "had the war . . . ended by a great Union victory a year ago to-day, slavery [would] have been left almost intact." Since that time, Stewart believed, each military setback had increased the North's hatred of slavery. "The nation was not at first ready or willing to kill the monster outright," he noted, "nor is it yet entirely prepared" for emancipation. "The Lord is nevertheless fast educating the whole people for this result. Our late reverses before Richmond have pushed the nation rapidly in that direction." The chaplain insisted that God "would have his own way . . . whether Presidents, Senators, and Generals, be willing or not. . . . We can still trust Him for right results from this great contest."[25]

Historians have affirmed Stewart's assessment that McClellan's defeat turned northern opinion in favor of a more aggressive war and some form of emancipation. What they have not done is demonstrate the specific ways that the actions of slaves helped shape McClellan's campaign and how those same actions played a pivotal role in helping to convince a broad range of Northerners that emancipation was a military necessity. Newspaper reports from the Peninsula, Confederate impressments, allegations that blacks were fighting alongside their masters, pragmatic choices by Union officers like Benjamin Butler, military intelligence provided by slaves, the forceful arguments of abolitionists and radicals, positive interactions between African Americans and Yankee soldiers, McClellan's failure, Union soldier fatigue, Lincoln's keen sense of public opinion, and his critical decisions, all combined to bring about emancipation. No one person or group of people freed the slaves: from the start of the war the actions and sentiments of a disparate cast of thousands advanced the military necessity argument, and all the elements potently converged in July 1862. Whether African Americans were unloading Union ships, providing military intelligence to the Federals, digging Confederate trenches, or even fighting beside their masters, the Peninsula Campaign had worked to their advantage. Slavery was born in the British colonies when a Dutch ship brought blacks to the Virginia Peninsula in 1619, and there, 242 years later, slavery began to die. For African Americans, their Peninsula Campaign proved to be a decisive victory.

NOTES

Abbreviations

CG   *Congressional Globe*

CWF   Colonial Williamsburg Foundation Archives, Oral History Collection, Williamsburg, Virginia

Duke   Duke University, William R. Perkins Library, Durham, North Carolina

GBMP George B. McClellan Papers, Library of Congress, Manuscripts Division, Washington, D.C.

LC   Library of Congress, Manuscripts Division, Washington, D.C.

LV   Library of Virginia, Richmond

OR   U.S. War Department, *The War of the Rebellion: A Compilation of the Official Records of the Union and Confederate Armies* (unless otherwise noted, all references are to series 1).

SHC   University of North Carolina, Southern Historical Collection, Chapel Hill

USAMHI U.S. Army Military History Institute, Carlisle Barracks, Pennsylvania

VHS   Virginia Historical Society, Richmond

WM   College of William and Mary, Manuscripts and Rare Books Department, Swem Library, Williamsburg, Virginia

Introduction

1. *Washington Post*, April 30, 2000; *New York Times*, November 15, 1997. See also Pitcaithley, "A Cosmic Threat," 168–86.

2. *Washington Post*, April 30, 2000 (italics added).

3. For an interesting consideration of Civil War interpretation as reflected in various forms of modern popular culture, see Gallagher, *Causes Won, Lost, and Forgotten*.

4. *Los Angeles Times*, April 7, 2010; *Washington Post*, April 8, 2010. Under heavy pressure, the governor apologized for the omission and altered the proclamation to acknowledge slavery's role in the Civil War.

5. Gallagher, "Lee to the Fore," 6–8; Cullen, *The Peninsula Campaign*; Allan, *Army of Northern Virginia in 1862*; Freeman, *Lee's Lieutenants*, vol. 1; Dowdey, *The Seven Days*; Sears, *To the Gates of Richmond*.

6. Gallagher, *The Richmond Campaign of 1862*; William J. Miller, *Peninsula Campaign of 1862*; Dougherty and Moore, *Peninsula Campaign of 1862*; Burton, *Extraordinary Circumstances*.

7. See, for example, Quarles, *Lincoln and the Negro*, 125–26; Grimsley, *Hard Hand of War*, 68–78; Gallagher, *Richmond Campaign of 1862*, 16–17; McPherson, *Battle Cry of Freedom*, 489–90; McPherson, *Crossroads of Freedom*, 41–71; Goodwin, *Team of Rivals*, 462; Donald, *Lincoln*, 358–60.

8. Gallagher, *The Union War*, 121–24, asserts that because historians have often failed to successfully blend military history with the war's social and political as-

pects, much of current Civil War historiography essentially presents two differing and unrelated Civil Wars. In this work I have attempted to avoid this problem.

9. Brown, *Negro in the American Rebellion*; George Washington Williams, *A History of Negro Troops*; Joseph T. Wilson, *Black Phalanx*.

10. Aptheker, *Negro in the Civil War*; Wiley, *Southern Negroes*; Quarles, *Negro in the Civil War*; Ervin Jordan, *Black Confederates*; McPherson, *Negro's Civil War*; Cornish, *Sable Arm*; Glatthaar, *Forged in Battle*; Trudeau, *Like Men of War*; Berlin et al., *Slaves No More*.

11. See, for example, Blackerby, *Blacks in Blue and Gray*; Barrow, *Forgotten Confederates*; Segars, *Black Southerners in Confederate Armies*; and Bergeron, *Black Southerners in Gray*. For an interesting consideration of why some groups and individuals promote these interpretations, see Levine, "Black Confederates and Neo-Confederates: In Search of a Usable Past," 187–211.

12. For a succinct explanation of the "Black confederate legend," as well as a concise and skillful dismantling of the argument by a professional historian, see Levine, "Black Confederates," 40–45, as well as the author's letter to *North and South*'s "Editorial Crossfire," 8–9. For fuller treatment, see Levine, *Confederate Emancipation*.

13. See Harding, *There Is a River*; Barbara J. Fields, "Who Freed the Slaves?" 178–81. The editors of the Freedmen and Southern Society project (whose indispensable collection of primary source documents is cited in this work as Berlin et al., *Freedom*) acknowledge the importance of the Union army, Lincoln, and political factors in the process of emancipation. Nevertheless, their focus is to demonstrate that slaves were the critical actors in achieving emancipation, and thus the project has become the most influential work in the promotion of the "self-emancipation thesis." For a succinct overview of the specifics of this thesis, see James M. McPherson, "Who Freed the Slaves?" in McPherson, *Drawn with a Sword*, 192–207. The author skillfully repudiates the thesis but goes to the opposite extreme by emphatically concluding that "Abraham Lincoln freed the slaves." Without discounting the importance of either the slaves or the president, Gallagher, *The Union War*, 141–50, reminds us that "the armies largely determined how and where freedom arrived in the Confederacy."

Chapter 1

1. *CG*, 37th Cong., 2nd sess., 1919, 2326.

2. Patterson, *Slavery and Social Death*, 287–91. See also Buckley, *Slaves in Red Coats*.

3. Berlin, *Many Thousands Gone*, 29–63, 109–41; Quarles, "Colonial Militia and Negro Manpower," 643–48. For early Virginia and its evolving slave codes, see especially Edmund S. Morgan, *American Slavery*.

4. Wood, *Black Majority*, 308–16; Quarles, "Colonial Militia and Negro Manpower," 648–51.

5. Quarles, *Negro in the American Revolution*, 18; Larry G. Bowman, "Virginia's Use of Blacks in the French and Indian War," 59; Anderson, *Crucible of War*, 159–60. See also Holton, *Forced Founders*, 137–38 and notes.

6. Quarles, *Negro in the American Revolution*, 19.

7. Ibid., 13–31; Mullin, *Flight and Rebellion*, 130–33; Holton, *Forced Founders*, 156–57.

8. Patterson, *Slavery and Social Death*, 292; Joseph Ellis, *American Creation*, 35.

9. Jackson, "Virginia Negro Soldiers," 250–60, 269–73; Quarles, *Negro in the American Revolution*, 94–102.

10. Frey, *Water from the Rock*, 163–68, 170.

11. Quarles, *Negro in the American Revolution*, vii.

12. Ibid., 170–71.

13. George Washington, *Writings of George Washington*, 23:262; Quarles, *Negro in the American Revolution*, 170–71; Ranlet, "The British, Slaves, and Smallpox in Revolutionary Virginia," 223–24; Frey, "Between Slavery and Freedom," 389–90; Joseph Plumb Martin, *Private Yankee Doodle*, 241–42.

14. Berlin, *Many Thousands Gone*, 277–78; Kulikoff, *Tobacco and Slaves*, 432–35.

15. George, "Mirage of Freedom," 429.

16. Cassell, "Slaves of the Chesapeake Bay Area," 145–46; George, "Mirage of Freedom," 433–34.

17. George, "Mirage of Freedom," 434–36; Cassell, "Slaves of the Chesapeake Bay Area," 152–55. However, instead of fighting, most of the slaves chose to be relocated to British possessions. Thousands were settled in this way. The largest group was some 2,000 ex-slaves who were sent to Halifax in early 1815.

18. Altoff, *Amongst My Best Men*, 122–30; Remini, *Battle of New Orleans*, 37–38; Cassell, "Slaves of the Chesapeake Bay Area," 154.

19. Lydia J. Morgan, *Emancipation in Virginia's Tobacco Belt*, 17–19, 26–27; Klein, *Slavery in the Americas*, 185, 188; Kimball, *American City, Southern Place*, 16–23; Takagi, *Rearing Wolves*, 16–18; Link, *Roots of Secession*, 30; Dew, *Ironmaker to the Confederacy*, 2.

20. Lydia J. Morgan, *Emancipation in Virginia's Tobacco Belt*, 26; Forrest, *Historical and Descriptive Sketches*, 330; Shearer Davis Bowman, "Conditional Unionism," 42–43; Takagi, *Rearing Wolves*, 72; Blair, *Virginia's Private War*, 13; Dubbs, *Defend This Old Town*, 13; Engs, *Freedom's First Generation*, 8.

21. Kennedy, *Population of the United States*, 516–18.

22. Takagi, *Rearing Wolves*, 74; Link, *Roots of Secession*, 38; Brewer, *Confederate Negro*, 4–5; Goldin, *Urban Slavery*, 129; Franklin and Schweninger, *Runaway Slaves*, 4; Jonathan D. Martin, *Divided Mastery*, 27–43; Dew, *Ironmaker to the Confederacy*, 22–23. Today, the remaining original buildings of the Tredegar Ironworks house the main visitor's center for the Richmond National Battlefield Park, as well as the American Civil War Center.

23. Kennedy, *Population of the United States*, 516–18.

24. Jackson, *Free Negro Labor*, 74–81; Berlin, *Slaves without Masters*, 238; Berlin et al., *Freedom*, 3:86.

25. Lydia J. Morgan, *Emancipation in Virginia's Tobacco Belt*, 26; Klein, *Slavery in the Americas*, 187; Berlin et al., *Freedom*, 3:86; Olmsted, *Cotton Kingdom*, 89; Shearer Davis Bowman, "Conditional Unionism," 43.

26. Lydia J. Morgan, *Emancipation in Virginia's Tobacco Belt*, 26; Oakes, *Rul-*

ing Race, 193, 197; Berlin et al., *Freedom*, 3:86; West, *When the Yankees Came*, 3; Quarstein, *Civil War on the Virginia Peninsula*, 9; Jones, "Recollections of Williamsburg," CWF.

27. Perdue, Barden, and Phillips, *Weevils in the Wheat*, 52, 84, 68. My book often quotes from this collection of WPA slave interviews. Some may question the reliability of these sources, as the ex-slaves were young during slavery and very advanced in years when the interviews were taken in the 1930s. However, I have chosen my sources with an eye toward disregarding those that seemed to be a product of legend and lore more than of genuine memory. While I cannot claim infallibility in selecting what to use and what to disregard, it should be noted that even in cases where an ex-slave was letting imagination get the best of him or her, the story is still valuable. After all, exaggerations are usually based on some grain of truth. John W. Blassingame, in the introduction to *Slave Testimony*, points out the unreliability of the interviews administered by white project workers. However, one of the strengths of *Weevils in the Wheat* is that black workers conducted most of the interviews included in the book. Still, historians must handle these sources carefully, and it is best to use them to illustrate a point rather than to clinch it. For a fuller discussion of the reliability of these sources, see the introduction to Perdue, Barden, and Phillips, *Weevils in the Wheat*; Woodward, "History from Slave Sources," 470–81; Blassingame, *Slave Testimony*, xlii–xlvi; and Escott, *Slavery Remembered*.

28. Oakes, *Ruling Race*, 218; Redpath, *Roving Editor*, 31; Douglass, *My Bondage*, 263–64. See also Tadman, *Speculators and Slaves*, 219–20.

29. Perdue, Barden, and Phillips, *Weevils in the Wheat*, 115.

30. Ibid., 259.

31. Ibid., 71, 116; Nicholls, "In the Light of Human Beings," 73, 69.

32. Baker, "Memoirs of Williamsburg," CWF. White resident Charles S. Jones recalled "the cage" as well, although he maintained that it was on the ground floor of a building near Williamsburg's courthouse. Jones, "Recollections of Williamsburg," CWF.

33. See, for example, Conrad and Meyer, "Economics of Slavery in the Antebellum South," 95–122; and Sutch, "The Breeding of Slaves for Sale and the Westward Expansion of Slavery, 1850–1860," 173–210. Michael Tadman, in *Speculators and Slaves*, presents an effective argument against a "widespread system of stud farms." However, his argument does not completely refute the theory that the practice occurred on a more limited scale.

34. Olmsted, *Cotton Kingdom*, 87–88; Shearer Davis Bowman, "Conditional Unionism," 50; Baker, "Memoirs of Williamsburg," CWF.

35. Perdue, Barden, and Phillips, *Weevils in the Wheat*, 84–85, 166. For a particularly interesting discussion of the degrading process of examining bodies in the slave market, see Johnson, *Soul by Soul*, 135–61.

36. Perdue, Barden, and Phillips, *Weevils in the Wheat*, 166; Tadman, *Speculators and Slaves*, 211–12; Shearer Davis Bowman, "Conditional Unionism," 32 (notes).

37. Perdue, Barden, and Phillips, *Weevils in the Wheat*, 68; Baker, "Memoirs of Williamsburg," CWF.

38. Link, *Roots of Secession*, 100–103; Perdue, Barden, and Phillips, *Weevils in the Wheat*, 272; Schwarz, *Slave Laws*, 140–41; Takagi, *Rearing Wolves*, 121.

39. Brewer, *Confederate Negro*, 5; Franklin and Schweninger, *Runaway Slaves*, 4, 33–37; Link, *Roots of Secession*, 249–50; Jonathan D. Martin, *Divided Mastery*, 174–78.

40. Takagi, *Rearing Wolves*, 121.

41. Link, *Roots of Secession*, 106; Schwarz, *Slave Laws*, 142–43, 145.

42. Blassingame, *Slave Community*, 41.

43. Olmsted, *Cotton Kingdom*, 100; Forrest, *Historical and Descriptive Sketches*, 418.

44. See Camp, *Closer to Freedom*, 35–59; and Perdue, Barden, and Phillips, *Weevils in the Wheat*, 67, 105.

45. West, *When the Yankees Came*, 56. See also Franklin and Schweninger, *Runaway Slaves*, 99–109.

46. Blassingame, *Slave Community*, 44–45; Camp, *Closer to Freedom*, 73–78; Perdue, Barden, and Phillips, *Weevils in the Wheat*, 241, 316, 119; Alho, *Religion of the Slaves*, 155.

47. Perdue, Barden, and Phillips, *Weevils in the Wheat*, 119; Randolph, *Sketches of Slave Life*, 30–31.

48. Stampp, *Peculiar Institution*, 214; Franklin and Schweninger, *Runaway Slaves*, 152–56; Perdue, Barden, and Phillips, *Weevils in the Wheat*, 93, 182–83, 267, 290; Camp, *Closer to Freedom*, 71–72.

49. Perdue, Barden, and Phillips, *Weevils in the Wheat*, 100, 117, 216–17; Rawick, *From Sundown to Sunup*, 107–8.

50. Perdue, Barden, and Phillips, *Weevils in the Wheat*, 117.

51. Shearer Davis Bowman, "Conditional Unionism," 51; Robert Page Waller Diary, November 17, 1861, WM. After exhaustive research into the diaries and letters of soldiers, Chandra Manning, in *What This Cruel War Was Over*, 38, found that similar "rumors of slave violence circulated throughout the [southern] army in the early days of the war."

52. *Richmond Daily Dispatch*, January 3–4, 1861.

53. Ibid.

Chapter 2

1. Allen Pinkerton to George B. McClellan, December 2, 1861 (A-32:14), GBMP.

2. Freeman, *Lee's Lieutenants*, 1:14; Freeman, *R. E. Lee*, 1:464, 472–77; Sears, *To the Gates of Richmond*, 27; Brewer, *Confederate Negro*, 131–34; Lee to Andrew Talcott, April 30, 1861, Talcott Family Papers, VHS.

3. Olmsted, *Cotton Kingdom*, 87; Brewer, *Confederate Negro*, 134.

4. *Petersburg Daily Express*, April 26, 1861; *Richmond Dispatch*, July 18, 1861.

5. John Washington, *John Washington's Civil War*, 36.

6. Diary of Richard Eppes, May 8, 1861, VHS.

7. Ibid.

8. William Eppes to Hill Carter, May 25, 1861, John Letcher Executive Papers, box 432, LV.

9. Ruffin, *Diary of Edmund Ruffin*, 2:35.

10. Paludan, *Presidency of Abraham Lincoln*, 51–56; McPherson, *Struggle for Equality*, 56.

11. *National Anti-Slavery Standard*, May 18, 1861; Paludan, *Presidency of Abraham Lincoln*, 51–56; McPherson, *Battle Cry of Freedom*, 261–62, 308–12; McPherson, *Struggle for Equality*, 56. Historians often use the label "radical Republicans" to denote a party faction that believed prosecution of the war required emancipation and embraced abolitionist moral arguments. The label distinguishes them from conservative Republicans (those who wanted the war carried out without destroying southern institutions) and moderates such as Lincoln. Although some abolitionists embraced and worked within the Republican Party, many others were skeptical and distanced themselves from the party.

12. McPherson, *Struggle for Equality*, 49.

13. Quarles, *Negro in the Civil War*, 46. See also *Richmond Dispatch*, June 24, 1861; and Perdue, Barden, and Phillips, *Weevils in the Wheat*, 149.

14. McPherson, *Battle Cry of Freedom*, 228; William Eppes to Hill Carter, May 25, 1861, John Letcher Executive Papers, box 432, LV. Dew, *Apostles of Disunion*, is perhaps the most powerful demonstration of how, in an effort to unify the white South in 1860–61, leaders used racially charged language depicting Lincoln and the Republicans as committed to emancipation, black equality, and even miscegenation.

15. William Eppes to Hill Carter, May 25, 1861, John Letcher Executive Papers, box 432, LV; Ruffin, *Diary of Edmund Ruffin*, 2:35–36.

16. Freeman, *Lee's Lieutenants*, 1:17; Freeman, *R. E. Lee*, 1:481, 486; Pinkerton to McClellan, December 2, 1861 (A-32:14), GBMP; *National Anti-Slavery Standard*, May 18, 1861.

17. Brewer, *Confederate Negro*, 132–33. For a full discussion of Civil War–era field fortifications and construction, see Mahan, *Treatise of Field Fortifications*.

18. Brewer, *Confederate Negro*, 133; Freemen, *R. E. Lee*, 1:490.

19. Pierce, "Contrabands at Fortress Monroe," 626–27; Parton, *General Butler in New Orleans*, 125, 132–33.

20. Pierce, "Contrabands at Fortress Monroe," 626–27; Parton, *General Butler in New Orleans*, 125, 132–33.

21. Pierce, "Contrabands at Fortress Monroe," 626–27; Parton, *General Butler in New Orleans*, 125, 132–33.

22. Pierce, "Contrabands at Fortress Monroe," 626–27; Parton, *General Butler in New Orleans*, 125, 132–33.

23. This conversation is justly famous and reconstructed in Butler, *Butler's Book*, 256–57. Its content is confirmed by his report in *OR*, 2:648–51. See also Marshall, *Private and Official Correspondence of Gen. Benjamin F. Butler*, 1:106–7; *New York Times*, May 27, 1861; and *New York Herald*, May 28, 1861.

24. *OR*, 2:652.

25. Pierce, "Contrabands at Fortress Monroe," 628; *National Anti-Slavery Standard*, June 8, 1861; *Boston Journal*, May 26, 1861; Quarles, *Negro in the Civil War*, 60–62.

26. Butler, *Private and Official Correspondence*, 1:113, 114.

27. Ibid., 1:116–17.

28. Ibid., 1:119; Browning, *Diary of Orville Hickman Browning*, 1:477–78.

29. Ruffin, *Diary of Edmund Ruffin*, 2:40; Parton, *General Butler in New Orleans*, 132–33.

30. The term "contraband" was initially a specific label for slaves who had been "confiscated" because they had labored for the Confederacy (as well as the families of these workers) but who were technically not free. Many of these slaves were runaways, but others had been abandoned by their owners when white civilians fled before the advance of Union armies. As such, the term is still useful for historians when specifically discussing these slaves. However, Kate Masur, in "A Rare Phenomenon of Philological Vegetation," reveals that during the war the term "contraband" quickly entered popular culture as a label for all southern blacks sheltered behind Union lines whether they or their family members had worked for the Confederacy or not, was frequently connected to racist stereotypes, and implied "poverty, dependence, and desperation." Moreover, contemporary illustrations and songs often depicted contrabands as "heterogeneous, disorganized, and in need of white supervision." Masur argues that the legal meaning the term initially carried was dubious, and thus the more influential use of the term was its cultural, not legal, connotation. The essay distinguishes the racial politics of the Democrats from that of the Republicans and abolitionists but it slights the fact that the term was frequently used in the context of praising, rather than denigrating, African Americans in the South. Nevertheless, Masur argues that in such instances, commentators often employed the phrase "intelligent contraband" so that the adjective "intelligent" would counterbalance the stereotypes connected to "contraband." Her work has shown that when not directly quoting primary sources, historians should use the term carefully and not as a broad label for southern blacks during the war.

31. *Chicago Tribune*, May 30, 1861; *Philadelphia Inquirer*, May 31, 1861.

32. *Boston Herald* quoted in *National Anti-Slavery Standard*, June 8, 1861; *New York Times*, May 31, 1861. Fort Monroe still stands today, housing the small but impressive Casemate Museum. The facility now includes interpretation of Fort Monroe's role in the process of emancipation, as well as information on the lives of the runaway slaves who were sheltered there. As of this writing, it appears that the federal government will soon make Fort Monroe a unit of the National Park Service, and thus the site will likely see an appropriate and much-warranted expansion of its historical interpretation.

33. Casdorph, *Prince John Magruder*, 119.

34. Ibid.; Blair, *Virginia's Private War*, 35–37; Freeman, *R. E. Lee*, 1:511; Freeman, *Lee's Lieutenants*, 1:16.

35. Brewer, *Confederate Negro*, 137.

36. Casdorph, *Prince John Magruder*, 119; Southwick, *A Duryee Zouave*, 37.

37. West, *When the Yankees Came*, 46–47, 53–54. West shows no signs of having wondered, as the reader must, if this mulatto boy, whom they "raised almost like a son," was in fact the elderly gentleman's son.

38. Ibid., 55.

39. Warner, *Generals in Blue*, 368–69; Vermont Colonization Society, *Forty-eighth Annual Report*, 27; Parton, *General Butler in New Orleans*, 164, 168. Later, when stationed in New Orleans, Phelps organized black troops before this became military policy and was ordered to disband the regiment. He then resigned in disgust. Meanwhile, the Confederate government labeled him an outlaw for having "organized and armed Negro slaves for military service against their masters." Perhaps out of spite, he later, once the United States reversed its policy, declined a commission as a major general of colored troops.

40. West, *When the Yankees Came*, 55.

41. Ibid., 55–56.

42. Ibid., 56–58. When Aunt Lucy and her husband reunited after the war, she was still carrying his clothes. They lived together in Hampton for the rest of their lives.

43. Casdorph, *Prince John Magruder*, 125–26.

44. Hess, *Field Armies and Fortifications*, 28–29.

45. Quarles, *Negro in the Civil War*, 78; Engs, *Freedom's First Generation*, 15. For a brief discussion of which battle was the first of the war, see Boatner, *Civil War Dictionary*, 63, 280.

46. Quarles, *Negro in the Civil War*, 78–79.

47. *New York Times*, June 13, 1861; Quarles, *Negro in the Civil War*, 79.

48. Butler, *Private and Official Correspondence*, 1:133; Parton, *General Butler in New Orleans*, 142; Hess, *Field Armies and Fortifications*, 29; Pierce, "Contrabands at Fortress Monroe," 628.

49. Hale, "Bethel Regiment," 96; Moore, *Civil War in Song and Story*, 481; Perdue, Barden, and Phillips, *Weevils in the Wheat*, 145.

50. Butler, *Private and Official Correspondence*, 1:138–39; Butler, *Butler's Book*, 274–75.

51. Freeman, *R. E. Lee*, 1:528; Berlin et al., *Freedom*, 1:684–85.

52. Pierce, "Contrabands at Fort Monroe," 633.

53. Ibid.

54. Ibid., 634, 638; *National Anti-Slavery Standard*, June 8, 1861.

55. Pierce, "Contrabands at Fort Monroe," 636.

56. Ibid., 637; Marks, *Peninsula Campaign in Virginia*, 99.

57. Pierce, "Contrabands at Fort Monroe," 638–39.

58. Ibid., 638.

59. Joseph T. Wilson, *Black Phalanx*, 483.

60. Pierce, "Contrabands at Fort Monroe," 638; *Principia*, September 14, 1861.

61. Pierce, "Contrabands at Fortress Monroe," 638.

62. *Principia*, October 12, 1861.

63. Pierce, "Contrabands at Fortress Monroe," 637.

64. Ibid., 636.

Chapter 3

1. *New York Times*, August 8, 1861; *Chicago Tribune*, August 8, 1861.

2. *Philadelphia Inquirer*, December 5, 1861.

3. Hess, *Field Armies and Fortifications*, 31.

4. *OR*, 2:501.

5. *Philadelphia Inquirer*, July 1, 1861; *Boston Herald*, July 25, 1861; *Chicago Tribune*, July 29, 1861.

6. *New York Times*, July 29, 1861, August 1, 1861; *Reading (Pa.) Journal* quoted in *Douglass' Monthly* 4 (March 1862): 612; *Charlotte Western Democrat*, July 30, August 6, 1861; *Daily Chicago Times* quoted in *Indianapolis Daily Sentinel*, July 27, 1861; *Principia*, August 3, 1861.

7. *Chicago Tribune*, July 29, 1861; *Boston Herald*, July 22, 1861; *Philadelphia Inquirer*, July 22, 23, 1861.

8. *National Anti-Slavery Standard*, August 3, 1861; *Indianapolis Star*, December 23, 1861; *Harper's Weekly*, May 10, 1862.

9. *Reading (Pa.) Journal* quoted in *Douglass' Monthly* 4 (March 1862): 612.

10. Siddali, *From Property to Person*, 59–77.

11. *CG*, 37th Cong., 1st sess., 218–19; Klung, *Lyman Trumbull*, 189, 195; Roske, *His Own Counsel*, 74–75.

12. *CG*, 37th Cong., 1st sess., 218–19; *New York Times*, July 23, 1861; Blaine, *Twenty Years of Congress*, 1:342.

13. *CG*, 37th Cong., 1st sess., 219; *CG*, 36th Cong., 1st sess., 1484.

14. *CG*, 37th Cong., 1st sess., 219, 224. Silvana Siddali, in *From Property to Person*, 59–77, downplays the influence of Manassas on the Senate bill, arguing that since Trumbull's amendment was offered the day before the battle, the results did not lead to the inclusion of slaves. However, the senators did not vote on the amendment until after the battle, and the debates clearly reveal that blacks fighting within Confederate ranks played a significant role in getting the bill passed.

15. McPherson, *Struggle for Equality*, 70–71; *National Anti-Slavery Standard*, August 3, 1861.

16. *Douglass' Monthly* 4 (September 1861): 516; *Liberator*, August 23, 1861.

17. *Principia*, September 21, 1861.

18. *New York Times*, September 7, 1861; *Chicago Tribune*, August 6, 1861.

19. Levine, "Black Confederates," 42.

20. Andrews, *The North Reports the Civil War*, 28; *Chicago Tribune*, August 1, 3, 6, 1861.

21. McPherson, *Battle Cry of Freedom*, 312.

22. Grimsley, *Hard Hand of War*, 32.

23. Butler, *Private and Official Correspondence*, 1:188–89.

24. Ibid.; *National Anti-Slavery Standard*, August 3, 10, 1861; *Baltimore American and Commercial Advertiser*, July 29, 1861; *Harper's Weekly*, August 17, 1861.

25. Butler, *Private and Official Correspondence*, 1:188–89.

26. Ibid.

27. *New York Times*, August 7, 12, 1861; Ruffin, *Diary of Edmund Ruffin*, 2:106.

28. Butler, *Private and Official Correspondence*, 1:201–3; *New York Herald*, August 12, 1861.

29. *OR*, 4:570; Casdorph, *Prince John Magruder*, 134; *Richmond Dispatch*, August 14, 1861.

30. Parton, *General Butler in New Orleans*, 165.

31. *National Anti-Slavery Standard*, September 7, 28, 1861; Diary of Richard Eppes, list of escaped slaves, VHS.

32. *Chicago Tribune*, November 7, 1861.

33. *National Anti-Slavery Standard*, September 28, 1861; *OR*, 4:616; Gerteis, *From Contraband to Freedman*, 19–20. Abolitionists soon began a school for the contrabands, which evolved into Hampton University.

34. *National Anti-Slavery Standard*, September 28, 1861.

35. *OR*, 4:636; Ruffin, *Diary of Edmund Ruffin*, 2:134–35.

36. Dr. John R. Purdie to T. M. R. Talcott, August 14, 1861, and Dr. William D. Southall to T. M. R. Talcott, August 14, 1861, Talcott Family Papers, VHS.

37. T. M. R. Talcott to John C. Pemberton, September 7, 1861, Talcott Family Papers, VHS; *OR*, 4:654.

38. *OR*, 4:654; Brewer, *Confederate Negro*, 192.

39. Donald, *Lincoln*, 314–17; Paludan, *Presidency of Abraham Lincoln*, 87. The president also feared that Frémont's order would offend slave owners in other Border States and put the weighty question of emancipation into the hands of military commanders, allowing them to overrule civilian authority.

40. McPherson, *Struggle for Equality*, 72–74; Paludan, *Presidency of Abraham Lincoln*, 87.

41. McPherson, *Struggle for Equality*, 72–81.

42. Beecher, *War and Emancipation*, 22, 24.

43. *CG*, 37th Cong., 2nd sess., 83; *New York Times*, November 28, 1861.

44. Cheever, *Salvation of the Country*, 16; White, *Abolition of Slavery*, 23–24.

45. Conway, *Rejected Stone*, 103; McPherson, *Struggle for Equality*, 63.

46. *New Bedford Mercury* quoted in *National Anti-Slavery Standard*, August 24, 1861; Cheever, *Salvation of the Country*, 5.

47. *New York Times*, October 2, 1861.

48. McPherson, *Struggle for Equality*, 76–81; Stewart, *Camp, March, and Battlefield*, 118; Conway, *Rejected Stone*, 112.

49. Conway, *Rejected Stone*, 68, 73; *CG*, 37th Cong., 2nd sess., 83; Boutwell, *Emancipation*, 7, 9.

50. *Chicago Tribune*, November 7, December 3, 1861; *Cincinnati Gazette*, December 7, 1861; *Daily Cleveland Herald*, December 7, 1861.

51. McPherson, *Struggle for Equality*, 81–82; *Detroit Free Press*, November 30, 1861. McPherson concludes that "the evidence of the newfound popularity, prestige, and influence of abolitionists in 1861–1862 is overwhelming."

52. McPherson, *Struggle for Equality*, 79; *Daily Chicago Times*, November 23, 1861.

53. *Boston Courier* quoted in *National Anti-Slavery Standard*, November 30, 1861; *National Anti-Slavery Standard*, September 28, 1861. See also *New York Her-*

ald, November 6, 8, 11, 29, 1861; and *Louisville Democrat* quoted in *Indianapolis Daily Sentinel*, December 6, 1861.

54. *Washington Sunday Morning Chronicle*, December 29, 1861; *Daily Chicago Times* quoted in *Indianapolis Daily Sentinel*, December 24, 1861; *Washington Daily Intelligencer*, December 2, 1861.

55. McClellan, *Civil War Papers*, 128; Grimsley, *Hard Hand of War*, 125.

56. Conway, *Rejected Stone*, 114.

57. Quarles, *Lincoln and the Negro*, 88–90; Donald, *Charles Sumner and the Rights of Man*, 48; Bogue, *Congressman's Civil War*, 172. The Republican strength in Congress was deceptive. The numbers do not reveal that the margin of victory for Republican candidates in many crucial districts was slim. In Congress and in the military, the Democrats remained an influential bastion of conservatism and strongly resisted the expansion of federal power. Paludan, *A People's Contest*, 88, 91–96.

58. Lincoln, *Collected Works*, 5:48–52. Lincoln's support for the colonization of African Americans was nothing new; he had long been an advocate of the idea, despite the fact that the vast majority of abolitionists, and, more important, of African Americans, widely denounced such schemes.

59. Ibid.; Siddali, *From Property to Person*, 126. The president also rejected the idea of arming blacks. Since the start of the war, it had become increasingly clear that Secretary of War Simon Cameron could not handle the job, and pressure was building to replace him. Sensing the direction of things, Cameron attempted to win over the radicals so that they would help protect his job. He did so by publicly calling for the arming of confiscated slaves. Lincoln was appalled, tried to prevent the publication of Cameron's report, and in his address to Congress was publicly rejecting both emancipation and the secretary's proposal.

60. *New York Herald*, December 4, 1861; *Boston Daily Advertiser*, December 4, 1861; *Detroit Free Press*, December 5, 1861.

61. *Illinois State Journal*, December 5, 1861; *Washington Daily Intelligencer*, December 4, 1861; *Baltimore American*, December 4, 6, 1861; *Washington Sunday Morning Chronicle*, December 15, 1861.

62. *New York Times*, December 4, 1861.

63. *Racine (Wis.) Weekly Journal*, December 11, 1861; *Chicago Tribune*, December 4, 1861.

64. *CG*, 37th Cong., 2nd sess., 18–19; *Illinois State Journal*, December 5, 1861; William Doubleday to Zachariah Chandler, December 6, 1861, Zachariah Chandler Papers, LC.

65. Pinkerton to McClellan, December 2, 1861 (A-32:14), GBMP.

66. Ibid.; Brewer, *Confederate Negro*, 138. Small remnants of these works are still visible in the eastern suburbs of Richmond. See, for example, the Chickahominy Bluffs Unit of Richmond National Battlefield Park.

67. Pinkerton to McClellan, December 2, 1861 (A-32:14), GBMP.

68. Ibid.

69. Ibid.; Fischel, *Secret War for the Union*, 117–18.

70. *OR*, 4:715.

71. Manning, *What This Cruel War Was Over*, 39–51, argues that by the end of 1861 significant numbers of soldiers in both the western and eastern armies were already starting to embrace emancipation. Manning believes this was because slavery was seen as the cause of the war, and thus it could not end until the institution was destroyed. Additionally, she argues that soldiers arrived at these sentiments due to their increasing exposure to the evils of slavery as they marched south. Nevertheless, she concedes that such beliefs were "not universal among the entire Union Army," nor were they "shared by most civilians, political leaders, or high ranking military officers."

72. *Indianapolis Journal*, November 26, 1861.

Chapter 4

1. *New York Times*, January 14, 16, 1862.

2. Ibid., January 16, 1862.

3. Ibid.

4. *New York Evening Post*, January 24, 1862; *Principia*, January 30, 1862. Advocates of the "Black Confederate" legend frequently cite Parker's testimony but usually fail to quote his qualifying language.

5. *New York Times*, December 25, 1861; *Chicago Tribune*, December 25, 1861; Fuller, *Chaplain Fuller*, 232; *OR*, 4:566.

6. *Philadelphia Inquirer*, December 25, 1861.

7. *Indianapolis Journal*, December 27, 1861.

8. See, for example, *Daily Cleveland Herald*, December 30, 1861; *Chicago Tribune*, December 30, 1861; *Liberator*, January 17, 1862; and *National Anti-Slavery Standard*, January 18, 1862.

9. *Chicago Tribune*, December 30, 1861.

10. Ibid.; *Philadelphia Inquirer*, February 12, 1862.

11. *Principia*, January 30, 1862; *CG*, 37th Cong., 2nd sess., 330.

12. *New York Times*, January 14, 1862; *Rochester Evening Express*, February 27, 1862; *Chicago Tribune*, March 19, 1862.

13. *Frank Leslie's Illustrated Newspaper*, March 1, 1862; *Chicago Tribune*, December 30, 1861; *North American and United States Gazette* (Philadelphia), December 17, 1861.

14. The previous November, the U.S. navy seized two Confederate forts controlling the Sea Islands around Port Royal Bay, South Carolina, and local plantation owners evacuated with Rebel forces. Masters left behind approximately 10,000 slaves. Abolitionists quickly sent missionaries to set up schools and help the government organize the abandoned slaves so that the cotton plantations could continue to function and bring in much-needed federal revenue. Secretary of the Treasury Salmon Chase sent Edward Pierce (who had first organized the black laborers at Fort Monroe) to help oversee the endeavor. For the best study on Port Royal, see Rose, *Rehearsal for Reconstruction*.

15. *Boston Journal* quoted in *New York Times*, February 9, 1862; *New York Times*, January 31, 1862.

16. *Philadelphia Inquirer*, February 4, 1862; *Chicago Tribune*, December 30, 1861; *Philadelphia Inquirer*, December 25, 1861.

17. *Philadelphia Inquirer*, February 4, 1862; *New York Times*, February 9, 1862.

18. *Philadelphia Inquirer*, January 1, February 3, 1862.

19. Haydon, *For Country, Cause, and Leader*, 212.

20. *Chicago Tribune*, January 7, 1862.

21. Tap, *Over Lincoln's Shoulder*, 11–17, 101–8. Controlled by radicals such as Benjamin Wade, Zachariah Chandler, and George Julian, the seven-man Committee on the Conduct of the War (consisting of three senators and four representatives) began holding meetings in the basement of the Capitol. Initially, they called witnesses to testify concerning Bull Run and Ball's Bluff, but they also took direct aim at McClellan's apparent inactivity and his conciliatory policy toward Southerners and their slaves.

22. Goodwin, *Team of Rivals*, 410–15; Donald, *Lincoln*, 333–34; Rafuse, *McClellan's War*, 177. Lincoln made the change in his cabinet because Simon Cameron had proven incapable of effectively managing the War Department, and accusations of corruption had swirled about him.

23. Pinkerton, *Spy of the Rebellion*, 344. Pinkerton's book is notorious for its imaginative interpretations and outright fabrications. As a primary source, it must be viewed with a judicious and cautious eye.

24. Fischel, *Secret War for the Union*, 113.

25. Ibid., 115.

26. These reports are located in the McClellan Papers, at the Library of Congress, and are based on interviews conducted by Pinkerton's staff with runaway slaves and free blacks during January, February, and March 1862. Some of Pinkerton's letters are undated, but each page in the library's collection is numbered. Pinkerton and staff used the nom de guerre "E. J. Allen" in signing the letters.

27. Pinkerton to McClellan, March 12, 1862, no. 9417, GBMP.

28. Pinkerton to McClellan, nos. 8784–89, GBMP.

29. Pinkerton to McClellan, February 20, 1862, no. 8960, GBMP.

30. Pinkerton to McClellan, February 10, 1862, nos. 8494–501, GBMP.

31. Pinkerton to McClellan, January 7, 1862, no. 7582, GBMP.

32. Brewster, *When This Cruel War Is Over*, 88, 92–94.

33. McPherson, *Struggle for Equality*, 97.

34. Fischel, *Secret War for the Union*, 123–27.

35. Ibid., 127. Pinkerton's and McClellan's calculation methods were famously flawed and, it has been argued, were designed to produce inflated numbers. Pinkerton counted enemy regiments and attributed approximately 700 men to each. This average was reasonable for Federal regiments early in the war, but the true Confederate average was somewhere around 500. Over time, Pinkerton relied less on this flawed method and increasingly turned to guesswork and rumor. Whatever McClellan's and Pinkerton's methods or motivations, it is unfair to place blame on black informants for their gross exaggerations. See Fischel, "Pinkerton and McClellan: Who Deceived Whom?" 115–42; and Fischel, *Secret War for the Union*, 581–87.

36. McClellan, *Papers of McClellan*, 196, 162–70.

37. Ibid., 162–70; Pinkerton to McClellan, December 2, 1861 (A-32:14), GBMP. For a detailed discussion of the formulation of McClellan's plans and his arguments and problems with the White House, see Sears, *To the Gates of Richmond*, 3–34.

38. Pinkerton, *Spy of the Rebellion*, 344–45.

39. Ibid.; Varon, *Southern Lady, Yankee Spy*, 74–75. In April, Confederate authorities arrested Webster and Lawton, but because Scobell did not seem suspicious, the officials released him. Webster was eventually executed by the Confederacy.

40. Brewer, *Confederate Negro*, 7; *Richmond Dispatch*, December 19, 1861.

41. *Richmond Dispatch*, December 31, 1861; *Richmond Examiner*, January 9, 1862.

42. *Richmond Examiner*, January 9, 1862; *Richmond Dispatch*, January 9, 20, 30, February 5, 1862.

43. *OR*, 9:32–33; Berlin et al., *Freedom*, 1:689.

44. These ads can be seen in the *Richmond Dispatch* and the *Richmond Enquirer* throughout the month of January 1862 starting on January 4 and in the *Richmond Whig* starting on January 10.

45. *OR*, 9:32–33.

46. William Roane Aylett to wife, February 26, 1862, Aylett Family Papers, VHS.

47. *OR*, 9:36.

48. Ibid.

49. Brewer, *Confederate Negro*, 140; *OR*, 9:40–43. For a provocative discussion of the Confederacy's impressment problems, see McCurry, *Confederate Reckoning*, 270–88. The author effectively demonstrates that owners feared that their slaves would abscond while working close to Union lines, that slaves themselves refused to serve, and that white Southerners strongly resisted and condemned impressments as a violation of owner rights. McCurry concludes that owner resistance to slave impressments was an indication that white Southerners were more concerned with property rights than with doing what was necessary to establish the Confederate nation. However, this argument must rest on the assumption that owners accepted that slave impressments were a military necessity. Masters could not fully comprehend the difficulties faced by military commanders and they consistently expressed confusion as to why white soldiers could not do the work, and thus it is likely that they did not accept (or want to accept) that slave impressments were necessary to win the war. White Southerners certainly proved willing to make many other difficult sacrifices they deemed necessary for establishing nationhood—even to the point of death.

50. Brewer, *Confederate Negro*, 7.

51. Pinkerton to McClellan, no. 8670, GBMP; *OR*, 9:57.

52. McPherson, *Battle Cry of Freedom*, 373.

53. Welles, "First Iron-Clad Monitor," 20; *New York Times*, January 31, 1862.

54. Welles, "First Iron-Clad Monitor," 20.

55. Ibid.

56. Ibid.; Welles, *Diary of Gideon Welles*, 1:62–65; Ervin Jordan, *Black Confederates*, 284.

57. Perdue, Barden, and Phillips, *Weevils in the Wheat*, 69, 86, 118.

58. Hay, *Inside Lincoln's White House*, 35; Sears, *To the Gates of Richmond*, 16.

59. Sears, *To the Gates of Richmond*, 17.

60. Goodwin, *Team of Rivals*, 428–31.

61. Sears, *To the Gates of Richmond*, 16–20.

62. For a discussion of the reasons for this decision, see Sears, *To the Gates of Richmond*, 12–13.

63. *Boston Herald*, March 18, 1862.

64. Pinkerton to McClellan, March 14, 1862, nos. 9560–63, GBMP.

65. Dubbs, *Defend This Old Town*, 60; John M. Galt II Diary, February 19, 1862, Galt Family Papers (I), WM.

66. Sears, *To the Gates of Richmond*, 12.

67. Pinkerton to McClellan, March 17, 1862, no. 9708, GBMP.

68. *New York Examiner* quoted in *Principia*, January 18, 1862.

69. Pinkerton to McClellan, March 14, 1862, nos. 9560–63, GBMP.

70. Pinkerton to McClellan, February 10, 1862, nos. 8506–10, GBMP.

71. Ibid., nos. 8638–48.

72. Ibid., no. 8683; *Lowell (Mass.) Daily Citizen and News*, February 5, 1862.

73. Pinkerton to McClellan, March 17, 1862, nos. 9693–99, GBMP.

74. Ibid.

75. Pinkerton to McClellan, March 27, 1862, nos. 10172–74, GBMP.

76. *Cincinnati Commercial* quoted in *Chicago Tribune*, March 25, 1862; *New York World* (semiweekly), March 21, 1862; *New York Times*, March 15, 1862.

77. *New York World* (semiweekly), March 21, 1862; *Cincinnati Commercial* quoted in *Chicago Tribune*, March 25, 1862. See also *New York Times*, March 12, 14, 1862.

78. *New York World* (semiweekly), March 21, 1862; *New York Times*, March 22, 1862.

79. *National Anti-Slavery Standard*, March 22, 1862; *New York Times*, March 15, 1862.

80. *Cincinnati Commercial* quoted in *Chicago Tribune*, March 25, 1862; *National Anti-Slavery Standard*, March 29, 1862.

81. *CG*, 37th Cong., 2nd sess., 1142–43; McPherson, *Struggle for Equality*, 96–97.

82. Tap, *Over Lincoln's Shoulder*, 114–15.

83. Fischel, *Secret War for the Union*, 118.

84. *OR*, 11:3, 393, 404, 412.

85. *OR*, 11:3, 478, 434, 475.

86. Ibid., 437; Brewer, *Confederate Negro*, 141.

87. Sears, *To the Gates of Richmond*, 35–39; Rafuse, *McClellan's War*, 203–5.

88. Sears, *To the Gates of Richmond*, 35–39; Rafuse, *McClellan's War*, 203–5.

89. McClellan, *McClellan's Own Story*, 149–51; Sears, *To the Gates of Richmond*, 40; Rafuse, *McClellan's War*, 206.

90. McClellan, *McClellan's Own Story*, 151; McClellan, *Papers of McClellan*, 235.

91. Sears, *To the Gates of Richmond*, 33–34, 39; Rafuse, *McClellan's War*, 202–3. T. Harry Williams, *Lincoln and the Radicals*, argues that the withholding of troops from McClellan was indeed a radical plot to sabotage the general's campaign and thus delay the war long enough to bring about emancipation. Williams's argument rests on a depiction of Lincoln as indecisive, easily manipulated, and "scared" by radical leaders into believing that the capital would be endangered if McDowell's corps were sent to McClellan. See ibid., 126–30. The evidence is highly circumstantial, and Hans L. Trefousse persuasively refutes it, in *Radical Republicans*, 193–94.

92. Lincoln, *Collected Works*, 5:182; McClellan, *Papers of McClellan*, 228, 229, 232; McClellan, *McClellan's Own Story*, 272. For a detailed description of Magruder's defense lines, see Hess, *Field Armies and Fortifications*, 78–81. The author describes the works as "one of the strongest defensive positions of the war."

93. Hess, *Field Armies and Fortifications*, 81. After detailing Magruder's battles with local slaveholders, McCurry, *Confederate Reckoning*, 270, concludes that "slave impressments failed to provide the needed element of strength" on the Peninsula. However, the author's examination of the Peninsula ends in March 1862. The argument does not take into account the slaves Magruder procured in late March and April or demonstrate that McClellan's campaign floundered in front of the formidable Confederate defenses largely constructed by impressed slave laborers.

Chapter 5

1. *National Anti-Slavery Standard*, April 19, 1862; Bell Halsey Miller Diary, March 20, 1862, Duke.

2. *Baltimore American and Commercial Advertiser*, April 5, 1862.

3. McClellan, *Papers of McClellan*, 246; James H. Mitchell to mother, April 6, 1862, James H. Mitchell Papers, USAMHI.

4. Walter J. Eames to wife, April 1, 8, 1862, Walter J. Eames Papers, USAMHI; *Philadelphia Inquirer*, April 16, 1862.

5. *Philadelphia Inquirer*, April 8, 15, 18, 19, 1862.

6. *Philadelphia Inquirer*, April 21, 22, 1862; *New York Herald* quoted in *Boston Herald*, April 26, 1862.

7. Parker, *Henry Wilson's Regiment*, 78–79.

8. *Philadelphia Inquirer*, April 19, 25, 1862; *Philadelphia Press*, April 24, 1862.

9. Sneden, *Eye of the Storm*, 47.

10. Wainwright, *Diary of Battle*, 35; Bell Halsey Miller Diary, March 25, 1862, Duke; Haydon, *For Country, Cause, and Leader*, 227; George Williamson Balloch to children, April 24, 1862, George Williamson Balloch Letters, Duke; For a discussion of how the needs of blacks behind Union lines were explained to northern children, as well as a consideration of the correspondence between Union soldiers and their children or younger siblings, see Marten, *Children's Civil War*, 42–45, 68–100.

11. Bell Halsey Miller Diary, March 20, 1862, Duke; *New York Herald* quoted in *National Anti-Slavery Standard*, April 19, 1862.

12. *New York Times*, April 9, 1862; *Philadelphia Inquirer*, April 17, 18, 1862.

13. *Baltimore American and Commercial Advertiser*, April 5, 1862.

14. *Detroit Free Press*, April 11, 1862.

15. *New York Herald*, April 6, 12, 1862; Auchmuty, *Letters of Richard Tylden Auchmuty*, 45; Andrews, *The North Reports the Civil War*, 197; Strong, *Diary of George Templeton Strong*, 3:216.

16. W. T. H. Brooks to father, April 20, 1862, W. T. H. Brooks Papers, USAMHI; *OR*, 11:1, 360; Goss, *Recollections of a Private*, 36; John Berry Diary, May 7, 1862, USAMHI.

17. *New York Herald*, April 23, 1862; *National Anti-Slavery Standard*, May 10, 1862.

18. *New York Herald*, April 30, 1862; *Philadelphia Public Ledger*, April 16, 1862; *Philadelphia Press*, April 24, May 2, 1862; *New York Times*, April 23, 1862.

19. Berlin et al., *Freedom*, 1:698–99. Apparently the problem persisted, because in September Confederate authorities required regimental adjutants to "inquire into and report all cases of slaves serving . . . without written authority from their masters." Once this information was compiled it was to be published in the newspapers so that masters could come claim their slaves. *OR*, series 4, 2:86.

20. See McCurry, *Confederate Reckoning*, 270–71.

21. Thomas Lewis Ware Diary, vol. 2, April 20, 21, 1862, SHC.

22. *OR*, 11:3, 465, 430.

23. *New York Herald*, April 23, 1862; *Illinois State Journal*, April 29, 1862.

24. *New York Tribune* quoted in *Chicago Tribune*, May 9, 1862.

25. Sears, *To the Gates of Richmond*, 50; Wainwright, *Diary of Battle*, 40; Bellard, *Gone for a Soldier*, 56–57.

26. Townsend, *Rustics in Rebellion*, 52; *New York Herald*, April 30, 1862; *Baltimore American and Commercial Advertiser*, May 3, 1862. See also *Boston Daily Advertiser*, May 3, 1862; and *Boston Daily Journal*, May 3, 1862.

27. Murray, *Letters from Berdan's Sharpshooters*, 21; Strong, *Diary of George Templeton Strong*, 3:216.

28. *OR*, 11:1, 382.

29. Brewster, *When This Cruel War Is Over*, 118.

30. Ibid., 113, 118–19; Murray, *Letters from Berdan's Sharpshooters*, 21.

31. *Philadelphia Inquirer*, April 25, 29, 1862; *New York Times*, April 27, 1862; *Baltimore American and Commercial Advertiser*, April 30, 1862; *Lowell (Mass.) Daily Citizen and News*, May 1, 1862.

32. *New York Times*, April 22, 1862; Haydon, *For Country, Cause, and Leader*, 219; *Boston Daily Journal*, April 21, May 1, 3, 1862; *Philadelphia Inquirer*, April 26, 1862.

33. *New York Times*, April 22, 1862; *Cincinnati Gazette*, May 2, 1862.

34. *Harper's Weekly*, May 10, 1862; Ervin Jordan, *Black Confederates*, 223.

35. Brewster, *When This Cruel War Is Over*, 114; *Philadelphia Inquirer*, April 26, 1862; *Boston Daily Journal*, April 21, 1862; James H. Mitchell to mother, April 25, 1862, James H. Mitchell Papers, USAMHI; *Chicago Tribune*, May 3, 1862.

36. *National Anti-Slavery Standard*, May 3, 1862.

37. *Philadelphia Inquirer*, April 29, 1862; *Baltimore American and Commercial Advertiser*, April 30, 1862; *Boston Daily Advertiser*, May 1, 1862; *Chicago Tribune*, May 3, 1862.

38. Paine, *Political Lessons of the Rebellion*, 19; Henry Wilson, *History of the Antislavery Measures*, 112–30.

39. Sumner, *Selected Letters*, 2:110; Henry Wilson, *History of the Antislavery Measures*, 112–30.

40. *CG*, 37th Cong., 2nd sess., 1802. For a brief discussion of how the Democrats politically used racist warnings about blacks moving north, see Paludan, *A People's Contest*, 95–96.

41. *CG*, 37th Cong., 2nd sess., 1896.

42. Grimsley, *Hard Hand of War*, 68–70, 78; Donald, *Charles Sumner and the Rights of Man*, 63. For a detailed discussion of the constitutional and legal debates surrounding the act, see Siddali, *From Property to Person*, 145–66.

43. *CG*, 37th Cong., 2nd sess., 1651.

44. *Boston Daily Journal*, April 26, 1862.

45. *CG*, 37th Cong., 2nd sess., 1652, 1801.

46. Ibid., 1797, 1790, 1918; Smith, *Schuyler Colfax*, 175–76.

47. *CG*, 37th Cong., 2nd sess., 1790, 1795; Beauregard, *Bingham of the Hills*, 53.

48. *Indianapolis Daily Sentinel*, April 28, 1862; *Boston Daily Advertiser*, April 7, 1862.

49. *North American and United States Gazette*, May 7, 1862; *Daily Cleveland Herald*, May 3, 1862; *Philadelphia Press*, May 1, 1862.

50. *Illinois State Journal*, April 15, 1862; *Baltimore American and Commercial Advertiser* quoted in *National Anti-Slavery Standard*, May 3, 1862.

51. Benjamin C. Stevens Diary, April 14, 1862, Duke.

52. *Philadelphia Press*, April 23, 1862; *Cincinnati Gazette*, May 2, 1862.

53. *OR*, 11:3, 117; George T. Stevens, *Three Years in the Sixth Corps*, 34–35.

54. Quarstein, "The Siege of Yorktown," 32; Sears, *To the Gates of Richmond*, 43, 45, 48.

55. Mitchell, *Civil War Soldiers*, 118; *Philadelphia Public Ledger*, April 28, 1862; *New York Times*, May 4, 6, 1862.

56. Trobriand, *Four Years with the Army of the Potomac*, 187–88; Judd, *Story of the Thirty-third NYS Vols*, 80–81; Erasmus Keyes testimony, *Report of the Joint Committee*, 1:600.

57. Uriah H. Painter testimony, *Report of the Joint Committee*, 1:283–84.

58. Parker, *Henry Wilson's Regiment*, 93; Sears, *To the Gates of Richmond*, 62; Trobriand, *Four Years with the Army of the Potomac*, 188.

59. John Berry Diary, May 7, 1862, USAMHI; James H. Mitchell to mother, May 14, 1862, James H. Mitchell Papers, USAMHI; George H. Selkirk to brother, May 7, 1862, George H. Selkirk Papers, USAMHI; Townsend, *Rustics in Rebellion*, 52. Many of these "monuments" are still in very fine condition, and visitors can see them today at sites like Lee's Mill, Skiffles Creek, Lee Hall, Fort Magruder, Williamsburg's "Redoubt Park," and especially at the Yorktown National Battlefield.

(To obtain an excellent modern map of these locations, visit http://www.civilwar traveler.com/EAST/VA/va-tidewater/peninsula.html). At Yorktown, the Park Service interprets the history of the Revolutionary battle, but in truth, many of the preserved fortifications are from the Civil War.

60. Freeman, *Lee's Lieutenants*, 1:148–55.

61. *Baltimore American and Commercial Advertiser*, May 6, 1862. The paper misidentified Lee as the Confederate commander. During the Yorktown siege, he was still acting as a military adviser to Jefferson Davis, and Joseph Johnston was in command of the southern army on the Peninsula. The *Baltimore American*'s editors would have agreed with one of historian Stephanie McCurry's points in *Confederate Reckoning*. Federal confiscation of southern slaves, she emphasizes, "was made possible by the Confederate state's decision to turn slave men into military laborers." McCurry, *Confederate Reckoning*, 271.

62. See Manning, *What This Cruel War Was Over*, 73.

Chapter 6

1. *Philadelphia Press*, May 6, 21, 1862.

2. James DeWitt Hankins to father, May 3, 1862, Hankins Family Papers, VHS.

3. Sears, *To the Gates of Richmond*, 70; *New York Herald*, May 7, 1862.

4. *OR*, 11:1, 533–35.

5. Ibid., 537; Uriah H. Painter testimony, *Report of the Joint Committee*, 1:284.

6. *OR*, 11:1, 512.

7. Ibid., 527; Sears, *To the Gates of Richmond*, 73.

8. Sears, *To the Gates of Richmond*, 73–74.

9. *OR*, 11:1, 535.

10. *Chicago Tribune*, May 15, 1862; *Boston Daily Journal*, May 12, 1862; Tucker, *Hancock the Superb*, 80.

11. Tucker, *Hancock the Superb*, 80–82; David M. Jordan, *Winfield Scott Hancock*, 43. Jordan's exceptional biography fails to acknowledge the role of slaves in the battle, indicating only that Smith and Sumner "had been informed" of the abandoned works.

12. *OR*, 11:1, 538, 540–41; Tucker, *Hancock the Superb*, 82–87; David M. Jordan, *Winfield Scott Hancock*, 43–44.

13. *OR*, 11:1, 538, 540–41; Tucker, *Hancock the Superb*, 82–87; David M. Jordan, *Winfield Scott Hancock*, 43–44.

14. *OR*, 11:1, 550–51.

15. *OR*, 11:1, 551; Tucker, *Hancock the Superb*, 87–88.

16. Tucker, *Hancock the Superb*, 89; *New York Herald*, May 8, 16, 1862; *New York Times*, May 7, 16, 1862; *Philadelphia Inquirer*, May 9, 1862.

17. *New York Herald*, May 9, 1862; *Chicago Tribune*, May 15, 1862.

18. *Boston Daily Journal*, May 12, 1862; *New York Times* quoted in *Chicago Tribune*, May 9, 1862; *Philadelphia Press*, May 7, 1862.

19. Sears, *To the Gates of Richmond*, 84–85; *OR*, 11:1, 615; Patrick McGlenn to John Brislin, June 3, 1862, and Francis Boland to John Brislin, June 14, 1862, John Brislin Papers, USAMHI.

20. Sears, *To the Gates of Richmond*, 86; *OR*, 11:1, 626.

21. Francis Boland to John Brislin, June 14, 1862, John Brislin Papers, USAMHI. It is telling that although Boland's close comrade Patrick McGlenn noted that the area around Eltham's Landing was deserted by whites and populated with only blacks, he did not mention any black troops in the ensuing fight. See Patrick Mc-Glenn to John Brislin, June 3, 1862, ibid.

22. Ruffin Thomson to father, May 24, 1862, Ruffin Thomson Diary, SHC.

23. Jack Foster to his master, October 12, 1862, April 10, May 19, 28, 1863, Tomkins Family Papers, VHS.

24. Quarles, *Negro in the Civil War*, 50; [Caffey], *Battlefields of the South*, 284. See also Faust, *This Republic of Suffering*, 90–91.

25. *OR*, 11:1, 617.

26. Lee, "Williamsburg in 1861," CWF; Jones, "Recollections of Williamsburg," CWF; Coleman, "Peninsular Campaign," WM.

27. Lee, "Williamsburg in 1861," CWF; Diary of Cynthia B. T. W. Coleman, WM; Hays, *Under the Red Patch*, 90.

28. Joinville, *Army of the Potomac*, 56; *Philadelphia Inquirer*, May 10, 1862; Comte de Paris, "We Prepare to Receive the Enemy Where We Stand," 22.

29. Joinville, *Army of the Potomac*, 56; *Boston Daily Journal*, May 12, 1862.

30. Hyde, *Following the Greek Cross*, 49; Hays, *Under the Red Patch*, 91; John A. Williams to sister, May 22, 1862, John A. Williams Papers, VHS.

31. Wainwright, *Diary of Battle*, 60.

32. *National Anti-Slavery Standard*, May 24, 1862; *Boston Daily Journal*, June 3, 1862.

33. *Philadelphia Inquirer* quoted in *National Anti-Slavery Standard*, May 31, 1862; Fisk, *Hard Marching Every Day*, 24; Walter J. Eames to wife, May 12, 25, 1862, Walter J. Eames Papers, USAMHI; *Philadelphia Press*, May 29, 1862; Baker, "Memoirs of Williamsburg," CWF.

34. *National Anti-Slavery Standard*, May 24, 1862; *Principia*, May 22, 1862; Fisk, *Hard Marching Every Day*, 24.

35. Diary of Cynthia B. T. W. Coleman, WM.

36. Harriette Cary Diary, May 21, 1862, WM; Diary of Cynthia B. T. W. Coleman, WM.

37. Coleman, "Peninsular Campaign," WM. Coleman's words here are a perfect illustration of what Eugene D. Genovese describes in *Roll, Jordan, Roll* as a "moment of truth. Could it be," Genovese writes, "that they had never known 'their people' at all? That they had been deceiving themselves? Yes, it could be, and it was." See ibid., 97–112.

38. Coleman, "Peninsular Campaign," WM.

39. *Detroit Free Press*, May 28, 1862. See also *Providence (R.I.) Post*, June 6, 1862.

40. *New York Times*, June 1, 1862; *Chicago Times*, May 24, 1862.

41. Regan, *Lost Civil War Diaries*, 51; *Albany (N.Y.) Evening Journal* quoted in *National Anti-Slavery Standard*, May 14, 1862; *Philadelphia Inquirer*, May 10, 1862.

42. Marks, *Peninsular Campaign in Virginia*, 171–75.

43. Ibid.

44. Regan, *Lost Civil War Diaries*, 51–52. See also *Richmond Dispatch*, May 23, 1862.

45. Cook, *Siege of Richmond*, 74–75.

46. Marten, "A Feeling of Restless Anxiety," 138–39. Bell I. Wiley's classic study of Union soldiers, *Life of Billy Yank*, maintains that the writings of Federal soldiers are filled with "expressions of unfriendliness" or even "intense hatred" of the blacks they encountered in the South. Wiley argued that as men grew tired of fighting, they used blacks as a convenient target for their frustrations because they were seen as the cause of the war. Soldier racism usually took the form of simple jokes, racial slurs, and pranks on blacks in their camps, but too often it also showed itself in acts of brutal violence. Physical torture and rape were not uncommon. Wiley attributed this treatment to prewar racial prejudices, especially among soldiers from midwestern states or of southern background, of which there was a higher concentration in the western armies. See *Life of Billy Yank*, 109–15; and Mitchell, *Civil War Soldiers*, 121. Nevertheless, as Chandra Manning notes in *What This Cruel War Was Over*, 50, the racist actions and assumptions of Union troops "did not necessarily indicate tolerance of slavery." Marten, in "A Feeling of Restless Anxiety," quotes *Philadelphia Press* correspondent Joel Cook to strengthen his argument that race relations between slaves and Union soldiers on the Peninsula were generally poor, yet the author fails to include Cook's assertion that although slaves were often teased, it was "very rare that they were quarreled with or in any way maltreated. Those in Government or private employ were never molested." Cook, *Siege of Richmond*, 75.

47. Robert A. Everett Diary, May 16, 1862, Robert A. Everett Papers, USAMHI; *Williamsburg Cavalier*, June 26, 30, 1862; Walter J. Eames to wife, May 16, 1862, Walter J. Eames Papers, USAMHI.

48. *Chicago Tribune*, May 29, 1862.

49. Luther C. Furst Diary, May 14, 1862, USAMHI; George T. Stevens, *Three Years in the Sixth Corps*, 59; Brewster, *When This Cruel War Is Over*, 133.

50. Bell Halsey Miller Diary, May 14, 1862, Duke; Walter J. Eames to wife, May 25, 1862, Walter J. Eames Papers, USAMHI.

51. Walter J. Eames to wife, May 25, 1862, Walter J. Eames Papers, USAMHI.

52. Rhodes, *All for the Union*, 67; Harriette Cary Diary, May 14, 1862, WM; Sarah Dandridge Cooke Duval Memoir, VHS; George T. Stevens, *Three Years in the Sixth Corps*, 59.

53. Banes, *History of the Philadelphia Brigade*, 58; Cook, *Siege of Richmond*, 85; Beach, *First New York Cavalry*, 116.

54. Perdue, Barden, and Phillips, *Weevils in the Wheat*, 277 (italics added); Beach, *First New York Cavalry*, 114.

55. Joseph D. Baker to sister, May 11, 1862, Joseph D. Baker Papers, USAMHI; Walter J. Eames to wife, May 18, 1862, Walter J. Eames Papers, USAMHI; Beach, *First New York Cavalry*, 114; Luther C. Furst Diary, May 19, 1862, USAMHI. For a lengthy discussion of how exposure to slavery's evils promoted emancipation sentiment among northern soldiers, see Manning, *What This Cruel War Was Over*.

56. Murray, *Letters from Berdan's Sharpshooters*, 55; Norton, *Army Letters*, 88.

57. See, for example, Gallagher, *The Union War*, 149–50.

58. Macnamara, *Story of the Ninth Regiment*, 87; *Philadelphia Inquirer*, May 15, 1862; Harriette Cary Diary, July 4, 1862, WM.

59. Norton, *Army Letters*, 79; *Philadelphia Inquirer*, May 15, 20, 1862.

60. *Philadelphia Inquirer*, May 24, 1862; *Philadelphia Press*, May 24, 1862.

61. Macnamara, *Story of the Ninth Regiment*, 87; *Philadelphia Inquirer*, May 24, 1862.

62. *Principia*, June 19, 1862; *National Anti-Slavery Standard*, May 21, 1862.

63. Sears, *To the Gates of Richmond*, 90–91.

64. Ibid., 93.

65. Brewer, *Confederate Negro*, 156–57. Today, the fortifications at Drewry's Bluff are preserved as a unit of the Richmond National Battlefield Park.

66. *Charleston Mercury*, May 10, 16, 1862.

67. *OR*, 11:3, 563.

68. Sears, *To the Gates of Richmond*, 94.

69. Brownlow, *Sketch of Parson Brownlow*, 22; *New York Herald*, May 11, 1862; *New York Times*, May 19, 1862.

70. *National Anti-Slavery Standard*, May 10, 17, 1862.

71. *Liberator*, May 16, 1862; *Chicago Tribune*, June 3, 1862.

72. *CG*, 37th Cong., 2nd sess., appendix, 184–86; Riddleberger, *George Washington Julian*, 133–34.

73. *CG*, 37th Cong., 2nd sess., 2196.

74. Ibid., 2196, 2326.

75. *Boston Herald*, May 21, 1862; *New York Herald*, May 22, 1862.

76. *CG*, 37th Cong., 2nd sess., appendix, 221, 243; *Detroit Free Press*, May 10, 1862.

77. *CG*, 37th Cong., 2nd sess., 2246; *CG*, 37th Cong., 2nd sess., appendix, 184–86.

78. Sumner, *Selected Letters*, 2:214; *CG*, 37th Cong., 2nd sess., appendix, 234.

79. *Philadelphia Press*, May 7, 15, 1862.

80. *CG*, 37th Cong., 2nd sess., appendix, 194.

81. Ibid., 178; *CG*, 37th Cong., 2nd sess., 2302.

82. *CG*, 37th Cong., 2nd sess., 2244; *CG*, 37th Cong., 2nd sess., appendix, 204.

83. *CG*, 37th Cong., 2nd sess., appendix, 204; *CG*, 37th Cong., 2nd sess., 2244.

84. *CG*, 37th Cong., 2nd sess., 2302.

85. Ibid.; *CG*, 37th Cong., 2nd sess., appendix, 204.

86. *CG*, 37th Cong., 2nd sess., 2253; Henry Wilson, *History of the Antislavery Measures*, 169–70.

87. *Boston Daily Journal*, June 7, 1862.

88. Ibid.

89. Sears, *To the Gates of Richmond*, 103–4; *New York Herald*, May 24, 1862.

90. James Graham to aunt, May 18, 1862, James Lee Graham Papers, USAMHI; *Baltimore American and Commercial Advertiser*, May 21, 1862; Luther C. Furst Diary, May 11, 1862, USAMHI.

91. *Philadelphia Inquirer*, May 19, 20, 1862; *New York World*, May 20, 1862.

92. Luther C. Furst Diary, May 11, 1862, USAMHI; Norton, *Army Letters*, 78–79; Auchmuty, *Letters of Richard Tylden Auchmuty*, 56; *Philadelphia Inquirer*, May 19, 1862.

93. Luther C. Furst Diary, May 11, 1862, USAMHI; Rhodes, *All for the Union*, 65–66; *Principia*, June 19, 1862; *Philadelphia Inquirer*, May 22, 1862.

94. *New York Herald*, May 20, 22, 1862.

95. *Boston Herald*, May 13, 1862; *Washington Sunday Morning Chronicle*, May 25, 1862; *Philadelphia Press*, May 6, 1862; Quarles, *Negro in the Civil War*, 81–82; Ervin Jordan, *Black Confederates*, 71–72.

96. *New York Herald*, May 28, 1862; Acton, "Dear Mollie," 17.

97. John Berry Diary, May 20, 1862, USAMHI.

98. McClellan, *Papers of George B. McClellan*, 128.

99. *New York Herald*, May 24, 1862.

100. Ibid.; *Boston Herald*, May 30, 1862; *Philadelphia Public Ledger*, May 8, 1862.

101. *New York Herald*, May 24, 1862; *Philadelphia Inquirer*, May 16, 20, 24, 1862; *Boston Daily Advertiser*, May 23, 1862.

Chapter 7

1. *New York Times*, June 3, 1862. For a brief discussion of how slaves viewed the death and destruction meted out against their masters as appropriate justice, see Faust, *This Republic of Suffering*, 51–52.

2. *Philadelphia Press*, June 5, 1862; Ruffin, *Diary of Edmund Ruffin*, 2:307.

3. Diary of Richard Eppes, lists of escaped slaves, VHS.

4. Ibid.; Perdue, Barden, and Phillips, *Weevils in the Wheat*, 269–71.

5. Diary of Richard Eppes, "Negroes Carried Off from Chesterfield County," VHS; Ruffin, *Diary of Edmund Ruffin*, 2:317.

6. Cook, *Siege of Richmond*, 96; *Philadelphia Press*, June 13, 1862.

7. Freeman, *Lee's Lieutenants*, 1:363; *OR*, 11:1, 32.

8. *OR*, 11:1, 32.

9. McClellan later maintained in his self-serving memoir that contrabands provided little usable information for military purposes (*McClellan's Own Story*, 253–54). However, the numerous official reports in which officers, including McClellan, credited African Americans with useful assistance (of which only a handful are cited in this work) more than refute the general's contention.

10. *New York Evening Post* quoted in *National Anti-Slavery Standard*, June 7, 1863; Brewster, *When This Cruel War Is Over*, 150.

11. *OR*, 11:1, 637–38; See other such examples on pages 11:667, 677, 711, 997, 999, and 11:2, 920, 930, 931, 949.

12. *OR*, 11:1, 675–76; *New York Times*, June 8, 1862; *Daily Cleveland Herald*, June 2, 1862.

13. *OR*, 11:1, 999–1000.

14. Sears, *To the Gates of Richmond*, 111–45; *OR*, 11:3, 217.

15. *Boston Journal* quoted in *National Anti-Slavery Standard*, June 5, 1862.

16. Green, *Chimborazo*, 47.

17. Ibid.

18. Ibid., ix, 10, 12; Brewer, *Confederate Negro*, 95–96. The Richmond National Battlefield Park includes a Civil War medical museum on the site of where Chimborazo once stood.

19. Lee, *Wartime Papers of Robert E. Lee*, 183–84; Davis, *Papers of Jefferson Davis*, 8:236.

20. *OR*, 11:3, 593.

21. *OR*, 11:3, 597.

22. *Principia*, June 12, 1862; Strong, *Diary of George Templeton Strong*, 3:229.

23. *New York Times*, June 1, 1862; *Philadelphia Inquirer*, June 18, 24, 1862. Most of the fortifications that protected Richmond in early 1862 are now gone, although a small portion can still be seen at the Chickahominy Bluffs unit of Richmond National Battlefield Park.

24. James H. Mitchell to mother, May 29, 1862, James H. Mitchell Papers, US-AMHI; Brewster, *When This Cruel Was Is Over*, 151; George H. Selkirk to mother, June 23, 1862, George H. Selkirk Papers, USAMHI.

25. *Chicago Tribune*, June 6, 1862; *Cincinnati Gazette*, June 6, 16, 1862; Sypher, *History of the Pennsylvania Reserve Corps*, 156–57.

26. *New York World*, June 17, 1862; *Washington Sunday Morning Chronicle*, June 22, 1862.

27. Jacob Heffelfinger Diary, June 11, 1862, USAMHI; Sypher, *History of the Pennsylvania Reserve Corps*, 193.

28. *New York Evening Post* quoted in *National Anti-Slavery Standard*, June 21, 1862; Rhodes, *All for the Union*, 67; *New York Times*, May 28, 1862.

29. Cook, *Siege of Richmond*, 96. "Stump speeches" were regular components of antebellum minstrel shows and featured white actors in black face ignorantly and comically misusing words. For an intriguing discussion of how northern stage productions depicted slaves and slavery, see Lawson, "Imagining Slavery." The author points out that for most Northerners the stage was their primary exposure to depictions of African Americans and the peculiar institution. Before the 1840s, plays often depicted enslaved characters who craftily struggled for power with their masters, and they sometimes violently attempted to break free. Even the famous Jim Crow character was a feisty rebel. Lawson demonstrates that it was not until the 1840s and 1850s (the era when most Union soldiers came of age) that plays and minstrel shows predominately lampooned slaves and freed blacks. Even performances with abolitionist themes depicted slaves as victims in need of rescue rather than as wily potential rebels. Yankees carried these racial assumptions with them into the South, but as at White House Landing, their exposure to actual slaves often challenged such perceptions.

30. Judd, *Story of the Thirty-third NYS Vols*, 115; Sydnor, "A Virginia Boy in the Sixties," 105.

31. Ruffin, *Diary of Edmund Ruffin*, 2:345–46; *Richmond Dispatch*, June 16, 1862.

32. *New York Herald*, May 27, 1862; George H. Selkirk to mother, June 23, 1862, George H. Selkirk Papers, USAMHI; *National Anti-Slavery Standard*, June 28, 1862; *New York Evening Post* quoted in *National Anti-Slavery Standard*, June 21, 1862.

33. *OR*, 11:1, 1038.

34. Ibid.; *New York Times*, June 20, 1862; *Richmond Dispatch*, July 5, 1862.

35. Cook, *Siege of Richmond*, 286; *OR*, 11:1, 1038; *Richmond Dispatch*, June 16, 1862; Hays, *Under the Red Patch*, 108.

36. *OR*, 11:1, 1018, 1019, 1030, 1034.

37. Ruffin, *Diary of Edmund Ruffin*, 2:345–46, 350–53.

38. *Richmond Dispatch*, June 7, 16, 1862.

39. Sumner, *Selected Letters*, 3:119–20; *New York Times*, June 5, 1862.

40. *New York Herald*, May 29, 1862; *CG*, 37th Cong., 2nd sess., 2919–20.

41. *New York Times*, June 24, 1862; McPherson, *Struggle for Equality*, 97.

42. McPherson, *Struggle for Equality*, 102–3, 108–9; *Principia*, June 12, 1862; Browning, *Diary of Orville Hickman Browning*, 1:550.

43. Lincoln, *Collected Works*, 5:222, 278–79; Garrison, *Letters of William Lloyd Garrison*, 5:97.

44. Welles, *Diary of Gideon Welles*, 1:71; Browning, *Diary of Orville Hickman Browning*, 1:555.

45. Chase, *Salmon P. Chase Papers*, 3:219. Lincoln may have already been thinking of using executive war powers to emancipate the slaves in rebellious states. See Donald, *Lincoln*, 363–64; Paludan, *Presidency of Abraham Lincoln*, 147; Franklin, *Emancipation Proclamation*, 34–37; and Guelzo, *Lincoln's Emancipation Proclamation*, 140–44. Nevertheless, as Chase suspected, whether Lincoln decided to do so or not hinged on the outcome of McClellan's campaign.

46. Burton, *Extraordinary Circumstances*, 36–37.

47. *New York Herald*, May 27, 1862; *Richmond Dispatch*, May 25, 1861; Diary of William Fanning Wickham, June 19, 1862, VHS; Sydnor, "A Virginia Boy in the Sixties," 105.

48. H. B. White to unknown, June 5, 1862, H. B. White Papers, SHC.

49. *New York Times*, May 28, 1862; T. E. Chase, *History of the Fifth Massachusetts Battery*, 285, 308; *Principia*, June 12, 1862.

50. Sears, *To the Gates of Richmond*, 182.

51. Fanny W. Gaines Tinsley Memoir, VHS.

52. Fitz John Porter to Randolph B. Marcy, June 24, 1862 (A-67:27), GBMP; Sears, *To the Gates of Richmond*, 189; *OR*, 11:1, 51; *OR*, 11:3, 257.

53. *Report of the Joint Committee*, 1:23; *OR*, 11:1, 51.

54. *OR*, 11:3, 257; Sears, *To the Gates of Richmond*, 191, 196; Burton, *Extraordinary Circumstances*, 57; Rafuse, *McClellan's War*, 221.

55. Sears, *To the Gates of Richmond*, 197.

56. [Caffey], *Battlefields of the South*, 284.

57. Sears, *To the Gates of Richmond*, 210–48; Rawick, *American Slave*, supplement, series 2, 9:8, 3616.

58. Fanny W. Gaines Tinsley Memoir, VHS.

59. Judd, *Story of the Thirty-third NYS Vols*, 124–25; John S. Tucker Diary, June 28, 1862, Richmond National Battlefield Park, Manuscripts Collection, vol. 17.

60. *Philadelphia Inquirer*, July 1, 1862; Benjamin E. Ashenfelter Papers, July 7, 1862, USAMHI; *New York Times*, July 2, 1862; Burton, *Extraordinary Circumstances*, 150–51.

61. *CG*, 37th Cong., 2nd sess., 2965, 2991.

62. Robert L. Dabney to Jediah Hotchkiss, April 22, 1896, Jediah Hotchkiss Papers, LC; Jones, "Seven Days around Richmond," 564.

63. Thomas Lewis Ware Diary, vol. 2, June 29, 1862, SHC; Ivy W. Duggan to *Sandersville Central Georgian*, July 8, 1862, Duggan Papers, Emory University, Robert W. Woodruff Library, Special Collections, Atlanta.

64. William B. Westervelt Diary, July 2, 1862, USAMHI; *Philadelphia Inquirer*, July 1, 1862; Sneden, *Eye of the Storm*, 81.

65. Today, Richmond National Battlefield Park encompasses many of the sites associated with the Seven Days Battles and provides driving and walking trails that connect and interpret each of the battle locations. Gaines' Mill and Malvern Hill are particularly well preserved.

66. Le Duc, *Recollections of a Civil War Quartermaster*, 84–85.

Chapter 8

1. Strong, *Diary of George Templeton Strong*, 3:236; *Philadelphia Inquirer*, July 3, 1862; *New York Times*, July 3, 4, 1862; McPherson, *Crossroads of Freedom*, 48.

2. *Cleveland Herald*, July 2, 1862.

3. *Philadelphia Press*, July 31, 1862.

4. Brewster, *When This Cruel War Is Over*, 163; Holmes, *Touched by Fire*, 56; Dunn, "On the Peninsular Campaign," 18; Benjamin Roher to wife, July 28, 1862, Benjamin Roher Papers, USAMHI; Clement D. Potts to mother, July 15, 1862, Clement D. Potts Papers, USAMHI; Jonathon P. Stowe Diary, July 8, 1862, USAMHI.

5. McAllister, *Civil War Letters*, 187; Auchmuty, *Letters of Richard Tylden Auchmuty*, 74; James C. Miller, "Serving under McClellan on the Peninsula in 62," 30; Reichardt, *Diary of Battery A*, 52; Robert A. Everett Diary, July 6, 1862, Robert A. Everett Papers, USAMHI; Charles Becker Diary, July 6, 16, 1862, Charles Becker Papers, USAMHI; John Berry Diary, July 2, 21, USAMHI.

6. Jonathon P. Stowe Diary, July 5, 1862, USAMHI; William J. Burns Diary, July 2, 1862, USAMHI; John Berry Diary, July 4, 1862, USAMHI; Benjamin Roher to wife, July 28, 1862, Benjamin Roher Papers, USAMHI; Perkins, "Letters Home," 116; Henry Gerrish Memoir, 14, USAMHI.

7. See, for example, Norton, *Army Letters*, 102.

8. See, for example, Auchmuty, *Letters of Richard Tylden Auchmuty*, 73.

9. George H. Selkirk to parents, July 1, 8, 1862, George H. Selkirk Papers, USAMHI; Joseph D. Baker to sister, August 2, 1862, Joseph D. Baker Papers, USAMHI.

10. George H. Selkirk to parents, July 1, 1862, George H. Selkirk Papers, USAMHI; Macnamara, *Story of the Ninth Regiment*, 174, 271; Sypher, *History of the Pennsylvania Reserve Corps*, 156–57.

11. *Indianapolis Journal*, July 28, 1862.

12. Ibid.; *New York World* (semiweekly), July 15, 1862.

13. McPherson, *Struggle for Equality*, 110–11; Douglass, *Frederick Douglass Papers*, series 1, 3:540–41; *National Anti-Slavery Standard*, July 12, 19, 1862.

14. *Detroit Free Press*, July 3, 1862; *Boston Daily Advertiser*, July 10, 1862.

15. McPherson, *Struggle for Equality*, 110; *Commercial Advertiser* (New York)

quoted in *New York Times*, July 14, 1862; *Boston Daily Journal*, July 12, 1862; *Washington Chronicle*, July 13, 1862.

16. *Philadelphia Public Ledger*, July 11, 1862; *Boston Herald*, July 18, 1862.

17. *Philadelphia Public Ledger*, July 11, 1862; Blair, "The Seven Days and the Radical Persuasion," 172; *Cincinnati Daily Commercial*, July 10, 11, 1862.

18. *New York World* (semiweekly), July 11, 1862; *New York Times*, July 17, 1862.

19. *Bangor (Maine) Daily Whig and Courier*, July 15, 1862; *New York Tribune* quoted in *National Anti-Slavery Standard*, July 26, 1862, and *Liberator*, August 8, 1862; *Chicago Tribune*, July 13, 1862; *Racine (Wis.) Weekly Journal*, July 9, 1862.

20. *Illinois State Journal*, July 12, 15, 17, 1862.

21. *Illinois State Journal*, July 17, 1862; *Bangor (Maine) Daily Whig and Courier*, July 15, 1862.

22. *CG*, 37th Cong., 2nd sess., 3198–230.

23. Ibid., 3391; Zachariah Chandler to wife, July 11, 1862, Zachariah Chandler Papers, LC.

24. *CG*, 37th Cong., 2nd sess., 3198–99.

25. *Daily Cleveland Herald*, July 14, 1862; *Philadelphia Press*, July 11, 1862.

26. *CG*, 37th Cong., 2nd sess., 3207, 3228; *Illinois State Journal*, July 15, 1862.

27. *CG*, 37th Cong., 2nd sess., 3342.

28. *CG*, 37th Cong., 2nd sess., 3229–30.

29. Sellers, "James R. Doolittle," 281–82, 293, 302–3, 305; James R. Doolittle Papers, LC; *Racine (Wis.) Weekly Journal*, May 7, 28, June 4, 1862.

30. *CG*, 37th Cong., 2nd sess., 3229–30.

31. *Chicago Tribune*, July 10, 11, 1862; *Baltimore American*, July 17, 1862; *Boston Herald*, July 14, 1862.

32. *New York Commercial Advertiser* quoted in *Cincinnati Gazette*, July 15, 1862.

33. *Philadelphia Inquirer*, July 10, 12, 1862.

34. Ibid.

35. *Philadelphia Press*, July 11, 1862; *Indianapolis Journal*, July 14, 1862; *Boston Herald*, July 14, 1862; *New York World*, July 15, 1862.

36. William Caldwell to father, July 15, 1862, Caldwell Family Papers, Rutherford B. Hayes Presidential Center, Fremont, Ohio. I am indebted to Kristopher Teters for sharing Caldwell's letter, which he discovered while researching his forthcoming work on Union officers and the process of emancipation on the ground in the Western Theater of war.

37. See Berlin et al., *Slaves No More*, 33–40.

38. William Caldwell to father, July 15, 1862, Caldwell Family Papers, Rutherford B. Hayes Presidential Center, Fremont, Ohio.

39. See McPherson, *For Cause and Comrades*, 117–20; and Manning, *What This Cruel War Was Over*, 72–79. Gallagher, *The Union War*, 76, maintains that while exposure to slavery did make some soldiers feel more compassion for southern blacks, other Federals had their existing racist prejudices hardened. The author concludes that "the exact proportion of these two responses defy precise calculation."

40. William Caldwell to father, July 15, 1862, Caldwell Family Papers, Rutherford B. Hayes Presidential Center, Fremont, Ohio.

41. Ibid.

42. McClellan, *Civil War Papers*, 333–45; Grimsley, *Hard Hand of War*, 74–75.

43. Grimsley, *Hard Hand of War*, 67–95, persuasively demonstrates the Peninsula Campaign's primary role in creating support for a "harder war" against the South.

44. Ibid.; Paludan, *Presidency of Abraham Lincoln*, 140–42.

45. Lincoln, *Collected Works*, 5:317–20, 7:282.

46. *Boston Daily Advertiser*, July 18, 1862; Lincoln, *Collected Works*, 7:282, 506–7. For a well-crafted review of the conflicting primary and secondary sources on the timing of Lincoln's emancipation decision, see Pinsker, "Lincoln's Summer of Emancipation."

47. Welles, *Diary of Gideon Welles*, 1:70–71; Welles, "History of Emancipation," 842–43; Goodwin, *Team of Rivals*, 462–63; Quarles, *Lincoln and the Negro*, 125–26.

48. Lincoln, *Collected Works*, 7:506–7.

49. Paludan, *Presidency of Abraham Lincoln*, 146–47; *New York Times*, July 23, 1862; *New York Tribune* quoted in *Washington Daily Intelligencer*, July 25, 1982.

50. Browning, *Diary of Orville Hickman Browning*, 1:558; Lincoln, *Collected Works*, 5:328–30; T. Harry Williams, *Lincoln and the Radicals*, 164–66; Trefousse, *Radical Republicans*, 218–22; Paludan, *Presidency of Abraham Lincoln*, 146–47; Syrett, *Civil War Confiscation Acts*, 53–54.

51. *Philadelphia Inquirer*, July 16, 1862; Perkins, "Letters Home," 123–24; Castleman, *Army of the Potomac*, 184.

52. *Boston Herald*, July 30, 1862; *Cincinnati Gazette*, July 24, 1862; *Detroit Free Press*, July 25, 1862; *Boston Daily Journal*, July 31, 1862.

53. Paludan, *Presidency of Abraham Lincoln*, 146–47; McPherson, *Battle Cry of Freedom*, 500; Grimsley, *Hard Hand of War*, 77–78. Blair, "Friend or Foe," demonstrates how moderates and conservatives purposely killed the bill's effectiveness by insisting on the treason element of the legislation. The author maintains that the final product was therefore more a product of the efforts of moderates and conservatives than of the radicals. For a comprehensive discussion of the weakness of the Second Confiscation Act, see Siddali, *From Property to Person*, 227–43. Eric Foner, *This Fiery Trial*, 215, interprets the Second Confiscation Act as requiring court proceedings only for nonslave forms of property and maintains that without court action slaves were thus irreversibly freed upon reaching Union lines. Such a distinction in the act is not nearly as clear as Foner asserts, however, as Siddali, *From Property to Person*, 233–34, demonstrates. Moreover, if a slaveholder tried to reclaim slave property from the Union army on the grounds that they had never supported the rebellion, the act expressly forbade military commanders from making a judgment in the case. Presumably, then, the final status of such slaves would indeed require court proceedings.

54. Sumner, *Selected Letters*, 2:122; Grimsley, *Hard Hand of War*, 78.

55. Two impressive recent studies of the Confiscation Acts, Siddali, *From Property to Person*, and John Syrett, *Civil War Confiscation Acts*, focus their respective

discussions on the legal and constitutional elements of the debates, the true motives of the radicals, shifting conceptions of slaves as legitimate forms of property, and the limitations and failures of the acts. While both note that the radicals argued that the measure was a military necessity, the focus of their works naturally leads them away from elaborating on specific ways it was painted as a military necessity. Thus, neither work engages the Peninsula Campaign in a substantive way.

56. *Boston Daily Journal*, July 25, 1862; *Philadelphia Inquirer*, July 24, 1862.

57. Fish, *Duty of the Hour*, 12–13.

58. *Philadelphia Inquirer*, July 24, 1862.

59. *Philadelphia Press*, July 18, 1862.

60. *Philadelphia Press*, July 21, 1862; *Detroit Free Press*, July 25, 1862; *Boston Daily Advertiser*, July 19, 1862; *Washington Daily Intelligencer*, July 25, 1862.

61. *National Anti-Slavery Standard*, July 19, 1862; *Philadelphia Inquirer*, July 17, 1862; Fish, *Duty of the Hour*, 8–10.

62. Lincoln, *Collected Works*, 5:341; Siddali, *From Property to Person*, 243–45; *New York World*, July 29, 1862; McPherson, *Struggle for Equality*, 111.

63. *Baltimore American*, August 6, 1862; *Illinois State Journal*, August 6, 1862; *Boston Herald*, August 6, 1862.

64. *Indianapolis Journal*, August 11, 1862.

65. *Boston Daily Journal*, July 28, 1862.

66. *Baltimore American*, July 29, 1862; *Cincinnati Gazette*, August 1, 1862.

67. *Philadelphia Press*, July 28, 1862; *Boston Daily Journal*, July 24, 1862; *Chicago Tribune*, August 2, 1862.

68. *Chicago Tribune*, July 28, 1862.

69. *Philadelphia Press*, July 28, 1862.

70. *Chicago Tribune*, August 2, 1862; *Philadelphia Press*, July 28, 1862.

71. *National Anti-Slavery Standard*, July 19, 1862; Fish, *Duty of the Hour*, 8–10.

72. *Cincinnati Gazette*, July 26, 1862; *Philadelphia Press*, July 31, 1862.

73. For a recent and comprehensive discussion of this famous cabinet meeting, see Goodwin, *Team of Rivals*, 464–68.

74. The release of the Preliminary Emancipation Proclamation does not fully explain the thirty-two lost Republican congressional seats in the fall of 1862. Other factors included stronger Democratic voter turnout—and especially the faltering military situation. Regardless, Republicans retained control of the House and actually gained five seats in the Senate. See Paludan, *A People's Contest*, 101–2. Gallman, *The North Fights the Civil War*, 129, argues that while resistance to emancipation was "substantial," it was "far less than it would have been" in 1861. Furthermore, if the election results in late 1862 "were a referendum on the Emancipation Proclamation, the popular judgment was still favorable. Much of this shift reflected the growing belief that emancipation would help win the war." For soldier responses to the proclamation, see McPherson, *For Cause and Comrades*, 120–30; and Manning, *What This Cruel War Was Over*, 81–95. Both scholars extensively researched soldier diaries and letters to reach their conclusions. Manning argues that although there was significant opposition to emancipation, it was ultimately embraced by soldiers, "partly because they knew that emancipa-

tion was necessary to save the Union, but also because they now recognized that it was necessary to make the Union worth saving." Gallagher, *The Union War*, 101–3, somewhat over-aggressively challenges Manning's methods and conclusions, insisting that only "a small minority of soldiers" embraced emancipation on moral grounds, that their initial reaction to the Emancipation Proclamation "included a great deal of opposition," and that eventually "by far the most common soldiers' response" was to embrace emancipation as a "useful or even necessary" means of winning the war. McPherson offers a similar, yet less dogmatic assessment, concluding that while pro-emancipation sentiment did ultimately predominate in the army, one of the main factors "that converted many soldiers to emancipation was a growing conviction that it really did hurt the enemy and help their own side." McPherson, *For Cause and Comrades*, 124–25.

Conclusion

1. *New York Times*, August 2, 1862; Thorndike, *Correspondence between General and Senator Sherman*, 156–57.

2. *Principia*, August 16, 1862; Garrison, *Letters of William Lloyd Garrison*, 5:107.

3. McPherson, *Struggle for Equality*, 112–16; *Principia*, August 9, 1862; Lincoln, *Collected Works*, 5:388–89; Goodwin, *Team of Rivals*, 471; Quarles, *Lincoln and the Negro*, 128–29; Guelzo, *Lincoln's Emancipation Proclamation*, 134–36; Pinsker, "Lincoln's Summer of Emancipation," 84. Historians such as Guelzo have praised Lincoln for his response to Greeley, but some have labeled it an example of his racism and unconcern for slaves. See, for example, DiLorenzo's highly problematic *The Real Lincoln*, 34–35. Lincoln's lifelong moral objections to slavery are clearly documented, as is his belief that in the absence of military necessity he had no legal means to interfere with slavery in states where it already existed. Moreover, such criticisms also fail to view events from the perspective of the summer of 1862. Lincoln had already decided to issue the Emancipation Proclamation based on military necessity and needed to ensure that the public would see it for what it was—and for which more people were willing to accept it as—a measure to win the war. Abolitionism divided the North; the goal of saving the Union united it. In this light, as Gary Gallagher argues in *The Union War*, 50–51, Lincoln's response to Greeley "stands as a straightforward expression" of his efforts to rally the North behind saving the Union and of his willingness to use emancipation as a military necessity.

4. Coski, *Army of the Potomac at Berkeley Plantation*, 17; *Baltimore American*, July 31, 1862; *Philadelphia Inquirer*, July 15, 1862; *New York Tribune* quoted in *National Anti-Slavery Standard*, August 9, 1862; *Principia*, August 16, 1862.

5. McClellan, *McClellan's Own Story*, 34; Ruffin, *Diary of Edmund Ruffin*, 2:386.

6. Parker, *Henry Wilson's Regiment*, 179; Shirley Plantation Journals, June 30, 1862, LC.

7. Norton, *Army Letters*, 101; Joseph D. Baker to mother, July 18, 1862, Joseph D. Baker Papers, USAMHI; *Boston Daily Journal*, July 12, 1862.

8. *Philadelphia Inquirer*, July 25, 1862.

9. Coski, *Army of the Potomac at Berkeley Plantation*, 17; *Philadelphia Inquirer*, July 31, 1862; George Williamson Balloch to children, George Williamson Balloch Letters, July 29, 1862, Duke. Today, the beautiful Shirley, Berkeley, and Westover Plantations are all well preserved and open to the public (at Westover only the grounds can be visited). Across the James River from the Peninsula, Richard Eppes's City Point Plantation is now a unit of the Petersburg National Battlefield Park.

10. William J. Burns Diary, July 31, 1862, USAMHI; William B. Westervelt Diary, July 31, 1862, USAMHI; George H. Selkirk to father, August 1, 1862, George H. Selkirk Papers, USAMHI.

11. *New York Tribune* quoted in *National Anti-Slavery Standard*, August 9, 1862; *OR*, 11:3, 327.

12. *Philadelphia Inquirer*, July 15, 31, 1862.

13. *Chicago Tribune*, July 26, 1862; *Bangor (Maine) Daily Whig and Courier*, August 12, 1862; *Baltimore American*, July 31, 1862.

14. *Baltimore American*, July 31, 1862; George H. Selkirk to Charles Selkirk, July 27, 1862, George H. Selkirk Papers, USAMHI; *Boston Herald*, August 5, 1862.

15. *Richmond Dispatch*, July 18, 1862.

16. William Barrett Sydnor to Thomas White Sydnor, July 2, 1862, William Barrett Sydnor Letter, VHS; John A. Williams to sisters, October 8, 1862, John A. Williams Papers, VHS.

17. Gregory, "Judge John M. Gregory to John Armistead, June 19, 1862," 187–90; unknown to Martha Tabb Robins, July 24, 1862, Bruce Family Papers, VHS.

18. Gregory, "Judge John M. Gregory to John Armistead, June 19, 1862," 187–90.

19. Sears, *To the Gates of Richmond*, 352–55.

20. *National Anti-Slavery Standard*, August 30, 1862; Charles C. Perkins Diaries, August 19, 1862, USAMHI; *New York Times*, August 20, 1862; Jones, "Recollections of Williamsburg," CWF.

21. Sneden, *Eye of the Storm*, 113; *New York Times*, August 20, 1862; Thomas T. Ellis, *Leaves from the Diary of an Army Surgeon*, 196.

22. *New York Times*, August 20, 1862; Marks, *Peninsular Campaign in Virginia*, 235; Reichardt, *Diary of Battery A*, 58; William E. Dunn to sister, September 10, 1862, William E. Dunn Papers, USAMHI.

23. *OR*, 11:3, 667; *OR*, 11:2, 939; Thomas T. Ellis, *Leaves from the Diary of an Army Surgeon*, 196.

24. Auditor of Public Accounts, Runaway and Escaped Slaves, Receipts and Reports, 1863, LV; *New York Times*, August 20, 1862; Coski, *Army of the Potomac at Berkeley Plantation*, 35; John Berry Diary, July 13, 1862, USAMHI; George E. Hagar Diary, USAMHI; Berlin et al., *Freedom*, 1:91; Coleman, "Peninsular Campaign," WM. Ayers and Nesbit, "Seeing Emancipation," 5–6, includes a graph that charts the daily percentage of content in the *Richmond Dispatch* that was devoted to fugitive slave advertisements during the war. The highest peak was reached during the last stages of the Peninsula Campaign and the Union occupation of White House Landing. The authors appropriately attribute the sharp increase of runaways to

the presence of the Army of the Potomac on the outskirts of Richmond, but the passage of the Second Confiscation Act and especially Lincoln's late July order for the military to enroll more black laborers (and McClellan's subsequent efforts to round up more slaves) are probably also highly significant factors in the spike.

25. Stewart, *Camp, March, and Battlefield*, 196–97.

BIBLIOGRAPHY

Primary Sources

MANUSCRIPTS COLLECTIONS
Atlanta, Georgia
    Emory University, Robert W. Woodruff Library, Special Collections
        Duggan Papers
Carlisle Barracks, Pennsylvania
    U.S. Army Military History Institute
        W. T. H. Brooks Papers
        Civil War Miscellaneous Collection
            Joseph D. Baker Papers
            Solomon F. Beals Papers
            Luther C. Furst Diary
            James Lee Graham Papers
            William B. Westervelt Diary
        Civil War Times Illustrated Collection of Civil War Papers
            John Berry Diary
            William E. Dunn Papers
            Henry Gerrish Memoir
            Jacob Heffelfinger Diary
            Charles C. Perkins Diaries
            Jonathon P. Stowe Diary
        Harrisburg Civil War Roundtable Collection
            Benjamin E. Ashenfelter Papers
            John Brislin Papers
            Clement D. Potts Papers
        Wendell W. Lang Jr. Collection
            George E. Hagar Diary
        Lewis Leigh Jr. Collection
            Robert A. Everett Papers
            Benjamin Roher Papers
        James H. Mitchell Papers
        Pennsylvania "Save the Flags" Civil War Collection
            Charles Becker Papers
            William J. Burns Diary
        George H. Selkirk Papers
        Murray J. Smith Collection
            Walter J. Eames Papers
Chapel Hill, North Carolina
    University of North Carolina, Southern Historical Collection
        Ruffin Thomson Diary

Thomas Lewis Ware Diary

H. B. White Papers

Durham, North Carolina

Duke University, William R. Perkins Library

George Williamson Balloch Letters

Bell Halsey Miller Diary

Benjamin C. Stevens Diary

Richmond, Virginia

Library of Virginia

Auditor of Public Accounts, Runaway and Escaped Slaves,
Receipts and Reports, 1863

John Letcher Executive Papers

Richmond National Battlefield Park, Manuscripts Collection

Volume 17: John S. Tucker Diary

Virginia Historical Society

Aylett Family Papers

Bruce Family Papers

Sarah Dandridge Cooke Duval Memoir

Eppes Family Muniments

Diary of Richard Eppes

Hankins Family Papers

Charles Tayloe Mason Papers

Selden Family Letters

William Barrett Sydnor Letter

Talcott Family Papers

Fanny W. Gaines Tinsley Memoir

Tomkins Family Papers

Wickham Family Papers

Diary of William Fanning Wickham

John A. Williams Papers

Washington, D.C.

Library of Congress, Manuscripts Division

Zachariah Chandler Papers

James R. Doolittle Papers

Jediah Hotchkiss Papers

George B. McClellan Papers

Shirley Plantation Journals

Papers of John Washington

Williamsburg, Virginia

College of William and Mary, Swem Library, Manuscripts
and Rare Books Department

Harriette Cary Diary

Benjamin Soddert Ewell Papers

Galt Family Papers

Tucker-Coleman Papers
  Diary of Cynthia B. T. W. Coleman
  Cynthia B. T. W. Coleman, "Peninsular Campaign"
  Robert Page Waller Diary
Colonial Williamsburg Foundation Archives, Oral History Collection
  Eliza Baker, "Memoirs of Williamsburg"
  Charles S. Jones, "Recollections of Williamsburg, Virginia, as It Was
    before the Civil War"
  Victoria Lee, "Williamsburg in 1861"

NEWSPAPERS AND MAGAZINES

Atlantic Monthly
*Baltimore American and Commercial
  Advertiser*
Bangor (Maine) Daily Whig and Courier
Boston Daily Advertiser
Boston Daily Journal
Boston Herald
Charleston Mercury
Charlotte Western Democrat
Chicago Times
Chicago Tribune
Cincinnati Daily Commercial
Cincinnati Gazette
Cleveland Herald
Detroit Free Press
Douglass' Monthly
Frank Leslie's Illustrated Newspaper
Harper's Weekly
Illinois State Journal
Indianapolis Daily Sentinel
Indianapolis Journal
Indianapolis Star
Liberator
Lowell (Mass.) Daily Citizen
Milwaukee Daily Sentinel
National Anti-Slavery Standard

New York Evening Post
New York Herald
New York Independent
New York Times
New York Tribune
New York World (semiweekly)
*North American and United States
  Gazette* (Philadelphia)
Petersburg Daily Press
Philadelphia Inquirer
Philadelphia Press
Philadelphia Public Ledger
Principia
Providence (R.I.) Post
Racine (Wis.) Weekly Journal
Richmond Daily Dispatch
Richmond Enquirer
Richmond Examiner
Richmond Sentinel
Richmond Whig (semiweekly)
Rochester (N.Y.) Evening Express
San Francisco Daily Evening Bulletin
Washington Daily National Intelligencer
Washington Sunday Morning Chronicle
Williamsburg Cavalier (published by
  the 5th Pennsylvania Cavalry)

GOVERNMENT DOCUMENTS

Congressional Globe. 46 vols. Washington, D.C.: Blair and Rives, 1834–73.
Kennedy, Joseph C. G. *Population of The United States in 1860; Compiled from the
  Original Returns of the Eighth Census under the Direction of the Secretary of the
  Interior.* Washington, D.C.: Government Printing Office, 1864.
Report of the Joint Committee on the Conduct of the War. 3 pts. Washington, D.C.:
  Government Printing Office, 1865.

U.S. War Department. *The War of the Rebellion: A Compilation of the Official Records of the Union and Confederate Armies*. 128 vols. Washington, D.C.: Government Printing Office, 1880–1901.

BOOKS, ARTICLES, AND OTHER PUBLISHED SOURCES

Acton, Edward A. "'Dear Mollie': Letters of Captain Edward A. Acton to His Wife, 1862." Edited by Mary Acton Hammond. *Pennsylvania Magazine of History and Biography* 89, no. 1 (January 1965): 3–51.

Auchmuty, Richard Tylden. *Letters of Richard Tylden Auchmuty, Fifth Corps, Army of the Potomac*. Edited by E.S.A. Privately printed, 1889.

Banes, Charles H. *History of the Philadelphia Brigade*. Philadelphia: J. B. Lippincott, 1876.

Bates, Edward. *Diary of Edward Bates, 1859–1866*. Washington, D.C.: American Historical Association, 1933.

Beach, William Harrison. *The First New York (Lincoln) Cavalry from April 19, 1861, to July 7, 1865*. Milwaukee: Burdick and Allen, 1902.

Beecher, Henry Ward. *War and Emancipation: A Thanksgiving Sermon, Preached in the Plymouth Church, Brooklyn, N.Y., on Thursday, November 21, 1861*. Philadelphia: T. B. Peterson, 1861.

Bellard, Alfred. *Gone for a Soldier: The Civil War Memoirs of Private Alfred Bellard*. Edited by David Herbert Donald. Boston: Little, Brown, 1975.

Berlin, Ira, Barbara J. Fields, Thavolia Glymph, Joseph P. Reidy, and Leslie S. Rowlands, eds. *Freedom: A Documentary History of Emancipation, 1861–1867*. Selected from the holdings of the National Archives of the United States. Ser. I, vol. 1: *The Destruction of Slavery*. New York: Cambridge University Press, 1985. Ser. I, vol. 3: *The Wartime Genesis of Free Labor: The Lower South*. Cambridge: Cambridge University Press, 1990.

Blaine, James G. *Twenty Years of Congress: From Lincoln to Garfield*. 2 vols. Norwich, Conn.: Henry Bill, 1884–86.

Blassingame, John W., ed. *Slave Testimony: Two Centuries of Letters, Speeches, Interviews, and Autobiographies*. Baton Rouge: Louisiana State University Press, 1977.

Boutwell, George S. *Emancipation: Its Justice, Expediency, and Necessity, as the Means of Securing a Speedy and Permanent Peace: An Address Delivered by Hon. George S. Boutwell, in Tremont Temple, Boston, under the Auspices of the Emancipation League, December 16, 1861*. Boston: Wright and Potter, 1861.

Brewster, Charles Harvey. *When This Cruel War Is Over: The Civil War Letters of Charles Harvey Brewster*. Edited by David Blight. Amherst: University of Massachusetts Press, 1992.

Browning, Orville Hickman. *Diary of Orville Hickman Browning*. 2 vols. Edited by Theodore Calvin Pease and James G. Randall. Springfield: Illinois State Historical Library, 1925–33.

Brownlow, William Gannaway. *Sketch of Parson Brownlow, and His Speeches at the Academy of Music and Cooper Institute, New York, May, 1862*. New York: E. O. Barker, 1862.

Butler, Benjamin. *Butler's Book*. Boston: A. M. Thayer, 1892.

———. *Private and Official Correspondence of Gen. Benjamin F. Butler during the Period of the Civil War*. 5 vols. Edited by Jessie Ames Marshall. Norwood, Mass.: Privately printed, 1917.

[Caffey, Thomas C.]. *Battlefields of the South, from Bull Run to Fredericksburgh . . . by an English Combatant*. New York: John Bradburn, 1864.

Castleman, Alfred L. *The Army of the Potomac behind the Scenes*. Milwaukee: Strickland, 1863.

Chase, Salmon P. *The Salmon P. Chase Papers*. 4 vols. Kent, Ohio: Kent State University Press, 1993–.

Chase, T. E. *History of the Fifth Massachusetts Battery*. Boston: Luther E. Cowles, 1902.

Cheever, George B. *Salvation of the Country Secured by Immediate Emancipation: A Discourse by Rev. George B. Cheever, D.D., Delivered in the Church of the Puritans, Sabbath Evening, Nov. 10, 1861*. New York: John A. Gray, 1861.

Conway, Moncure. *The Rejected Stone; or Insurrection vs. Resurrection in America*. Boston: Welch, Bigelow, 1861.

Cook, Joel. *The Siege of Richmond: A Narrative of the Military Operations of Major-General George B. McClellan during the Months of May and June, 1862*. Philadelphia: George W. Childs, 1862.

Davis, Jefferson. *The Papers of Jefferson Davis*. 10 vols. Edited by Lynda Lasswell Crist and Mary Seaton Dix. Baton Rouge: Louisiana State University Press, 1995.

Douglass, Frederick. *The Frederick Douglass Papers*. 5 vols. Edited by John W. Blassingame. New Haven, Conn.: Yale University Press, 1979–92.

———. *My Bondage and My Freedom*. New York: Miller, Orton, and Mulligan, 1855.

Dunn, William E. "On the Peninsular Campaign: Civil War Letters from William E. Dunn." *Civil War Times Illustrated* 14, no. 1 (July 1975): 14–19.

Ellis, Thomas T. *Leaves from the Diary of an Army Surgeon; or, Incidents of Field, Camp, and Hospital Life*. New York: John Bradburn, 1863.

Fish, Henry Clay. *Duty of the Hour; or, Lessons from Our Reverses: A Discourse*. New York: Sheldon, 1862.

Fisk, Wilbur. *Hard Marching Every Day: Civil War Letters of Private Wilbur Fisk, 1861–1865*. Edited by Emil Rosenblatt and Ruth Rosenblatt. Lawrence: University Press of Kansas, 1992.

Forrest, William S. *Historical and Descriptive Sketches of Norfolk and Vicinity*. Philadelphia: Lindsay and Blakiston, 1853.

Fuller, Richard F. *Chaplain Fuller; Being a Life Sketch of a New England Clergyman and Army Chaplain*. Boston: Walker, Wise, 1863.

Garrison, William Lloyd. *The Letters of William Lloyd Garrison*. 5 vols. Edited by Walter M. Merrill. Cambridge, Mass.: Harvard University Press, 1979.

Goss, Warren Lee. *Recollections of a Private*. New York: Thomas Y. Crowell, 1890.

Gregory, John M. "Judge John M. Gregory to John Armistead, June 19, 1862." *Tyler's Quarterly Genealogical and Historical Magazine* 10 (1929): 187–90.

Hale, Edward J. "The Bethel Regiment: The First N.C. Volunteers." In *Histories of the Several Regiments and Battalions from North Carolina in the Great War, 1861–65: Written by Members of the Respective Commands*, edited by Walter Clark, 1:69–107. Raleigh: E. M. Uzzell, 1901.

Hay, John. *Inside Lincoln's White House: The Complete Civil War Diary of John Hay.* Carbondale: Southern Illinois University Press, 1977.

Haydon, Charles B. *For Country, Cause, and Leader: The Civil War Journal of Charles B. Haydon.* Edited by Stephen Sears. New York: Ticknor and Fields, 1993.

Hays, Gilbert Adams. *Under the Red Patch: Story of the Sixty-third Regiment, Pennsylvania Volunteers, 1861–1865.* Pittsburgh: Market Review, 1908.

Holmes, Oliver Wendell, Jr. *Touched by Fire: Civil War Letters and Diary of Oliver Wendell Holmes Jr.* Edited by Mark DeWolfe Howe. New York: Fordham University Press, 2000.

Hyde, Thomas W. *Following the Greek Cross; or, Memories of the Sixth Army Corps.* Boston: Houghton Mifflin, 1895.

Joinville, Prince de. *Album of Paintings by the Prince de Joinville, 1861–1862.* New York: Atheneum, 1964.

———. *The Army of the Potomac: Its Organization, Its Commander, and Its Campaign.* New York: Anson D. F. Randolph, 1862.

Jones, William. "Seven Days around Richmond." *Southern Historical Society Papers* 9 (1881): 557–70.

Judd, David W. *The Story of the Thirty-third NYS Vols.* Rochester, N.Y.: Benton and Andrews, 1864.

Julian, George. *Political Recollections.* New York: Jansen, McClung, 1884.

Le Duc, William G. *Recollections of a Civil War Quartermaster.* St. Paul, Minn.: North Central Publishing Company, 1963.

Lee, Robert E. *The Wartime Papers of Robert E. Lee.* Edited by Clifford Dowdey and Louis Manarin. New York: Bramhill House, 1961.

Lincoln, Abraham. *The Collected Works of Lincoln.* 9 vols. Edited by Roy P. Basler. New Brunswick, N.J.: Rutgers University Press, 1953–55.

Macnamara, Daniel G. *The Story of the Ninth Regiment Massachusetts Volunteer Infantry.* Boston: E. B. Stillings, 1899.

Mahan, D. H. *A Treatise of Field Fortifications and Other Subjects Connected with the Duties of the Field Engineer.* 2nd ed. London: Bosworth, 1847.

Marks, James J. *The Peninsula Campaign in Virginia; or, Incidents and Scenes on the Battle-fields and in Richmond.* Philadelphia: Lippincott, 1864.

Martin, Joseph Plumb. *Private Yankee Doodle: A Narrative of Some of the Adventures, Dangers, and Sufferings of a Revolutionary Soldier.* Edited by George F. Scheer. Boston: Little, Brown, 1962.

McAllister, Robert. *Civil War Letters of General Robert McAllister.* Edited by James I. Robertson Jr. New Brunswick, N.J.: Rutgers University Press, 1965.

McClellan, George. *The Civil War Papers of George B. McClellan: Selected Correspondence, 1860–1865.* Edited by Stephen W. Sears. New York: Ticknor and Fields, 1989.

———. *McClellan's Own Story: The War for the Union, the Soldiers Who Fought It, the Civilians Who Directed It, and His Relations to It and to Them*. New York: C. L. Webster, 1887.

Miller, James C. "Serving under McClellan on the Peninsula in 62." *Civil War Times Illustrated* 8, no. 3 (June 1969): 24–30.

Moore, Frank, ed. *Civil War in Song and Story: Anecdotes, Poetry, and Incidents of the War, North and South, 1860–1865*. New York: Publication Office, Bible House, 1867.

Murray, R. L., ed. *Letters from Berdan's Sharpshooters*. New York: Benedum Books, 2005.

Norton, Oliver Wilcox. *Army Letters, 1861–1865*. Chicago: O. L. Deming, 1903.

Olmsted, Frederick Law. *The Cotton Kingdom: A Traveler's Observations on Cotton and Slavery in the American Slave States*. New York: Mason Brothers, 1862.

Paine, Levi L. *Political Lessons of the Rebellion: A Sermon Delivered at Farmington, Connecticut, on Fast Day, April 18, 1862*. Farmington, Conn.: S. S. Cowles, 1862.

Paris, Comte de. "'We Prepare to Receive the Enemy Where We Stand': The Journal of the Comte de Paris." Edited by Mark Grimsley. *Civil War Times Illustrated* 24, no. 3 (May 1985): 18–26.

Parker, John L. *Henry Wilson's Regiment: History of the Twenty-second Massachusetts Infantry, the Second Company Sharpshooters, and the Third Light Battery, in the War of the Rebellion*. Boston: Regimental Association, 1887.

Parton, James. *General Butler in New Orleans*. New York: Mason Brothers, 1864.

Perdue, Charles, Jr., Thomas E. Barden, and Robert K. Phillips, eds. *Weevils in the Wheat: Interviews with Virginia Ex-Slaves*. Charlottesville: University Press of Virginia, 1976.

Perkins, Charles E. "Letters Home: Sergeant Charles E. Perkins in Virginia, 1862." Edited by Ray Henshaw and Glenn W. LaFantasie. *Rhode Island History* 39 (November 1980): 106–31.

Pickerwill, W. N. *History of the Third Indiana Cavalry*. Indianapolis: Aetna, 1906.

Pierce, Edward. "The Contrabands at Fortress Monroe." *Atlantic Monthly* 7 (November 1861): 626–40.

Pinkerton, Allen. *The Spy of the Rebellion; Being a True History of the Spy System of the United States Army during the Late Rebellion*. New York: G. W. Dillingham, 1888.

Randolph, Peter. *Sketches of Slave Life; or, Illustrations of the Peculiar Institution*. Boston: Self-published, 1855.

Rawick, George. *The American Slave: A Composite Autobiography*. 19 vols. Westport, Conn.: Greenwood Press, 1979.

Redpath, James. *The Roving Editor; or Talks with Slaves in the Southern States*. New York: Negro Universities Press, 1968.

Regan, Timothy J. *The Lost Civil War Diaries: The Diaries of Corporal Timothy J. Regan*. Edited by David C. Newton and Kenneth J. Pluskat. Victoria, B.C.: Trafford, 2003.

Reichardt, Theodore. *Diary of Battery A, First Regiment, Rhode Island Light Artillery*. Providence, R.I.: N. Bangs, 1865.

Rhodes, Elisha Hunt. *All for the Union: The Diary and Letters of Elisha Hunt Rhodes*. Edited by Robert Hunt Rhodes. New York: Orion Books, 1991.

Ruffin, Edmund. *The Diary of Edmund Ruffin*. 3 vols. Edited by William Kaufman Scarborough. Baton Rouge: Louisiana State University Press, 1972–89.

———. "A Sketch of the Progress of Agriculture in Virginia." *Farmer's Register* 3 (1835).

Sneden, Robert Knox. *Eye of the Storm: A Civil War Odyssey*. Edited by Charles F. Bryan Jr. and Nelson D. Lankford. New York: Free Press, 2000.

Southwick, Thomas P. *A Duryee Zouave*. Washington, D.C.: Acme, 1930.

Stevens, George T. *Three Years in the Sixth Corps*. New York: D. Van Nostrand, 1870.

Stevens, Thaddeus. *Selected Papers of Thaddeus Stevens*. 2 vols. Edited by Beverly Wilson Palmer and Holly Byers Ochoa. Pittsburgh: University of Pittsburgh Press, 1997.

Stewart, Rev. A. M. *Camp, March, and Battlefield; or, Three Years and a Half with the Army of the Potomac*. Philadelphia: James B. Rodgers, 1865.

Strong, George Templeton. *The Diary of George Templeton Strong*. 4 vols. Edited by Allan Nevins and Milton Halsey Thomas. New York: Macmillan, 1952.

Sumner, Charles. *The Selected Letters of Charles Sumner*. 2 vols. Edited by Beverly Wilson Palmer. Boston: Northeastern University Press, 1990.

Sydnor, Henry Clinton. "A Virginia Boy in the Sixties." *Confederate Veteran* 20 (March 1912): 105–7.

Sypher, Josiah Rinehart. *History of the Pennsylvania Reserve Corps*. Lancaster, Pa.: Elias Barr, 1865.

Thorndike, Rachel Sherman, ed. *Correspondence between General and Senator Sherman from 1837 to 1891*. New York: Charles Scribner's, 1894.

Townsend, George Alfred. *Rustics in Rebellion: A Yankee Reporter on the Road to Richmond*. Chapel Hill: University of North Carolina Press, 1950.

Trobriand, Regis de. *Four Years with the Army of the Potomac*. Translated by George K. Dauchy. Boston: Ticknor, 1889.

Vermont Colonization Society. *The Forty-eighth Annual Report of the Vermont Colonization Society Together with the Address of Gen. J. W. Phelps, at the Annual Meeting in Montpelier, October 17th, 1867*. Montpelier, Vt.: Burlington, 1867.

Wainwright, Charles S. *A Diary of Battle: The Personal Journals of Colonel Charles S. Wainwright, 1861–1865*. New York: Harcourt, Brace and World, 1962.

Washington, George. *The Writings of George Washington from the Original Manuscript Sources, 1745–1799*. 37 vols. Edited by John C. Fitzpatrick. Washington D.C.: Government Printing Office, 1931–44.

Washington, John. *John Washington's Civil War: A Slave Narrative*. Edited by Crandall Shifflett. Baton Rouge: Louisiana State University Press, 2008.

Welles, Gideon. *Diary of Gideon Welles, Secretary of the Navy under Lincoln and Johnson*. 3 vols. Boston: Houghton Mifflin, 1911.

———. "The First Iron-Clad Monitor." In *The Annals of the War Written by Leading Participants North and South*, edited by Alexander K. McClure, 17–31. Philadelphia: Times Publishing Company, 1879.

———. "The History of Emancipation." *Galaxy* 14 (December 1872): 838–51.

West, George Benjamin. *When the Yankees Came: Civil War and Reconstruction on the Virginia Peninsula.* Edited by Parke Rouse Jr. Richmond: Deitz Press, 1977.

Wheeler, Richard, ed. *Sword over Richmond: An Eyewitness History of McClellan's Peninsula Campaign.* New York: Fairfax Press, 1986.

White, Andrew Dickson. *Abolition of Slavery the Right of Government under the War Power.* Boston: R. F. Walcutt, 1861.

Wilson, Henry. *History of the Antislavery Measures of the Thirty-seventh and Thirty-eighth United-States Congresses, 1861–64.* Boston: Walker, Wise, 1864.

———. *History of the Rise and Fall of the Slave Power in America.* Vol. 2. Boston: Houghton Mifflin, 1877.

Secondary Sources

Alho, Olli. *The Religion of the Slaves: A Study of the Religious Tradition and Behavior of Plantation Slaves in the United States, 1830–1865.* Helsinki: Suomalainen Tiedeakatemia, 1976.

Allan, William. *The Army of Northern Virginia in 1862.* Boston: Wright and Potter, 1899.

Altoff, Gerald T. *Amongst My Best Men: African-Americans and the War of 1812.* Put-in-Bay, Ohio: Perry Group, 1996.

Anderson, Fred. *Crucible of War: The Seven Years' War and the Fate of Empire in British North America, 1754–1766.* New York: Alfred A. Knopf, 2000.

Andrews, J. Cutler. *The North Reports the Civil War.* Pittsburgh: University of Pittsburgh Press, 1955.

Aptheker, Herbert. *The Negro in the Civil War.* New York: New York International Publishers, 1938.

Ayers, Edward, and Scott Nesbit. "Seeing Emancipation: Scale and Freedom in the American South." *Journal of the Civil War Era* 1, no. 1 (March 2011): 3–24.

Ayers, Edward, and John C. Willis, eds. *The Edge of the South: Life in Nineteenth-Century Virginia.* Charlottesville: University Press of Virginia, 1991.

Barrow, Charles K., ed. *Forgotten Confederates: An Anthology about Black Southerners.* Murfreesboro, Tenn.: Southern Heritage Press, 1998.

Beauregard, Erving. *Bingham of the Hills: Politician and Diplomat Extraordinary.* New York: Peter Lang, 1989.

Bergeron, Arthur W., ed. *Black Southerners in Gray: Essays about Afro-Americans in Confederate Armies.* Redondo Beach, Calif.: Rank and File Publications, 1994.

Berlin, Ira. *Many Thousands Gone: The First Two Centuries of Slavery in North America.* Cambridge, Mass.: Harvard University Press, 1998.

———. *Slaves without Masters: The Free Negro in the Antebellum South.* New York: Pantheon, 1974.

Berlin, Ira, Barbara J. Fields, Steven F. Miller, Joseph P. Reidy, and Leslie S. Rowlands. *Slaves No More: Three Essays on Emancipation and the Civil War.* New York: Cambridge University Press, 1992.

Berlin, Ira, and Ronald Hoffman, eds. *Slavery and Freedom in the Age of the American Revolution.* Charlottesville: University Press of Virginia, 1983.

Blackerby, H. C. *Blacks in Blue and Gray: Afro-American Service in the Civil War.* Tuscaloosa, Ala.: Portals Press, 1979.

Blair, William Alan. "Friend or Foe: Treason and the Second Confiscation Act." In *Wars within a War: Controversy and Conflict over the America Civil War,* edited by Joan Waugh and Gary W. Gallagher, 27–51. Chapel Hill: University of North Carolina Press, 2009.

———. "The Seven Days and the Radical Persuasion: Convincing Moderates in the North of the Need for a Hard War." In *The Richmond Campaign of 1862: Peninsula and the Seven Days,* ed. Gary W. Gallagher, 153–180. Chapel Hill: University of North Carolina Press, 2000.

———. *Virginia's Private War: Feeding Body and Soul in the Confederacy.* New York: Oxford University Press, 1998.

Blassingame, John W. *The Slave Community: Plantation Life in the Antebellum South.* New York: Oxford University Press, 1979.

Boatner, Mark M. *The Civil War Dictionary.* New York: D. McKay, 1959.

Bogue, Allan G. *The Congressman's Civil War.* New York: Cambridge University Press, 1989.

Bowman, Larry G. "Virginia's Use of Blacks in the French and Indian War." *Western Pennsylvania Historical Magazine* 53 (1970): 57–63.

Bowman, Shearer Davis. "Conditional Unionism and Slavery in Virginia, 1860–1861: The Case of Dr. Richard Eppes." *Virginia Magazine of History and Biography* 96 (January 1988): 31–54.

Breen, T. H. "A Changing Labor Force and Race Relations in Virginia, 1660–1710." *Journal of Social History* 7 (Fall 1973): 2–25.

Brewer, James H. *The Confederate Negro: Virginia's Craftsmen and Military Laborers, 1861–1865.* Durham, N.C.: Duke University Press, 1969.

Brown, William Wells. *The Negro in the American Rebellion: His Heroism and His Fidelity.* Boston: A. G. Brown, 1880.

Buckley, Roger Norman. *Slaves in Red Coats: The British West India Regiments, 1795–1815.* New Haven, Conn.: Yale University Press, 1979.

Burton, Brian K. *Extraordinary Circumstances: The Seven Days Battles.* Bloomington: Indiana University Press, 2001.

Camp, Stephanie M. H. *Closer to Freedom: Enslaved Women and Everyday Resistance in the Antebellum South.* Chapel Hill: University of North Carolina Press, 2004.

Casdorph, Peter. *Prince John Magruder: His Life and Campaigns.* New York: John Wiley, 1996.

Cassel, Frank. "Slaves of the Chesapeake Bay Area and the War of 1812." *Journal of Negro History* 57 (April 1972): 144–55.

Conrad, A. H., and J. R. Meyer. "The Economics of Slavery in the Antebellum South." *Journal of Political Economy* 66 (1958): 95–122.

Cooper, Frederick. *Plantation Slavery on the East Coast of Africa.* New Haven, Conn.: Yale University Press, 1977.

Cornish, Dudley T. *The Sable Arm: Negro Troops in the Union Army, 1861–1865.* New York: Longmans, Green, 1956.

Coski, John M. *The Army of the Potomac at Berkeley Plantation: The Harrison's Landing Occupation of 1862*. Richmond: J. M. Coski, 1989.

Cullen, Joseph P. *The Peninsula Campaign, 1862: McClellan and Lee Struggle for Richmond*. New York: Bonanza Books, 1973.

Dew, Charles B. *Apostles of Disunion: Southern Secession Commissioners and the Causes of the Civil War*. Charlottesville: University Press of Virginia, 2001.

———. *Ironmaker to the Confederacy: Joseph R. Anderson and the Tredegar Iron Works*. New Haven, Conn.: Yale University Press, 1966.

DiLorenzo, Thomas J. *The Real Lincoln: A New Look at Abraham Lincoln, His Agenda, and an Unnecessary War*. Roseville, Calif.: Forum, 2002.

Donald, David H. *Charles Sumner and the Rights of Man*. New York: Knopf, 1970.

———. *Lincoln*. London: Jonathan Cape, 1995.

Dornbusch, Charles E. *Military Bibliography of the Civil War*. 3 vols. New York: New York Public Library, 1961–72.

Dougherty, Kevin, and J. Michael Moore. *The Peninsula Campaign of 1862: A Military Analysis*. Oxford: University Press of Mississippi, 2005.

Dowdey, Clifford. *The Seven Days: The Emergence of Lee*. Boston: Little, Brown, 1964.

Dubbs, Carol Kettenburg. *Defend This Old Town: Williamsburg during the Civil War*. Baton Rouge: Louisiana State University Press, 2002.

Ellis, Joseph. *American Creation: Triumphs and Tragedies at the Founding of the Republic*. New York: Alfred A. Knopf, 2007.

Engerman, Stanley L., and Eugene D. Genovese, eds. *Race and Slavery in the Western Hemisphere: Quantitative Studies*. Princeton, N.J.: Princeton University Press, 1975.

Engs, Robert Francis. *Freedom's First Generation: Black Hampton, Virginia, 1861–1890*. Philadelphia: University of Pennsylvania Press, 1979.

Escott, Paul D. *Slavery Remembered: A Record of Twentieth-Century Slave Narratives*. Chapel Hill: University of North Carolina Press, 1979.

Faust, Drew Gilpin. *This Republic of Suffering: Death and the American Civil War*. New York, Alfred A. Knopf, 2008.

Fields, Barbara Jean. "Who Freed the Slaves?" In Geoffrey C. Ward, Ric Burns, and Ken Burns, *The Civil War: An Illustrated History*, 178–81. New York: Alfred A. Knopf, 1990.

Fischel, Edwin. "Pinkerton and McClellan: Who Deceived Whom?" *Civil War History* 34, no. 2 (June 1988): 115–42.

———. *The Secret War for the Union: The Untold Story of Military Intelligence in the Civil War*. Boston: Houghton Mifflin, 1996.

Foner, Eric. *The Fiery Trial: Abraham Lincoln and American Slavery*. New York: W.W. Norton and Company, 2010.

Foote, Shelby. *The Civil War: A Narrative*. 3 vols. New York: Random House, 1958.

Franklin, John Hope. *The Emancipation Proclamation*. New York: Doubleday, 1963.

Franklin, John Hope, and Loren Schweninger. *Runaway Slaves: Rebels on the Plantations*. New York: Oxford University Press, 1999.

Freeman, Douglas S. *Lee's Lieutenants: A Study in Command*. 3 vols. New York: Scribner's, 1942–44.

——. *R. E. Lee: A Biography*. 4 vols. New York: Scribner's, 1936–42.

Frey, Sylvia. "Between Slavery and Freedom: Virginia Blacks in the American Revolution." *Journal of Southern History* (1983): 375–98.

——. *Water from the Rock: Black Resistance in a Revolutionary Age*. Princeton, N.J.: Princeton University Press, 1991.

Gallagher, Gary W. *Causes Won, Lost, and Forgotten: How Hollywood and Popular Art Shape What We Know about the Civil War*. Chapel Hill: University of North Carolina Press, 2007.

——. "Lee to the Fore." *Civil War: The Magazine of the Civil War Society* (June 1995): 6–8.

——. *The Union War*. Cambridge, Mass.: Harvard University Press, 2011.

——, ed. *The Richmond Campaign of 1862: The Peninsula and the Seven Days*. Chapel Hill: University of North Carolina Press, 2000.

Gallman, J. Matthew. *The North Fights the Civil War: The Home Front*. Chicago: Ivan R. Dee, 1994.

Genovese, Eugene. *Roll, Jordan, Roll: The World the Slaves Made*. New York: Vintage Books, 1974.

George, Christopher T. "Mirage of Freedom: African Americans in the War of 1812." *Maryland Historical Magazine* 91 (Winter 1996): 427–50.

Gerteis, Louis. *From Contraband to Freedman: Federal Policy toward Southern Blacks, 1861–1865*. Westport, Conn.: Greenwood Press, 1973.

Glatthaar, Joseph T. *Forged in Battle: The Civil War Alliance of Black Soldiers and White Officers*. New York: Free Press, 1990.

Goldin, Claudia Dale. *Urban Slavery in the American South, 1820–1860: A Quantitative History*. Chicago: University of Chicago Press, 1976.

Goodwin, Doris Kearns. *Team of Rivals: The Political Genius of Abraham Lincoln*. New York: Simon and Schuster, 2005.

Green, Carol C. *Chimborazo: The Confederacy's Largest Hospital*. Knoxville: University of Tennessee Press, 2004.

Grimsley, Mark. *The Hard Hand of War: Union Military Policy toward Southern Civilians, 1861–1865*. Cambridge: Cambridge University Press, 1995.

Guelzo, Allen. *Lincoln's Emancipation Proclamation: The End of Slavery in America*. New York: Simon and Schuster, 2004.

Harding, Vincent. *There Is a River: The Black Struggle for Freedom in America*. New York: Harcourt Brace Jovanovich, 1981.

Hess, Earl J. *Field Armies and Fortifications: The Eastern Campaigns, 1861–1864*. Chapel Hill: University of North Carolina Press, 2005.

Holton, Woody. *Forced Founders: Indians, Debtors, Slaves, and the Making of the American Revolution in Virginia*. Chapel Hill: University of North Carolina Press, 1999.

Jackson, Luther Porter. *Free Negro Labor and Property Holding in Virginia, 1830–1860*. New York: D. Appleton–Century, 1942.

———. "Virginia Negro Soldiers and Seamen in the American Revolution." *Journal of Negro History* 27 (1942): 247–87.

Johnson, Walter. *Soul by Soul: Life inside the Antebellum Slave Market*. Cambridge, Mass.: Harvard University Press, 1999.

Jordan, David M. *Winfield Scott Hancock: A Soldier's Life*. Bloomington: Indiana University Press, 1988.

Jordan, Ervin. *Black Confederates and Afro-Yankees in Civil War Virginia*. Charlottesville: University Press of Virginia, 1995.

Kimball, Gregg D. *American City, Southern Place: A Cultural History of Antebellum Richmond*. Athens: University of Georgia Press, 2000.

Klein, Herbert. *Slavery in the Americas: A Comparative Study of Virginia and Cuba*. Chicago: University of Chicago Press, 1967.

Klung, Mark M. *Lyman Trumbull: Conservative Radical*. New York: Barnes, 1965.

Kulikoff, Allen. *Tobacco and Slaves: The Development of Southern Cultures in the Chesapeake, 1680–1800*. Chapel Hill: University of North Carolina Press, 1986.

Lawson, Melinda. "Imagining Slavery: Representations of the Peculiar Institution on the Northern Stage, 1776–1860." *Journal of the Civil War Era* 1, no. 1 (March 2011): 25–55.

Levine, Bruce. "Black Confederates." *North and South* 10, no. 2 (July 2007): 40–45.

———. "Black Confederates and Neo-Confederates: In Search of a Usable Past." In *Race, Slavery, and Public History: The Tough Stuff of American Memory*, edited by James Oliver Horton and Lois E. Horton, 187–211. New York: New Press, 2006.

———. *Confederate Emancipation: Southern Plans to Free and Arm Slaves during the Civil War*. New York: Oxford University Press, 2007.

———. "Editorial Crossfire." *North and South* 10, no. 5 (March 2008): 8–9.

Link, William A. *Roots of Secession: Slavery and Politics in Antebellum Virginia*. Chapel Hill: University of North Carolina Press, 2003.

Lovejoy, Paul E. *Transformations in Slavery: A History of Slavery in Africa*. New York: Cambridge University Press, 1983.

Manning, Chandra. *What This Cruel War Was Over: Soldiers, Slavery, and the Civil War*. New York: Knopf, 2007.

Marten, James. *The Children's Civil War*. Chapel Hill: University of North Carolina Press, 1998.

———. "A Feeling of Restless Anxiety: Loyalty and Race in the Peninsula Campaign and Beyond." In *The Richmond Campaign of 1862: Peninsula and the Seven Days*, ed. Gary W. Gallagher, 121–152. Chapel Hill: University of North Carolina Press, 2000.

Martin, Jonathan D. *Divided Mastery: Slave Hiring in the American South*. Cambridge, Mass.: Harvard University Press, 2004.

Masur, Kate. "'A Rare Phenomenon of Philological Vegetation': The Word 'Contraband' and the Meanings of Emancipation in the United States." *Journal of American History* (March 2007): 1050–84.

McCurry, Stephanie. *Confederate Reckoning: Power and Politics in the Civil War South*. Cambridge, Mass.: Harvard University Press, 2010.

McPherson, James M. *Battle Cry of Freedom: The Civil War Era*. New York: Oxford University Press, 1988.

———. *Crossroads of Freedom: Antietam, 1862*. New York: Oxford University Press, 2002.

———. *Drawn with a Sword: Reflections on the American Civil War*. New York: Oxford University Press, 1997.

———. *For Cause and Comrades: Why Men Fought in the Civil War*. New York: Oxford University Press, 1997.

———. *The Negro's Civil War*. New York: Vintage, 1965.

———. *The Struggle for Equality: Abolitionists and the Negro in the Civil War and Reconstruction*. Princeton, N.J.: Princeton University Press, 1964.

Michel, Gregg L. "From Slavery to Freedom, Hickory Hill, 1850–80." In *The Edge of the South: Life in Nineteenth Century Virginia*, edited by Edward L. Ayers and John C. Willis, 109–33. Charlottesville: University Press of Virginia, 1991.

Miller, William J., ed. *The Peninsula Campaign of 1862: Yorktown to the Seven Days*. 2 vols. Campbell, Calif.: Savas, 1997.

Mitchell, Reid. *Civil War Soldiers*. New York: Viking, 1988.

Mohr, Clarence L. "Southern Blacks in the Civil War: A Century of Historiography." *Journal of Negro History* 69 (1974): 177–95.

Morgan, Edmund S. *American Slavery, American Freedom: The Ordeal of Colonial Virginia*. New York: Norton, 1975.

Morgan, Lydia J. *Emancipation in Virginia's Tobacco Belt, 1850–1870*. Athens: University of Georgia Press, 1992.

Mullin, Gerald. *Flight and Rebellion: Slave Resistance in Eighteenth-Century Virginia*. New York: Oxford University Press, 1972.

Nicholls, Michael. "'In the Light of Human Beings': Richard Eppes and the Island Plantation Code of Laws." *Virginia Magazine of History and Biography* 90 (1982): 67–78.

Oakes, James. *The Ruling Race: A History of American Slaveholders*. New York: Knopf, 1982.

Paludan, Phillip Shaw. *A People's Contest: The Union and Civil War, 1861–1865*. 2nd ed. Lawrence: University Press of Kansas, 1996.

———. *The Presidency of Abraham Lincoln*. Lawrence: University Press of Kansas, 1994.

Patterson, Orlando. *Slavery and Social Death: A Comparative Study*. Cambridge, Mass.: Harvard University Press, 1982.

Pinsker, Matthew. "Lincoln's Summer of Emancipation." In *Lincoln and Freedom: Slavery, Emancipation, and the Thirteenth Amendment*, edited by Harold Holzer and Sara Vaughn Gabbard, 79–99. Carbondale: Southern Illinois University Press, 2007.

Pitcaithley, Dwight T. "'A Cosmic Threat': The National Park Service Addresses the Causes of the American Civil War." In *Slavery and Public History: The Tough Stuff of American Memory*, edited by James Oliver Horton and Lois E. Horton, 168–86. New York: New Press, 2006.

Quarles, Benjamin. "The Colonial Militia and Negro Manpower." *Mississippi Valley Historical Review* 45 (1959): 643–52.

——. *Lincoln and the Negro.* New York: Oxford University Press, 1962.

——. *The Negro in the American Revolution.* Chapel Hill: University of North Carolina Press, 1961.

——. *The Negro in the Civil War.* Boston: Little, Brown, 1969.

Quarstein, John V. *The Civil War on the Virginia Peninsula.* Dover, N.H.: Arcadia, 1997.

——. "The Siege of Yorktown and Engagements along the Warwick River." *Civil War: The Magazine of the Civil War Society* 51 (June 1995): 29–34.

Raboteau, Albert J. *Slave Religion: The "Invisible Institution" in the Antebellum South.* New York: Oxford University Press, 1978.

Rafuse, Ethan S. *McClellan's War: The Failure of Moderation in the Struggle for the Union.* Bloomington: Indiana University Press, 2005.

Ranlet, Phillip. "The British, Slaves, and Smallpox in Revolutionary Virginia." *Journal of Negro History* 84 (Summer 1999): 217–26.

Rawick, George. *From Sundown to Sunup: The Making of the Black Community.* Westport, Conn.: Greenwood, 1972.

Remini, Robert V. *The Battle of New Orleans.* New York: Penguin, 2001.

Riddleberger, Patrick W. *George Washington Julian, Radical Republican: A Study in Nineteenth-Century Politics and Reform.* Indianapolis: Indiana Historical Society, 1966.

Robinson, William M., Jr. "Drewry's Bluff: Naval Defense of Richmond, 1862." *Civil War History* 7, no. 2 (June 1961): 167–75.

Rose, Willie Lee. *Rehearsal for Reconstruction: The Port Royal Experiment.* Indianapolis: Bobbs-Merrill, 1964.

Roske, Ralph J. *"His Own Counsel": The Life and Times of Lyman Trumbull.* Reno: University of Nevada Press, 1979.

Schwarz, Philip J. *Slave Laws in Virginia.* Athens: University of Georgia Press, 1996.

Sears, Stephen. *To the Gates of Richmond: The Peninsula Campaign.* New York: Ticknor and Fields, 1992.

Segars, J. H. *Black Southerners in Confederate Armies.* Madison, Ga.: Southern Lion Books, 2001.

Sellers, James Lee. "James R. Doolittle." *Wisconsin Magazine of History* 17, no. 2 (March 1933): 277–306.

Siddali, Silvana R. *From Property to Person: Slavery and the Confiscation Acts, 1861–1862.* Baton Rouge: Louisiana State University Press, 2005.

Smith, Willard H. *Schuyler Colfax: The Changing Fortunes of a Political Idol.* Indianapolis: Indiana Historical Bureau, 1952.

Stampp, Kenneth. *The Peculiar Institution: Slavery in the Ante-bellum South.* New York: Knopf, 1956.

Sutch, Richard. "The Breeding of Slaves for Sale and the Westward Expansion of Slavery, 1850–1860." In *Race and Slavery in the Western Hemisphere:*

Quantitative Studies, edited by Stanley L. Engerman and Eugene D. Genovese, 173–210. Princeton, N.J.: Princeton University Press, 1975.

Syrett, John. *The Civil War Confiscation Acts: Failing to Reconstruct the South*. New York: Fordham University Press, 2005.

Tadman, Michael. *Speculators and Slaves: Masters, Traders, and Slaves in the Old South*. Madison: University of Wisconsin Press, 1990.

Takagi, Midori. *Rearing Wolves to Our Own Destruction: Slavery in Richmond, Virginia, 1792–1865*. Charlottesville: University Press of Virginia, 1999.

Tap, Bruce. *Over Lincoln's Shoulder: The Committee on the Conduct of the War*. Lawrence: University Press of Kansas, 1998.

Thornton, John. *Africa and Africans in the Making of the Atlantic, 1400–1800*. New York: Cambridge University Press, 1998.

Traylor, Alan. *American Colonies*. New York: Viking, 2001.

Trefousse, Hans L. *The Radical Republicans: Lincoln's Vanguard for Racial Justice*. New York: Knopf, 1969.

Trudeau, Noah Andre. *Like Men of War: Black Troops in the Civil War*. Boston: Little, Brown, 1998.

Tucker, Glenn. *Hancock the Superb*. Indianapolis: Bobbs-Merrill, 1960.

Varon, Elizabeth R. *Southern Lady, Yankee Spy: The True Story of Elizabeth Van Lew, a Union Agent in the Heart of the Confederacy*. New York: Oxford University Press, 2003.

Vaughan, Alden T. "The Origins Debate: Slavery and Racism in Seventeenth-Century Virginia." *Virginia Magazine of History and Biography* 97 (1989): 311–54.

Wade, Richard C. *Slavery in the Cities: The South, 1820–1860*. New York: Oxford University Press, 1964.

Warner, Ezra J. *Generals in Blue: Lives of the Union Commanders*. Baton Rouge: Louisiana State University Press, 1964.

Wiley, Bell Irvin. *Life of Billy Yank: The Common Soldier of the Union*. Indianapolis: Bobbs-Merrill, 1952.

———. *The Life of Johnny Reb: The Common Soldier of the Confederacy*. Indianapolis: Bobbs-Merrill, 1943.

———. *Southern Negroes, 1861–1865*. New York: Rhinehart, 1938.

Williams, George Washington. *A History of Negro Troops in the War of the Rebellion*. New York: Harper, 1888.

Williams, T. Harry. *Lincoln and the Radicals*. Madison: University of Wisconsin Press, 1941.

Wilson, Joseph T. *The Black Phalanx*. Hartford, Conn.: American Publishing Company, 1888.

Wood, Peter H. *Black Majority: Negroes in Colonial South Carolina from 1670 through the Stono Rebellion*. New York: Knopf, 1974.

Woodward, C. Vann. "History from Slave Sources: A Review Article." *American Historical Review* 79 (April 1974): 470–81.

ACKNOWLEDGMENTS

Indirectly, this project began in 1989 when as a college student I went to the movie theater and saw *Glory*. I always had had a fascination with history but not an especially strong interest in the Civil War. I understood that the primary cause of the conflict was the South's desire to preserve slavery, but that meant little to me as a white Alabamian. When I thought about or discussed the Civil War at all, I tended to celebrate the South's valiant struggle against great odds. In short, I rooted for the home team. But *Glory* changed that. The opening battle scene was immediately engrossing, and the film's powerful depiction of runaway slaves fighting for freedom pulled me into a world that in many ways I have never left. When teardrops slid from Denzel Washington's eye as his defiant character was being whipped, I realized that the Civil War involved something more profound than just southern military heroics. I was exhilarated when Morgan Freeman's character stopped to speak to young black children who were admiring the African American soldiers as they handsomely marched by. "That's right honeys," he announced, "ain't no dream. We runaway slaves but we come back fighting men!" During the black prayer meeting the night before the final battle scene, I choked up as Washington asked rhetorically, "We men, ain't we?" When day dawned in the movie's last scene and the Confederate flag still flew triumphantly over Fort Wagner, my heart plummeted, and I instantly knew that I would never view the Civil War the same. Thus, as melodramatic as it may sound, it is only fitting that I begin my acknowledgments by thanking everyone involved with the production of the movie *Glory*.

My interest in the Civil War broadened in time, especially when I began visiting battlefield sites. There is something indefinably special about connecting to the past by standing on hallowed grounds, and I hope that this book demonstrates my conviction that the Civil War's social and political dimensions are best understood within the context of the war's military events (and vice versa). In 1995, thanks to the suggestion of Peter S. Carmichael (then a seasonal park ranger, now director of Gettysburg's Civil War Institute), Edward Sanders recruited me as a volunteer at the Richmond National Battlefield Park, and that eventually led to my first job for which my college degree prepared me (that is a special blessing when you are a history major). Working as a seasonal park ranger, I learned more about the Civil War and the Peninsula Campaign from conversations on the battlefields with my friends and colleagues than I could have ever learned on my own. World War II veteran and Park Service volunteer Jim Gates was a dear friend who always encouraged my endeavors. I wish he had lived to see this book published, because he would have been proud and no doubt would have helped promote it to visitors at the Cold Harbor visitors' center. Robert E. L. Krick made his impressive collection of soldier manuscripts available to me and at the last minute helped me with the maps featured in this book. I simply cannot thank David Ruth and Michael Andrus enough for being the best bosses I have ever had, always finding work for me, and saving me from substitute teaching when I was first looking for college teaching positions.

While I was working on my master's degree at Virginia Commonwealth University, Philip J. Schwarz was the first to see the merit in this topic, and if not for him the project would have never moved forward. I thank him for his friendship, direction, and encouragement at a time when other scholars warned me away from what appeared to be an unworkable subject. Much of what I have learned about Virginia and slavery is a product of his insight and tutelage. My pursuit of a doctorate brought me home to the University of Alabama, and its history department provided an excellent learning environment and continues to be supportive of my career (Roll Tide!). I am grateful for the department's financial assistantships and for awarding me the Gary B. Mills Prize. Lawrence F. Kohl, and especially my adviser George C. Rable, never seemed to lose faith in me, even when my early work was clearly lacking. They pushed me to ask bigger questions of my evidence, patiently improved my writing, and offered ample and encouraging praise when they felt I deserved it. They continue to be the biggest champions of this book, and I feel truly blessed to have worked with them. I have never asked a favor of George that he did not happily and speedily do, and he has frequently aided me in ways that I never even expected. I will never be able to repay my debt to him for his kindness, guidance, and friendship.

George introduced me to David Perry, the editor in chief at the University of North Carolina Press, and touted my work to Gary W. Gallagher. Both men became immediately interested in my manuscript, and their cogent suggestions and ideas immeasurably improved the final product. The press's anonymous readers tactfully pointed out some potential pitfalls in my interpretations and revealed the need for additional details that have subsequently strengthened this work. The staff at the Press was extremely helpful and patient with a first-time author. Zach Read and Paul Betz in particular received an annoying barrage of e-mailed questions from me, but they quickly answered each of them helpfully, guided me through the process, and effectively handled all of my problems. Dorothea Anderson's skillful copyediting saved me from some embarrassing inconsistencies, typos, and just plain errors. Any that remain in the final product are mine, and mine alone.

I owe an enormous debt to the staffs at all the libraries and repositories in which I conducted research, but particularly to the Virginia Historical Society, whose staff generously provided me with a Mellon Research Fellowship and whose professionalism, efficiency, and excellent finding aids are second to none. The interlibrary loan department at the University of Alabama's Gorgas Library quickly located and obtained every item I requested—particularly important for my use of the Civil War era newspapers, which in many ways form the backbone of this work. (Thankfully, they did not complain too much when I frequently took more time with the borrowed material than was allowed.) The U.S. Army Military History Institute in Carlisle, Pennsylvania, houses an enormous collection of soldier diaries and letters, provides an especially comfortable and efficient facility for researchers, and has a particularly knowledgeable staff. This book is immensely stronger because of them.

I would be remiss not to thank all the students I have had the pleasure of teaching over the last fourteen years. I truly never understood history and its purposes more than when I started teaching and responding to student questions. The classroom is in many ways a refuge for me, and the interactions with my students over the years have kept me motivated and inspired.

Special thanks to my friends, who kept me entertained and got me through some difficult times. Kevin Windham, Jonathon Hooks, Brooke and Justin Turner, Lauren and Joe Danielson, Heather and Michael Hoekstra, Gina Pearson, Brittney Miller, Melissa Landa, and Katie Kowitz all provided invaluable friendship, diversions, and encouragement, which made the grueling process of writing a book more endurable. The guys in our "history nerd tour group" are great travel companions and have never complained no matter how many times I have cajoled them into trips to the Virginia Peninsula and Colonial Williamsburg (and trust me, there have been numerous times). Christian McWhirter never once told me that he was tired of discussing my ideas, and our conversations helped me to sharpen the focus of this work. His wonderful wife and my friend, Corrin, used her artistic and computer skills to help with my illustrations at the very last moment. As all my friends know, Kristopher Teters never tires of discussing the Civil War, and he helped me work through some of my thorniest historical questions. Sitting on the grounds at Berkeley Plantation where the Union army had camped in 1862, he and I had a conversation that caused the proverbial lightbulb to pop on in my head regarding one of this book's main interpretive points.

Last, and most important, I thank my family. My dog, Jackson, was my constant companion for close to sixteen years, and I greatly depended on him to brighten my mood and keep me sane. I miss him terribly. My brother, sister-in-law, and nephews were an important source of amusement, encouragement, and love. Although only one of my grandparents lived to see this book published, they all had a profound impact on shaping the person I have become, and I carry each of them with me every day. I inherited my personality and passion for history from my dad. I lost him to cancer while researching this work, and it saddens me that he did not live to see it on the shelf. Nevertheless, I know he is looking down with pride. Of course, no one is prouder than my mother, and I thank her above all for instilling my values and supporting my goals.

as label for runaway slaves, 38, 235 (n. 30). *See also* African Americans
Conway, Martin F., 64
Conway, Moncure, 65–66, 69, 215–16
Cook, Joel, 140, 144, 174–75, 176, 249 (n. 46)
Cooper, Peter, 209
Cooper Institute, 75–76, 78
Cox, Samuel S., 152
Crittenden, Charles, 116

Davidson, John W., 112
Davis, Frank C., 168
Davis, Jefferson, 56, 158–59, 171
Davis, William, 75–76
DeLong, Harrison, 111, 112
Doolittle, James, 199–200
Douglass, Frederick, 18, 55, 194
Drake, Charles D., 209
Drewry's Bluff, Battle of, 148–49
Duell, Rodolphus Holland, 117
Duggan, Ivy W., 187
Dunmore's Proclamation, 11
Dunn, William E., 223
Dunn, William M., 55
Duval, Sandra Dandridge Cooke, 143

Eames, Walter J., 103, 136, 141, 142–43, 144
Ellet, Robert, 18, 20, 91
Ellis, Franklin, 169
Ellis, Thomas T., 222–23
Eltham's Landing, Battle of, 131–32, 248 (n. 21)
Emancipation: Northern resistance to, 30–31; Northern support for, 240 (n. 71), 257 (n. 74); and Peninsula Campaign, 197–214, 227; and warfare, 10, 13–15, 224. *See also* Military necessity argument
Emancipation Proclamation, 212–14, 227, 256 (n. 46), 257 (n. 74)
Eppes, Richard, 19, 20, 25, 29–30, 61, 164, 259 (n. 9)
Eppes, William, 29–30, 32

Ethiopian Regiment, 11
Evans, James, 87
Everett, Robert A., 141, 191
Ewell, Benjamin, 88

Farnsworth, John F., 211
Fish, Henry C., 207–8, 212
Fisk, Wilbur, 136
Forbes, Edwin, 131 (ill.)
Forney, John W., 118–19, 130, 153–54, 191, 201, 208, 212
Fort Magruder, 126, 129, 246–47 (n. 59)
Fort Monroe, 28, 36 (ill.), 58, 59 (ill.), 85, 92, 97, 140, 216, 235 (n. 32); African American laborers at, 44–48, 50, 60, 62, 65, 79–80, 80 (ill.), 102, 103, 105, 205–6, 223; slaves escaping to, 33–39, 38 (ill.), 75, 79–81, 102, 164
Foster, Jack, 133
Franklin, William, 131–32
Free blacks. *See* African Americans: free
Frémont, John C., 63–64, 238 (n. 39)
Fuller, Richard F., 77
Furst, Luther C., 142, 144–45, 157

Gaines, William, 181–82, 221
Gaines' Mill, Battle of, 185, 254 (n. 65)
Galt, John Minson, 93
Garlick's Landing, Va., 159–61, 176, 199
Garner, Cornelius, 24
Garrison, William Lloyd, 55, 78, 150, 180, 215
Georgia troops: 12th infantry, 182–83; 15th infantry, 110, 187
Gerrish, Henry, 192
Glendale, Battle of, 188, 226
Glory (motion picture), 2, 277
Gloucester, Va., 12, 24, 27, 63, 72, 81, 99
Goodell, William, 67
Gosline, John M., 132
Goss, Warren Lee, 108
Graham, James, 157
Grandy, Charles, 18, 19, 24, 25, 91
Grant, Ulysses S., 93, 107, 123
Greeley, Horace, 215, 216–17